The complete guide to TEST CRICKET *in the* EIGHTIES

MARCUS BERKMANN

PARTRIDGE PRESS

LONDON · NEW YORK · TORONTO · SYDNEY · AUCKLAND

TRANSWORLD PUBLISHERS LTD
61–63 Uxbridge Road, London W5 5SA

TRANSWORLD PUBLISHERS (AUSTRALIA) PTY LTD
15–23 Helles Avenue, Moorebank, NSW 2170

TRANSWORLD PUBLISHERS (NZ) LTD
Cnr Moselle and Waipareira Aves,
Henderson, Auckland

Published 1990 by Partridge Press
a division of Transworld Publishers Ltd

British Library Cataloguing in Publication Data
Berkmann, Marcus, *1960–*
Deloitte ratings : complete guide to test cricket in the eighties.
1. Cricket. Test matches, history
I. Title
796.35865

ISBN 1–85225–134–4
ISBN 1–85225–097–6 pbk

Cover and Book Design by
Christie Archer Design, London

Typeset by Photoprint, Torquay, Devon

Printed in Great Britain at
The Bath Press, Avon

PICTURE CREDITS
Patrick Eagar pp 10, 32, 36, 79, 107, 145 *left & right*, 159, 213 *right*, 219, 247, 254; AllSport/Adrian Murrell pp 3, 59, 115, 193, 213 *left*, 250, 260; AllSport/Ben Radford p 235; AllSport pp 91, 241.

FOREWORD

Deloitte Ratings have come a long way since their public announcement in 1987 and since Deloitte in the UK began applying their computer expertise to this new ratings system. It is gratifying for me that the Ratings (now known as the Coopers Deloitte Ratings*) are sufficiently valued to be used to provide the statistical justification for this entertaining and informative book looking back at Test cricket in the eighties.

Some elements of the Ratings have worked out more or less exactly the way they were envisaged, such as the greater volatility of player placings as compared with traditional averages and the wider gap between 'big match temperament' players and those who only seem to thrive when the going is somewhat easier.

The pleasant surprises include the early recognition of overseas talent which often remained under wraps overlong and the considerable accuracy of the Ratings when used to compare the relative strengths of Test playing countries.

Happily it seems that the cricketing public retain a healthy appetite for comparing the relative merits of teams and individual players and it has been fun to devise and remain associated with the Deloitte Ratings which have added a new statistical dimension to the debate.

Ted Dexter
March 1990

*Deloitte Haskins & Sells and Coopers & Lybrand merged in the UK in April 1990 to form Coopers & Lybrand Deloitte. The new firm is colloquially known as Coopers Deloitte.

ACKNOWLEDGEMENTS

The author would like to thank Coopers Deloitte for the Ratings information and the use of their Macintosh II for the graphs; the devisers of the system, Rob Eastaway and Gordon Vince for their time and encouragement; Esther Kaposi for lunch; Mike Richardson for his invaluable research material; Debbie Beckerman and Jennie Bull for their forbearance; and *Wisden Cricketer's Almanack*, without which civilization would crumble.

CONTENTS

Abbreviations

*	Captain
†	Vice-Captain
NE	New Entry
RE	Re-Entry
A	Australia
E	England
I	India
P	Pakistan
NZ	New Zealand
SL	Sri Lanka
WI	West Indies

INTRODUCTION

So what is a Deloitte Rating? Where did it come from, and why?

Originally the brainchild of England's chairman of selectors, Ted Dexter, the ratings seek to provide an index of current Test form for every player operating at international level, both for batting and bowling. Ratings range between 0 and 1000 (and are usually nearer 0 than 1000), and are updated after every Test match. As they place greater emphasis on recent form than past successes (or failures), they tend to fluctuate more.

They are not, it should be emphasized straight away, designed to supersede averages. The simple act of dividing the number of runs scored by the number of times out may seem a rather crude calculation in this complex age, but it remains by far the most (and possibly the only) reliable method of assessing a player's career in the long term. The Deloitte Ratings are necessarily more ephemeral. They assess a player less on what he did in 1981 than on what he did last week – and so are perhaps a more reliable guide to what he may do next week. Or perhaps they may not be. Cricket, fortunately, is less predictable than that.

The ratings system is therefore a guide to form, not the final word on selection. (Mr Dexter's part in the proceedings should not be taken too literally.) This does not render them uninteresting, of course. Indeed, the desire to put things in order is a fundamental human urge, to which cricket followers are especially prone. The ratings are just another fascinating statistic, to join the many other fascinating statistics that we already love and cherish. And, just as we would argue over who we would choose for our World Teams past and present, so the Deloitte Ratings have their own opinion. (Whether you agree with their findings, of course, is another matter entirely.)

But as well as being fun, the ratings can also tell us a great deal. Who were the great players of the Eighties? Who were the greatest? Averages tell one story, but the ratings are in many ways more subtle. As well as incorporating the bald facts (173 not out, 3 for 36), they also take account of the result, the team scores, the conditions, the opposition and sundry other factors. A century is worth more in a tense low-scoring victory than in a dreary high-scoring draw at Faisalabad (why is it always Faisalabad?). A bowler gets more points for taking Javed Miandad's wicket than, say, Derek Pringle's. A batsman gets more points for hitting a six off Richard Hadlee than off, say, Derek Pringle.

Of course the ratings are not perfect, and can never be so. The computer programs which calculate the ratings necessarily incorporate weightings that, by their very nature, are no more than estimations – admittedly by people who love cricket and know all about it. Since the ratings were launched in 1987, the algorithms have been tinkered with on a couple of occasions to remove obvious anomalies (which is why some of the figures in this book may not tally with those in earlier published sources). When, for instance, the nineteen-year-old Indian leg-spinner Narendra Hirwani took 16 wickets in his first Test against the West Indies, he leapt straight into the top five – which was a bit much even for the programmers. Now, players don't achieve a full rating until they have played ten innings or taken 40 wickets (although they get a 90 per cent rating after 30 wickets). Until they pass those thresholds – and many don't – their ratings are reduced by a gradually decreasing percentage – so Hirwani, for instance, now comes in at 9th. With the publication of this book, though, the algorithms have been set in stone: these are the numbers that count, and they won't change.

So what do the ratings mean? The following bands are not definitive, but they provide reasonable guidelines, both for batting and bowling. When you get fully engrossed, as I seem to have become, you begin to see untold subtleties between 450 and 480 – but that may be a joy yet to come.

850–1000 Exceptional, world-class performances, probably over some period of time. No single 10-wicket match gets you into this bracket – you have to work for it. The players who get here are pretty exceptional – those who stay (Richards, Marshall, Hadlee) virtually superhuman.

700–850 World-class performances from players who would make most people's World Teams. Most, that is, but not all.

550–700 Good solid Test performer. Probably a team regular, but not exactly spoken of in hushed tones.

400–550 The Twilight Zone. Old players come here to retire, while new players often spend a lengthy apprenticeship here. In-and-out players, the ones who never quite establish themselves but always seem to play about twenty Tests before a bright spark appears to steal their place, make this their home.

Below 400 In trouble. A drop below 400 often indicates that it's time to chuck it all in and open a pub.

Without anyone really intending it, 400 has become the accepted threshold of success in the ratings. None of the graphs would dream of showing anyone whose rating fell below this figure (or who had never got that high in the first place) – which causes the occasional problem, especially when, for instance, one comes to chronicling the recent record of the England team. But we have found that 400 has an uncanny tendency to sort the sheep from the goats – and indeed the rabbits.

The book covers the last decade of Test cricket, which has also been the busiest – 247 Tests in all, equivalent to the number played between 1877 and 1935. To encompass its scope, the Deloitte team backdated the ratings to the late Seventies, choosing as their cut-off point the emergence of the Packer circus back in 1978. That sorry episode probably influenced international cricket more than anything that has happened since – for that was when the needs of television became paramount and the inexorable rise of the one-day international began. This book, as it deals only with the full five-day game, totally ignores one-day internationals, partly because no-one can ever remember the results a week later, let alone six or seven years later, and partly because they're essentially a different form of cricket entirely, emphasizing efficiency over flair and quick 30s over slow 100s. Test cricket is what counts, and that's why we are looking at it.

The ratings, as we use them, ignore decimals – although fortunately the computer is more thorough, which explains why two players can appear to be on the same score but one is a place higher than the other. Each player who takes part in a Test, whether he bats or bowls or doesn't do anything, is given a rating. Players retain their ratings after they have been dropped or injured, or even when they retire, but ratings decay by 1 per cent for every game missed. After eighteen months' absence from the Test arena, the player vanishes from the lists completely. (Surprisingly few return.) There are around 150 players in each list at any one time.

Batting ratings, you will notice, are generally higher than bowling ratings – at least in the world top twenties. This is for a very simple reason – there are more batsmen than bowlers. We toyed with the notion of using a world top thirty for batsmen, but the generally minor differences between 10th and 20th positions – usually no more than 80–90 points – are even more trivial lower down: the chart becomes so volatile that there's nothing particularly interesting to be read from it. But it is certainly far harder to get into the higher echelons of the batting lists than the bowling lists – all-rounders make the latter top twenty frequently, the former very rarely indeed.

For each series of three Tests or more, two Rising Star awards are given for the player on each side whose ratings have gone up by the greatest margin, although only points scored above 400 are deemed to count. Thus, for England against Australia in 1989 the winners were Robin Smith, up 321 from 425 to 746, and Mark Taylor, up 357 to 757, although he actually rose 599 on his pre-series rating. These two, in fact, won £2,500 each from Deloittes – sadly, earlier Rising Stars will not be able to claim similar sums. The awards do, however, provide an interesting if sometimes amusingly unfair indication of each series' leading performers.

After the main bulk of the book – the ups and downs of individual players through every series played in the Eighties – there's a brief records section, which discusses the leading batsmen, bowlers and all-rounders of the age. There are no team ratings, as we have yet to come up with a convincing formula for one, but this gap may be filled in future volumes. A more intense technical discussion of the Deloitte algorithms follows at the end for lovers of pointless detail (or masochists).

If nothing else, writing this book has made me realize just how much Test cricket is played – far too much, in short – and that in England we tend to underestimate the achievements of those who prosper overseas while we freeze at home in winter. It's arguable that the Deloitte Ratings have helped people over here understand just how good Richie Richardson and Dilip Vengsarkar are – without their having to come over here and prove it to us. The ratings provide an international perspective to a sport that is increasingly dominated by narrow national concerns – the desire of English counties to make as much money as possible, for instance, and the desire of the Pakistan authorities to win all their home Test matches, whatever the cost. But more importantly, they are something else for cricket fans to pore over and argue over – a vital function indeed.

Finally, I must stress that although all the figures in this book come straight from the Coopers Deloitte computer, the comment and interpretation that go with them are my own. If you disagree with the latter, you should blame me.

Marcus Berkmann
April 1990

ABOUT THE GRAPHS

Each of the graphs shows the top performers – either batsmen or bowlers – for each country at the end of each English season (1980, 1981, 1982 etc.) and each world season (1980–81, 1981–82, 1982–83 etc.).* In most cases I have plotted the paths of all batsmen with ratings over 500 and all bowlers with ratings over 400, although occasionally this varies (for example, for Sri Lanka's first Test matches, where I have been a little more generous). Each player is denoted by his own specific graph line (which carries over from series to series), and by a square, round or triangular marker for each new rating. Markers are filled in black for the player's rating at the beginning of the season, and for any Tests he misses during the season. If he misses an entire series, his graph line does not appear at all. (As a result, for instance, Neil Foster appears more often in the graphs than Graham Dilley, although Dilley played more Tests – Foster had a tendency to play just one Test of a series, while Dilley played fewer series but had longer spells in the team.) Some graphs can appear a little busy, but then if three or four players in a side are mediocre enough all to have scores in the early 500s (England's team is a regular offender), that's their fault, not the ratings'. If ratings are sufficiently bunched to make it impossible to tell whether or not a player actually took part in a Test, remember that for each match missed, the rating drops by about 1 per cent – a gentle and distinctive slope on the graph. (Of course, this does not necessarily work the other way – you don't have to miss a game to deteriorate by about 1 per cent. You can just play badly . . . .)

*These are usually about September and May respectively.

WORLD TOP TWENTY AS AT APRIL 1980

BATTING

1.	Javed Miandad (Pakistan)	883
2.	S.M. Gavaskar (India)	882
3.	A.R. Border (Australia)	881
4.	I.V.A. Richards (West Indies)	874
5.	G.S. Chappell (Australia)	869
6.	I.T. Botham (England)	796
7.	D.I. Gower (England)	782
8.	B.A. Edgar (New Zealand)	769
9.	D.L. Haynes (West Indies)	753
10.	G.P. Howarth (New Zealand)	752
11.	G. Boycott (England)	732
12.	Taslim Arif (Pakistan)	719
13.	K.J. Hughes (Australia)	714
14.	A.I. Kallicharran (West Indies)	697
15.	C.G. Greenidge (West Indies)	676
16.	Wasim Raja (Pakistan)	673
17.	G.A. Gooch (England)	671
18.	Majid Khan (Pakistan)	665
19.	D.B. Vengsarkar (India)	656
20.	B.M. Laird (Australia)	643

BOWLING

1.	I.T. Botham (England)	907
2.	Kapil Dev (India)	875
3.	C.E.H. Croft (West Indies)	795
4.	J. Garner (West Indies)	795
5.	D.R. Doshi (India)	787
6.	M. Hendrick (England)	770
7.	M.A. Holding (West Indies)	730
8.	R.J. Hadlee (New Zealand)	726
9.	D.K. Lillee (Australia)	714
10.	G. Dymock (Australia)	713
11.	A.M.E. Roberts (West Indies)	689
12.	Imran Khan (Pakistan)	688
13.	R.G.D. Willis (England)	661
14.	R.M. Hogg (Australia)	658
15.	P.H. Edmonds (England)	650
16.	D.L. Underwood (England)	638
17.	J.K. Lever (England)	638
18.	J.R. Thomson (Australia)	623
19.	A.G. Hurst (Australia)	620
20.	C.M. Old (England)	589

If the batting has a familiar ring to it, that's because six of the top nine (and in all, nine of the twenty) were still playing Test cricket – and excelling at it – a decade later. For most, of course, these were the first flowerings of what turned into long and prolific careers – of those nine survivors, only Viv Richards was already well established at the top of the list. The bowlers, naturally enough, have shown rather less longevity – only Kapil Dev, Botham, Hadlee and (under duress) Imran made it anywhere near the end of the decade. But then the fact that these four players dominated the intervening ten years may well have had something to do with it.

The preceding winter was, nevertheless, unduly hectic. In all, twenty-five Test matches were played between September 1979 and March 1980, with most teams appearing to fly around the world at least once. The merry-go-round began with six Tests between India and Australia crowbarred rather hurriedly into September and October so that the Aussies would be back home in time for their own domestic season. This was the last series played before the Australian Board of Control 'reached their historic compromise with' Mr Packer's World Series Cricket organization, and their team was not dissimilar to the pallid-looking 2nd XI that had been brushed aside by England the previous winter. Not surprisingly, Australia went down 2–0, the first series they had ever lost to India. Allan Border's rating dropped from 919 to 735 over the series, and he was held to have done quite well. Of the other batsmen, only Hughes and (marginally) Yallop improved their ratings, each scoring a century in the tests. Geoff Dymock was the greatest success, with 24 wickets in the series and a jump from 309 to 649. But Hogg fell away badly, his 906 (earned against Brearley's side) declining to 748.

The Indians, meanwhile, had a great old time, with Viswanath scoring 518 runs at 74 and rising to 4th in the ratings with 842. Gavaskar had for him a moderate series, but remained 2nd with 904. Biggest success with the ball, naturally enough, was Kapil Dev, with 28 wickets and a final rating of 764.

No sooner had Australia skittled back home in mild disgrace (they didn't win a single game on the tour), than Pakistan turned up for six more Tests. India again won 2–0, as the Pakistanis' great batting side of the Seventies began visibly to decline. With a consistent flow of runs, if no enormous innings, Wasim Raja was the visitors' best batsman, and bumped up his rating accordingly, from 486 to 684. Otherwise, only Miandad, as ever, was at all consistent, although no doubt disgruntled to be given out lbw five times in the series, something that would never have been allowed to happen at home. As so often when they are doing badly, the Pakistan side was racked by internal squabbling; nevertheless, Imran Khan and Sikander Bakht kept the Indian batsmen in check.

We move on, then, to the Australian season, where the home team played three Tests each against England and the West Indies, interrupted, of course, by innumerable one-day games. By this stage the Packer players were back in Test match cricket, and the strong Australians not surprisingly munched up England 3–0, with the returning Chappell brothers scoring piles of runs. Dennis Lillee's return to Test cricket was no less profitable (23 wickets), while for England Botham (19 wickets) was the leading performer. But for all their new-found strength, Australia were no match for the West Indies, who won 2–0, helped by their latest fearsome quartet of fast bowlers, Roberts, Garner, Holding and Croft, and Richards' 386 runs in four innings. It was a fine revenge for the 5–1 pasting they had received at the hands of Lillee and Thomson four years earlier.

Not that they had much time to savour their triumph. Next on the schedule was New Zealand vs West Indies, an ill-tempered series which is now remembered mainly for Holding kicking over the stumps when an umpire didn't raise the required digit. New Zealand in fact won the series 1–0, their first ever series win at home, but the West Indian management thought the umpires were to blame, rather than the fact that they just didn't play very well. The series' greatest success was Bruce Edgar, who with 241 runs at 60.25 bumped up his rating from 444 (46th) to 769 (8th), while Howarth consolidated his position in the top twenty. Haynes too had a good series (587 to 753).

England, meanwhile, had decamped to Bombay for the Golden Jubilee Test, and beat India by 10 wickets – or at least Botham did, with a brilliant 114 and 13 wickets, the latter performance edging him in front of Kapil Dev in the ratings. But after sixteen Tests in seven months, India were not surprisingly a little stale, and in this game just about turned up at the edges.

Which left only another swift series between Pakistan and Australia, squeezed unceremoniously into March. Asif Iqbal having retired from Test cricket after the disastrous Indian tour, Javed Miandad took over the captaincy, and now unendangered by lbw decisions, led his team to a more satisfactory 1–0 triumph. In traditional fashion, the first Test was won on a vicious turner, with spinners Tauseef Ahmed and Iqbal Qasim taking 18 of Australia's wickets, after which the pitches miraculously became perfect for batting, and not quite so perfect for forcing a result. Majid and Javed took predictable advantage, while wicketkeeper Taslim Arif scored one of history's less memorable double centuries to push him briefly up the ratings (he only played six Tests in all). Of the Australians, Border averaged 131 (with two centuries in the third Test) and Chappell 76, while the bowlers suffered, Dennis Lillee taking only 3 wickets at 101 and dropping three places in the ratings.

Was this enough Test cricket for one winter? At the time everyone seemed to think it was far too much, but all was conveniently forgotten four years later when the game's administrators (assisted by the world's major airlines) managed to schedule twenty-eight Test matches over the 1983-84 season, plus the usual 9,000 or so one-dayers. But never mind – let's move on to the 1980 season itself.

DeloitteRATINGS

1980

ENGLAND vs WEST INDIES

First Test (Trent Bridge, 5–10 June) West Indies won by 2 wickets
England 1st Innings: 263 (Botham 57, Woolmer 46, Roberts 5–72, Garner 3–44)
West Indies 1st Innings: 308 (Richards 64, D.L. Murray 64, Greenidge 53, Willis 4–82, Botham 3–50)
England 2nd Innings: 252 (Boycott 75, Garner 4–30, Roberts 3–57)
West Indies 2nd Innings: 209 for 8 (Haynes 62, Richards 48, Willis 5–65)

Second Test (Lord's, 19–24 June) Match Drawn
England 1st Innings: 269 (Gooch 123, Tavaré 42, Holding 6–67, Garner 4–36)
West Indies 1st Innings: 518 (Haynes 184, Richards 145, Lloyd 56, Willis 3–103, Botham 3–145)
England 2nd Innings: 133 for 2 (Boycott 49 not out, Gooch 47)

Third Test (Old Trafford, 10–15 July) Match Drawn
England 1st Innings: 150 (Rose 70, Roberts 3–23, Garner 3–34, Marshall 3–36)
West Indies 1st Innings: 260 (Lloyd 101, Richards 65, Emburey 3–20, Dilley 3–47, Botham 3–64)
England 2nd Innings: 391 for 7 (Boycott 86, Willey 62 not out, Gatting 56, Holding 3–100)

Fourth Test (The Oval, 24–29 July) Match Drawn
England 1st Innings: 370 (Gooch 83, Boycott 53, Rose 50, Gatting 48, Croft 3–97)
West Indies 1st Innings: 265 (Bacchus 61, Garner 46, Marshall 45, Dilley 4–57)
England 2nd Innings: 209 for 9 declared (Willey 100 not out, Rose 41)

Fifth Test (Headingley, 7–12 August) Match Drawn
England 1st Innings: 143 (Bairstow 40, Croft 3–35, Garner 3–41)
West Indies 1st Innings: 245 (Haynes 42, Dilley 4–79)
England 2nd Innings: 227 for 6 (Gooch 55, Boycott 47, Rose 43 not out, Marshall 3–42)

1980

Captains: England – I.T. Botham
West Indies – C.H. Lloyd (1st–4th Tests), I.V. A. Richards (5th Test)

Débuts: England – C.J. Tavaré (1st Test)

Rising Stars: England – B.C. Rose (+123 batting)
West Indies – J. Garner (+99 bowling)

Under Botham's youthful leadership, England went down 1–0 to the rampaging West Indies, a result that at the time was considered a calamity, although compared to the blackwashes later in the decade it now seems like little more than a mild setback. Although Gooch was the most convincing batsman against the fearsome Windies pace quartet, he never seemed to make quite enough runs against them – the talk was always of imperious 45s rather than 145s. But if he and Boycott managed to keep their heads above water, the form of England's other two leading batsmen suffered. Gower was dropped after a calamitous first Test, while Botham's rating dropped almost 200 points in a gradual but inexorable decline. Although there were four other batsmen with ratings over 400 (Miller, Randall, the retired Brearley and Bob Taylor), none was used, and until the arrival later in the season of Brian Rose, enjoying perhaps the best form of his career, the batting was in a sorry state. England's bowlers also suffered, with all the bowlers used in the first Test, Botham apart, losing their place at some point during the series. Emburey's 6 wickets at 13.83 pushed him up from 333 to 508, but by the fifth Test, only Botham had a rating over 700. This was in contrast to the West Indies, who in addition to the high-flying Garner, had Croft, Holding and Roberts, plus the promise of the then little-known Malcolm Marshall, who improved his rating from 52 (from three unsuccessful Tests against India in the Packer days of 1978–79) to 269. The batsmen too were more consistent, even if Greenidge and Kallicharran both had relatively disappointing tours. But no-one on either side could compare with Richards, who reached some sort of peak on this tour, even for someone of his remarkable gifts. The editor of *Wisden*, John Woodcock, not someone prone to intemperate remarks, said that 'Sir Gary Sobers was the last most powerful single influence on the game; before that, Sir Donald Bradman was.' In the end, England were saved from abject humiliation by some brave performances and much timely rain.

ENGLAND vs AUSTRALIA

Centenary Test (Lord's, 28 August–2 September) Match Drawn

Australia 1st Innings: 385 for 5 declared (K.J. Hughes 117, Wood 112, Border 56 not out, Chappell 47, Old 3–91)
England 1st Innings: 205 (Boycott 62, Gower 45, Pascoe 5–59, Lillee 4–43)
Australia 2nd Innings: 189 for 4 declared (Hughes 84, G.S. Chappell 59 not out, Old 3–47)
England 2nd Innings: 244 for 3 (Boycott 128 not out, Gatting 51 not out)

Captains: England – I.T. Botham
Australia – G.S. Chappell

Débuts: England – C.W.J. Athey

Joel Garner at Headingley, trying to remember the last time he conceded a run.

1980

Remembered mainly for the many hundreds of cricketing veterans who were hauled up before the cameras to reminisce drunkenly about the old days, this was an otherwise disappointing match, almost ruined by rain, and with no performance to match Derek Randall's heroic 174 in the Melbourne Centenary Test of 1977. Consistently outplayed by a spirited Australian team, England were finally faced with a target of 370 to win in 350 minutes, and thanks no doubt to the presence of the débutant Athey in the side, they never even considered having a go at it. Earlier, English bowling ratings had suffered as all the bowlers besides Old were taken apart by Wood, Hughes and Chappell, while only the in-form Boycott and, to a lesser extent, Gower, made any impression for the home team. Botham chimed in with a brief but entertaining 0 as England collapsed from 137 for 2 in their first innings to 205. But although the Aussies tried manfully to engineer a result, the deadly combination of rain, bad light and G. Boycott managed to deny them. Only a mildly risible scuffle between incensed MCC members and a beleaguered umpire Constant brought everyone out of their reverie.

WORLD TOP TWENTY AFTER 1980

BATTING

(3)	1.	A.R. Border (Australia)	903	(+22)
(4)	2.	I.V.A. Richards (West Indies)	902	(+28)
(1)	3.	Javed Miandad (Pakistan)	883	
(2)	4.	S.M. Gavaskar (India)	882	
(5)	5.	G.S. Chappell (Australia)	862	(−7)
(9)	6.	D.L. Haynes (West Indies)	813	(+60)
(11)	7.	G. Boycott (England)	806	(+74)
(13)	8.	K.J. Hughes (Australia)	785	(+71)
(8)	9.	B.A. Edgar (New Zealand)	769	
(10)	10.	G.P. Howarth (New Zealand)	752	
(12)	11.	Taslim Arif (Pakistan)	719	
(7)	12.	D.I. Gower (England)	679	(−103)
(16)	13.	Wasim Raja (Pakistan)	673	
(18)	14.	Majid Khan (Pakistan)	665	
(19)	15.	D.B. Vengsarkar (India)	656	
(22)	16.	C.H. Lloyd (West Indies)	642	(+20)
(21)	17.	G.R. Viswanath (India)	635	
(17)	18.	G.A. Gooch (England)	631	(−40)
(15)	19.	C.G. Greenidge (West Indies)	618	(−58)
(14)	20.	A.I. Kallicharran (West Indies)	616	(−81)

BOWLING

(1)	1.	I.T. Botham (England)	896 (−11)
(4)	2.	J. Garner (West Indies)	894 (+99)
(2)	3.	Kapil Dev (India)	875
(5)	4.	D.R. Doshi (India)	787
(9)	5.	D.K. Lillee (Australia)	752 (+38)
(11)	6.	A.M.E. Roberts (West Indies)	730 (+41)
(3)	7.	C.E.H. Croft (West Indies)	729 (−66)
(8)	8.	R.J. Hadlee (New Zealand)	726
(10)	9.	G. Dymock (Australia)	706 (−7)
(12)	10.	Imran Khan (Pakistan)	688
(7)	11.	M.A. Holding (West Indies)	674 (−56)
(13)	12.	R.G.D. Willis (England)	668 (+7)
(14)	13.	R.M. Hogg (Australia)	652 (−6)
(6)	14.	M. Hendrick (England)	650 (−120)
(20)	15.	C.M. Old (England)	635 (+46)
(18)	16.	J.R. Thomson (Australia)	616 (−7)
(19)	17.	A.G. Hurst (Australia)	614 (−6)
(15)	18.	P.H. Edmonds (England)	612 (−38)
(21)	19.	Sikander Bakht (Pakistan)	579
(16)	20.	D.L. Underwood (England)	576 (−62)

Border's superb performance in the Centenary Test lifted him to the top of the ratings for the first time, just pushing him ahead of Richards. Hughes' piles of runs at Lord's and Boycott's good form across the summer pushed them back into the top ten, but Gower's disappointments were reflected in his much reduced rating while Botham's loss of touch saw him drop from 6th to 23rd and a rating of 605. Bruce Laird also dropped out of the top twenty, allowing Viswanath and Lloyd back in. Gooch, who had had such a good series against the West Indies, dropped five places after the Centenary Test when he scored just 8 and 16.

Even though Botham's batting rate was on the slide, he remained the leading bowler, albeit by just 2 points from his Somerset pal Joel Garner. Croft's slow start in the Test series cost him vital points, and Holding, averaging over 30, also dropped back. But the biggest fall from grace was Mike Hendrick, who lost his place after taking just 2 for 141 in the first two Tests against the West Indies and then did little better against the Aussies. Dymock, Hogg, Thomson, Hurst and Edmonds lost points by the simple but flawless method of not being picked. Lever, dropped after the first Test, lost his place in the top twenty, replaced by Pakistan's Sikander Bakht.

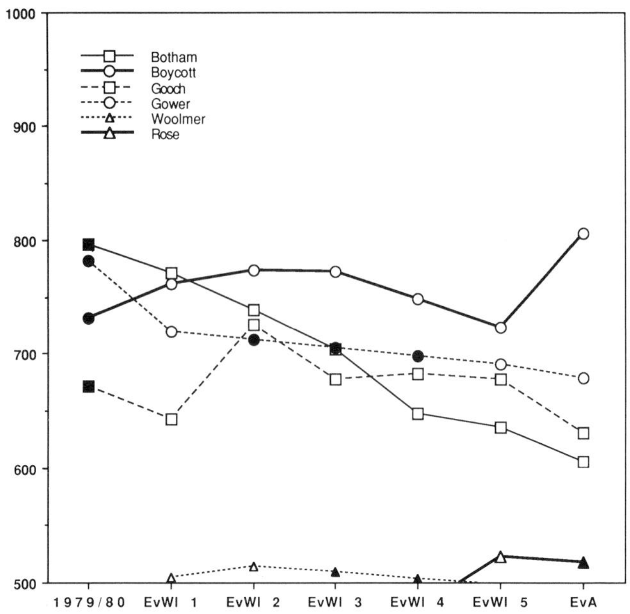
ENGLAND BATSMEN 1980
1000
900
800
700
600
500
Botham
Boycott
Gooch
Gower
Woolmer
Rose
1979/80
EvWI 1
EvWI 2
EvWI 3
EvWI 4
EvWI 5
EvA

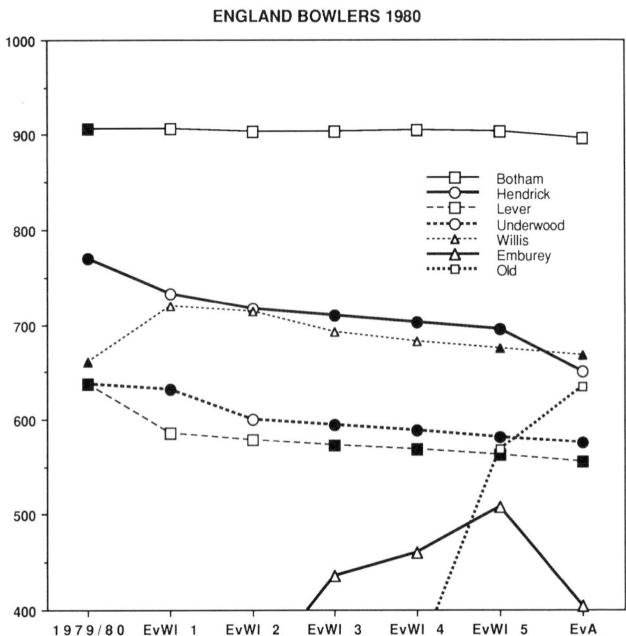
ENGLAND BOWLERS 1980
1000
900
800
700
600
500
400
Botham
Hendrick
Lever
Underwood
Willis
Emburey
Old
1979/80
EvWI 1
EvWI 2
EvWI 3
EvWI 4
EvWI 5
EvA

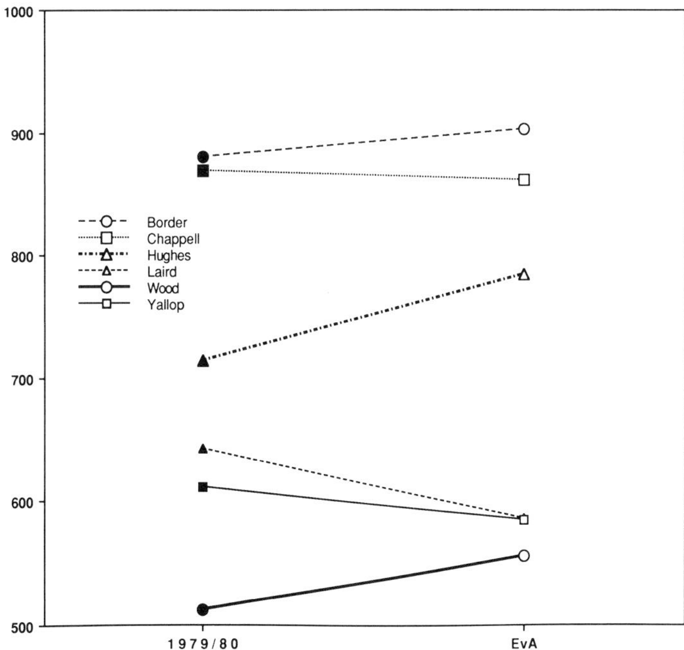
AUSTRALIA BATSMEN 1980
1000
900
800
700
600
500
Border
Chappell
Hughes
Laird
Wood
Yallop
1979/80
EvA

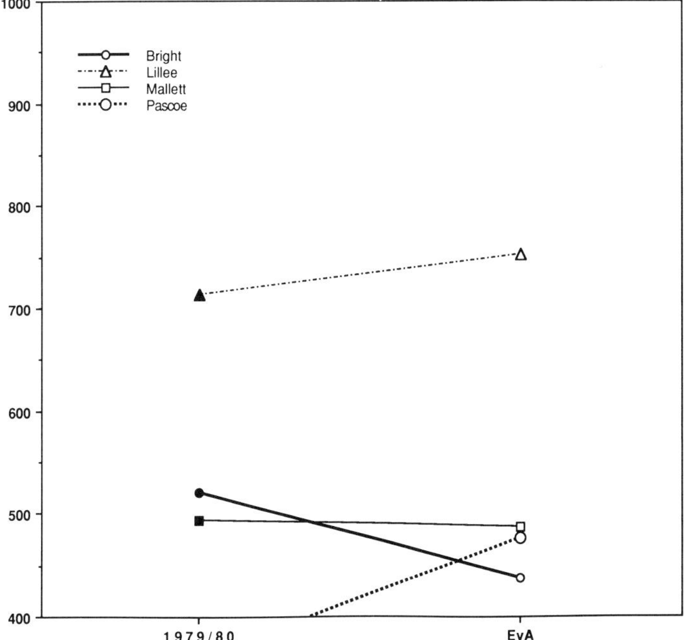
AUSTRALIA BOWLERS 1980
1000
900
800
700
600
500
400
Bright
Lillee
Mallett
Pascoe
1979/80
EvA

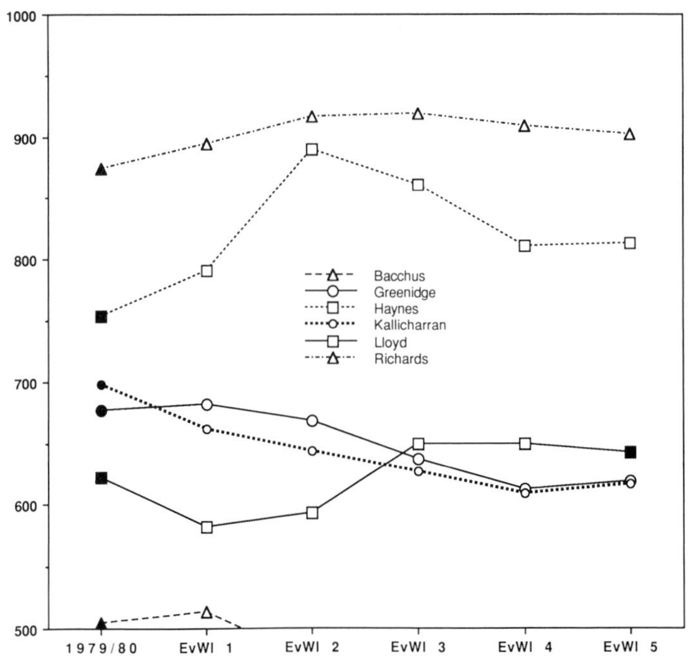
WEST INDIES BATSMEN 1980
1000
900
800
700
600
500
Bacchus
Greenidge
Haynes
Kallicharran
Lloyd
Richards
1979/80
EvWI 1
EvWI 2
EvWI 3
EvWI 4
EvWI 5

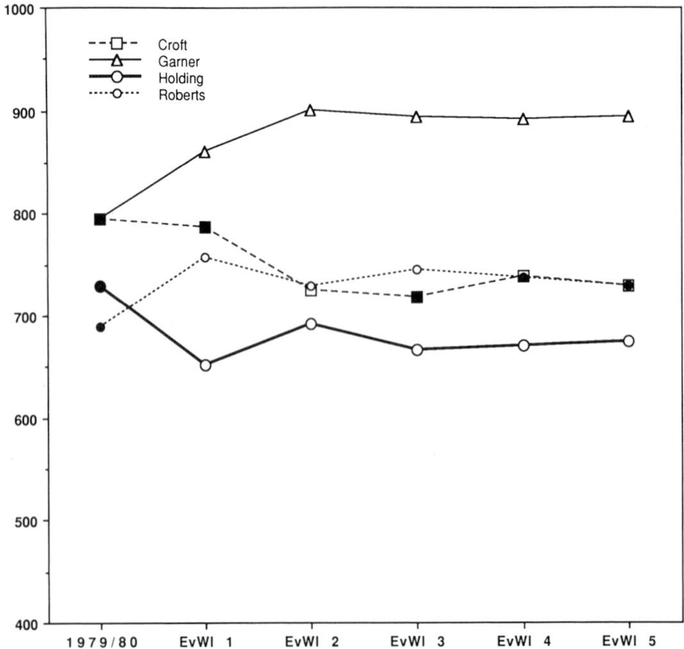
WEST INDIES BOWLERS 1980
1000
900
800
700
600
500
400
Croft
Garner
Holding
Roberts
1979/80
EvWI 1
EvWI 2
EvWI 3
EvWI 4
EvWI 5

1980–81

PAKISTAN vs WEST INDIES

First Test (Lahore, 24–29 November) Match Drawn
Pakistan 1st Innings: 369 (Imran Khan 123, Wasim Raja 76, Sarfraz Nawaz 55, Croft 3–88, Marshall 3–91)
West Indies 1st Innings: 297 (Richards 75, D.A. Murray 50, Gomes 43, Haynes 40, Abdul Qadir 4–131)
Pakistan 2nd Innings: 156 for 7 (Majid Khan 62 not out, Clarke 3–26)

Second Test (Faisalabad, 8–12 December) West Indies won by 156 runs
West Indies 1st Innings: 235 (Richards 72, Bacchus 45, Nazir Junior 5–44, Abdul Qadir 3–48)
Pakistan 1st Innings: 176 (Javed Miandad 50, Clarke 3–28)
West Indies 2nd Innings: 242 (Richards 67, Iqbal Qasim 6–89, Nazir Junior 3–76)
Pakistan 2nd Innings: 145 (Marshall 4–25, Croft 3–29)

Third Test (Karachi, 22–27 December) Match Drawn
Pakistan 1st Innings: 128 (Javed Miandad 60, Clarke 4–27, Croft 3–27)
West Indies 1st Innings: 169 (Gomes 61, D.A. Murray 42, Iqbal Qasim 4–48, Imran Khan 4–66)
Pakistan 2nd Innings: 204 for 9 (Wasim Raja 77 not out, Croft 3–50)

Fourth Test (Multan, 30 December–4 January) Match Drawn
West Indies 1st Innings: 249 (Richards 120 not out, Imran Khan 5–62)
Pakistan 1st Innings: 166 (Javed Miandad 57, Majid Khan 41, Garner 4–38)
West Indies 2nd Innings: 116 for 5 (Nazir Junior 3–35)

Captains: Pakistan – Javed Miandad
West Indies – C.H. Lloyd

Débuts: Pakistan – Mansoor Akhtar (1st Test), Ijaz Faqih (3rd Test)
West Indies – R. Nanan (2nd Test)

Rising Stars: Pakistan – Nazir Junior (+165 bowling)
West Indies – S.T. Clarke (+238 bowling)

The irrepressible Javed Miandad, scything another 4.

By winning 1–0, the West Indies not only took their first ever series in Pakistan, but also recorded the first victory by any visiting team since November 1969, when New Zealand had taken one. Such a result was an impressive achievement given some tricky spinning wickets, the stony faces of the local umpires and the tendentiousness of the local rain gods. Yet it was West Indies' fearsome fast bowlers, as ever, who made the difference between the two teams. Although the left-arm spinner Iqbal Qasim took 17 wickets and the off-spinner Nazir Junior (previously known as Mohammad Nazir) only one less, both at just under 18, the quickies – in the shape of Garner, Croft, Marshall and, standing in for the injured Holding, Sylvester Clarke – took 54 Pakistan wickets between them. Only Richards, still in top form, and Wasim Raja (assisted by some courageous not outs) prospered to any degree, although Javed Miandad played a couple of notable captain's innings. The ratings bear all this out – most of the batsmen's dropped, most of the bowlers' climbed, while Richards' 927 after the final test was the highest of the Eighties so far.

AUSTRALIA vs NEW ZEALAND

First Test (Brisbane, 28–30 November) Australia won by 10 wickets
New Zealand 1st Innings: 225 (Howarth 65, Parker 52, Higgs 4–59, Pascoe 3–41)
Australia 1st Innings: 305 (Wood 111, Cairns 5–87, Hadlee 3–83)

New Zealand 2nd Innings: 142 (Edgar 51, Hadlee 51 not out, Lillee 6–53)
Australia 2nd Innings: 63 for no wicket

Second Test (Perth, 12–14 December) Australia won by 8 wickets
New Zealand 1st Innings: 196 (Coney 71, Burgess 43, Lillee 5–63, Pascoe 3–61)
Australia 1st Innings: 265 (R.W. Marsh 91, Walters 55, Hadlee 5–87, Cairns 4–88)
New Zealand 2nd Innings: 121 (Higgs 4–25)
Australia 2nd Innings: 55 for 2

Third Test (Melbourne, 26–30 December) Match Drawn
Australia 1st Innings: 321 (Walters 107, K.J. Hughes 51, Border 45, Chappell 42, Coney 3–28, Hadlee 3–89)
New Zealand 1st Innings: 317 (Howarth 65, Parker 56, Coney 55 not out, Burgess 49, Hogg 4–60, Pascoe 3–75, Higgs 3–87)
Australia 2nd Innings: 188 (Chappell 78, Hadlee 6–57)
New Zealand 2nd Innings: 128 for 6 (Wright 44)

Captains: Australia – G.S. Chappell
New Zealand – G.P. Howarth (1st & 3rd Tests), M.G. Burgess (2nd Test)

Débuts: Australia – G.F. Lawson (1st Test)
New Zealand – J.G. Bracewell, I.D.S. Smith (1st Test)

Rising Stars: Australia – J.D. Higgs (+72 bowling)
New Zealand – R.J. Hadlee (+66 bowling)

The second Australian season of post-Packer double tours saw visits from India and New Zealand – a slightly less starry line-up than the previous year, but then even Mr Packer couldn't have the Ashes fought for on an annual basis, much as no doubt he would have liked to. The centrepiece for the season was, of course, the interminable series of one-day games, but the Test series tottered on in the background, with the New Zealanders outclassed by some penetrative bowling from Lillee, Hogg and Pascoe. In a generally low-scoring series, none of the visiting batsmen made much of an impression, with only Coney averaging over 40, and Edgar's rating in particular suffered appropriately. For Australia, Geoff Lawson made a nervous début in the first Test and was then dropped, but the other bowlers performed admirably, while the batsmen took full advantage of New Zealand's less than hostile bowling (John Bracewell, after his first three Tests, had a bowling rating of 16), with centuries from the euphonious Australian combination of Wood and Walters. The exception was Border, who scored no more than 45 and dropped to 4th in the world list. Player of the series was Richard Hadlee, the mainstay of the New Zealand attack (as he would remain throughout the 1980s) who took 19 wickets at 19.15 and pushed his bowling rating to just below 800.

AUSTRALIA vs INDIA

First Test (Sydney, 2–4 January) Australia won by an innings and 4 runs
India 1st Innings: 201 (Patil 65 retired hurt, Pascoe 4–61, Lillee 4–86)
Australia 1st Innings: 406 (Chappell 204, Walters 67, Kapil Dev 5–97, Ghavri 5–107)
India 2nd Innings: 201 (Kirmani 43 not out, Higgs 4–45, Lillee 3–79)

Second Test (Adelaide, 23–27 January) Match Drawn
Australia 1st Innings: 528 (K.J. Hughes 213, Wood 125, Border 57, Yadav 4–143, Doshi 4–146)
India 1st Innings: 419 (Patil 174, Chauhan 97, Yashpal Sharma 47, Lillee 4–80)
Australia 2nd Innings: 221 for 7 declared (Hughes 53, Chappell 52, Doshi 3–49)
India 2nd Innings: 135 for 8 (Pascoe 3–32)

Third Test (Melbourne, 7–11 February) India won by 59 runs
India 1st Innings: 237 (Viswanath 114, Lillee 4–65, Pascoe 3–29)
Australia 1st Innings: 419 (Border 124, Walters 78, Chappell 76, R.W. Marsh 45, Doshi 3–109)

India 2nd Innings: 324 (Chauhan 85, Gavaskar 70, Lillee 4–104)
Australia 2nd Innings: 83 (Kapil Dev 5–28, Ghavri 2–10)

Captains: Australia – G.S. Chappell
India – S.M. Gavaskar

Débuts: None

Rising Stars: Australia – K.D. Walters (+410 batting)
India – S.M. Patil (+262 batting)

India's series against Australia was rather less one-sided than New Zealand's, although after the first Test, it looked, if anything, that it would be even more so. Greg Chappell had just notched up the highest individual score by an Australian against them (beating Don Bradman's 201 a mere thirty-three years earlier), and Lillee, Pascoe and the leg-spinner Higgs had scythed through some brittle Indian batting to record an innings win. Australia quickly gained the upper hand in the second Test too, when Gavaskar put them in, saw Wood dropped on 0, and then watched as the home team compiled 528 runs. But Patil, whose 65 in the first Test had been cut short when Pascoe bopped him with a short one, rose to the challenge superbly with an aggressive 174, and in the final Test India squared the series when Australia fell apart against Kapil Dev and Ghavri. Of Indian batsmen, though, only Patil, who averaged over 62, and the old-stager Chauhan saw their ratings flourish. The Australian figures, with Walters leaping an astonishing 429 points to 5th in the world, were altogether sturdier – by the series' end, they boasted four of the world's top eight batsmen, with the top Indian, Gavaskar, down to 9th. Of the bowlers, Pascoe leapt to 9th in the world, while Lillee (4th) and Kapil Dev (2nd) maintained their excellent records.

WEST INDIES vs ENGLAND

First Test (Port-Of-Spain, Trinidad, 13–18 February) West Indies won by an innings and 79 runs
West Indies 1st Innings: 426 for 9 (Haynes 96, Greenidge 84, Lloyd 64, Roberts 50 not out, D.A. Murray 46, Emburey 5–124)
England 1st Innings: 178 (Gower 48, Gooch 41, Croft 5–40)
England 2nd Innings: 169 (Boycott 70, Holding 3–38, Roberts 3–41)

Third Test (Bridgetown, Barbados, 13–18 March) West Indies won by 298 runs
West Indies 1st Innings: 265 (Lloyd 100, Gomes 58, Botham 4–77, Dilley 3–51, Jackman 3–65)
England 1st Innings: 122 (Croft 4–39, Holding 3–16)
West Indies 2nd Innings: 379 for 7 declared (Richards 182 not out, Lloyd 66, Botham 3–102)
England 2nd Innings: 224 (Gooch 116, Gower 54, Croft 3–65)

Fourth Test (St Johns, Antigua, 27 March–1 April) Match Drawn
England 1st Innings: 271 (Willey 102 not out, Croft 6–74)
West Indies 1st Innings: 468 for 9 declared (Richards 114, Mattis 71, Greenidge 63, Lloyd 58, Holding 58 not out, Botham 4–127, Stevenson 3–111)
England 2nd Innings: 234 for 3 (Boycott 104 not out, Gooch 83)

Fifth Test (Kingston, Jamaica, 10–15 April) Match Drawn
England 1st Innings: 285 (Gooch 153, Boycott 40, Holding 5–56)
West Indies 1st Innings: 442 (Lloyd 95, Gomes 90 not out, Haynes 84, Greenidge 62, Dilley 4–116)
England 2nd Innings: 302 for 6 (Gower 154 not out, Willey 67)

Captains: West Indies – C.H. Lloyd
England – I.T. Botham

Débuts: West Indies – E.H. Mattis (1st Test)
England – P.R. Downton (1st Test), R.O. Butcher, R.D. Jackman (3rd Test)

Rising Stars: West Indies – C.H. Lloyd (+143 batting)
England – G.A. Gooch (+139 batting)

The famous 'Jackman series' (not something the great Surrey appealer would wish to be remembered for), during which for the first time a Test match was called off because the host nation objected to an England player's connections with South Africa. Why Robin Jackman was singled out by the Guyanese government was never entirely clear, as a number of other England players had also played and coached there, but perhaps the 'Bairstow series' didn't have quite the same ring to it. Nevertheless, the second Test was called off, thus reducing England's losing margin to a relatively respectable 2–0.

It seems uncharacteristically adventurous, in retrospect, that of England's party, five players were under twenty-three – Gatting, Athey, Dilley, Downton and Gower. The last three all enhanced their reputations, and Gower, Gooch and Willey, who all averaged between 48 and 58, showed that it was possible to bat against the West Indian quickies after all. Their ratings flourished appropriately, with the first two moving up into the top ten on the world table, and Willey entering the top thirty for the first time. That said, the pitches did not favour intense pace as much as they came to on later tours, and there were none of the usual moans about umpiring. Where England suffered was in their bowling. Willis was injured and had to go home, and although Dilley was clearly improving – his rating passed 400 for the first time in the final Test – and Emburey bowled superbly in the first Test, Botham's performance declined under the strains of captaincy, while Old was as injury-prone as ever.

But in the main England were simply outclassed by the bowling of Roberts, Holding, Garner and Croft and the batting of Richards (340 runs at 85) and Lloyd, whose lowest score in the series was 58. Richards broke his own record when his rating climbed to 934 for the third and fourth Tests, the highest batting rating ever recorded. And when Roberts lost form towards the end of the series, who was there to replace him but Malcolm Marshall? Sylvester Clarke, who had had such a good series in Pakistan, couldn't even get into the side.

England probably did as well as they could have expected to, especially after the sudden death of their coach Ken Barrington during the Barbados Test. Their ratings, under the circumstances, bore up well – rather better than they would in later West Indian series, at least.

NEW ZEALAND vs INDIA

First Test (Wellington, 21–25 February) New Zealand won by 62 runs
New Zealand 1st Innings: 375 (Howarth 137 not out, Reid 46, Shastri 3–54, Kapil Dev 3–112)
India 1st Innings: 223 (Patil 64, Cairns 5–33, Troup 3–43)
New Zealand 2nd Innings: 100 (Kapil Dev 4–34, Shastri 3–9)
India 2nd Innings: 190 (Patil 42, Hadlee 4–65)

Second Test (Christchurch, 6–11 March) Match Drawn
India 1st Innings: 255 (Chauhan 78, Vengsarkar 61, Gavaskar 53, Hadlee 5–47)
New Zealand 1st Innings: 286 for 5 (Reid 123 not out, Edgar 49)

Third Test (Auckland, 13–18 March) Match Drawn
India 1st Innings: 238 (Kirmani 78, Yadav 43, Bracewell 4–61, Cairns 3–37)
New Zealand 1st Innings: 366 (Wright 110, Reid 74, Coney 65, Cairns 41, Shastri 5–125)
India 2nd Innings: 284 (Patil 57, Vengsarkar 52 not out, Viswanath 46, Bracewell 5–75, Cairns 3–47)
New Zealand 2nd Innings: 95 for 5 (Edwards 47)

Captains: New Zealand – G.P. Howarth
India – S.M. Gavaskar

Débuts: New Zealand – M.C. Snedden (1st Test)
India – K. Azad, R.J. Shastri, Yograj Singh (1st Test), T.E. Srinivasan (3rd Test)

Rising Stars: New Zealand – J.G. Wright (+139 batting)
India – R.J. Shastri (+60 bowling)

Just to polish off an exhausting winter, India, who had just beaten Australia at Melbourne, came to New Zealand, and through poor batting and a series of unfortunate injuries, managed to lose this brief series. New Zealand, who themselves had been well beaten in

Australia, now played with determination and spirit, Howarth's century in the first Test pushing his rating up to 853, while Wright also flourished, thanks to his 110 in the final Test. Cairns, for once, overshadowed Hadlee with the ball, and saw his own rating rise by 129. But the real star of the series was the left-handed batsman John Reid, returning to Test cricket two years after an inauspicious début against Pakistan. With a century in the rain-ruined second Test, and 74 in the third, he quickly leapt to 511 in the ratings. As for the Indian batsmen, only Chauhan and Viswanath rose at all (and then not by much), while Gavaskar (down 74) and Kapil Dev (down 82 to a measley 348) had a poor series. The nineteen-year-old Shastri was more successful – his 15 wickets at 18.5 gave him a rating after three Tests of 460 – but otherwise the only bowler to maintain his status was Doshi. Did anyone say there's too much Test cricket?

WORLD TOP TWENTY AFTER 1980–81

BATTING

(2)	1.	I.V.A. Richards (West Indies)	930 (+28)
(5)	2.	G.S. Chappell (Australia)	886 (+24)
(3)	3.	Javed Miandad (Pakistan)	873 (−10)
(1)	4.	A.R. Border (Australia)	833 (−70)
NE	5.	K.D. Walters (Australia)	810
(13)	6.	Wasim Raja (Pakistan)	801 (+128)
(8)	7.	K.J. Hughes (Australia)	792 (+7)
(7)	8.	G. Boycott (England)	783 (−23)
(12)	9.	D.I. Gower (England)	777 (+98)
(18)	10.	G.A. Gooch (England)	770 (+139)
(16)	11.	C.H. Lloyd (West Indies)	759 (+117)
(10)	12.	G.P. Howarth (New Zealand)	754 (+2)
(11)	13.	Taslim Arif (Pakistan)	750 (+31)
(4)	14.	S.M. Gavaskar (India)	710 (−172)
(6)	15.	D.L. Haynes (West Indies)	693 (−120)
(68)	16.	S.M. Patil (India)	674 (+385)
(15)	17.	D.B. Vengsarkar (India)	648 (−8)
(14)	18.	Majid Khan (Pakistan)	639 (−26)
(19)	19.	C.G. Greenidge (West Indies)	619 (+1)
NE	20.	H.A. Gomes (West Indies)	619

BOWLING

(7)	1.	C.E.H. Croft (West Indies)	869 (+140)
(5)	2.	D.K. Lillee (Australia)	824 (+72)
(1)	3.	I.T. Botham (England)	814 (−82)

(2)	4.	J. Garner (West Indies)	809 (−85)
(3)	5.	Kapil Dev (India)	808 (−67)
(8)	6.	R.J. Hadlee (New Zealand)	778 (+52)
(4)	7.	D.R. Doshi (India)	748 (−41)
(11)	8.	M.A. Holding (West Indies)	742 (+68)
(31)	9.	L.S. Pascoe (Australia)	736 (+259)
NE	10.	S.T. Clarke (West Indies)	733
(13)	11.	R.M. Hogg (Australia)	696 (+44)
(22)	12.	Iqbal Qasim (Pakistan)	670 (+95)
(10)	13.	Imran Khan (Pakistan)	670 (−18)
(9)	14.	G. Dymock (Australia)	665 (−31)
(6)	15.	A.M.E. Roberts (West Indies)	657 (−73)
(12)	16.	R.G.D. Willis (England)	642 (−26)
(14)	17.	M. Hendrick (England)	650 (−120)
(15)	18.	C.M. Old (England)	606 (−29)
(16)	19.	J.R. Thomson (Australia)	580 (−36)
(17)	20.	A.G. Hurst (Australia)	578 (−36)

With heaps of runs scored against first England in England, then Pakistan in Pakistan and then poor old England at home again, it's hardly surprising that Viv Richards was setting new records for the batting ratings in 1980–81. Greg Chappell also benefited from a purple patch, but perhaps the biggest surprise in the top twenty batsmen is the renaissance of Doug Walters, who scored piles of runs against both India and New Zealand. Good winters for Wasim Raja, Gooch and Clive Lloyd were also reflected in the ratings. Patil and Gomes were the other new entries, replacing Bruce Edgar (9th to 22nd), Gundappa Viswanath (17th to 24th) and Alvin Kallicharran (20th to 30th after being dropped by the West Indies). Coney and Wright of New Zealand remained just outside the top twenty, while Botham had now dropped to 36th. And what of England's brightest new hope, C.W.J. Athey (3 Tests, 17 runs at 2.83)? Right down at 133rd, with a rating of 44.

For the bowlers, Colin Croft's 24 wickets against England at just under 19 pushed him to the top of the list, while Sylvester Clarke's successful Pakistan tour propelled him into the top ten for the first time. With four of their quickies in the top ten, and Andy Roberts at 15th, the West Indies' pre-eminence was unquestioned. Botham, despite relatively average bowling performances in the West Indies and the collapse of his batting form, was still in the top three, while England's next highest bowlers on that tour were Old (18th), Miller (32nd), Dilley (33rd) and Emburey (48th, behind Javed Miandad). Rarely had the side's bowling resources been thinner. Meanwhile, Len Pascoe's good form had finally paid off, and Iqbal Qasim's 17 wickets against the West Indies brought him into the top twenty too. Out were Phil Edmonds (who hadn't played for eighteen months and so was out of the ratings altogether), Sikander Bakht (19th to 26th) and Derek Underwood (20th to 24th).

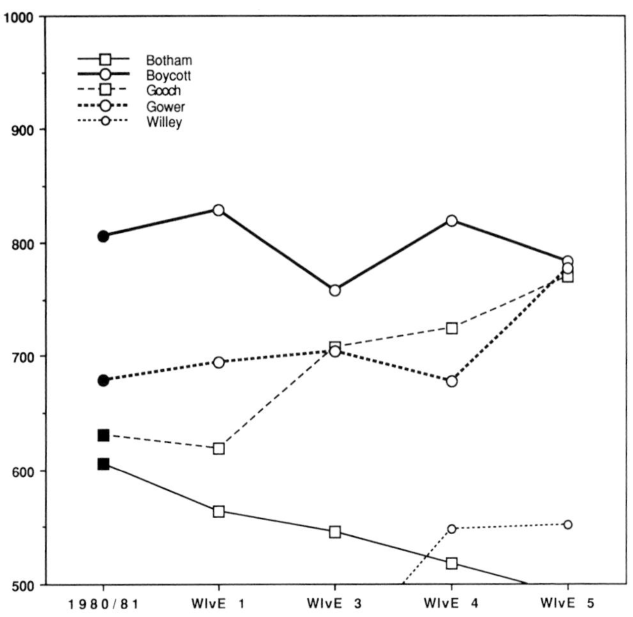
ENGLAND BATSMEN 1980/81
1000
900
800
700
600
500
Botham
Boycott
Gooch
Gower
Willey
1980/81
WIvE 1
WIvE 3
WIvE 4
WIvE 5

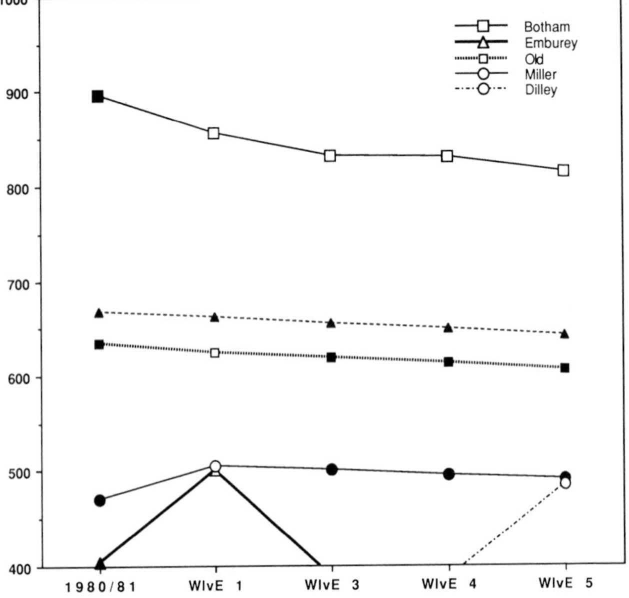
ENGLAND BOWLERS 1980/81
1000
900
800
700
600
500
400
Botham
Emburey
Old
Miller
Dilley
1980/81
WIvE 1
WIvE 3
WIvE 4
WIvE 5

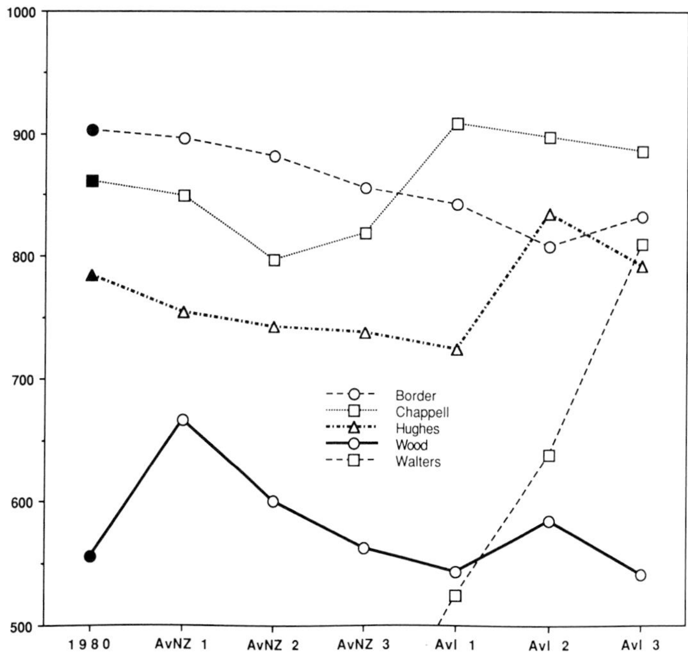
AUSTRALIA BATSMEN 1980/81
1000
900
800
700
600
500
1980
AvNZ 1
AvNZ 2
AvNZ 3
AvI 1
AvI 2
AvI 3
Border
Chappell
Hughes
Wood
Walters

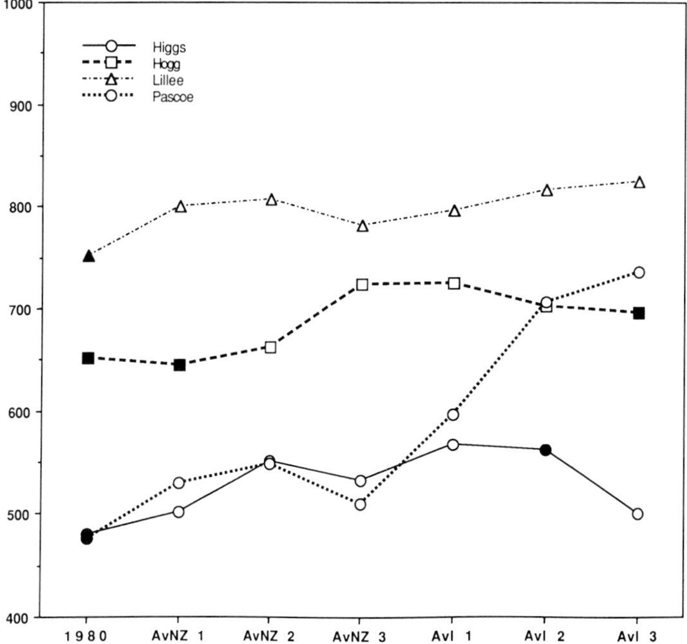
AUSTRALIA BOWLERS 1980/81
1000
900
800
700
600
500
400
1980
AvNZ 1
AvNZ 2
AvNZ 3
AvI 1
AvI 2
AvI 3
Higgs
Hogg
Lillee
Pascoe

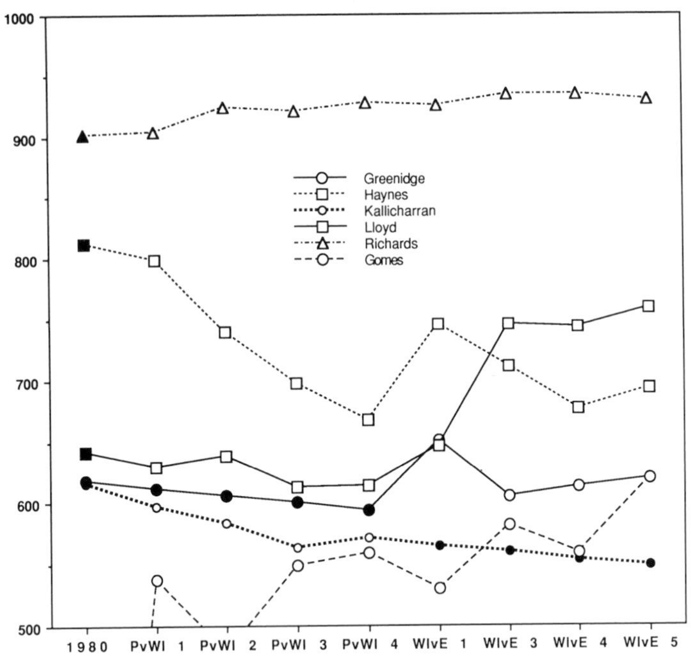
WEST INDIES BATSMEN 1980/81
1000
900
800
700
600
500
Greenidge
Haynes
Kallicharran
Lloyd
Richards
Gomes
1980
PvWI 1
PvWI 2
PvWI 3
PvWI 4
WIvE 1
WIvE 3
WIvE 4
WIvE 5

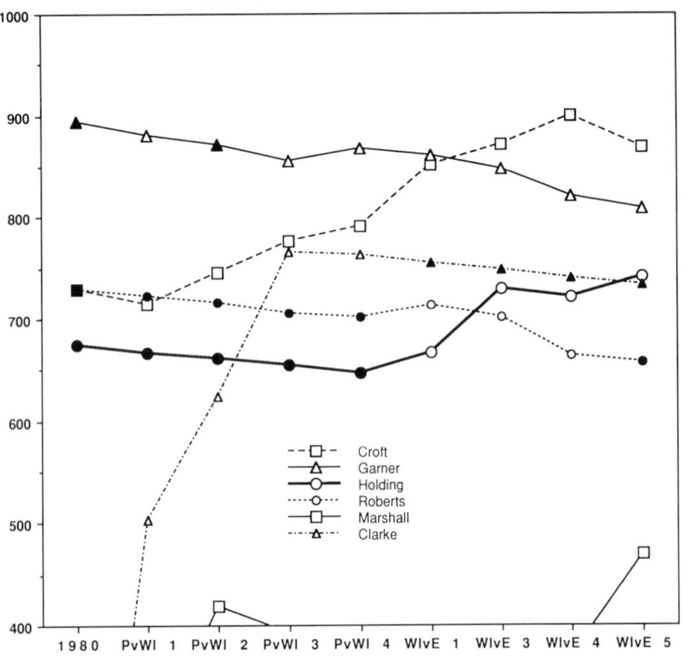
WEST INDIES BOWLERS 1980/81
1000
900
800
700
600
500
400
Croft
Garner
Holding
Roberts
Marshall
Clarke
1980
PvWI 1
PvWI 2
PvWI 3
PvWI 4
WIvE 1
WIvE 3
WIvE 4
WIvE 5

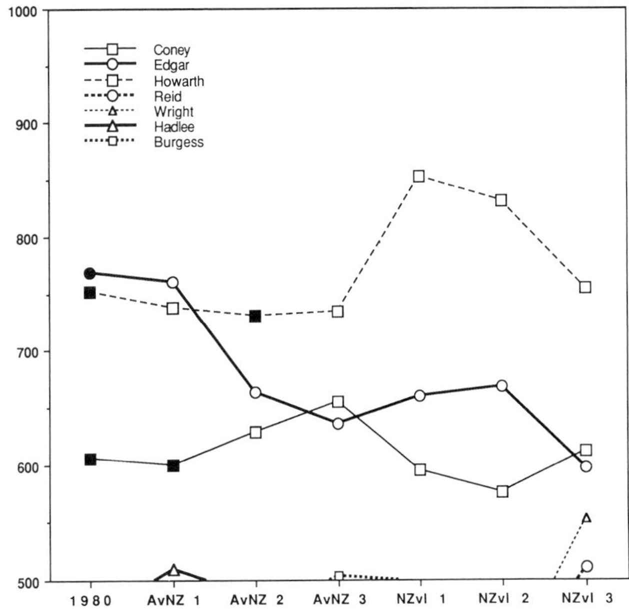
NEW ZEALAND BATSMEN 1980/81
Coney
Edgar
Howarth
Reid
Wright
Hadlee
Burgess
1000
900
800
700
600
500
1980
AvNZ 1
AvNZ 2
AvNZ 3
NZvI 1
NZvI 2
NZvI 3

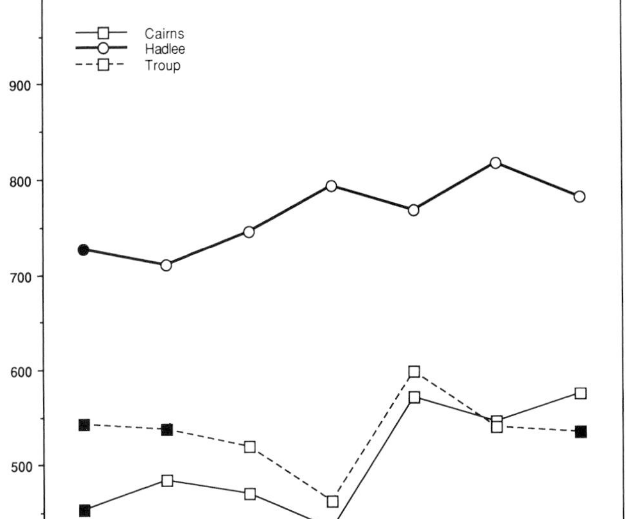
NEW ZEALAND BOWLERS 1980/81
Cairns
Hadlee
Troup
1000
900
800
700
600
500
400
1980
AvNZ 1
AvNZ 2
AvNZ 3
NZvI 1
NZvI 2
NZvI 3

INDIA BATSMEN 1980/81

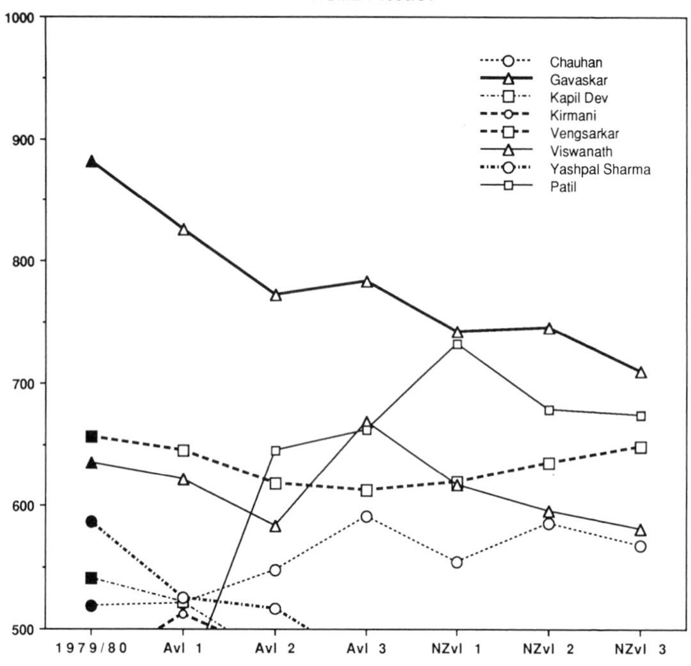
1000
900
800
700
600
500
Chauhan
Gavaskar
Kapil Dev
Kirmani
Vengsarkar
Viswanath
Yashpal Sharma
Patil
1979/80
Avl 1
Avl 2
Avl 3
NZvl 1
NZvl 2
NZvl 3

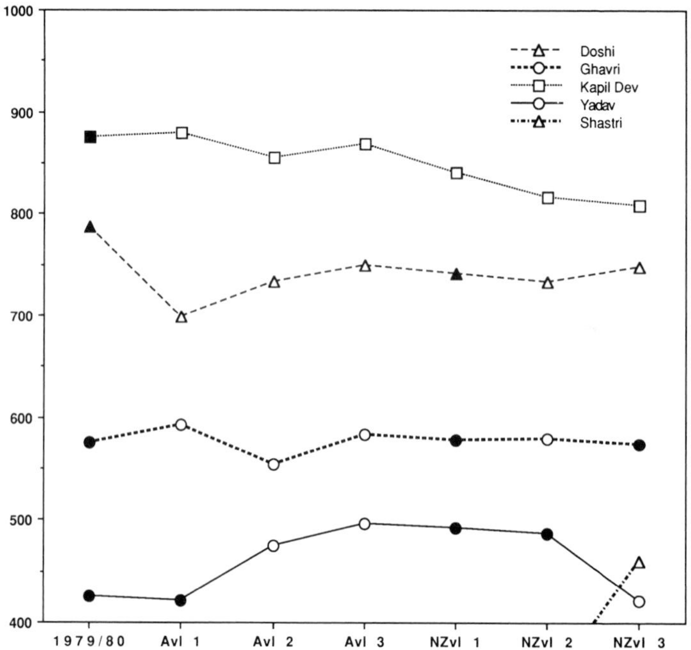
INDIA BOWLERS 1980/81
1000
900
800
700
600
500
400
Doshi
Ghavri
Kapil Dev
Yadav
Shastri
1979/80
Avl 1
Avl 2
Avl 3
NZvl 1
NZvl 2
NZvl 3

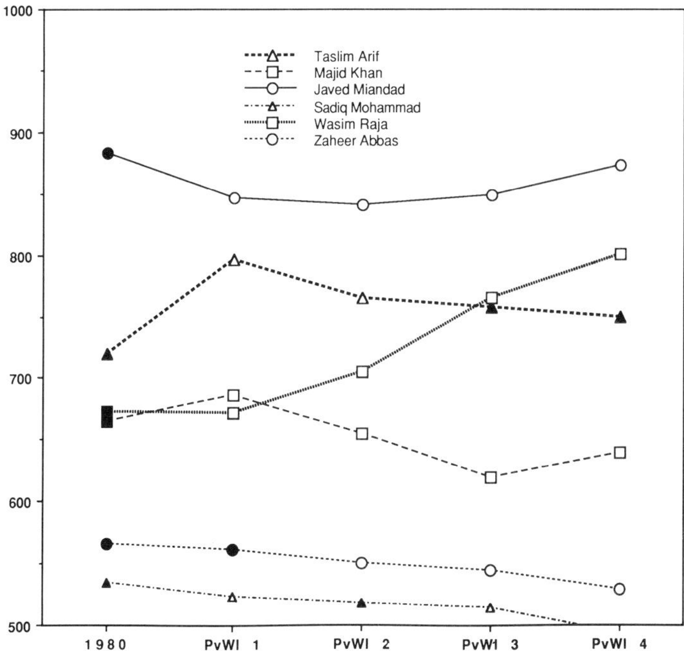
PAKISTAN BATSMEN 1980/81
1000
900
800
700
600
500
Taslim Arif
Majid Khan
Javed Miandad
Sadiq Mohammad
Wasim Raja
Zaheer Abbas
1980
PvWI 1
PvWI 2
PvWI 3
PvWI 4

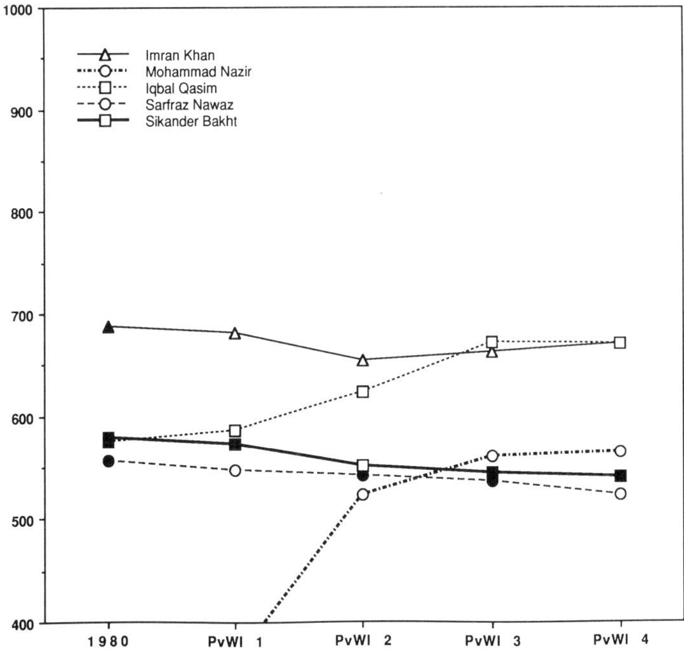
PAKISTAN BOWLERS 1980/81
1000
900
800
700
600
500
400
Imran Khan
Mohammad Nazir
Iqbal Qasim
Sarfraz Nawaz
Sikander Bakht
1980
PvWI 1
PvWI 2
PvWI 3
PvWI 4

1981

ENGLAND vs AUSTRALIA

First Test (Trent Bridge, 18–21 June) Australia won by 4 wickets
England 1st Innings: 185 (Gatting 52, Alderman 4–68, Lillee 3–34, Hogg 3–47)
Australia 1st Innings: 179 (Border 63, Dilley 3–38, Willis 3–47)
England 2nd Innings: 125 (Lillee 5–46, Alderman 5–62)
Australia 2nd Innings: 132 for 6 (Dilley 4–24)

Second Test (Lord's, 2–7 July) Match Drawn
England 1st Innings: 311 (Willey 82, Gatting 59, Gooch 44, Lawson 7–81)
Australia 1st Innings: 345 (Border 64, R.W. Marsh 47, Wood 44, K.J. Hughes 42, Lillee 40 not out, Willis 3–50, Dilley 3–106)
England 2nd Innings: 265 for 8 declared (Gower 89, Boycott 60, Bright 3–67, Lillee 3–82)
Australia 2nd Innings: 90 for 4 (Wood 62 not out)

Third Test (Headingley, 16–21 July) England won by 18 runs
Australia 1st Innings: 401 for 9 declared (Dyson 102, K.J. Hughes 89, Yallop 58, Botham 6–95)
England 1st Innings: 174 (Botham 50, Lillee 4–49, Lawson 3–32, Alderman 3–59)
England 2nd Innings: 356 (Botham 149 not out, Dilley 56, Boycott 46, Alderman 6–135, Lillee 3–94)
Australia 2nd Innings: 111 (Willis 8–43)

Fourth Test (Edgbaston, 30 July–2 August) England won by 29 runs
England 1st Innings: 189 (Brearley 48, Alderman 5–42)
Australia 1st Innings: 258 (K.J. Hughes 47, Kent 46, Emburey 4–43, Old 3–44)
England 2nd Innings: 219 (Bright 5–68, Alderman 3–65)
Australia 2nd Innings: 121 (Border 40, Botham 5–11)

Fifth Test (Old Trafford, 13–17 August) England won by 103 runs
England 1st Innings: 231 (Tavaré 69, Allott 52 not out, Lillee 4–55, Alderman 4–88)
Australia 1st Innings: 130 (Kent 52, Willis 4–63, Botham 3–28)
England 2nd Innings: 404 (Botham 118, Tavaré 78, Knott 59, Emburey 57, Alderman 5–109)

Australia 2nd Innings: 402 (Border 123 not out, Yallop 114, R.W. Marsh 47, K.J. Hughes 43, Willis 3–96)

Sixth Test (The Oval, 27 August–1 September) Match Drawn
Australia 1st Innings: 352 (Border 106 not out, Wood 66, Kent 54, Botham 6–125, Willis 4–91)
England 1st Innings: 314 (Boycott 137, Gatting 53, Lillee 7–89, Alderman 3–84)
Australia 2nd Innings: 344 for 9 declared (Wellham 103, Border 84, R.W. Marsh 52, Hendrick 4–82, Botham 4–128)
England 2nd Innings: 261 for 7 (Knott 70 not out, Gatting 56, Brearley 51, Lillee 4–70)

Captains: England – I.T. Botham (1st & 2nd Tests), J.M. Brearley (3rd–6th Tests)
Australia – K.J. Hughes

Débuts: England – P.J.W. Allott (5th Test), P.W.G. Parker (6th Test)
Australia – T.M. Alderman, T.M. Chappell (1st Test), M.F. Kent (4th Test), M.R. Whitney (5th Test), D.M. Wellham (6th Test)

Rising Stars: England – I.T. Botham (+166 batting)
Australia – T.M. Alderman (+332 bowling)

One of the most famous of all Test series, certainly in England, where it was one of the few in the Eighties they actually won. Botham's finest hour was preceded by the inglorious end to his captaincy after the Lord's Test, when he made 0 and the MCC members refused to clap him into the pavilion. 'Send for Brearley!' was the cry, and the selectors paid heed, the old brainbox returning for Headingley and perhaps England's most bizarre Test win this century. Or at least, the most bizarre until the following Test at Edgbaston.

The volatility of the ratings – which are of course a measurement of form rather than lasting success – was never better shown than during this remarkable series. The leaps and bounds of Terry Alderman, for instance, with an impressive initial rating of 447 on his début and a peak after the fifth of 751, reflected the importance of his record 42 wickets in the series, while Lillee maintained his own lofty status with 39 wickets and, after the first Test, a new personal high of 870. Border also did well, jumping 69 to pass 900 for the first time since the Centenary Test, but the other batsmen either trod water or declined notably. In particular, the absence of Greg Chappell (still smarting after the controversies of his captaincy the previous Australian summer – most memorably the famous 'grubber' he instructed his brother Trevor to bowl at the end of a hard fought one-day match against New Zealand) fatally weakened the top half of the order. Even Martin Kent's successful introduction (416 after three Tests) was small consolation.

But it was England whose ratings really wobbled about, as indeed did their performances. After a disastrous first Test and an inconclusive second, Botham's batting had plummeted to a (for him) dismal 452, lower even than Gatting, who at this stage in his career was averaging about 22. At Headingley, though, Botham's rating leapt 210 points to its highest for a year, and after a further peak (for his Edgbaston century) settled at a rather more respectable 657. The Kent dasher Tavaré, meanwhile, recalled for the fifth Test, jumped from 124 to 518, which can't be too far away from the number of minutes we watched him bat during those long dour days. Brearley bobbled around 400 as usual, but Gooch and Gower had one of their bad years. Curiously enough Allott, who made his début as a bowler but proceeded to score his maiden first-class fifty instead, ended the series with a higher batting rating (282) than bowling rating (208). Dilley, meanwhile, confirmed his England status at the first Test, moving up 170 points with his 7 inexpensive wickets, while his 56 at Headingley gave him a higher batting rating than the just dropped Bob Woolmer. Oddly, Willis' remarkable bowling at Headingley gave him only 40 extra points, an odd anomaly that confirms my suspicion that it's rather easier to get batting points on this system than bowling points. Unless you're Botham, of course.

WORLD TOP TWENTY AFTER 1981

BATTING

(1)	1.	I.V.A. Richards (West Indies)	930
(4)	2.	A.R. Border (Australia)	902 (+69)
(3)	3.	Javed Miandad (Pakistan)	873
(2)	4.	G.S. Chappell (Australia)	834 (−52)
(6)	5.	Wasim Raja (Pakistan)	801
(5)	6.	K.D. Walters (Australia)	763 (−47)
(11)	7.	C.H. Lloyd (West Indies)	759
(12)	8.	G.P. Howarth (New Zealand)	754
(13)	9.	Taslim Arif (Pakistan)	750
(8)	10.	G. Boycott (England)	742 (−41)
(14)	11.	S.M. Gavaskar (India)	710
(15)	12.	D.L. Haynes (West Indies)	693
(16)	13.	S.M. Patil (India)	674
(9)	14.	D.I. Gower (England)	671 (−106)
(36)	15.	I.T. Botham (England)	657 (+166)
(7)	16.	K.J. Hughes (Australia)	651 (−141)

(17)	17.	D.B. Vengsarkar (India)	648
(18)	18.	Majid Khan (Pakistan)	639
(19)	19.	C.G. Greenidge (West Indies)	619
(20)	20.	H.A. Gomes (West Indies)	619

BOWLING

(1)	1.	C.E.H. Croft (West Indies)	869
(2)	2.	D.K. Lillee (Australia)	837 (+13)
(3)	3.	I.T. Botham (England)	827 (+13)
(4)	4.	J. Garner (West Indies)	809
(5)	5.	Kapil Dev (India)	808
(6)	6.	R.J. Hadlee (New Zealand)	778
(7)	7.	D.R. Doshi (India)	748
(8)	8.	M.A. Holding (West Indies)	742
(10)	9.	S.T. Clarke (West Indies)	733
NE	10.	T.M. Alderman (Australia)	732
(9)	11.	L.S. Pascoe (Australia)	693 (−47)
(12)	12.	Iqbal Qasim (Pakistan)	670
(13)	13.	Imran Khan (Pakistan)	670
(16)	14.	R.G.D. Willis (England)	670 (+28)
(15)	15.	A.M.E. Roberts (West Indies)	657
(33)	16.	G.R. Dilley (England)	632 (+147)
(18)	17.	C.M. Old (England)	593 (−13)
(11)	18.	R.M. Hogg (Australia)	587 (−107)
(21)	19.	K.D. Ghavri (India)	574
(22)	20.	B.L. Cairns (New Zealand)	571

Border's fine form in the Ashes series paid off with a rise to second place, but notice the one new entry at number 15. Chappell and Walters dropped by the usual dint of not going on tour, while the declines of Gower, Hughes and Gooch were there for all to see. Well, not Gooch's, as he had dropped out of the twenty altogether, falling from 10th to 23rd with a thumping loss of 181 points.

As for the bowlers, Lillee and Botham maintained their places while Alderman did well to sneak into the top ten in only six Tests. Dilley's improvement overshadowed a general drop in points levels, allowing Ghavri and Cairns to sneak into the twenty without doing anything at all – a neat trick. Leaving the top rank was Hendrick, whose loss of 84 valuable points meant a drop from 17th to 21st, plus the three Australian bowlers Dymock, Thomson and Hurst, none of whom had been picked in the preceding eighteen months.

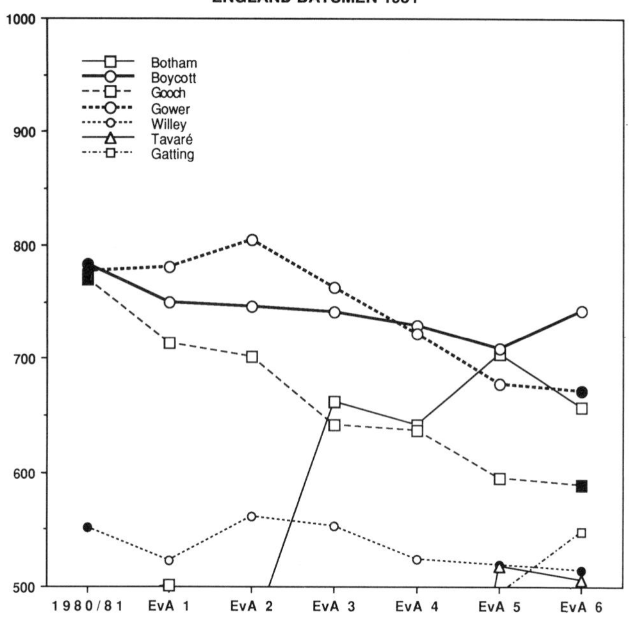
ENGLAND BATSMEN 1981
1000
900
800
700
600
500
Botham
Boycott
Gooch
Gower
Willey
Tavaré
Gatting
1980/81
EvA 1
EvA 2
EvA 3
EvA 4
EvA 5
EvA 6

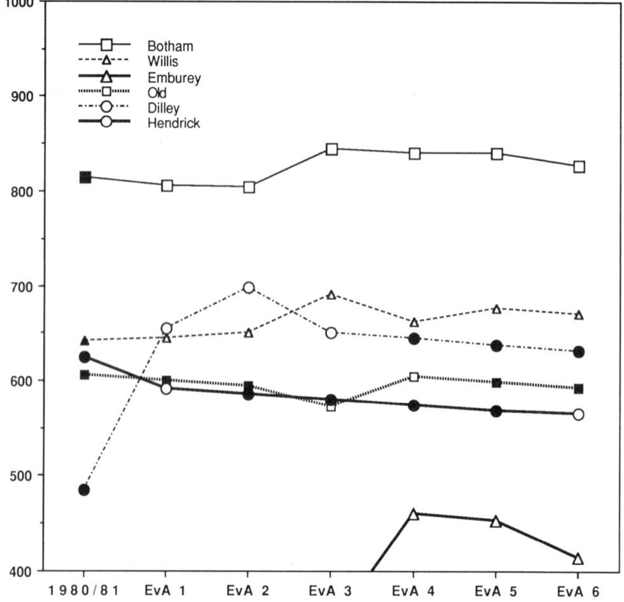
ENGLAND BOWLERS 1981
1000
900
800
700
600
500
400
Botham
Willis
Emburey
Old
Dilley
Hendrick
1980/81
EvA 1
EvA 2
EvA 3
EvA 4
EvA 5
EvA 6

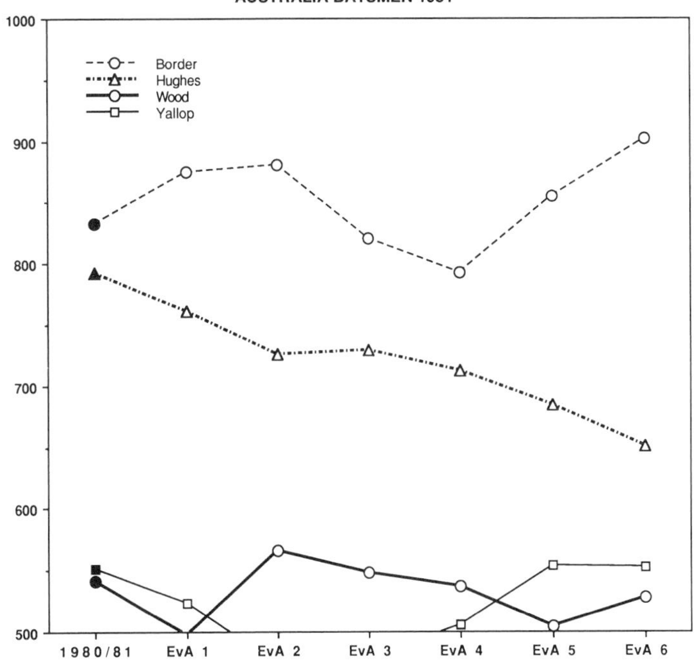
AUSTRALIA BATSMEN 1981
Border
Hughes
Wood
Yallop
1000
900
800
700
600
500
1980/81
EvA 1
EvA 2
EvA 3
EvA 4
EvA 5
EvA 6

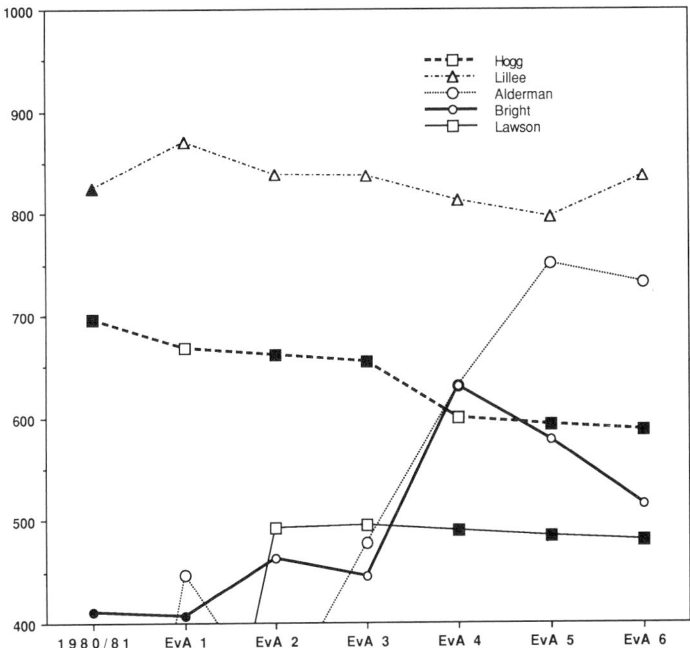
AUSTRALIA BOWLERS 1981
Hogg
Lillee
Alderman
Bright
Lawson
1000
900
800
700
600
500
400
1980/81
EvA 1
EvA 2
EvA 3
EvA 4
EvA 5
EvA 6

1981–82

AUSTRALIA vs PAKISTAN

First Test (Perth, 13–17 November) Australia won by 286 runs
Australia 1st Innings: 180 (Imran Kahn 4–66)
Pakistan 1st Innings: 62 (Lillee 5–18, Alderman 4–36)
Australia 2nd Innings: 424 for 8 declared (K.J. Hughes 106, Laird 85, Wood 49, Marsh 47, Imran Khan 3–90)
Pakistan 2nd Innings: 256 (Javed Miandad 79, Wasim Raja 48, Yardley 6–84)

Second Test (Brisbane, 27 November–1 December) Australia won by 10 wickets
Pakistan 1st Innings: 291 (Zaheer Abbas 80, Wasim Raja 43, Lillee 5–81)
Australia 1st Innings: 512 for 9 declared (Chappell 201, Wood 72, Laird 44, Imran Khan 4–92)
Pakistan 2nd Innings: 223 (Mohsin Khan 43, Lillee 4–51, Yardley 4–77)
Australia 2nd Innings: 3 for no wicket

Third Test (Melbourne, 11–15 December) Pakistan won by an innings and 82 runs
Pakistan 1st Innings: 500 (Mudassar Nazar 95, Zaheer Abbas 90, Majid Khan 74, Imran Khan 70 not out, Javed Miandad 62, Wasim Raja 50, Yardley 7–187)
Australia 1st Innings: 293 (Wood 100, Imran Khan 3–41, Iqbal Qasim 3–104)
Australia 2nd Innings: 125 (Laird 52, Iqbal Qasim 4–44, Sarfraz Nawaz 3–11)

Captains: Australia – G.S. Chappell
Pakistan – Javed Miandad

Début: Pakistan – Rizwan-uz-Zaman (1st Test)

Rising Stars: Australia – B. Yardley (+168 bowling)
Pakistan – Mudassar Nazar (+71 batting)

With the one-day mania at its height – Pakistan and West Indies were the visitors for Australia's now annual World Series Cup competition

– no-one was too bothered about the Tests, which were played to a total of less than 90,000 spectators. But there were some good performances nonetheless from both sides. For Pakistan, Imran (16 wickets at 19.5 – up 56 points) and Iqbal Qasim (10 at 23.5 – up 32 points) kept the bowling afloat, but their batting was as mercurial as ever, ranging from 62 all out at Perth (their lowest total against anyone) to 500 on a poor MCG pitch, with runs from most of the top order. Zaheer topped the averages with 56.66, and rose 70 in the ratings, and Mudassar had a few good knocks, but otherwise few players did more than consolidate.

The Australians, though, looked a much better side with Chappell back in charge, even though for once Border failed (average 16, top score 37, down 99 points in the process) and the side as a whole played poorly at Melbourne. Chappell, Wood and the returning Laird all averaged around 50, and the latter two gained 75 and 120 points for their troubles. But all was overshadowed by the huge barney that Lillee and cheery old Javed Miandad enjoyed at Perth, when the Australian kicked the Pakistani and the Pakistani threatened the Australian with his bat. Good clean fun, and Dennis got his revenge during the following Test, with a scorecard entry that would never be permitted in the subcontinent: Javed Miandad lbw b Lillee 38.

INDIA vs ENGLAND

First Test (Bombay, 27 November–1 December) India won by 138 runs
India 1st Innings: 179 (Gavaskar 55, Dilley 4–47, Botham 4–72)
England 1st Innings: 166 (Boycott 60, Tavaré 56, Doshi 5–39)
India 2nd Innings: 227 (Kapil Dev 46, Botham 5–61)
England 2nd Innings: 102 (Madan Lal 5–23, Kapil Dev 5–70)

Second Test (Bangalore, 9–14 December) Match Drawn
England 1st Innings: 400 (Gower 82, Gooch 58, Botham 55, Dilley 52, Shastri 4–83, Kapil Dev 3–136)
India 1st Innings: 428 (Gavaskar 172, Srikkanth 65, Kapil Dev 59, Vengsarkar 43, Lever 5–100, Underwood 3–88)
England 2nd Innings: 174 for 3 (Boycott 50, Gooch 40)

Third Test (Delhi, 23–28 December) Match Drawn
England 1st Innings: 476 (Tavaré 149, Boycott 105, Gooch 71, Botham 66, Fletcher 51, Madan Lal 5–85)
India 1st Innings: 487 (Viswanath 107, Shastri 93, Kirmani 67, Gavaskar 46, Madan Lal 44)

Kapil Dev in full flourish.

England 2nd Innings: 68 for no wicket

Fourth Test (Calcutta, 1–6 January) Match Drawn
England 1st Innings: 248 (Fletcher 69, Botham 58, Gooch 47, Kapil Dev 6–91)
India 1st Innings: 208 (Vengsarkar 70, Gavaskar 42, Underwood 3–45)
England 2nd Innings: 265 for 5 declared (Gower 74, Gooch 63, Fletcher 60 not out)
India 2nd Innings: 170 for 3 (Gavaskar 83 not out)

Fifth Test (Madras, 13–18 January) Match Drawn
India 1st Innings: 481 for 4 declared (Viswanath 222, Yashpal Sharma 140, Vengsarkar 71 retired hurt)
England 1st Innings: 328 (Gooch 127, Gower 64, Botham 52, Doshi 4–69, Kapil Dev 3–88, Shastri 3–104)
India 2nd Innings: 160 for 3 (Pranab Roy 60 not out)

Sixth Test (Kanpur, 30 January–4 February) Match Drawn
England 1st Innings: 378 for 9 declared (Botham 142, Gower 85, Gooch 58, Doshi 4–81)
India 1st Innings: 377 for 7 (Kapil Dev 116, Viswanath 74, Yashpal Sharma 55 not out, Gavaskar 52, Willis 3–75)

Captains: India – S.M. Gavaskar
England – K.W.R. Fletcher

Débuts: India – K. Srikkanth (1st Test), A. Malhotra, Pranab Roy (5th Test)

Rising Stars: India – Kapil Dev (+146 batting)
England – C.J. Tavaré (+100 batting)

Although probably gruesomely tedious actually to watch – India, having won the first Test with ease, were content to see through the remainder of the series with boring draw after boring draw – England's eighth tour of the country was rather more notable for the political hubbub that sought to undermine it. First there was doubt that the tour would go ahead at all, with both Boycott and Geoff Cook objected to by the Indian authorities for their South African connections. Then, at the end of the tour, it turned out that Boycott had been instrumental in the arrangement of a 'rebel' tour to South Africa by a group of fifteen England cricketers under the auspices of South African Breweries. All the players, eleven of whom had played for England in the preceding eighteen months, were banned from international cricket for three years.

It may be instructive to give the ratings of those eleven (those above 250, at least) and their world placings at the time:

BATTING	Rating	World ranking
Boycott	718	12th
Gooch	685	15th
Willey	484	40th
Knott	401	50th
Woolmer	366	55th
Larkins	267	69th
Emburey	265	70th

BOWLING	Rating	World ranking
Old	558	20th
Lever	554	21st
Hendrick	533	25th
Underwood	504	30th
Emburey	403	38th

Compare these with those who stayed – Botham (742, 7th), Gower (710, 13th), Tavaré (606, 23rd), new captain Fletcher (492, 37th) and Gatting (459, 43rd) of the batsmen, and of the bowlers, Botham again (738, 7th), Willis (669, 13th), Dilley (509, 29th) and Miller (434, 37th) – and it's easy to see how important the losses were, even taking into consideration the relatively elderly nature of the rebel party. The figures also illustrate just why England came to rely so much on Botham in subsequent series.

These, though, were the positions at the end of the six Tests in India, by which time most of England's batsmen had improved their ratings and most of England's bowlers had seen theirs decline. For other than the first calamitous Test, when England recorded the lowest total by a visiting country in India, the batting held up well, with Gooch and Botham both averaging over 50. Botham's bowling, on the other hand, fell away badly after a good start at Bombay, with only 8 wickets in the final five Tests at 65 – enough for his rating to fall 100 points. For the first time he ended a tour with a higher batting rating than bowling rating. Dilley's batting rating also fell as attempts were made to groom him into an all-rounder – his recent position in the England team (11) shows how well that worked. Poor Allott played only one Test, was hit for 135 without taking a wicket, and saw his rating collapse to 58. Tavaré's steady batting gave him the Rising Star award (or at least it would have done, had it existed at the time).

For India, most of the batsmen prospered, as pitches were prepared with the draw (rather than the spectators) in mind. Viswanath's partnership of 316 with Yashpal broke sundry records, as well as the England's bowlers' hearts, but neither could disturb Gavaskar at the top of his country's ratings, as he rose 88 to 798 and 5th in the world. Doshi's 22 wickets at 21 pushed him up to 3rd, leading one to wonder whether we might well have underestimated him at the time. Kapil Dev's rather more expensive wickets did his bowling rating no favours (down 104 to 704) but his batting rating prospered, and he too was a Rising Star. But what a dreary series.

AUSTRALIA vs WEST INDIES

First Test (Melbourne, 26–30 December) Australia won by 58 runs
Australia 1st Innings: 198 (K.J. Hughes 100 not out, Holding 5–45)
West Indies 1st Innings: 201 (Gomes 55, Dujon 41, Lillee 7–83)
Australia 2nd Innings: 222 (Border 66, Laird 64, Wood 46, Holding 6–62, Garner 3–37)
West Indies 2nd Innings: 161 (Dujon 43, Yardley 4–38, Lillee 3–44)

Second Test (Sydney, 2–6 January) Match Drawn
West Indies 1st Innings: 384 (Gomes 126, Greenidge 66, Richards 44, Dujon 44, Lloyd 40, Lillee 4–119, Yardley 3–87, Thomson 3–93)
Australia 1st Innings: 267 (Wood 63, Border 53 not out, Yardley 45, Holding 5–64)
West Indies 2nd Innings: 255 (Lloyd 57, Haynes 51, Dujon 48, Gomes 43, Yardley 7–98)

Australia 2nd Innings: 200 for 4 (Dyson 127 not out)

Third Test (Adelaide, 30 January–3 February) West Indies won by 5 wickets
Australia 1st Innings: 238 (Border 78, Chappell 61, Holding 5–72, Roberts 4–43)
West Indies 1st Innings: 389 (Gomes 124 not out, Lloyd 53, Dujon 51, Richards 42, Roberts 42, Yardley 5–132, Thomson 4–112)
Australia 2nd Innings: 386 (Border 126, Hughes 84, Laird 78, Garner 5–56, Holding 3–70)
West Indies 2nd Innings: 239 for 5 (Lloyd 77 not out, Greenidge 52, Richards 50, Pascoe 3–84)

Captains: Australia – G.S. Chappell
West Indies – C.H. Lloyd

Débuts: West Indies – P.J.L. Dujon (1st Test)

Rising Stars: Australia – B. Yardley (+107 bowling)
West Indies – P.J.L. Dujon (+232 batting)

Intimations of West Indies' mortality come around about once every four or five years. Then the rumblings begin, and people start suggesting, quietly if rather smugly, that perhaps the West Indies are finally in decline, and it won't be long before Sri Lanka are beating them, or even England. The usual basis for this is that they have lost a Test match, and indeed when they did lose one in Australia in 1981–82, Henry Blofeld and the rest consulted their tea–leaves and found the Windies wanting. Were they complacent? Had they lost the will to win? Or more to the point, were they sick to death of all those one-day games?

But whatever the reason, the West Indies did finally lose a Test in Australia – although it wasn't long (about four weeks) before they won one again. Superb bowling by Lillee and Yardley was the difference in this case, and indeed, in that first Test Lillee notched up his 85th wicket in 1981, a new record. In fact, the two sides ended the series with the top two bowlers in the world – Lillee (who was merely maintaining his position) and Holding, who rose to 2nd after taking 24 wickets in the three games at 14.33. But although Garner still hung on in there, Croft, Roberts and Clarke were far less impressive than usual.

The batting, meanwhile, was dominated by Gomes, whose 393 runs at 78 (and a regular place at last) propelled him from 619 to 844 and 4th in the world; Lloyd, who certainly hadn't lost *his* will to win; and Dujon, the reserve wicketkeeper, who until David Murray was injured after the second Test, played as a specialist batsman. Greenidge, Haynes and Richards, by contrast, had a poor series, with Richards averaging just 26. Lucky old Australia.

Clive Lloyd in characteristic pose, after another savage square cut.

The Australian batting, as so often, was held together by Border, who had the second highest aggregate and average (336 at 67) after Gomes. Dyson too made his mark, rising to his highest personal rating, 526, after a staunch match-saving century in the second Test. But Chappell was out of sorts, with four successive noughts in one-day matches and Tests. Yardley, meanwhile, won the Rising Star award for the second successive series (with his best ever figures in the second Test), and moved up to 12th in the world. But was anyone interested? Just before the third Test the managing director of the Packer-owned company that was marketing Australian cricket doubted that Test matches could survive in the long term. With everybody writing off the West Indies, it was clearly the season for wishful thinking.

SRI LANKA vs ENGLAND

Inaugural Test (Colombo, 17–21 February) England won by 7 wickets

Sri Lanka 1st Innings: 218 (Madugalle 65, Ranatunga 54, Underwood 5–28, Botham 3–28)
England 1st Innings: 223 (Gower 89, Fletcher 45, de Mel 4–70, D.S. de Silva 3–54)
Sri Lanka 2nd Innings: 175 (Dias 77, Emburey 6–33, Underwood 3–67)
England 2nd Innings: 171 for 3 (Tavaré 85, Gower 42 not out)

Captains: Sri Lanka – B. Warnapura
England – K.W.R. Fletcher

Débuts: Sri Lanka – the whole lot
England – G. Cook

Gower's superb performance in Sri Lanka's inaugural Test did not just help win the match – it pushed him seven places up the world list to 7th, with 797. The highest batsman for the Sri Lankans, on the other hand, was Madugalle at 77th. Not that you can expect to wow the ratings after just one Test (the Sri Lankans would do rather better later on in the decade). The relatively small number of Sri Lankans to have a rating at all at this point (eleven, if you hadn't guessed) contrasts interestingly with the thirty-one England could boast – testimony, surely, to the selectoral processes of the time (and of most times since, come to that). Most of those who played, though, did not take full advantage of Test cricket's weakest outfit to bump up their averages or their ratings – Botham failed on both counts, and besides Gower, no-one but Tavaré (who recorded a new high, 641, and was even stumped!) acquitted himself especially well. And poor Allott, wicketless again, saw his rating fall further to just 44.

NEW ZEALAND vs AUSTRALIA

First Test (Wellington, 26 February–2 March) Match Drawn
New Zealand 1st Innings: 266 (Howarth 58 not out, Edgar 55, Yardley 3–49)
Australia 1st Innings: 85 for 1 (Wood 41)

Second Test (Auckland, 12–16 March) New Zealand won by 5 wickets
Australia 1st Innings: 210 (Troup 4–82)
New Zealand 1st Innings: 387 (Edgar 161, Coney 73, Howarth 56, Yardley 4–142, Lillee 3–106)
Australia 2nd Innings: 280 (Wood 100, Hadlee 5–63, Cairns 3–85)
New Zealand 2nd Innings: 109 for 5 (Yardley 2–40)

Third Test (Christchurch, 19–22 March) Australia won by 8 wickets
Australia 1st Innings: 353 (Chappell 176, Wood 64, Hadlee 6–100)
New Zealand 1st Innings: 149 (Hadlee 40, Thomson 4–51, Lillee 3–13)
New Zealand 2nd Innings: 272 (Wright 141, Howarth 41, Yardley 4–80, Border 3–20)
Australia 2nd Innings: 69 for 2

Captains: New Zealand – G.P. Howarth
Australia – G.S. Chappell

Début: New Zealand – M.D. Crowe (1st Test)

Rising Stars: New Zealand – B.A. Edgar (+117 batting)
Australia – G.S. Chappell (+106 batting)

This was a rather more cheerful series than the notorious 'underarm' series of the previous year, dominated by some excellent individual performances by members of two otherwise well-matched teams. Large centuries by Chappell, Edgar and Wright did their ratings no harm at all, Chappell's pushing him back into the world top ten after a previously disappointing summer. But with too many of Australia's frontline batsmen badly out of form – Hughes averaged less than 10 and Border (uncharacteristically) less than 15 – the brittleness of the batting cost Chappell's side the second Test – only their second ever defeat by New Zealand. (Equally bizarrely, Wood and Laird's 106 stand in the second innings was Australia's first ever three-figure opening partnership in New Zealand.) But the Aussies made amends in the final Test, when it was New Zealand's turn to bat and bowl ineptly. Hadlee, as ever, was the star of the home side's bowling, his 14 wickets bringing him up to 4th in the world by the series' end. The Australians, with Lillee never fully fit and Alderman struggling for form, relied increasingly on Yardley, who continued his magnificent season with 13 wickets. An interesting début was that of Martin Crowe, who played all three Tests but scored just 20 runs, top score 9, to end with a rating of just 48. In other countries that might have been the end of his career, but as we all know, Crowe went on to become one of the best players in the world. A lesson to be learnt here perhaps?

PAKISTAN vs SRI LANKA

First Test (Karachi, 5–10 March) Pakistan won by 204 runs
Pakistan 1st Innings: 396 (Haroon Rashid 153, Rashid Khan 59, Tahir Naqqash 57, Rizwan-uz-Zaman 42, D.S. de Silva 4–102, de Mel 3–124)

Sri Lanka 1st Innings: 344 (Wettimuny 71, Mendis 54, Dias 53, Tahir Naqqash 3–83)
Pakistan 2nd Innings: 301 for 4 declared (Salim Malik 100 not out, Javed Miandad 92, Iqbal Qasim 56, D.S. de Silva 3–99)
Sri Lanka 2nd Innings: 149 (Iqbal Qasim 4–27)

Second Test (Faisalabad, 14–19 March) Match Drawn
Sri Lanka 1st Innings: 454 (Wettimuny 157, Dias 98, Madugalle 91, Iqbal Qasim 6–141, Rizwan-uz-Zaman 3–26)

Pakistan 1st Innings: 270 (Ashraf Ali 58, Rashid Khan 43 not out, D.S. de Silva 4–103)
Sri Lanka 2nd Innings: 154 for 8 declared (Goonatillake 56, Tauseef Ahmed 3–18)
Pakistan 2nd Innings: 186 for 7 (Mohsin Khan 74, D.S. de Silva 5–59)

Third Test (Lahore, 22–27 March) Pakistan won by an innings and 102 runs
Sri Lanka 1st Innings: 240 (Dias 109, Imran Khan 8–58)
Pakistan 1st Innings: 500 for 7 declared (Zaheer Abbas 134, Mohsin Khan 129, Majid Khan 63, Ashraf Ali 45 not out, de Mel 3–120, Ratnayeke 3–121)
Sri Lanka 2nd Innings: 158 (Wettimuny 41, Imran Khan 6–58, Tauseef Ahmed 4–58)

Captains: Pakistan – Javed Miandad
Sri Lanka – B. Warnapura (1st & 3rd Tests), L.R.D. Mendis (2nd Test)

Débuts: Pakistan – Rashid Khan, Salim Malik, Salim Yousuf, Tahir Naqqash (1st Test), Ashraf Ali (2nd Test)
Sri Lanka – J.R. Ratnayeke (1st Test), A.N. Ranasinghe (2nd Test), R.S.A. Jayasekera, R.G.C.E. Wijesuriya (3rd Test)

Rising Stars: Pakistan – Mohsin Khan (+148 batting)
Sri Lanka – R.L. Dias (+155 batting)

A couple of minutes or so after they had finished their first Test against England, the Sri Lankans were on a plane and off to Pakistan for their first overseas tour, with three Tests and three one-day internationals squeezed into five weeks. In fact this was a bit of a 'who he?' series, for as well as the Sri Lankans, the Pakistan team too had an unfamiliar look to it. Objecting to Javed Miandad's rather excitable captaincy, the ten players who had played under him in the previous Test in Australia went on strike and refused to play unless someone else took over for the tour of England later in the year. Pakistan's Mr Pad-Up finally relented after the second Test, but not before a host of young players had made their débuts – most notably the eighteen-year-old Salim Malik, who scored a century in his first Test. Back at full strength for the third Test, Pakistan predictably wiped the floor with the poor Sri Lankans, Imran Khan's 14 wickets bumping him up to 6th in the world. But some of the visiting team did prosper in the series – Wettimuny scored his country's first Test century, and Dias the second, while the legspinner D.S. de Silva was by some distance his team's most penetrative bowler. But a quick glance at the graph shows the disparity between the two teams, and Sri Lanka could not really complain at the final 2–0 scoreline.

WORLD TOP TWENTY AFTER 1981–82

BATTING

(1)	1.	I.V.A. Richards (West Indies)	908 (−22)
(20)	2.	H.A. Gomes (West Indies)	844 (+225)
(2)	3.	A.R. Border (Australia)	837 (−65)
(7)	4.	C.H. Lloyd (West Indies)	835 (+76)
(11)	5.	S.M. Gavaskar (India)	798 (+88)
(14)	6.	D.I. Gower (England)	797 (+128)
(4)	7.	G.S. Chappell (Australia)	794 (−40)
(3)	8.	Javed Miandad (Pakistan)	775 (−98)
(8)	9.	G.P. Howarth (New Zealand)	765 (+11)
(15)	10.	I.T. Botham (England)	719 (+62)
(22)	11.	B.A. Edgar (New Zealand)	714 (+117)
(10)	12.	G. Boycott (England)	711 (−31)
(9)	13.	Taslim Arif (Pakistan)	706 (−44)
(6)	14.	K.D. Walters (Australia)	697 (−66)
(5)	15.	Wasim Raja (Pakistan)	678 (−123)
(32)	16.	B.M. Laird (Australia)	667 (+148)
(24)	17.	G.R. Viswanath (India)	666 (+84)
(23)	18.	G.A. Gooch (England)	663 (+74)
(16)	19.	K.J. Hughes (Australia)	658 (+7)
(17)	20.	D.B. Vengsarkar (India)	654 (+6)

BOWLING

(8)	1.	M.A. Holding (West Indies)	865 (+123)
(2)	2.	D.K. Lillee (Australia)	859 (+22)
(7)	3.	D.R. Doshi (India)	832 (+84)
(6)	4.	R.J. Hadlee (New Zealand)	803 (+25)
(4)	5.	J. Garner (West Indies)	798 (−21)
(13)	6.	Imran Khan (Pakistan)	796 (+126)
(1)	7.	C.E.H. Croft (West Indies)	776 (−93)
(3)	8.	I.T. Botham (England)	728 (−99)

(12)	9.	Iqbal Qasim (Pakistan)	706 (+36)
(5)	10.	Kapil Dev (India)	704 (−104)
(41)	11.	B. Yardley (Australia)	691 (+323)
(15)	12.	A.M.E. Roberts (West Indies)	686 (+29)
(14)	13.	R.G.D. Willis (England)	663 (−7)
(9)	14.	S.T. Clarke (West Indies)	660 (−73)
(11)	15.	L.S. Pascoe (Australia)	632 (−61)
(10)	16.	T.M. Alderman (Australia)	580 (−152)
(17)	17.	C.M. Old (England)	553 (−40)
(24)	18.	G.B. Troup (New Zealand)	553 (+22)
(28)	19.	J.K. Lever (England)	549 (+46)
(25)	20.	Sarfraz Nawaz (Pakistan)	548 (+25)

A quiet season it certainly wasn't. With nineteen Tests played, nine involving Australia, the two top twenties showed more than the odd minor adjustment. The advance of Larry Gomes, the return to form of Edgar and the return to Test cricket of Laird were perhaps the most noticeable developments in the batting chart, but possibly more remarkable was the eclipse (however temporary) of the West Indies' opening pair, Haynes and Greenidge. Both dropped out of the twenty, Haynes down 75 from 12th to 25th and Greenidge (illustrating a general upswing in the ratings) losing only 6 points but falling from 19th to 26th. Also out was Majid Khan (for the last time), down from 18th to 27th as his glorious form of previous years began to desert him, and Sandeep Patil, whose meteoric rise was followed by a similarly swift fall, from 13th to 31st in just six Tests. The much mooted decline of the West Indies, meanwhile, was shown to be completely illusory, with Richards, Gomes and Lloyd all in the top four and Holding at the head of the bowling list, displacing his countryman Croft. Note too the first appearance of Imran Khan in the top ten (for it was around now that his bowling acquired its fearsome reputation) and the substantial rise of Yardley. Otherwise it's much the same faces as usual – Hadlee, Garner, Lillee, Doshi and of course, Botham, the only man ever to be in both top tens at the same time. Willis, if anything, seems surprisingly low at 13th, but the big surprises are Troup and Lever, whose rises illustrate just how crowded it was down there in the 500s – there were fourteen players between Old on 553 and Tauseef Ahmed on 502. These included four who had left the twenty – Lance Cairns of New Zealand (down from 20th to 21st), Ghavri of India (19th to 23rd), Hogg of Australia (who hadn't played that season because of injury, and fell from 18th to 24th), and most spectacularly of all Dilley, whose disappointing form in India sent him spiralling down from 16th to 31st. Tough game, this cricket.

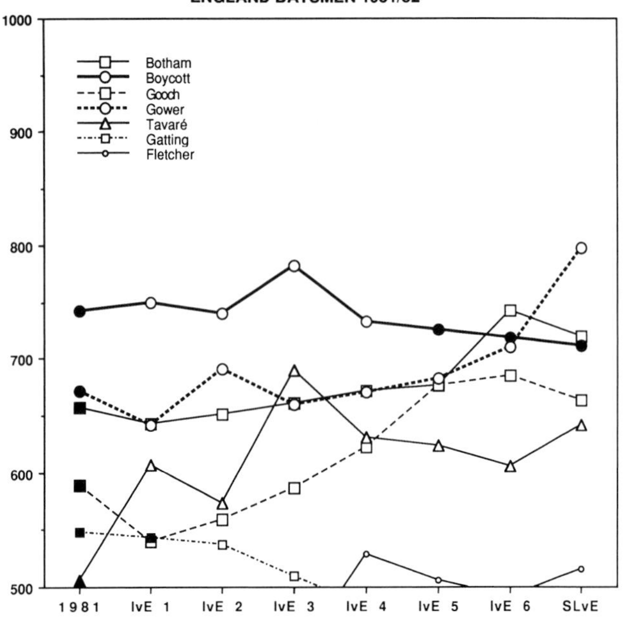
ENGLAND BATSMEN 1981/82
1000
900
800
700
600
500
Botham
Boycott
Gooch
Gower
Tavaré
Gatting
Fletcher
1981
IvE 1
IvE 2
IvE 3
IvE 4
IvE 5
IvE 6
SLvE

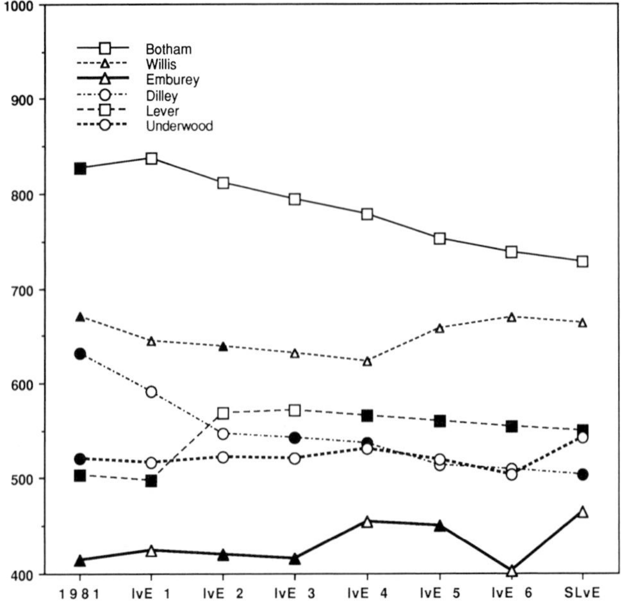
ENGLAND BOWLERS 1981/82
1000
900
800
700
600
500
400
Botham
Willis
Emburey
Dilley
Lever
Underwood
1981
IvE 1
IvE 2
IvE 3
IvE 4
IvE 5
IvE 6
SLvE

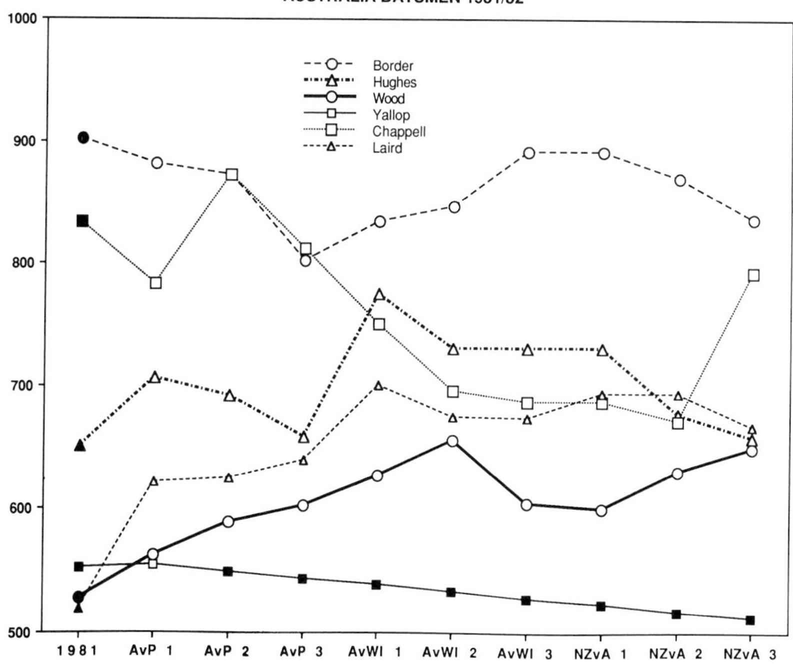

AUSTRALIA BOWLERS 1981/82

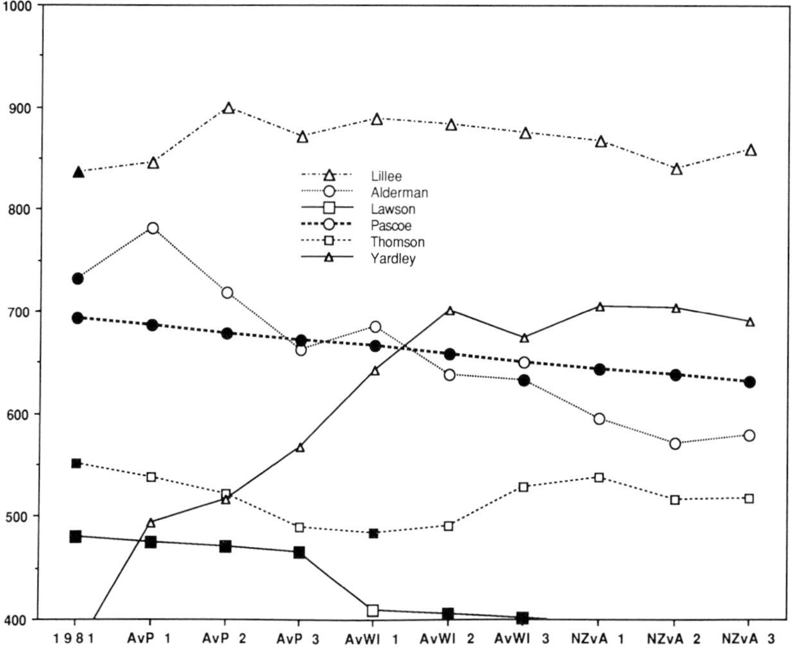

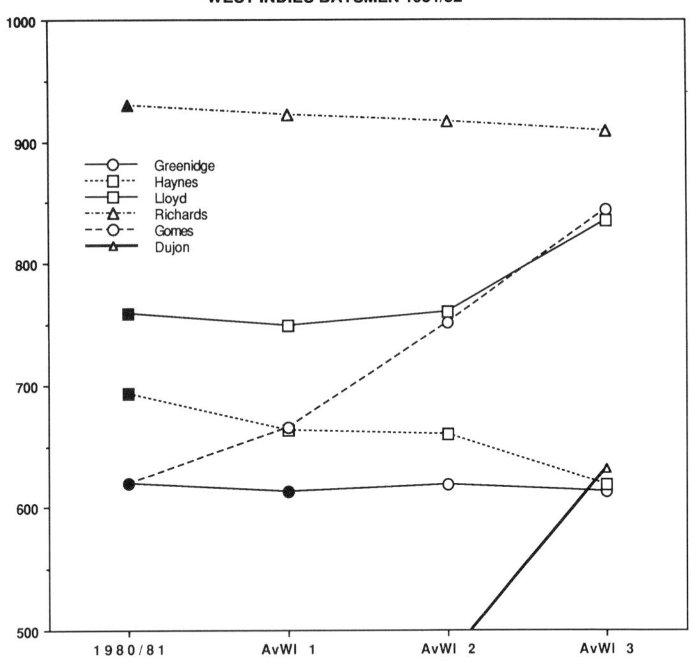
WEST INDIES BATSMEN 1981/82
1000
900
800
700
600
500
Greenidge
Haynes
Lloyd
Richards
Gomes
Dujon
1980/81
AvWI 1
AvWI 2
AvWI 3

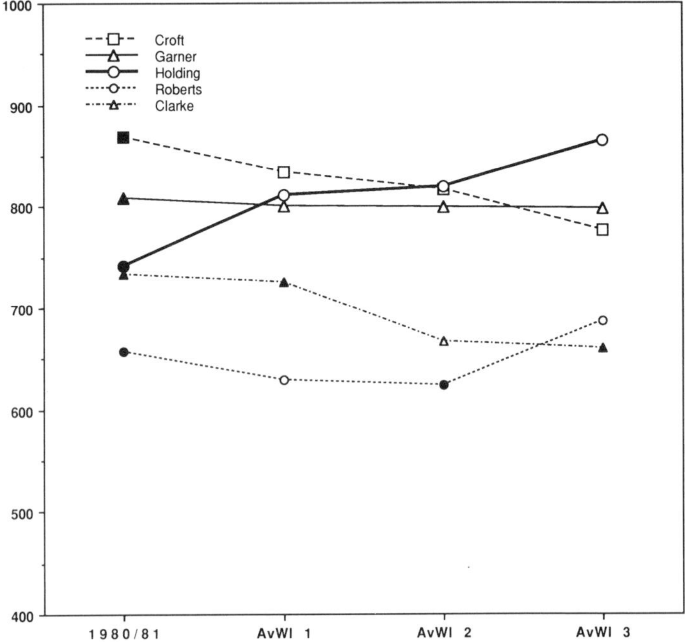
WEST INDIES BOWLERS 1981/82
1000
900
800
700
600
500
400
Croft
Garner
Holding
Roberts
Clarke
1980/81
AvWI 1
AvWI 2
AvWI 3

NEW ZEALAND BATSMEN 1981/82

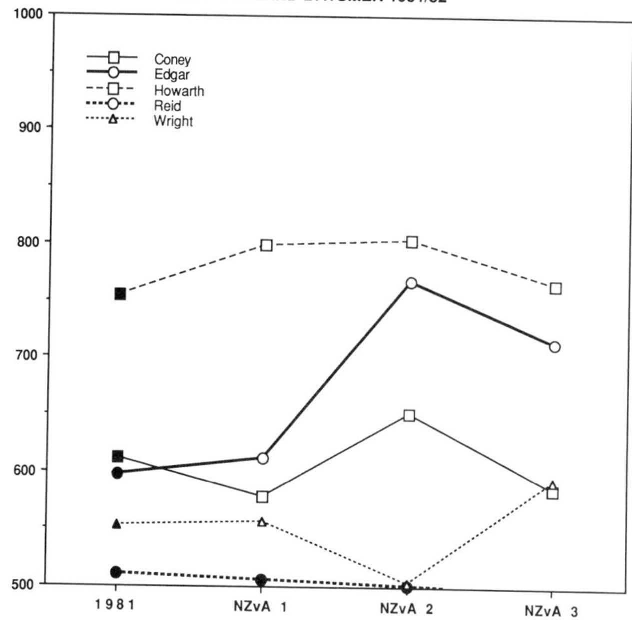
1000
900
800
700
600
500
Coney
Edgar
Howarth
Reid
Wright
1981
NZvA 1
NZvA 2
NZvA 3

NEW ZEALAND BOWLERS 1981/82

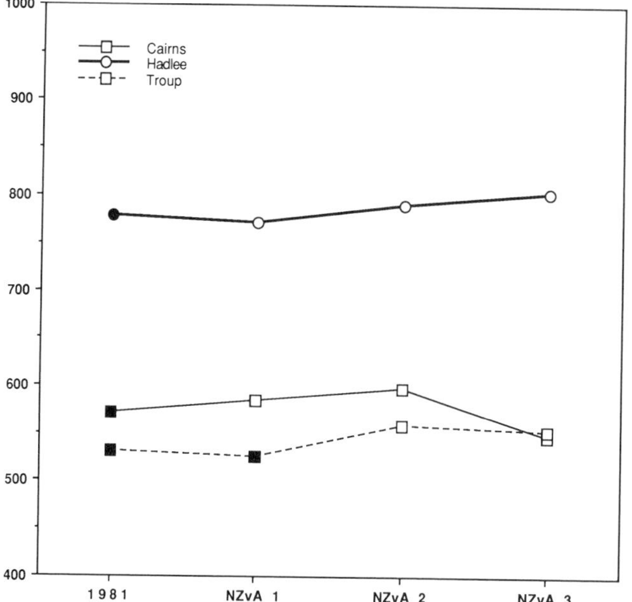
1000
900
800
700
600
500
400
Cairns
Hadlee
Troup
1981
NZvA 1
NZvA 2
NZvA 3

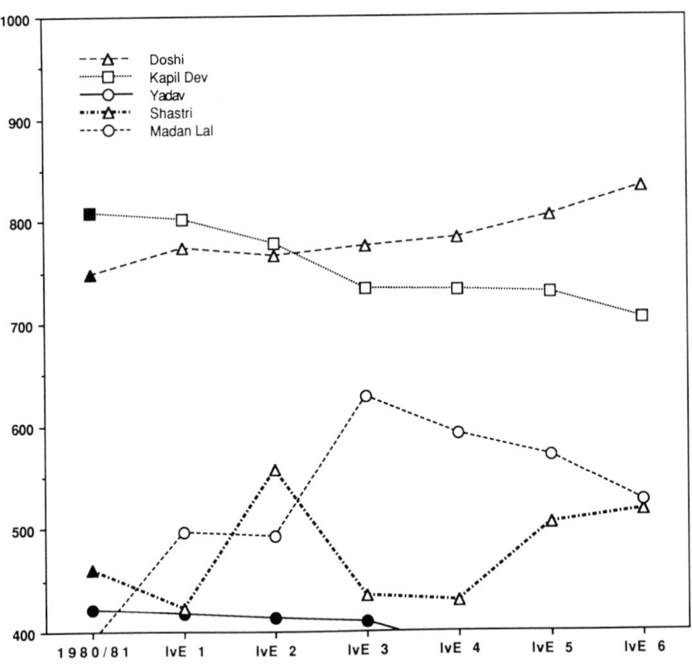
INDIA BOWLERS 1981/82
1000
900
800
700
600
500
400
Doshi
Kapil Dev
Yadav
Shastri
Madan Lal
1980/81
IvE 1
IvE 2
IvE 3
IvE 4
IvE 5
IvE 6

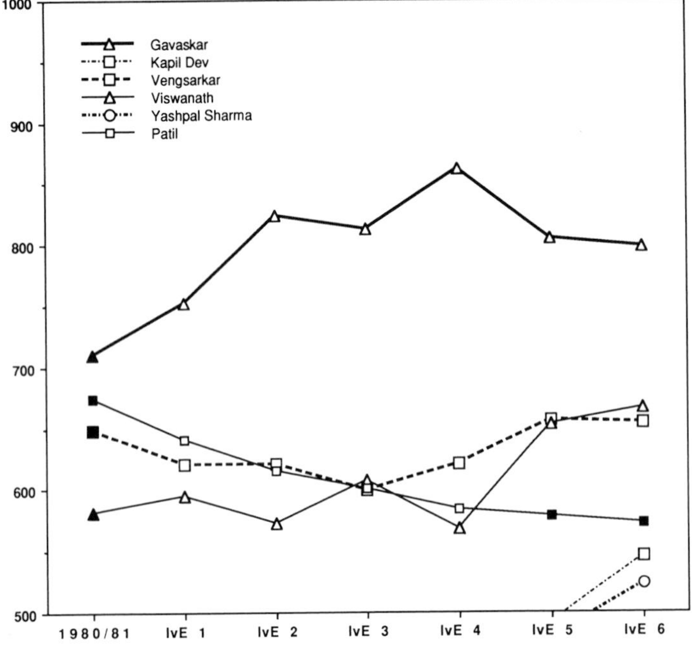
INDIA BATSMEN 1981/82
1000
900
800
700
600
500
Gavaskar
Kapil Dev
Vengsarkar
Viswanath
Yashpal Sharma
Patil
1980/81
IvE 1
IvE 2
IvE 3
IvE 4
IvE 5
IvE 6

PAKISTAN BATSMEN 1981/82

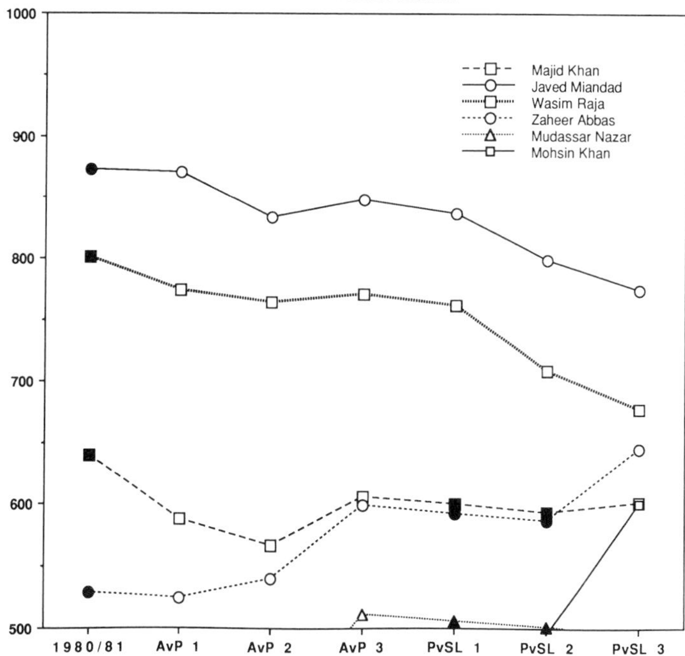
Majid Khan
Javed Miandad
Wasim Raja
Zaheer Abbas
Mudassar Nazar
Mohsin Khan
1000
900
800
700
600
500
1980/81
AvP 1
AvP 2
AvP 3
PvSL 1
PvSL 2
PvSL 3

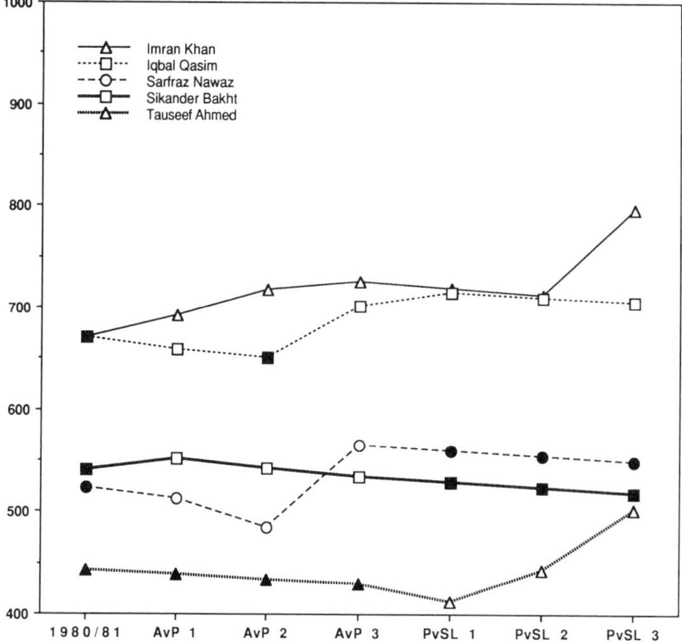
PAKISTAN BOWLERS 1981/82
Imran Khan
Iqbal Qasim
Sarfraz Nawaz
Sikander Bakht
Tauseef Ahmed
1000
900
800
700
600
500
400
1980/81
AvP 1
AvP 2
AvP 3
PvSL 1
PvSL 2
PvSL 3

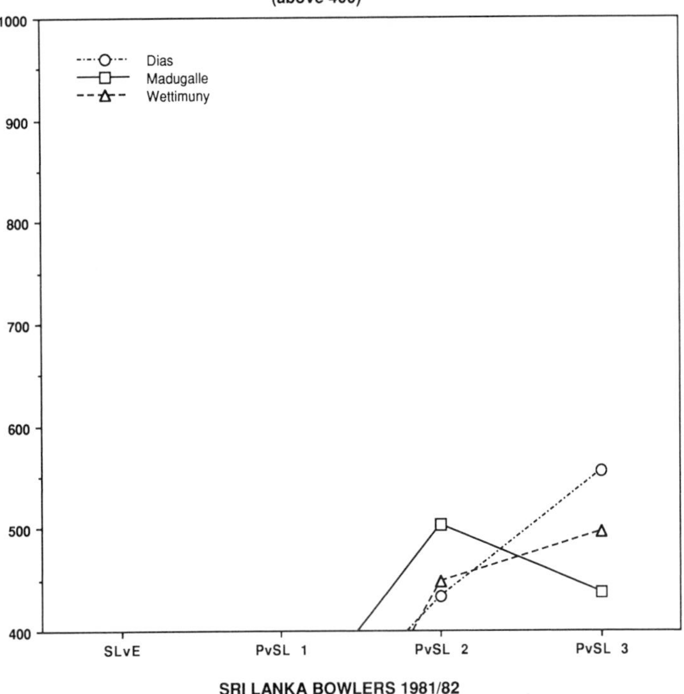
SRI LANKA BATSMEN 1981/82
(above 400)
1000
900
800
700
600
500
400
Dias
Madugalle
Wettimuny
SLvE
PvSL 1
PvSL 2
PvSL 3

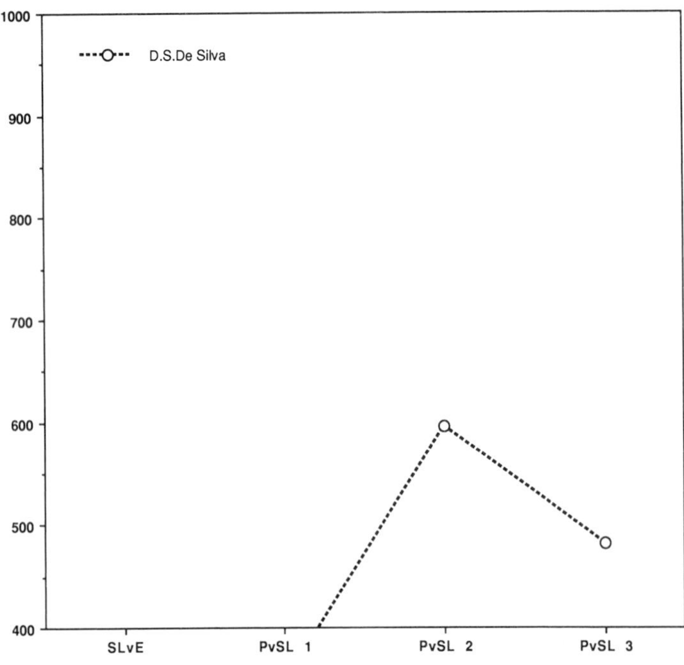
SRI LANKA BOWLERS 1981/82
1000
900
800
700
600
500
400
D.S.De Silva
SLvE
PvSL 1
PvSL 2
PvSL 3

1982

ENGLAND vs INDIA

First Test (Lord's, 10–15 June) England won by 7 wickets
England 1st Innings: 433 (Randall 126, Botham 67, Edmonds 64, Allott 41 not out, Kapil Dev 5–125, Madan Lal 3–99)
India 1st Innings: 128 (Gavaskar 48, Kapil Dev 41, Botham 5–46, Willis 3–41)
India 2nd Innings: 369 (Vengsarkar 157, Kapil Dev 89, Willis 6–101)
England 2nd Innings: 67 for 3 (Kapil Dev 3–43)

Second Test (Old Trafford, 24–28 June) Match Drawn
England 1st Innings: 425 (Botham 128, Miller 98, G. Cook 66, Tavaré 57, Doshi 6–102, Madan Lal 3–104)
India 1st Innings: 379 for 8 (Patil 129 not out, Kapil Dev 65, Kirmani 58, Viswanath 54, Edmonds 3–94)

Third Test (The Oval, 8–13 July) Match Drawn
England 1st Innings: 594 (Botham 208, Lamb 107, Randall 95, G. Cook 50, Gower 47, Doshi 4–175, Shastri 3–109)
India 1st Innings: 410 (Kapil Dev 97, Shastri 66, Patil 62, Viswanath 56, Kirmani 43, Willis 3–78, Edmonds 3–89)
England 2nd Innings: 191 for 3 declared (Tavaré 75 not out, Lamb 45, Gower 45)
India 2nd Innings: 111 for 3 (Viswanath 75 not out)

Captains: England – R.G.D. Willis
India – S.M. Gavaskar

Débuts: England – A.J. Lamb, D.R. Pringle (1st Test)
India – G.A. Parkar (1st Test), S.V. Nayak (2nd Test)

Rising Stars: England – I.T. Botham (+152 batting)
India – S.M. Patil (+102 batting)

When Gavaskar's confident Indian side were crushing Fletcher's England in Bombay in 1981–82, it was, remarkably enough, their last victory for over three years. When they came to England shortly after, they looked a much less impressive outfit than the previous winter's result had perhaps led us to believe. Most of the younger players found it hard to adapt to English conditions, and some of the older ones were not in especially good form – Gavaskar himself didn't even make a 50. The bowling was too thin, with Kapil Dev and Doshi holding the attack together (and sometimes not) for the whole tour.

That said, there were again some superb individual performances. Patil's 129 not out in the second Test was all the more remarkable for the poor form that had preceded it. It was a magnificent innings, during which he moved from 73 to 104 in nine balls. At one stage he hit Willis for 24 off an over (4,4,4,0,4,4,4 – the third delivery was a no-ball), equalling Andy Roberts' Test record. Kapil Dev was in similar form throughout the series. Although he never reached 100, his 41, 89, 65 and 97 were all superb exhibitions of big hitting. The 89 came off only fifty-five balls.

England, meanwhile, made hay against some unimpressive Indian bowling. If it was sad not to find out what Gooch would have made of them, English supporters nevertheless had the joy of seeing Randall recalled to the team and immediately score a gritty 126, after England had collapsed a little feebly to 166 for 6. Botham was in even more prodigious form, looking at times impossible to dismiss. Lamb's début was rather more successful than Pringle's – their batting and bowling ratings stood at 362 and 277 respectively by the end of the series. Willis' 15 wickets at 22 pushed his rating up 73 points, and sent him into the world top ten for the first time (at 8th). Botham's 871 batting rating at the end of the series (his best yet) left him behind only his friend Richards. Miller just avoided his maiden first-class century for the umpteenth time, while Allott's 2 wickets at 73.5 increased his rating encouragingly to 58. An entertaining series.

ENGLAND vs PAKISTAN

First Test (Edgbaston, 29 July–1 August) England won by 113 runs
England 1st Innings: 272 (Gower 74, Tavaré 54, Miller 47, Imran Khan 7–52)
Pakistan 1st Innings: 251 (Mansoor Akhtar 58, Zaheer Abbas 40, I.A. Greig 4–53)
England 2nd Innings: 291 (Randall 105, Taylor 54, Tahir Naqqash 5–40)
Pakistan 2nd Innings: 199 (Imran Khan 65, Botham 4–70)

Second Test (Lord's, 12–16 August) Pakistan won by 10 wickets
Pakistan 1st Innings: 428 (Mohsin Khan 200, Zaheer Abbas 75, Mansoor Akhtar 57, Jackman 4–110, Botham 3–148)
England 1st Innings: 227 (Abdul Qadir 4–39, Sarfraz Nawaz 3–56)
England 2nd Innings: 276 (Tavaré 82, Botham 69, Mudassar Nazar 6–32)

Pakistan 2nd Innings: 77 for no wicket (Mohsin Khan 39 not out)

Third Test (Headingley, 26–31 August) England won by 3 wickets
Pakistan 1st Innings: 275 (Imran Khan 67 not out, Mudassar Nazar 65, Javed Miandad 54, Botham 4–70, Jackman 3–74, Willis 3–76)
England 1st Innings: 256 (Gower 74, Botham 57, Imran Khan 5–49)
Pakistan 2nd Innings: 199 (Javed Miandad 52, Imran Khan 46, Botham 5–74, Willis 3–55)
England 2nd Innings: 219 for 7 (Fowler 86, Mudassar Nazar 4–55, Imran Khan 3–66)

Captains: England – R.G.D. Willis (1st & 3rd Tests), D.I. Gower (2nd Test)
Pakistan – Imran Khan

Débuts: England – I.A. Grieg, E.E. Hemmings (1st Test), G. Fowler, V.J. Marks (3rd Test)

Rising Stars: England – R.W. Taylor (+50 batting)
Pakistan – Mudassar Nazar (+128 bowling)

This brief but curious series eventually came out in England's favour, by a score of two Tests to one, but Pakistan were markedly more difficult opposition than the Indians had been earlier in the summer. As well as Imran Khan, now moving into the most successful phase of his career, they had the devilish leg-spin of Abdul Qadir, whose reputation preceded him, and who took untold millions of wickets in the county matches. In fact, Qadir had rather modest figures in the Tests – 10 wickets at 40.6 – and by the end of the series had a rating of just 345 (below Robin Jackman, for instance), but he consistently befuddled the English batsmen, and his most successful spell (4–39 in the Second Test) coincided with his team's only victory. In that Test Gower, in charge for the first time in place of the injured Willis, had one of the weakest bowling attacks ever foisted upon an England captain: Botham (670), Jackman (351), Pringle (191), Ian Grieg (112) and Hemmings (58). Mohsin scored 200 (giving him a rating of 805) and Pakistan won by 10 wickets.

In the other tests, though, the touring side were constantly undermined by the mercurial nature of their batting. No-one else besides Mohsin scored more than 75, and only he and Imran Khan, with a series of more circumspect innings lower in the order, saw their batting ratings rise. Mudassar, who dropped 42 points in the series, nevertheless had the consolation of a radically improved bowling rating, his supposedly amiable medium pace gleaning 10 wickets at 10.4 and a rise from 119 to 528 in the bowling ratings, making him (in ratings terms) a genuine all-rounder. Imran's bowling also went from strength to strength – 824 made him third in the world behind Holding and Lillee.

The England batsmen also found things hard going – few series can have been won with no-one averaging more than 36. Randall's solid century in the first Test, though, was crucial (and it increased his rating to 598, its highest yet), and Tavaré's steadiness helped him maintain his rating. But Lamb was a disappointment, with an average of 8 and a final rating of just 299, and Gatting yet again failed to make the expected breakthrough. This was also the season in which Trevor Jesty scored eight centuries for Hampshire, and yet was still not picked for England – an odd anomaly that still ranks as one of England's dafter selection errors of the decade. In the end, though, England did well to win, and the solid application of Willis and Botham had as much to do with that as anything.

WORLD TOP TWENTY AFTER 1982

BATTING

(1)	1.	I.V.A. Richards (West Indies)	908
(2)	2.	H.A. Gomes (West Indies)	844
(3)	3.	A.R. Border (Australia)	837
(4)	4.	C.H. Lloyd (West Indies)	835
(7)	5.	G.S. Chappell (Australia)	794
(10)	6.	I.T. Botham (England)	783 (+64)
(9)	7.	G.P. Howarth (New Zealand)	765
(8)	8.	Javed Miandad (Pakistan)	752 (−23)
(5)	9.	S.M. Gavaskar (India)	751 (−47)
(6)	10.	D.I. Gower (England)	739 (−58)
(11)	11.	B.A. Edgar (New Zealand)	714
(28)	12.	Mohsin Khan (Pakistan)	711 (+111)
(31)	13.	S.M. Patil (India)	674 (+102)
(12)	14.	G. Boycott (England)	670 (−14)
(16)	15.	B.M. Laird (Australia)	667
(17)	16.	G.R. Viswanath (India)	659 (−7)
(19)	17.	K.J. Hughes (Australia)	658
(21)	18.	G.M. Wood (Australia)	650
(23)	19.	C.J. Tavaré (England)	643 (+2)
(15)	20.	Wasim Raja (Pakistan)	639 (−39)

BOWLING

(1)	1.	M.A. Holding (West Indies)	865
(2)	2.	D.K. Lillee (Australia)	859
(6)	3.	Imran Khan (Pakistan)	824 (+28)
(4)	4.	R.J. Hadlee (New Zealand)	803
(5)	5.	J. Garner (West Indies)	798

(3)	6.	D.R. Doshi (India)	777 (−55)
(7)	7.	C.E.H. Croft (West Indies)	776
(13)	8.	R.G.D. Willis (England)	745 (+82)
(8)	9.	I.T. Botham (England)	727 (−1)
(11)	10.	B. Yardley (Australia)	691
(12)	11.	A.M.E. Roberts (West Indies)	686
(9)	12.	Iqbal Qasim (Pakistan)	685 (−21)
(14)	13.	S.T. Clarke (West Indies)	660
(10)	14.	Kapil Dev (India)	651 (−53)
(15)	15.	L.S. Pascoe (Australia)	632
(16)	16.	T.M. Alderman (Australia)	580
(18)	17.	G.B. Troup (New Zealand)	553
(20)	18.	Sarfraz Nawaz (Pakistan)	547 (−1)
(21)	19.	B.L. Cairns (New Zealand)	547
(24)	20.	R.M. Hogg (Australia)	536

If the upper reaches of the batting chart were unaffected by the Indian and Pakistani tours of England, there were many changes lower down. The renaissance of Patil and Mohsin's double century brought them both comfortably into the top twenty, replacing Vengsarkar (who only dropped from 20th to 21st) and Gooch, down to 24th, his rating gradually being eroded by his South African adventure. Also out were the enigmatic Taslim Arif, whose eighteen months were up, and Australia's Doug Walters, who had retired, while creeping in at the bottom were Graeme Wood and the Kent dasher. Botham's return to form made him England's top batsman (not that there was a lot of opposition on that score), while Wasim Raja played in just one Test – unlucky for someone who was, as far as the ratings were concerned, his country's third best batsman.

The bowling top twenty lost Old and Lever, rebels both, and gained Cairns and Hogg, neither of whom had bowled a ball since the previous chart. In an otherwise static listing, Imran and Willis benefited from their successful summers, while Doshi dropped back a little. Iqbal Qasim, at the start of the summer, 9th in the world, was kept out of the Pakistan Test side by Abdul Qadir, then 42nd. And just outside the twenty, Mudassar Nazar, ensuring that no-one would underestimate his slow-to-medium pace wobblers ever again.

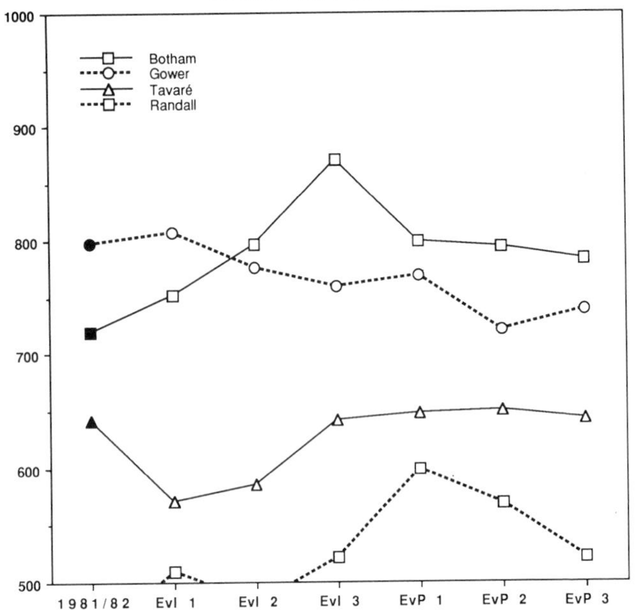
ENGLAND BATSMEN 1982
Botham
Gower
Tavaré
Randall
1000
900
800
700
600
500
1981/82
EvI 1
EvI 2
EvI 3
EvP 1
EvP 2
EvP 3

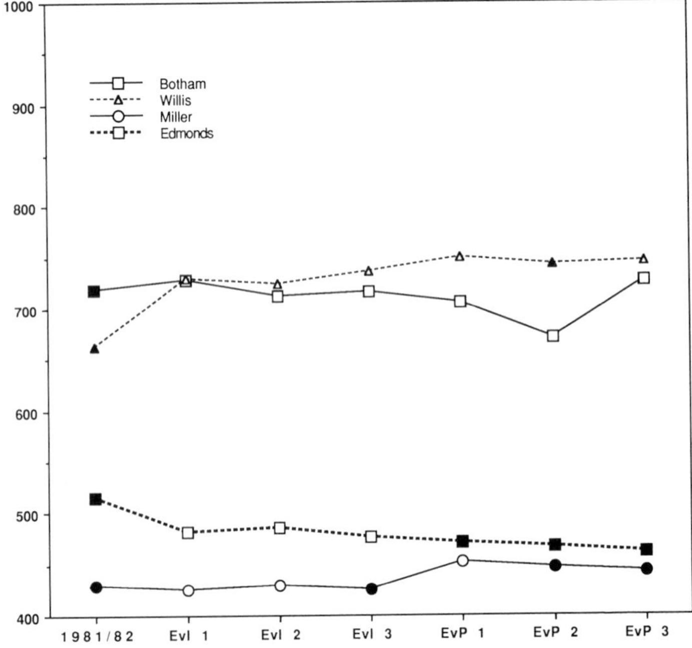
ENGLAND BOWLERS 1982
Botham
Willis
Miller
Edmonds
1000
900
800
700
600
500
400
1981/82
EvI 1
EvI 2
EvI 3
EvP 1
EvP 2
EvP 3

INDIA BATSMEN 1982

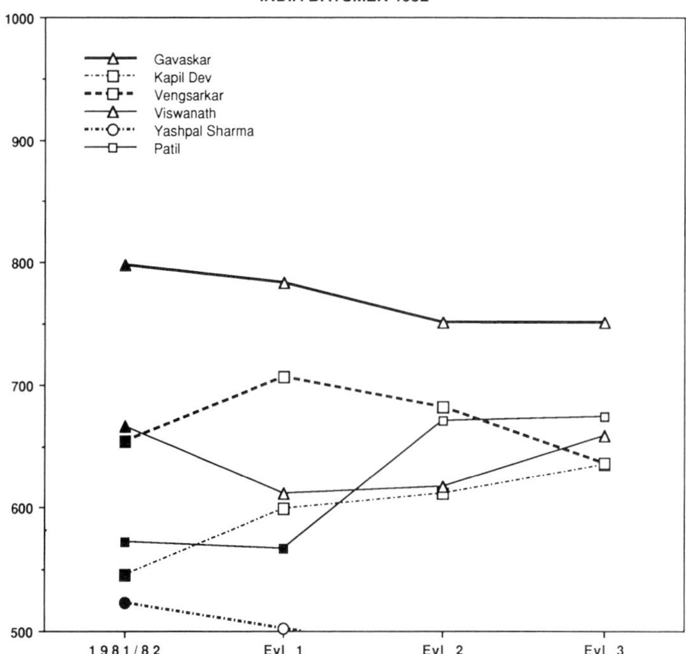
Gavaskar
Kapil Dev
Vengsarkar
Viswanath
Yashpal Sharma
Patil
1000
900
800
700
600
500
1981/82
Evl 1
Evl 2
Evl 3

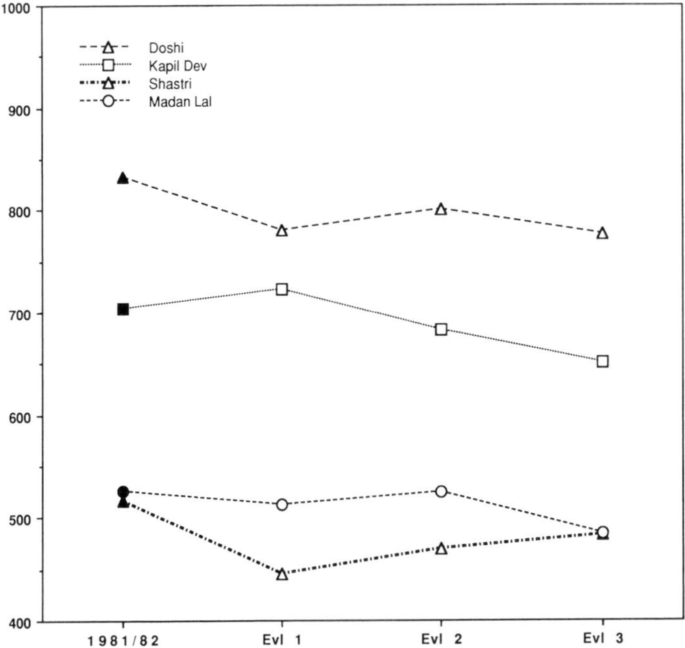
INDIA BOWLERS 1982
Doshi
Kapil Dev
Shastri
Madan Lal
1000
900
800
700
600
500
400
1981/82
Evl 1
Evl 2
Evl 3

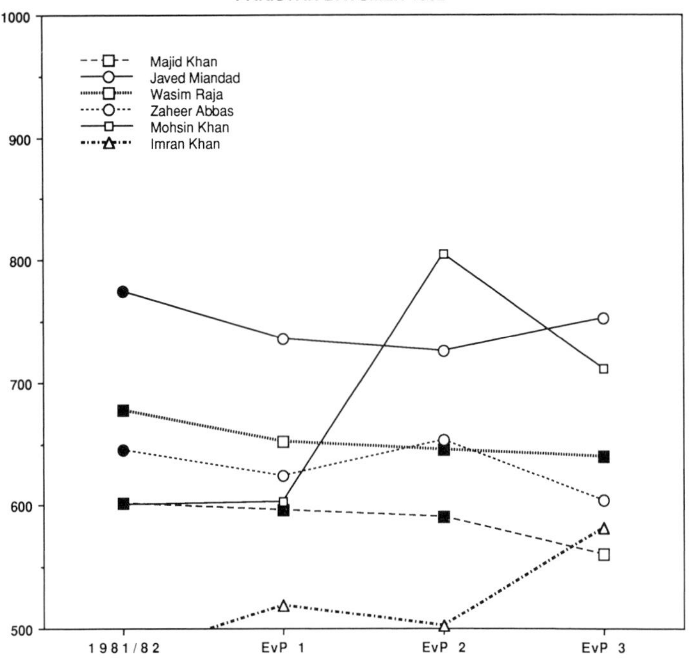
PAKISTAN BATSMEN 1982
1000
900
800
700
600
500
Majid Khan
Javed Miandad
Wasim Raja
Zaheer Abbas
Mohsin Khan
Imran Khan
1981/82
EvP 1
EvP 2
EvP 3

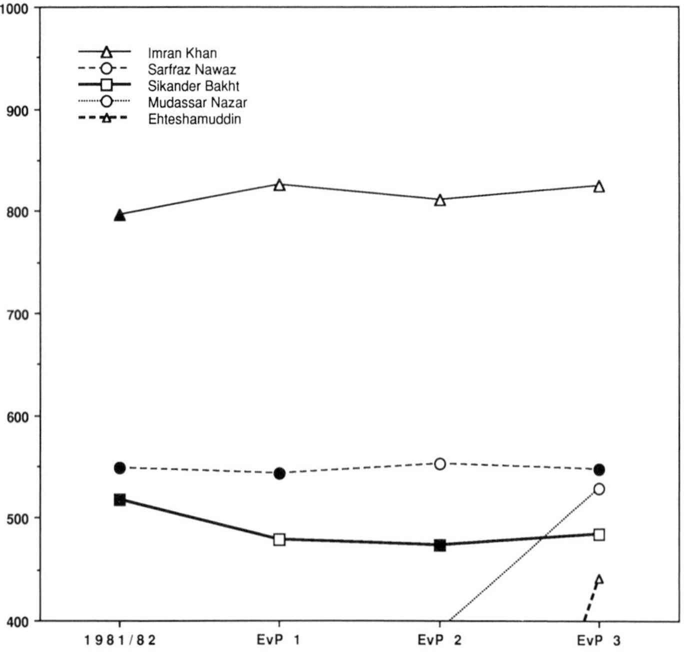
PAKISTAN BOWLERS 1982
1000
900
800
700
600
500
400
Imran Khan
Sarfraz Nawaz
Sikander Bakht
Mudassar Nazar
Ehteshamuddin
1981/82
EvP 1
EvP 2
EvP 3

1982–83

INDIA vs SRI LANKA

Inaugural Test (Madras, 17–22 September) Match Drawn
Sri Lanka 1st Innings: 346 (Mendis 105, Dias 60, Doshi 5–85, Kapil Dev 3–97)
India 1st Innings: 566 for 6 declared (Gavaskar 155, Patil 114 not out, Vengsarkar 90, Arun Lal 63)
Sri Lanka 2nd Innings: 394 (Mendis 105, Dias 97, Ranasinghe 77, D.S. de Silva 46 not out, Kapil Dev 5–110, Doshi 3–147)
India 2nd Innings: 135 for 7 (Patil 46, de Mel 5–68)

Captains: India – S.M. Gavaskar
Sri Lanka – B. Warnapura

Débuts: India – Arun Lal, R.S. Shukla

This was the match in which the Sri Lankans came of age as a Test-playing country. With Mendis scoring a century in each innings – only Sir Donald Bradman and Everton Weekes had ever done that against India before – and Dias also playing fluently, the visitors each achieved an eminently honourable draw and did their individual ratings no harm in the process. Indeed, Mendis climbed from 258 to 557 purely on the strength of this match, from 73rd in the world to 33rd. But Dias, with 709 (up 154), became Sri Lanka's first batsman to hit the top twenty, and that only in his fifth Test. Of the Indians, Patil's fluent scoring pushed him up to 11th and Gavaskar moved back up to 6th. Playing against Sri Lankans has its perils, though: Viswanath's two failures (9 and 2) cost him 50 points and sent him plummeting to 27th. Perhaps he should have had the weekend off.

PAKISTAN vs AUSTRALIA

First Test (Karachi, 22–27 September) Pakistan won by 9 wickets
Australia 1st Innings: 284 (Dyson 87, Border 55, K.J. Hughes 54, Tahir Naqqash 4–61)

Pakistan 1st Innings: 419 for 9 declared (Zaheer Abbas 91, Haroon Rashid 82, Mohsin Khan 58, Mudassar Nazar 52 not out, Bright 3–96)
Australia 2nd Innings: 179 (Abdul Qadir 5–76)
Pakistan 2nd Innings: 47 for 1

Second Test (Faisalabad, 30 September–5 October) Pakistan won by an innings and 3 runs
Pakistan 1st Innings: 501 for 6 declared (Zaheer Abbas 126, Mansoor Akhtar 111, Mudassar Nazar 79, Mohsin Khan 76, Haroon Rashid 51, Lawson 4–97)
Australia 1st Innings: 168 (Wood 49, Abdul Qadir 4–76)
Australia 2nd Innings: 330 (Ritchie 106 not out, Laird 60, Dyson 43, Abdul Qadir 7–142)

Third Test (Lahore, October 14–19) Pakistan won by 9 wickets
Australia 1st Innings: 316 (Wood 85, Lawson 57 not out, Yardley 40, Imran Khan 4–45, Jalal-ud-Din 3–77)
Pakistan 1st Innings: 467 for 7 declared (Javed Miandad 138, Mohsin Khan 135, Zaheer Abbas 52)
Australia 2nd Innings: 214 (Dyson 51, Imran Khan 4–35)
Pakistan 2nd Innings: 64 for 1 (Mudassar Nazar 39 not out)

Captains: Pakistan – Imran Khan
Australia – K.J. Hughes

Débuts: Pakistan – Jalal-ud-Din (3rd Test)
Australia – G.M. Ritchie (1st Test)

Rising Stars: Pakistan – Abdul Qadir (+232 bowling)
Australia – G.F. Lawson (+176 bowling)

After their narrow defeat in England, Pakistan were clearly in the mood when the Australians – without Lillee, Chappell and Pascoe for a variety of personal reasons – arrived in September. And studying their ratings as a team, you can see why they overwhelmed a by no means incompetent Aussie side. Here is their batting order for the second Test (when they were at full strength):

Mohsin Khan	batting rating: 747	
Mudassar Nazar	batting rating: 505	bowling rating: 502
Mansoor Akhtar	batting rating: 514	
Javed Miandad	batting rating: 708	
Zaheer Abbas	batting rating: 691	
Haroon Rashid	batting rating: 508	
*Imran Khan	batting rating: 569	bowling rating: 839
Tahir Naqqash		bowling rating: 323

Imran Khan, the world's top bowler in 1982–83, and no mean performer with the bat.

†Wasim Bari	batting rating: 246	
Abdul Qadir		bowling rating: 636
Iqbal Qasim		bowling rating: 663

None of the top seven batsmen had a rating of less than 500, and of the bowlers only Tahir Naqqash was out of the top twenty-five (Sikander, although he rated 474, was having a poor season and had been dropped). In the event, Australia won none of the nine matches they played – they lost all three Tests and the two one-day internationals that were completed (riots won the third), and drew their three other first class matches. But the difference between the two sides was, in many ways, summed up by Abdul Qadir's rating and its substantial rise after the second Test. With a record 22 wickets in the series – after Imran had insisted, against the selectors' wishes, on his inclusion – Pakistan's greatest living appealer rose from a modest 345 in the ratings to 632 (40th in the world to 14th). The Pakistani batsmen also contributed, with Mohsin's century at Lahore edging him past 800 for the second time, to 4th in the world behind the West Indian trio of Richards, Gomes and Lloyd. Imran's bowling was even more successful – his 13 wickets at 13 gave him a rating of 868, and the number one spot for the first time.

The Australians, by contrast, had a dreadful time. The only incumbent batsman to increase his rating was Dyson, by just 32, while Border left the top ten in something of a hurry. Ritchie was a gain, though, and quickly climbed to 347. Of their bowlers, only Lawson (9 wickets at 33) took more than 3 wickets in the entire series – 576 (up 187) represented by far his highest rating to date. Yardley was particularly ineffective (2 for 209 in 53 overs), surprisingly so after his triumphs of the previous season. By the third Test, Australia's best rated players were the ones they had left behind. Their 3–0 defeat was only the second time they had lost every Test in a rubber. Not once did they succeed in bowling out the opposition.

AUSTRALIA vs ENGLAND

First Test (Perth, 12–17 November) Match Drawn
England 1st Innings: 411 (Tavaré 89, Randall 78, Gower 72, Lamb 46, Yardley 5–107, Lillee 3–96)
Australia 1st Innings: 424 for 9 declared (Chappell 117, K.J. Hughes 62, Hookes 56, Dyson 52, Lawson 50, Miller 4–70, Willis 3–95)
England 2nd Innings: 358 (Randall 115, Lamb 56, Pringle 47 not out, Lawson 5–108, Yardley 3–101)
Australia 2nd Innings: 73 for 2

Second Test (Brisbane, 26 November–1 December) Australia won by 7 wickets
England 1st Innings: 219 (Lamb 72, Botham 40, Lawson 6–47)
Australia 1st Innings: 341 (Wessels 162, Chappell 53, Yardley 53, Willis 5–66, Botham 3–105)
England 2nd Innings: 309 (Fowler 83, Miller 60, Thomson 5–73, Lawson 5–87)
Australia 2nd Innings: 190 for 3 (Hookes 66 not out, Wessels 46)

Third Test (Adelaide, 10–15 December) Australia won by 8 wickets
Australia 1st Innings: 438 (Chappell 115, K.J. Hughes 88, Wessels 44, Dyson 44, Botham 4–112)
England 1st Innings: 216 (Lamb 82, Gower 60, Lawson 4–56, Thomson 3–51)

England 2nd Innings: 304 (Gower 114, Botham 58, Lawson 5–66)
Australia 2nd Innings: 83 for 2 (Dyson 37 not out)

Fourth Test (Melbourne, 26–30 December) England won by 3 runs
England 1st Innings: 284 (Tavaré 89, Lamb 83, Hogg 4–69, Yardley 4–89)
Australia 1st Innings: 287 (K.J. Hughes 66, Hookes 53, R.W. Marsh 53, Wessels 47, Willis 3–38, Miller 3–44)
England 2nd Innings: 294 (Fowler 65, Botham 46, Pringle 42, Lawson 4–66, Hogg 3–64, Thomson 3–74)
Australia 2nd Innings: 288 (Hookes 68, Border 62 not out, K.J. Hughes 48, Cowans 6–77)

Fifth Test (Sydney, 2–7 January) Match Drawn
Australia 1st Innings: 314 (Border 89, Dyson 79, Botham 4–75, Hemmings 3–68)
England 1st Innings: 237 (Gower 70, Randall 70, Thomson 5–50, Lawson 3–70)
Australia 2nd Innings: 382 (K.J. Hughes 137, Border 83, Wessels 53, R.W. Marsh 41, Hemmings 3–116, Miller 3–133)
England 2nd Innings: 314 for 7 (Hemmings 95, Randall 44, Yardley 4–139)

Captains: Australia – G.S. Chappell
England – R.G.D. Willis

Débuts: Australia – C.G. Rackemann, K.C. Wessels (2nd Test)
England – N.G. Cowans (1st Test)

Rising Stars: Australia – G.F. Lawson (+314 bowling)
England – A.J. Lamb (+159 batting)

With half of their first choice team playing in South Africa, and a further third of it not picked for any obvious reason, England did quite well to lose only 2–1 in Australia. Trevor Jesty remained unchosen, as did Mike Gatting, and instead of taking Phil Edmonds, the selectors preferred three off-spinners, presumably for variety. But the real shortages were in opening batsmen (Boycott and Gooch having gone to South Africa) and fast bowlers. The openers, such as they were, scarcely ever gave the innings a good start – in eight of their ten innings a wicket fell before 15 runs were scored. Cook, who started on a rating of 248, averaged only 9 and fell sadly to 225, while Tavaré, opening against his inclinations, averaged 21.8 and dropped 102 rating points. Fowler flourished to some extent, climbing from 257 to 537 during the series, but was injured just as he seemed to be finding his true form.

The middle-order did rather better. Although Gower dropped a little in the ratings, he scored more runs than anyone on either side, bar Kim Hughes. Randall and Lamb also performed well, with Randall reaching his personal career peak of 613 after his century at Perth and Lamb jumping from 299 to 558. Botham, though, was in one of his well-built periods, and as his rating tends to vary in inverse proportion to his poundage, he didn't exactly prosper. His 18 wickets were expensive and his runs few and far between, although he did pass 1,000 for the calendar year (as did Gower) in the third Test.

The other bowlers, Willis aside, were impressive only in patches. Cowans' match-winning performance in the now legendary fourth Test lifted his rating from 13 to 405, but all the others remained at best static. Pringle hit the unearthly heights of 199 in that same Test, but then was dropped in favour of Hemmings, whose batting rating (324) then overtook his bowling rating (291).

The Australian batsmen were rather more consistent. Kepler Wessels' remarkable first series lifted him to 627 after just four Tests, and into the world top twenty. Hughes averaged 67, while Hookes' recall pushed him over 400 for the first time. Border, whose rating had declined after the third Test to an unprecedently modest 657, recovered after his 62 at the Melbourne Test. But again it was the bowlers who really made the difference – even after Lillee and Alderman had both been injured after the first Test (Alderman after unsuccessfully rugby-tackling an errant spectator). Lawson, Thomson and Hogg performed admirably. Lawson's 34 wickets were the series' outstanding achievement, but the enormous rise in his rating (he hit number one by the end of the rubber) reflects the quality of many of the batsmen he dismissed. Yardley too grabbed his now standard pile of wickets, if at rather greater cost (36.04) than usual.

The series will be remembered, though, mainly for that horribly gripping fourth Test, when after a tenth wicket stand of 70 with Allan Border, Jeff Thomson edged a Botham long hop (but what else?) to Tavaré, who parried it to Miller, and England won by three runs. All four innings' totals, uniquely, were within ten runs of each other. The only closer result, at the time, had been the tied Test between Australia and West Indies in 1960–61, and no doubt the Cardiac Units of most British hospitals were well patronized that night (the result came through at about two in the morning). Even Pringle, who scored 42 in the second innings, contributed to the victory, but the Ashes were lost a week later at Sydney, as Australia regained them for the first time since 1977.

PAKISTAN vs INDIA

First Test (Lahore, 10–15 December) Match Drawn
Pakistan 1st Innings: 485 (Zaheer Abbas 215, Mohsin Khan 94, Mudassar Nazar 50, Doshi 5–90, Madan Lal 3–101)
India 1st Innings: 379 (Amarnath 109 not out, Gavaskar 83, Patil 68, Arun Lal 51, Sarfraz Nawaz 4–63, Imran Khan 3–68)
Pakistan 2nd Innings: 135 for 1 (Mohsin Khan 101 not out)

Second Test (Karachi, 23–28 December) Pakistan won by an innings and 86 runs
India 1st Innings: 169 (Kapil Dev 73, Abdul Qadir 4–67, Imran Khan 3–19)
Pakistan 1st Innings: 452 (Zaheer Abbas 186, Mudassar Nazar 119, Kapil Dev 5–102, Madan Lal 3–129)
India 2nd Innings: 197 (Vengsarkar 79, Madan Lal 52 not out, Gavaskar 42, Imran Khan 8–60)

Third Test (Faisalabad, 3–8 January) Pakistan won by 10 wickets
India 1st Innings: 372 (Patil 85, Kirmani 66, Madan Lal 54, Viswanath 53, Kapil Dev 41, Imran Khan 6–99)
Pakistan 1st Innings: 652 (Zaheer Abbas 168, Javed Miandad 126, Imran Khan 117, Salim Malik 107, Kapil Dev 7–220)
India 2nd Innings: 286 (Gavaskar 127 not out, Amarnath 78, Imran Khan 5–82, Sarfraz Nawaz 4–79)
Pakistan 2nd Innings: 10 for no wicket

Fourth Test (Hyderabad, 14–19 January) Pakistan won by an innings and 119 runs
Pakistan 1st Innings: 581 for 3 declared (Javed Miandad 280 not out, Mudassar Nazar 231)
India 1st Innings: 189 (Sandhu 71, Amarnath 61, Imran Khan 6–35, Sarfraz Nawaz 3–56)
India 2nd Innings: 273 (Amarnath 64, Gavaskar 60, Vengsarkar 58 not out, Sarfraz Nawaz 4–85)

Fifth Test (Lahore 23–28 January) Match Drawn
Pakistan 1st Innings: 323 (Mudassar Nazar 152 not out, Javed Miandad 85, Kapil Dev 8–85)
India 1st Innings: 235 for 3 (Amarnath 120, Yashpal Sharma 63 not out)

Sixth Test (Karachi, 30 January – 4 February) Match Drawn
India 1st Innings: 393 for 8 declared (Shastri 128, Vengsarkar 89, Imran Khan 3–65)

Pakistan 1st Innings: 420 for 6 declared (Mudassar Nazar 152, Mohsin Khan 91, Javed Miandad 47, Zaheer Abbas 43)
India 2nd Innings: 224 for 2 (Amarnath 103 not out, Gavaskar 67)

Captains: Pakistan – Imran Khan
India – S.M. Gavaskar

Débuts: Maninder Singh (2nd Test), B.S. Sandhu (4th Test), T.A.P. Sekar (5th Test)

Rising Stars: Pakistan – Mudassar Nazar (+231 batting)
India – M. Amarnath (+271 batting)

Far from being the usual festival of high-scoring draws that series between these neighbouring nations usually deteriorate into, this particular series was almost embarrassingly one-sided, and that side wasn't India. After crushing the Australians, the rampant Pakistan side welcomed their next-door neighbours with ill-disguised glee, and proceeded to smash them all over the place. Only rain in the first and fifth Tests, and Karachi's traditional crowd disturbances in the sixth, prevented the home team from recording more than three victories in the series, and of those, by far India's best performance came in the third Test, when they contrived to force Pakistan to bat again. They might have preferred, though, to provide a more testing second innings target than 8.

For the Pakistanis, runs flowed as never before. Mudassar scored four centuries and Zaheer, no doubt irritated by suggestions that he was, well, past it, patted off a further three. For Javed Miandad, with a mere two centuries (if no lbw decisions), it was a quieter series. The aggregates for these three, though – 761, 650 and 594 respectively – did set a new record for the top three batsmen in any Test series. And when Mudassar and Javed put on 451 together at Hyderabad, they not only broke the world third wicket record, but also equalled Bradman and Ponsford's record for any wicket.

None of this, naturally, did their ratings much harm. Mudassar, indeed, won his third Rising Star award in a year, while Zaheer jumped from 697 to 871 and third in the world. Salim Malik, given an extended spell in the Test side for the first time, averaged 30 and rose from 216 to 345, while poor Mohsin averaged over 56 and still saw his rating fall 59. Javed Miandad, with 876, moved up to second in the world, behind Richards.

For all the runs records, though, it was Imran's bowling feats that won the actual series. Forty wickets at 13.95 pushed him up from 868 to 915, the highest bowling rating yet recorded and by 25 points (from Lawson) the best in the world. In the second Test, for instance, fearsome swift stuff reduced the Indians in their second innings from 102 for one to 114 for seven, and Imran took 8 for 60 – all but one of them bowled or lbw. Indian ratings suffered. By the end of the series Patil had been dropped, and all the main batsmen besides Amarnath, recalled after three years, and Yashpal Sharma saw their ratings fall. The bowlers too were outclassed. Maninder Singh, at the time India's youngest ever Test débutant (17 years 193 days), ended his first game with batting and bowling ratings of 0 and 0 – no runs, no wickets, no ratings. His bowling rating rallied to 8 the following game, when he took a wicket, but dropped back to 7 after 0–135 in the fourth Test. A flurry of wickets (2) in the fifth Test sent him hurtling up to 33, but he ended the series with a rating of 27 and a career average of 148. India picked someone even younger four months later.

WEST INDIES vs INDIA

First Test (Kingston, Jamaica, 23–28 February) West Indies won by 4 wickets
India 1st Innings: 251 (Sandhu 68, Yashpal Sharma 63, Roberts 4–61)
West Indies 1st Innings: 254 (Greenidge 70, Shastri 4–43, Kapil Dev 4–45)
India 2nd Innings: 174 (Amarnath 40, Roberts 5–39, Marshall 3–56)
West Indies 2nd Innings: 173 for 6 (Richards 61, Greenidge 42, Kapil Dev 4–73)

Second Test (Port-of-Spain, Trinidad, 11–16 March) Match Drawn
India 1st Innings: 175 (Amarnath 58, Shastri 42, Marshall 5–37, Roberts 3–72)
West Indies 1st Innings: 394 (Lloyd 143, Gomes 123, Kapil Dev 3–91)
India 2nd Innings: 469 for 7 (Amarnath 117, Kapil Dev 100 not out, Yashpal Sharma 50, Vengsarkar 45)

Third Test (Georgetown, Guyana, 31 March – 5 April) Match Drawn
West Indies 1st Innings: 470 (Richards 109, Lloyd 81, Greenidge 70, Dujon 47, Haynes 46, Sandhu 3–87)
India 1st Innings: 284 for 3 (Gavaskar 147 not out, Vengsarkar 62)

Fourth Test (Bridgetown, Barbados, 15–20 April) West Indies won by 10 wickets
India 1st Innings: 209 (Amarnath 91, Roberts 4–48)
West Indies 1st Innings: 486 (Logie 130, Haynes 92, Richards 80, Greenidge 57, Lloyd 50, Kapil Dev 3–76, Venkataraghavan 3–146)
India 2nd Innings: 277 (Amarnath 80, Gaekwad 55, Roberts 4–31)
West Indies 2nd Innings: 1 for no wicket

Fifth Test (St John's, Antigua, 28 April–3 May) Match Drawn
India 1st Innings: 457 (Shastri 102, Kapil Dev 98, Vengsarkar 94, Amarnath 54, Marshall 4–87)
West Indies 1st Innings: 550 (Greenidge 154 retired not out, Haynes 136, Dujon 110, Lloyd 106, Madan Lal 3–105)
India 2nd Innings: 247 for 5 (Amarnath 116, Gaekwad 72)

Captains: West Indies – C.H. Lloyd
India – Kapil Dev

Débuts: West Indies – A.L. Logie (1st Test), W.W. Davis (5th Test)
India – L. Sivaramakrishnan (5th Test)

Rising Stars: West Indies – M.D. Marshall (+218 bowling)
India – M. Amarnath (+158 batting)

What's the last thing you want when you have just been unceremoniously stuffed by your nearest neighbour and deadliest cricket rival (in this case Pakistan)? Yes, a long trip to the West Indies, with their battery of quickies, unreliable pitches and umpires who don't regard five bouncers an over as 'intimidatory bowling'. From the frying pan straight into the core of the sun, India cannot have been too optimistic when they arrived for their fifth tour of the Windies in February 1983, even though their dismal performance in Pakistan had resulted in a few changes – Gavaskar had been replaced as captain by Kapil Dev, while two of the team's longest serving stalwarts, Doshi and Viswanath, had been left behind altogether, Viswanath thus ending a unique run of eighty-seven consecutive Tests.

None of this, though, had much bearing on the result: they were still stuffed. Although rain ruined the third Test, the West Indies won two of the remaining four and were never in any trouble in the other two. From the first over it was backs to the wall for India – gritty failure was the order of the day.

For two Indian players, though, the series was something of a personal triumph. Mohinder Amarnath, who had prospered in Pakistan, continued his fine form – with two centuries and a further four fifties, his aggregate of 598 was twice that of any other member of his own team, and nearly 200 more than any of the opposition (who admittedly didn't have to bat as often). And Kapil Dev, second in the batting averages with 42 and, with 17 wickets at 25, by far the most successful bowler, led very much from the front. For the rest, life was hard and unrewarding. Maninder Singh, with 2 wickets for 192 in his first three Tests, watched his rating hurtle up to 42. Sandhu, picked as a bowler, scored lots of runs but found taking wickets rather more challenging. Gaekwad, recalled once more as India sought a reliable opening partner for Gavaskar, failed again. Even Gavaskar struggled.

And all this when the West Indies, as they themselves would admit, were not really on song. Holding and Garner, tired by their Australian seasons, were less effective than usual – Garner was even dropped in favour of Winston Davis for the fifth Test. And Richards himself averaged a mere 47.

Even so, all the top seven West Indian batsmen scored centuries, including the youthful Logie, whose 130 made up for a succession of failures in the other Tests and pushed his rating to a respectable 310. If he hadn't been dropped in that innings when on 7, he'd have scored just 44 runs in the series, at an average of under 8. Would he still be in the side now, one wonders.

But with Clarke and Croft whisked off to South Africa for the latest rebel tour (and banned for life in the West Indies for their trouble), the bowling was dominated by Andy Roberts (24 wickets) and Malcolm Marshall (21 wickets), who beforehand had been unable to keep a regular place in the side. Odd, that, isn't it? England or Australian players go off to South Africa, and their national teams are decimated. A West Indian team goes there as well, and who gets his chance as a result? Malcolm Marshall. Such is the grim inevitability of fate.

NEW ZEALAND vs SRI LANKA

First Test (Christchurch, 4–6 March) New Zealand won by an innings and 25 runs
New Zealand 1st Innings: 344 (Lees 89, Coney 84, J.R. Ratnayeke 3–93)
Sri Lanka 1st Innings: 144 (S. Wettimuny 63 not out, Hadlee 4–33, Cairns 4–49)
Sri Lanka 2nd Innings: 175 (D.S. de Silva 52, Fernando 46, Cairns 4–47, Chatfield 3–40, Snedden 3–48)

Second Test (Wellington, 11–15 March) New Zealand won by 6 wickets
Sri Lanka 1st Innings: 240 (Madugalle 79, de Silva 61, Chatfield 4–66)
New Zealand 1st Innings: 201 (Cairns 45, John 5–60, R.J. Ratnayake 4–81)
Sri Lanka 2nd Innings: 93 (Hadlee 4–34, Chatfield 3–15, Snedden 3–21)

New Zealand 2nd Innings: 134 for 4 (Edgar 47 not out)

Captains: New Zealand– G.P. Howarth
Sri Lanka – D.S. de Silva

1982–83

Débuts: New Zealand– J.J. Crowe (1st Test)
Sri Lanka – R.G. de Alwis, E.R.N.S. Fernando, Y. Goonasekera, S. Jeganathan, V.B. John, R.J. Ratnayake, M. de S. Wettimuny (1st Test), S.A.R. Silva (2nd Test)

The Sri Lankans' first tour of Australia and New Zealand – as a full Test-playing nation, that is – culminated in two Tests (their first two) against New Zealand, which the home team won convincingly. The Sri Lankans' lack of bowling above trundly medium pace, and the absence through injury of their two most accomplished players, Mendis and Dias, fatally undermined their efforts, and the New Zealand seamers took predictable advantage. Hadlee, Chatfield (recalled after a year's absence), Cairns and Snedden shared the wickets almost equally, and even at the end of the series only de Silva, Madugalle and Sidath Wettimuny of those who played had batting ratings above 150. The only Sri Lankan bowler to make much impact was one of the new boys, John, whose 8 wickets at 17.87 gave him a rating of 366. Glenn Turner's comeback to Test cricket after six years in the commentary booth was not noticeably successful.

SRI LANKA vs AUSTRALIA

Inaugural Test (Kandy, 22–26 April) Australia won by an innings and 38 runs
Australia 1st Innings: 514 for 4 declared (Hookes 143 not out, Wessels 141, Yallop 98, Chappell 66, Border 43 not out)
Sri Lanka 1st Innings: 271 (Ranatunga 90, Mendis 74, Yardley 5–88)
Sri Lanka 2nd Innings: 205 (Wettimuny 96, Hogan 5–66)

Captains: Sri Lanka – L.R.D. Mendis
Australia – G.S. Chappell

Débuts: Sri Lanka – R.P.W. Guneratne
Australia – T.G. Hogan, R.D.Woolley

With Dias and Mendis back to full fitness, and Australia shorn of Kim Hughes, Rodney Marsh, Jeff Thomson and Geoff Lawson (all 'unavailable' for one reason of another), you might have expected Sri Lanka to do a little better in their inaugural Test against Australia, especially as it was on home territory. But no, they were taken to the cleaners once more. Lillee, having missed most of the season through injury, was back, and Greg Chappell returned as captain. Of the top six batsmen, only Wood failed, although such was the weakness of the Sri

Lankan attack that Chappell's 66 was not enough to stop his rating dropping 3 points. But Hookes' first Test century was more profitable, and Hogan, on his début, amassed a creditable 373 bowling points. After the rigours of their tour to Pakistan earlier in the summer, the Australians were no doubt delighted to have a relatively easy run of it.

WORLD TOP TWENTY AFTER 1982–83

BATTING

(1)	1.	I.V.A. Richards (West Indies)	878 (−30)
(8)	2.	Javed Miandad (Pakistan)	876 (+124)
(27)	3.	Zaheer Abbas (Pakistan)	871 (+267)
(4)	4.	C.H. Lloyd (West Indies)	812 (−23)
NE	5.	M. Amarnath (India)	775
NE	6.	K.C. Wessels (Australia)	763
(39)	7.	Mudassar Nazar (Pakistan)	761 (+307)
(12)	8.	Mohsin Khan (Pakistan)	742 (+31)
(3)	9.	A.R. Border (Australia)	741 (−96)
(11)	10.	B.A. Edgar (New Zealand)	740 (+26)
(5)	11.	G.S. Chappell (Australia)	740 (−54)
(2)	12.	H.A. Gomes (West Indies)	734 (−110)
(10)	13.	D.I. Gower (England)	729 (−10)
(7)	14.	G.P. Howarth (New Zealand)	701 (−64)
(26)	15.	C.G. Greenidge (West Indies)	700 (+87)
(17)	16.	K.J. Hughes (Australia)	699 (+41)
(23)	17.	P.J.L. Dujon (West Indies)	698 (+66)
(6)	18.	I.T. Botham (England)	672 (−111)
(9)	19.	S.M. Gavaskar (India)	653 (−98)
(25)	20.	D.L. Haynes (West Indies)	651 (+33)

BOWLING

(3)	1.	Imran Khan (Pakistan)	915 (+91)
(39)	2.	G.F. Lawson (Australia)	881 (+392)
(4)	3.	R.J. Hadlee (New Zealand)	800 (−3)
(1)	4.	M.A. Holding (West Indies)	792 (−73)
(2)	5.	D.K. Lillee (Australia)	766 (−93)
(8)	6.	R.G.D. Willis (England)	763 (+18)
(11)	7.	A.M.E. Roberts (West Indies)	752 (+66)
(5)	8.	J. Garner (West Indies)	740 (−58)
(7)	9.	C.E.H. Croft (West Indies)	738 (−38)
(14)	10.	Kapil Dev (India)	679 (+28)
NE	11.	M.D. Marshall (West Indies)	674
(9)	12.	I.T. Botham (England)	653 (−74)
(13)	13.	S.T. Clarke (West Indies)	628 (−32)

(12)	14.	Iqbal Qasim (Pakistan)	624 (−61)
(6)	15.	D.R. Doshi (India)	620 (−157)
(10)	16.	B. Yardley (Australia)	597 (−94)
(23)	17.	J.R. Thomson (Australia)	585 (+67)
(15)	18.	L.S. Pascoe (Australia)	577 (−55)
(19)	19.	B.L. Cairns (New Zealand)	565 (+18)
(18)	20.	Sarfraz Nawaz (Pakistan)	560 (+13)

Pakistan's busy (nine Tests) and successful season was reflected in the rise of Javed and, perhaps more surprisingly, Zaheer to the top three in the batting chart, a mere smattering of points behind the Great Viv. Amarnath's comeback and Wessels' sudden transformation from South African to loyal Australian (he was to revert some years later) also caused upheaveals in the top ten. Pakistan, with four batsmen in the top ten, were now clearly the strongest batting team, ahead of the West Indies. The poverty of India's and England's batting resources was similarly revealed, as Patil, Viswanath, Boycott and Tavaré went tumbling out of the twenty. Boycott's drop from 14th to 21st came about simply because he wasn't playing. But the others each plummeted more than 100 points after more than averagely disastrous seasons – Patil to 32nd, Tavaré to 41st, and Viswanath (who ominously had been on 666 at the end of the 1982 season) to a dismal 46th. Also gone, Wasim Raja (to 30th), Bruce Laird (37th) and Graeme Wood (39th).

The calmer waters of the bowling ratings, meanwhile, welcomed the hugely improved Geoff Lawson, whose bags of wickets against Pakistan and England made him the highest new entry yet seen. Malcolm Marshall's return (he admittedly only missed one series, but that had been enough for him to drop out of the ratings altogether on the 18-month rule) and Jeff Thomson's return to form meant it was goodbye to Troup of New Zealand (down a mere 11 points but four places to 21st), Rodney Hogg (22nd) and the injured Terry Alderman (25th). For Botham, it had been a disappointing season. As *Wisden* put it, 'He left behind in Australia many past cricketers and present judges who have yet to be convinced that he is a great all-rounder.'

ENGLAND BATSMEN 1982/83

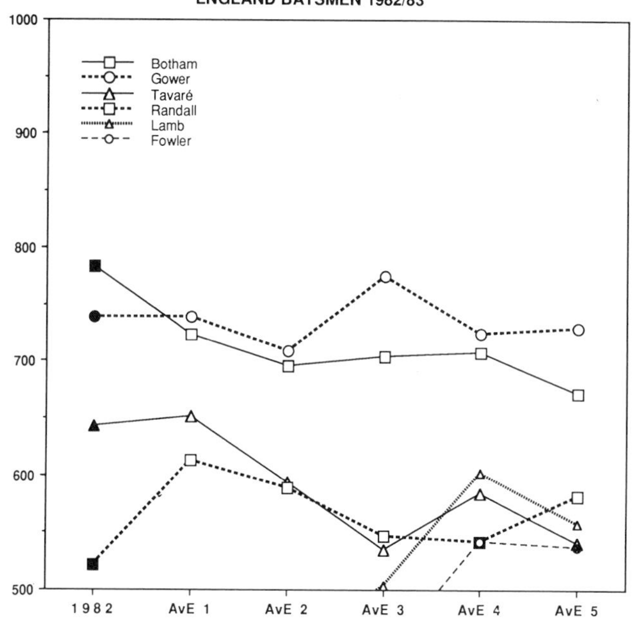
1000
900
800
700
600
500
Botham
Gower
Tavaré
Randall
Lamb
Fowler
1982
AvE 1
AvE 2
AvE 3
AvE 4
AvE 5

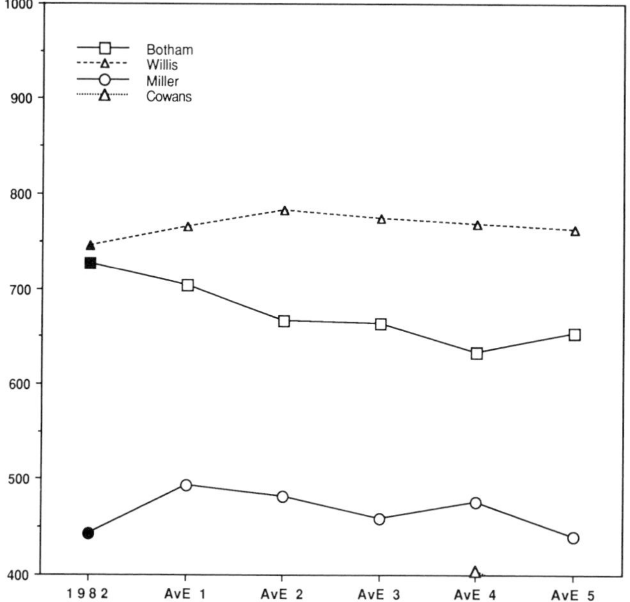
ENGLAND BOWLERS 1982/83
1000
900
800
700
600
500
400
Botham
Willis
Miller
Cowans
1982
AvE 1
AvE 2
AvE 3
AvE 4
AvE 5

AUSTRALIAN BATSMEN 1982/83

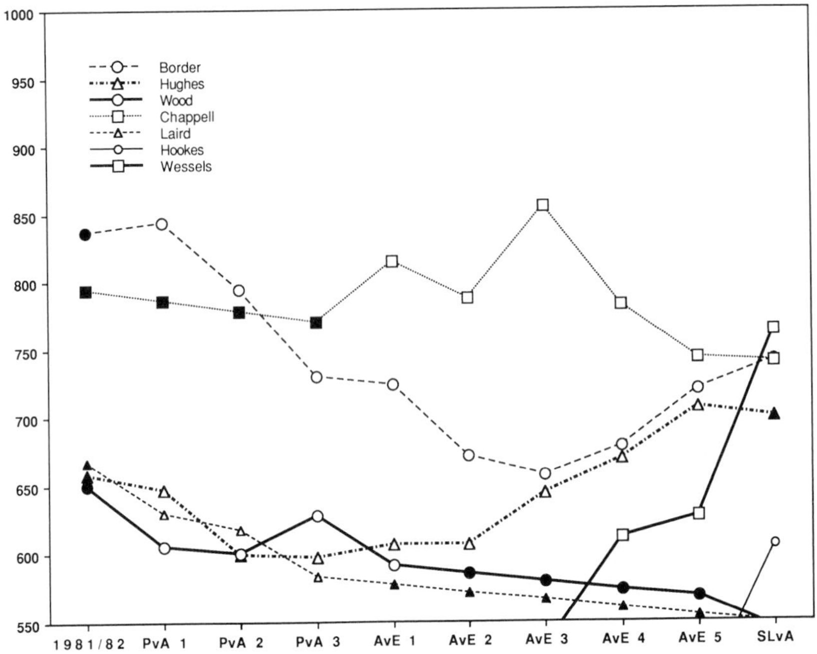

1000
950
900
850
800
750
700
650
600
550
Border
Hughes
Wood
Chappell
Laird
Hookes
Wessels
1981/82
PvA 1
PvA 2
PvA 3
AvE 1
AvE 2
AvE 3
AvE 4
AvE 5
SLvA

AUSTRALIAN BOWLERS 1982/83

1000
900
800
700
600
500
400
Lillee
Alderman
Lawson
Thomson
Yardley
Hogg
Bright
1981/82
PvA 1
PvA 2
PvA 3
AvE 1
AvE 2
AvE 3
AvE 4
AvE 5
SLvA

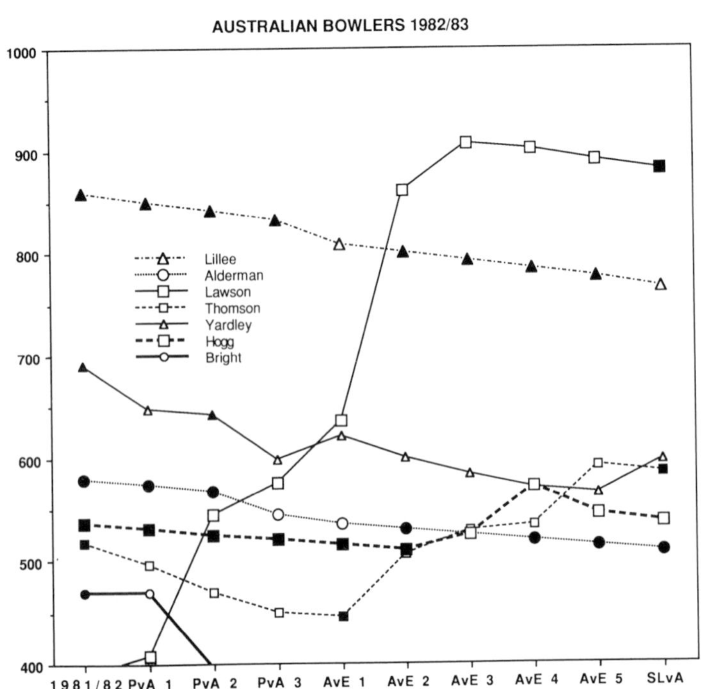

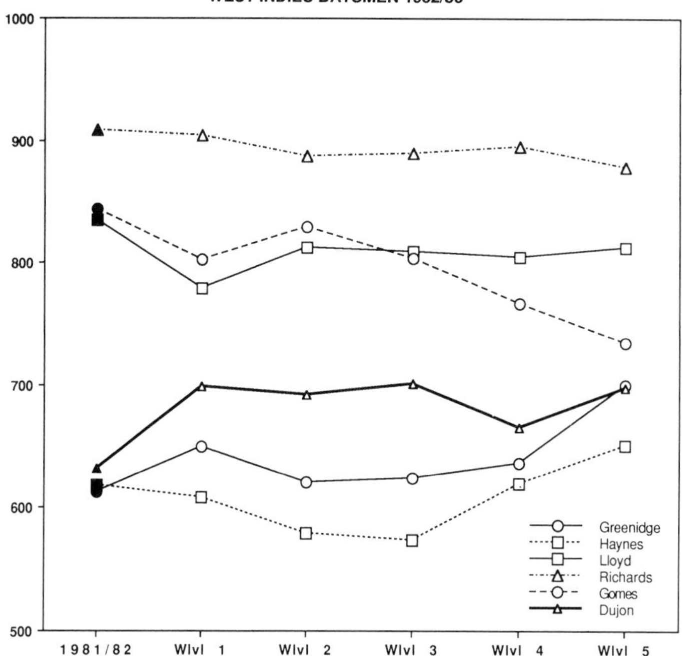
WEST INDIES BATSMEN 1982/83
1000
900
800
700
600
500
1981/82
WIvI 1
WIvI 2
WIvI 3
WIvI 4
WIvI 5
Greenidge
Haynes
Lloyd
Richards
Gomes
Dujon

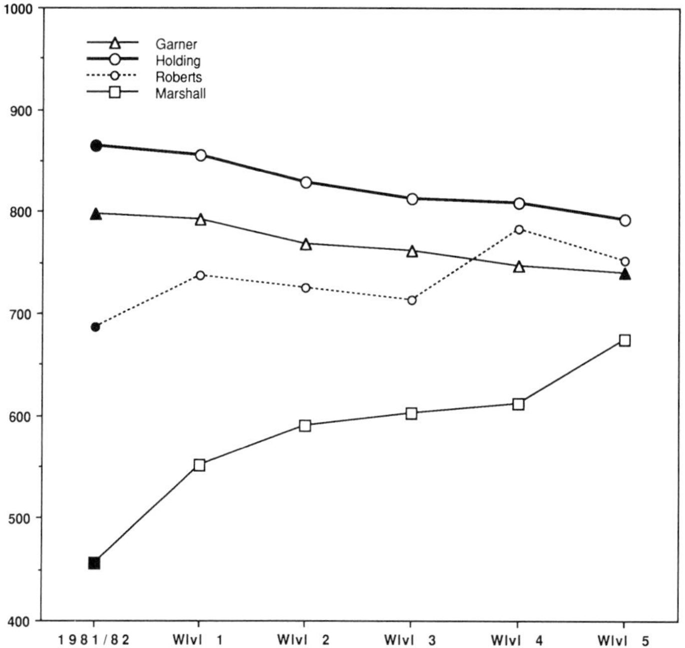
WEST INDIES BOWLERS 1982/83
1000
900
800
700
600
500
400
1981/82
WIvI 1
WIvI 2
WIvI 3
WIvI 4
WIvI 5
Garner
Holding
Roberts
Marshall

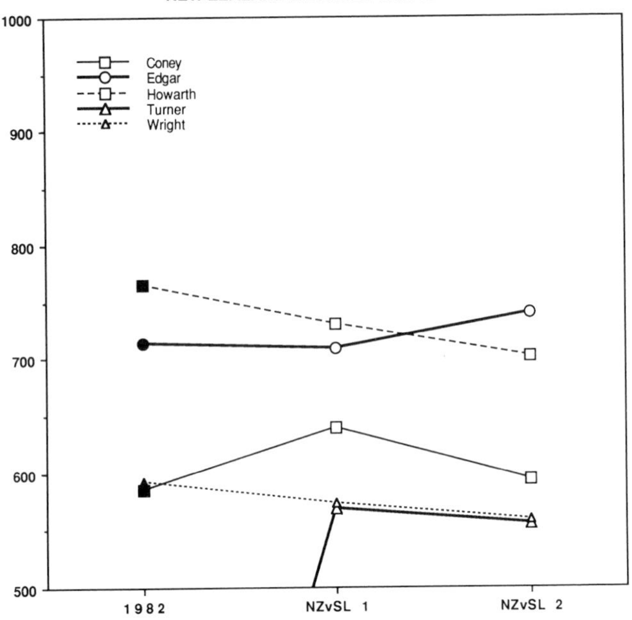
NEW ZEALAND BATSMEN 1982/83
1000
900
800
700
600
500
Coney
Edgar
Howarth
Turner
Wright
1982
NZvSL 1
NZvSL 2

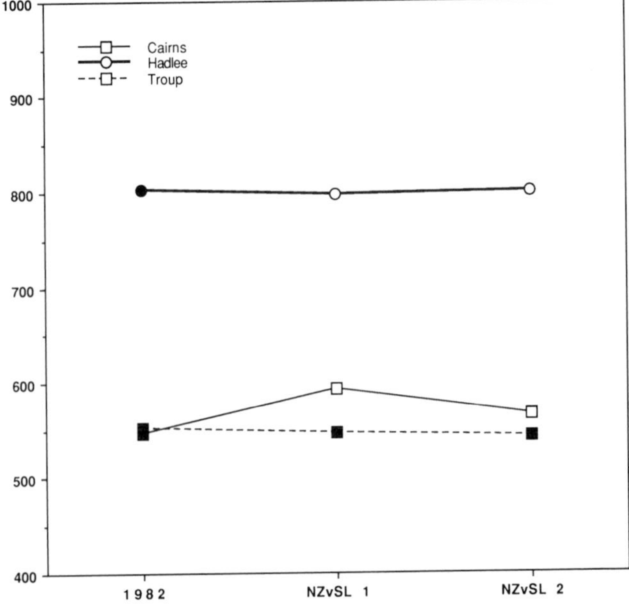
NEW ZEALAND BOWLERS 1982/83
1000
900
800
700
600
500
400
Cairns
Hadlee
Troup
1982
NZvSL 1
NZvSL 2

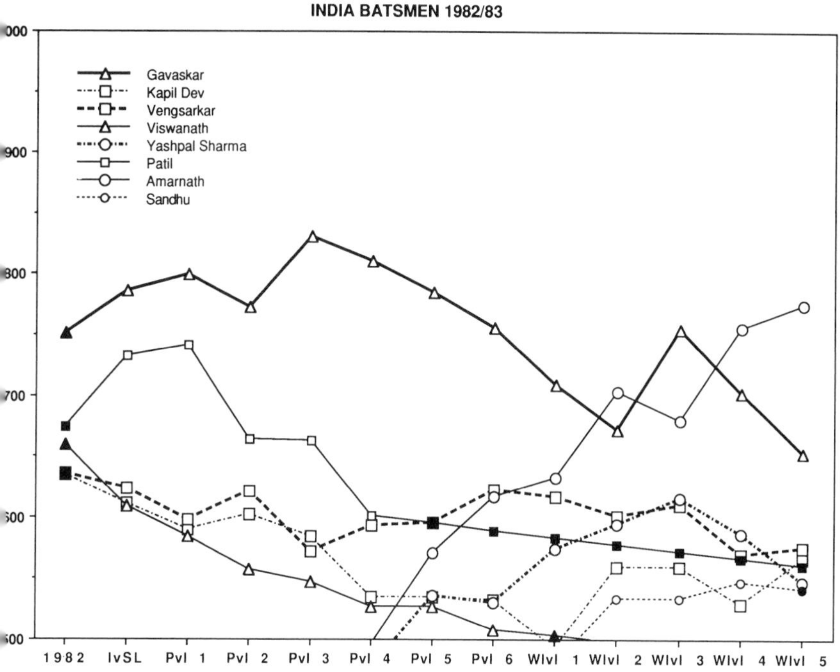

INDIA BATSMEN 1982/83

Gavaskar
Kapil Dev
Vengsarkar
Viswanath
Yashpal Sharma
Patil
Amarnath
Sandhu

1000
900
800
700
600
500

1982 IvSL Pvl 1 Pvl 2 Pvl 3 Pvl 4 Pvl 5 Pvl 6 WIvl 1 WIvl 2 WIvl 3 WIvl 4 WIvl 5

INDIA BOWLERS 1982/83

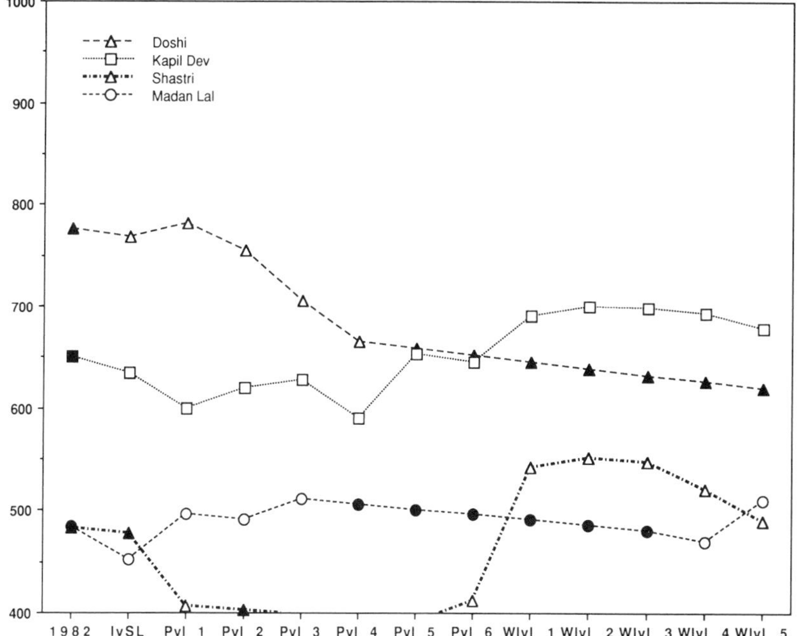

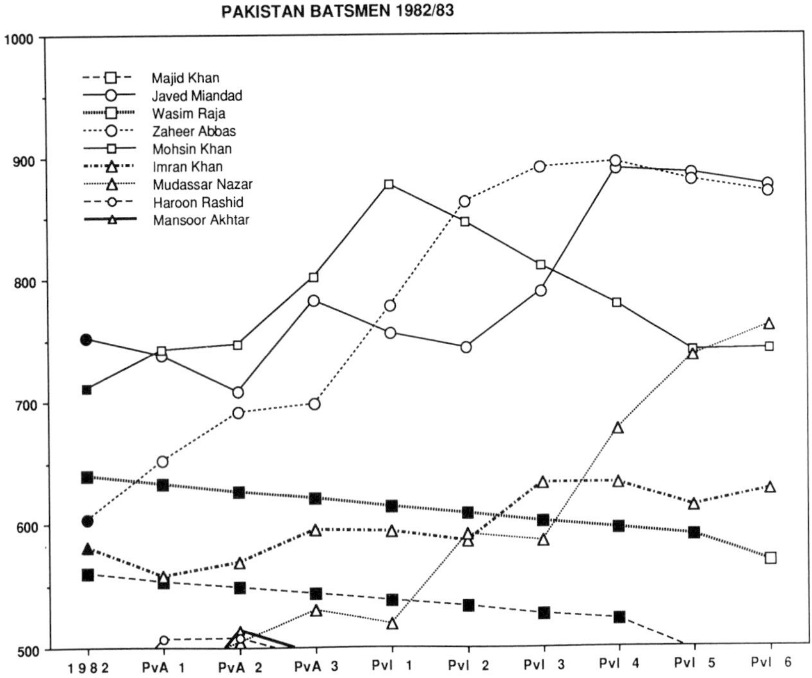
PAKISTAN BATSMEN 1982/83
Majid Khan
Javed Miandad
Wasim Raja
Zaheer Abbas
Mohsin Khan
Imran Khan
Mudassar Nazar
Haroon Rashid
Mansoor Akhtar
1000
900
800
700
600
500
1982
PvA 1
PvA 2
PvA 3
PvI 1
PvI 2
PvI 3
PvI 4
PvI 5
PvI 6

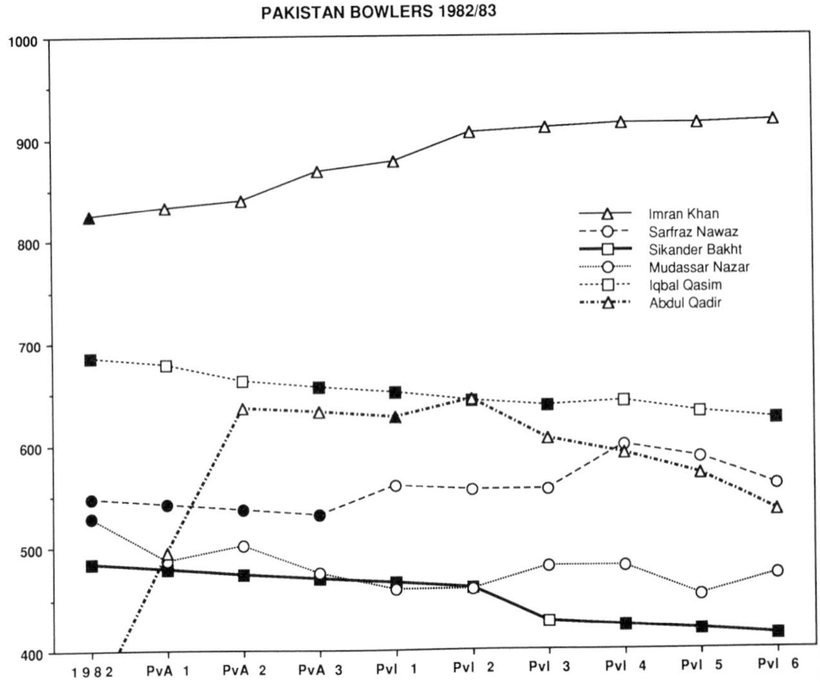
PAKISTAN BOWLERS 1982/83
Imran Khan
Sarfraz Nawaz
Sikander Bakht
Mudassar Nazar
Iqbal Qasim
Abdul Qadir
1000
900
800
700
600
500
400
1982
PvA 1
PvA 2
PvA 3
PvI 1
PvI 2
PvI 3
PvI 4
PvI 5
PvI 6

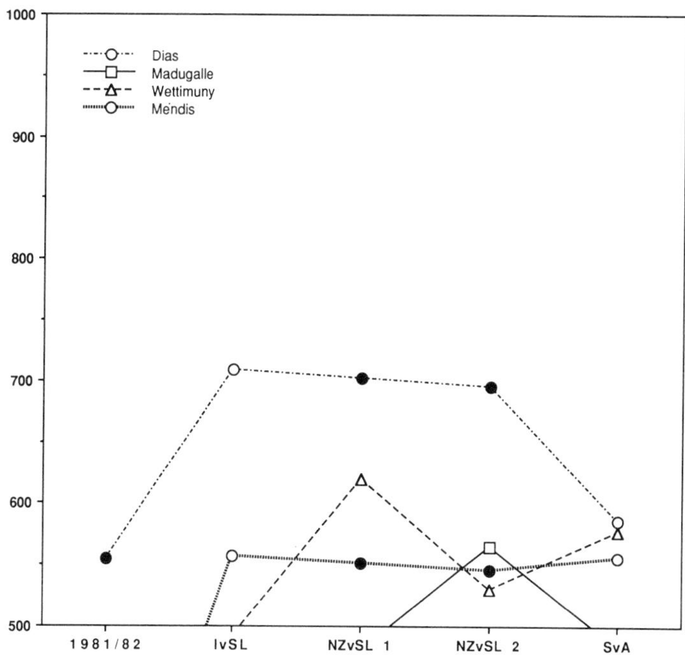
SRI LANKA BATSMEN 1982/83
Dias
Madugalle
Wettimuny
Mendis
1000
900
800
700
600
500
1981/82
IvSL
NZvSL 1
NZvSL 2
SvA

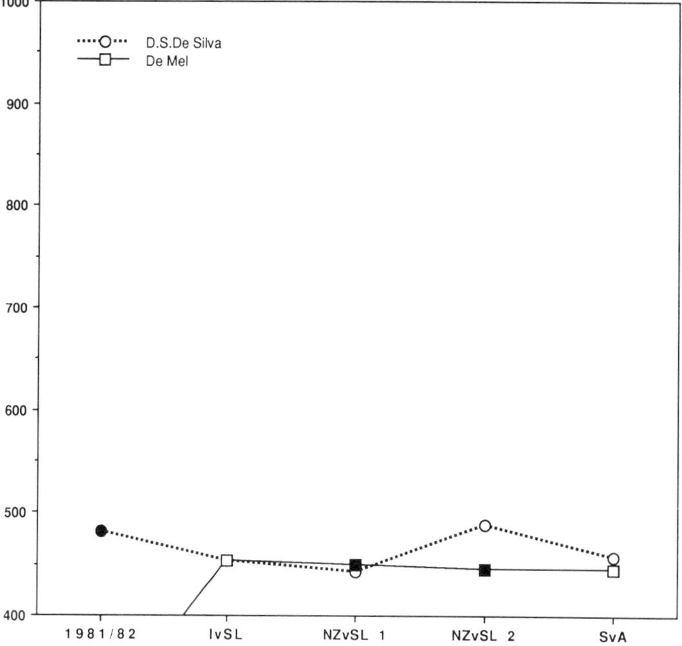
SRI LANKA BOWLERS 1982/83
D.S.De Silva
De Mel
1000
900
800
700
600
500
400
1981/82
IvSL
NZvSL 1
NZvSL 2
SvA

1983

ENGLAND vs NEW ZEALAND

First Test (The Oval, 14–18 July) England won by 189 runs
England 1st Innings: 209 (Randall 75 not out, Tavaré 45, Hadlee 6–53)
New Zealand 1st Innings: 196 (Hadlee 84, Coney 44, Willis 4–43, Botham 4–62)
England 2nd Innings: 446 for 6 declared (Tavaré 109, Fowler 105, Lamb 102 not out)
New Zealand 2nd Innings: 270 (Wright 88, Howarth 67, Marks 3–78, Edmonds 3–101)

Second Test (Headingley, 28 July–1 August) New Zealand won by 5 wickets
England 1st Innings: 225 (Tavaré 69, Lamb 58, Cairns 7–74)
New Zealand 1st Innings: 377 (Wright 93, Edgar 84, Hadlee 75, Willis 4–57, Cowans 3–88)
England 2nd Innings: 252 (Gower 112 not out, Chatfield 5–95, Cairns 3–70)
New Zealand 2nd Innings: 103 for 5 (Willis 5–35)

Third Test (Lord's, 11–15 August) England won by 127 runs
England 1st Innings: 326 (Gower 108, Gatting 81, Tavaré 51, Hadlee 5–93)
New Zealand 1st Innings: 191 (Edgar 70, M.D. Crowe 46, N.G.B. Cook 5–35, Botham 4–50)
England 2nd Innings: 211 (Botham 61, C.L. Smith 43, Chatfield 3–29, Hadlee 3–42, Gray 3–73)
New Zealand 2nd Innings: 219 (Coney 68, Willis 3–24, N.G.B. Cook 3–90)

Fourth Test (Trent Bridge, 25–29 August) England won by 165 runs
England 1st Innings: 420 (Botham 103, Randall 83, Gower 72, Bracewell 4–108, Snedden 3–69)
New Zealand 1st Innings: 207 (Edgar 62, N.G.B. Cook 5–63, Cowans 3–74)
England 2nd Innings: 297 (Lamb 137 not out, Hadlee 4–85)
New Zealand 2nd Innings: 345 (Hadlee 92 not out, Edgar 76, Coney 68, N.G.B. Cook 4–87, Cowans 3–95)

Nick Cook tossing one up in the decisive fourth Test. Umpire Bird looks on, gripped.

Captains: England – R.G.D. Willis
New Zealand – G.P. Howarth

Débuts: England – N.G.B. Cook, N.A Foster, C.L. Smith (3rd Test)
New Zealand – E.J. Gray (3rd Test), T.J. Franklin (4th Test)

Rising Stars: England – N.G.B. Cook (+240 bowling)
New Zealand – R.J. Hadlee (+130 batting)

After being knocked out in the group stages of the Prudential World Cup (India went on to win it, beating West Indies in the final), New Zealand stayed in England for a four-Test series, which they lost 3–1. That one victory, though, was their first ever in a Test in England, after seventeen defeats and eleven draws. Under Willis' determined leadership, England were much the better team, and in Lamb and Gower had the two most successful batsmen on either side. Lamb, with 392 runs at over 65 (including two centuries), improved his rating from 558 to 741, while Gower's 404 runs pushed him to 820 and 4th in the world, his best position yet. Fowler and Tavaré's opening partnership of 223 in the first Test was not only a record for the series, but the first time both England's openers had made a century in the same innings since 1960. And when Randall and Botham both rediscovered their form in the final Test and took the New Zealand bowling apart, the result was some of the most pleasurable England batting seen for years.

But perhaps the most decisive intervention was that of Nick Cook, the left-arm spinner who took 17 wickets in his first two Tests and immediately found himself the 11th best bowler on the planet.

Botham, though, was relatively disappointing with the ball, especially in the lost second Test, when his bowling was so poor in the first innings that Willis declined to use him for more than one ball in the second. Cowans, whose 12 wickets cost more than 37 runs each, failed to crack the 400 barrier, and ended the series on 387. Willis' 9–92 match analysis at Headingley was, surprisingly, the best of his career. Was he the best Test bowler never to take 10 wickets in a match?

The New Zealanders were hampered by Glenn Turner's refusal to take part in anything other than the World Cup, and by a lack of a suitably swift bowler to back up Hadlee. Although Cairns' 7–74 was his country's best return against England (and his own personal best), Chatfield and Snedden were disappointing. Most of the batsmen, though thriving in the county matches, struggled in the Tests – the twenty-year-old Martin Crowe, for instance, scored three centuries during the tour as a whole, but could manage no more than 46 in the Tests. His rating still climbed (to 276), although as it had been 47 before the series it didn't really have much choice.

In the main the batting was held up by Hadlee, who averaged over 50 with a number of sparkly late-order innings, and the obdurate Edgar. Hadlee also had a good series with the ball, taking a record 21 wickets, although his relatively minor role in the victory at Headingley (he didn't take a wicket in either innings) may have contributed to the slight drop in his ratings. Besides, 800 is a difficult standard for any bowler to keep up, even Hadlee. But never mind – New Zealand were too busy lulling England into a false sense of security for their return tour later in the year.

WORLD TOP TWENTY AFTER 1983

BATTING

(1)	1.	I.V.A. Richards (West Indies)	878
(2)	2.	Javed Miandad (Pakistan)	876
(3)	3.	Zaheer Abbas (Pakistan)	871
(13)	4.	D.I. Gower (England)	820 (+91)
(4)	5.	C.H. Lloyd (West Indies)	812
(5)	6.	M. Amarnath (India)	775
(6)	7.	K.C. Wessels (Australia)	763
(10)	8.	B.A. Edgar (New Zealand)	762 (+22)
(7)	9.	Mudassar Nazar (Pakistan)	761
(8)	10.	Mohsin Khan (Pakistan)	742
(34)	11.	A.J. Lamb (England)	741 (+183)
(9)	12.	A.R. Border (Australia)	741
(11)	13.	G.S. Chappell (Australia)	740

(12)	14.	H.A. Gomes (West Indies)	734
(15)	15.	C.G. Greenidge (West Indies)	700
(16)	16.	K.J. Hughes (Australia)	699
(17)	17.	P.J.L. Dujon (West Indies)	698
(18)	18.	I.T. Botham (England)	681 (+9)
(19)	19.	S.M. Gavaskar (India)	653
(20)	20.	D.L. Haynes (West Indies)	651

BOWLING

(1)	1.	Imran Khan (Pakistan)	915
(2)	2.	G.F. Lawson (Australia)	881
(6)	3.	R.G.D. Willis (England)	833 (+70)
(4)	4.	M.A. Holding (West Indies)	792
(5)	5.	D.K. Lillee (Australia)	766
(7)	6.	A.M.E. Roberts (West Indies)	752
(3)	7.	R.J. Hadlee (New Zealand)	749 (−51)
(8)	8.	J. Garner (West Indies)	740
(10)	9.	Kapil Dev (India)	679
(11)	10.	M.D. Marshall (West Indies)	674
NE	11.	N.G.B. Cook (England)	640
(14)	12.	Iqbal Qasim (Pakistan)	624
(15)	13.	D.R. Doshi (India)	620
(16)	14.	B. Yardley (Australia)	597
(12)	15.	I.T. Botham (England)	592 (−61)
(17)	16.	J.R. Thomson (Australia)	585
(19)	17.	B.L. Cairns (New Zealand)	580 (+15)
(20)	18.	Sarfraz Nawaz (Pakistan)	560
(22)	19.	R.M. Hogg (Australia)	536
(23)	20.	Abdul Qadir (Pakistan)	534

Not an amazing amount of difference between this and the last chart, but then a mere four Tests had been played, and neither teams involved were exactly the best the world had to offer. Nevertheless the successes of Lamb and Gower had their reward, making England's batting order look rather sturdier than for some time – especially with Randall, Tavaré and Fowler at 25th, 26th and 32nd respectively. Howarth's disappointing tour had its corollary, however, as he lost 95 points and fell to 23rd. Coney, meanwhile, was at 22nd, Wright at 28th and Hadlee at 31st.

The bowling ratings also reflected the upsurge in England's fortunes. Cook's swift advance almost distracts from Willis' superb achievement – bowling better than ever, he had achieved the best rating of his career. Ejected from the twenty, on the 18-month rule, were Len Pascoe of Australia and the two West Indian rebels, Colin Croft and Sylvester Clarke. Hogg and Abdul Qadir, without doing anything very much, stepped in to replace them.

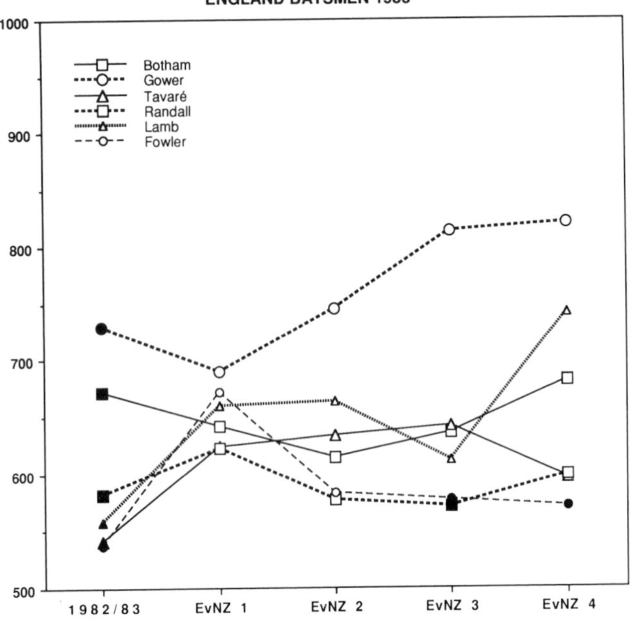
ENGLAND BATSMEN 1983
1000
900
800
700
600
500
Botham
Gower
Tavaré
Randall
Lamb
Fowler
1982/83
EvNZ 1
EvNZ 2
EvNZ 3
EvNZ 4

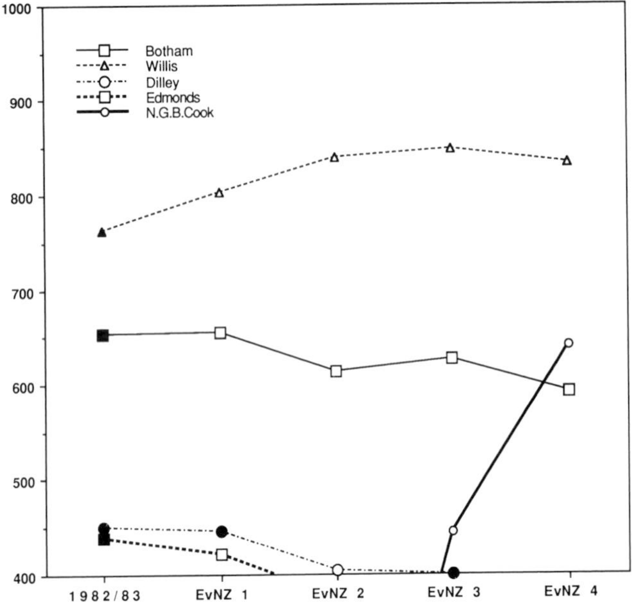
ENGLAND BOWLERS 1983
1000
900
800
700
600
500
400
Botham
Willis
Dilley
Edmonds
N.G.B.Cook
1982/83
EvNZ 1
EvNZ 2
EvNZ 3
EvNZ 4

NEW ZEALAND BATSMEN 1983

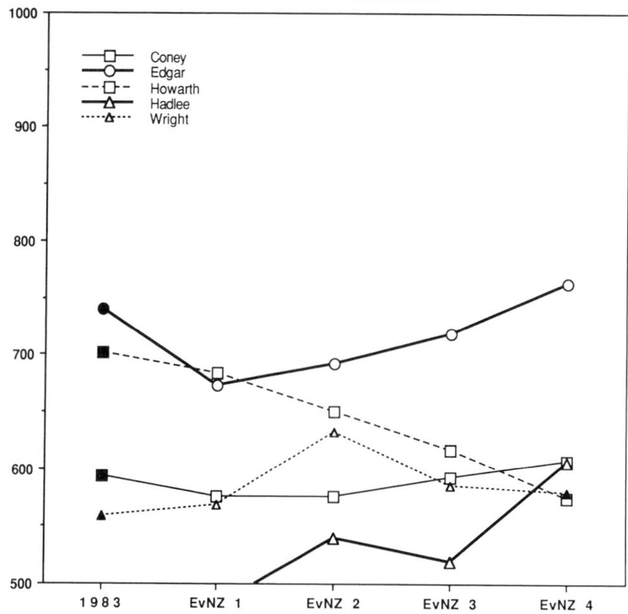
1000
900
800
700
600
500
Coney
Edgar
Howarth
Hadlee
Wright
1983
EvNZ 1
EvNZ 2
EvNZ 3
EvNZ 4

NEW ZEALAND BOWLERS 1983

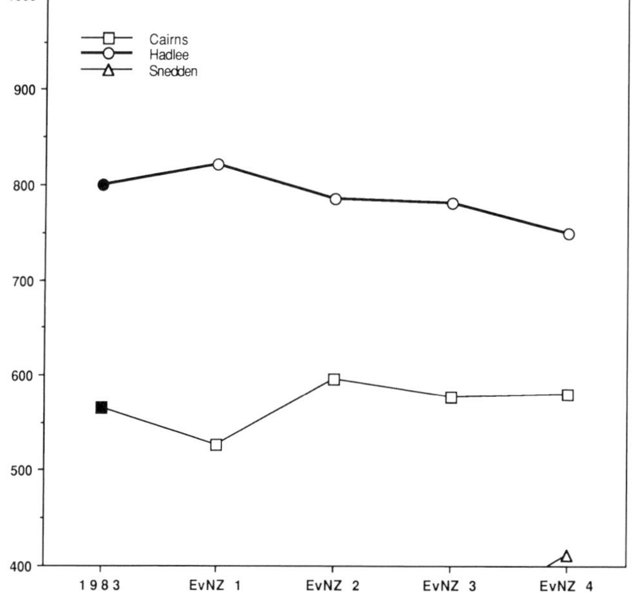
1000
900
800
700
600
500
400
Cairns
Hadlee
Snedden
1983
EvNZ 1
EvNZ 2
EvNZ 3
EvNZ 4

1983-84

INDIA vs PAKISTAN

First Test (Bangalore, 14–19 September) Match Drawn
India 1st Innings: 275 (Binny 83 not out, Madan Lal 74, Gavaskar 42, Tahir Naqqash 5–76, Mudassar Nazar 3–44)
Pakistan 1st Innings: 288 (Javed Miandad 99, Wasim Bari 64, Kapil Dev 5–68, Madan Lal 3–72)
India 2nd Innings: 176 for no wicket (Gavaskar 103 not out, Gaekwad 66 not out)

Second Test (Jullundur, 24–29 September) Match Drawn
Pakistan 1st Innings: 337 (Wasim Raja 125, Javed Miandad 66, Zaheer Abbas 49, Kapil Dev 4–80, Shastri 3–63)
India 1st Innings: 374 (Gaekwad 201, Binny 54, Wasim Raja 4–50, Azeem Hafeez 3–65)
Pakistan 2nd Innings: 16 for no wicket

Third Test (Nagpur, 5–10 October) Match Drawn
India 1st Innings: 245 (Shastri 52, Gavaskar 50, Azeem Hafeez 4–58)
Pakistan 1st Innings: 322 (Zaheer Abbas 85, Mudassar Nazar 78, Javed Miandad 60, Mohsin Khan 44, Shastri 5–75, Kapil Dev 3–68)
India 2nd Innings: 262 for 8 declared (Gavaskar 64, Vengsarkar 40, Mohammad Nazir 5–72)
Pakistan 2nd Innings: 42 for 1

Captains: India – Kapil Dev
Pakistan – Zaheer Abbas

Débuts: India – A. Raghuram Bhat (3rd Test)
Pakistan – Azeem Hafeez (1st Test), Qasim Omar, Shoaib Mohammad (2nd Test)

Rising Stars: India – R.J. Shastri (+99 bowling)
Pakistan – Mohammad Nazir (+89 bowling)

If it begins to look as though India and Pakistan were playing each other on an annual basis, that's because they were. The idea was to exchange short visits of three Tests at the beginning of each season, with Pakistan visiting India first in 1984–85. This arrangement didn't last long, though – the public, possibly sated by the ridiculous amount of Test cricket being played then (and since) in the sub-continent, showed little interest, and the second and final such tour, the following year, was cut short when Mrs Gandhi was assassinated.

This first tour was no less inconclusive, though ruined not by political upheaval but more prosaically by the weather. The first Test lost seven hours to rain, so that Pakistan's first innings eventually wound up at lunch on the final day. Gavaskar naturally continued to the death, to notch up one of his less relevant Test centuries. The second Test too surrendered seven hours to the downpours, and the third four and a half, suffering in addition from some drearily defensive captaincy from Zaheer Abbas.

Not perhaps one of nature's leaders, Zaheer had been drafted in to replace Imran Khan, whose stress facture of the shin was deemed to need six months' rest. Also absent were Abdul Qadir and Sarfraz Nawaz, both in 'disagreement' with their cricket board. Thus weakened, Pakistan gave an extended run to a young left-arm pace bowler, Azeem Hafeez, whose 10 wickets at 31 earned him a rating after three Tests of 363. The veteran off-spinner Mohammad Nazir came back for a final fling (after yet another name change) and earned the Rising Star award. Of the more established players, Salim Malik scored just 5 runs in two Tests (he was ill for the second) and dropped to 309 in the ratings, while Mohsin Khan was sadly off-form. Javed Miandad's 4-point jump edged him ahead of Viv Richards at the head of the world table.

India, meanwhile, were shaping up for a full-blooded series against the West Indies, and so were probably quite pleased not to be over-pressed by their neighbours. Gaekwad, who was dropped twice on the way to his double century, finally broke the 400 barrier, although Patil's decline continued and Vengsarkar didn't even play until the third Test. India's main batting success was in fact Binny, whose average of 137 didn't save him from being dropped for the third Test – another of India's profusion of bowlers who could bat a bit, but couldn't seem to bowl, he had taken just 2 wickets. Kapil Dev and Shastri, though, consolidated their reputations as world class all-rounders.

INDIA vs WEST INDIES

First Test (Kanpur, 21–25 October) West Indies won by an innings and 83 runs
West Indies 1st Innings: 454 (Greenidge 194, Marshall 92, Dujon 81, Kapil Dev 4–99)
India 1st Innings: 207 (Madan Lal 63 not out, Marshall 4–19, Holding 3–37)

India 2nd Innings: 164 (Vengsarkar 65, Shastri 46 not out, Marshall 4–47, Davis 3–46, Holding 3–59)

Second Test (Delhi, 29 October–3 November) Match Drawn
India 1st Innings: 464 (Vengsarkar 159, Gavaskar 121, Binny 52, Shastri 49, Holding 4–107, Daniel 3–86)
West Indies 1st Innings: 384 (Lloyd 103, Richards 67, Logie 63, Kapil Dev 6–77)
India 2nd Innings: 233 (Vengsarkar 63, Daniel 3–38, Marshall 3–52)
West Indies 2nd Innings: 120 for 2 (Greenidge 72 not out)

Third Test (Ahmedabad, 12–16 November) West Indies won by 138 runs
West Indies 1st Innings: 281 (Dujon 98, Lloyd 68, Maninder Singh 4–85, Binny 3–18)
India 1st Innings: 241 (Gavaskar 90, Daniel 5–39)
West Indies 2nd Innings: 201 (Holding 58, Kapil Dev 9–83)
India 2nd Innings: 103 (Holding 4–30, Davis 3–21)

Fourth Test (Bombay, 24–29 November) Match Drawn
India 1st Innings: 463 (Vengsarkar 100, Shastri 77, Binny 65, Gaekwad 48, Kirmani 43 not out, Holding 5–102, Marshall 3–88)
West Indies 1st Innings: 393 (Richards 120, Dujon 84, Lloyd 67, Haynes 55, Yadav 5–131)
India 2nd Innings: 173 for 5 declared (Malhotra 72 not out)
West Indies 2nd Innings: 104 for 4

Fifth Test (Calcutta, 10–14 December) West Indies won by an innings and 46 runs
India 1st Innings: 241 (Kapil Dev 69, Kirmani 49, Binny 44, Roberts 3–56, Holding 3–59, Marshall 3–65)
West Indies 1st Innings: 377 (Lloyd 161 not out, Roberts 68, Marshall 54, Kapil Dev 4–91, Yadav 3–80)
India 2nd Innings: 90 (Marshall 6–37, Holding 3–29)

Sixth Test (Madras, 24–29 December) Match Drawn
West Indies 1st Innings: 313 (Dujon 62, Maninder Singh 3–41, Kapil Dev 3–44)
India 1st Innings: 451 for 8 declared (Gavaskar 236 not out, Shastri 72, Kirmani 63 not out, Marshall 5–72)
West Indies 2nd Innings: 64 for 1

Captains: India – Kapil Dev
West Indies – C.H. Lloyd

Débuts: India – Navjot Singh (3rd Test)
West Indies – E.A.E. Baptiste (1st Test), R.B. Richardson (4th Test), R.A. Harper (5th Test)

Rising Stars: India – Kapil Dev (+98 bowling)
West Indies – M.D. Marshall (+162 bowling)

When you're finding it hard to beat anyone, it's always the West Indies you seem to find yourself playing next. Or at least, such was the case for India, who effortlessly stretched their winless streak to a record twenty-nine Tests. The West Indies, inspired as so often by Malcolm Marshall, imperiously swatted the home side 3–0 in the Tests, and won all five of the one-day internationals, as if to prove that India's victory in the World Cup the previous June had been a one-off after all. Marshall, with a record 33 wickets (at 18.81), improved his rating from 674 to 846, which meant that in his last eleven Tests, all against India, it had risen 380 points. If it had trouble increasing any further as the series wound on, that may have something to do with the rapidly decreasing batting ratings of the players he was so consistently getting out.

Holding's 30 wickets proved less profitable in rating terms – up just 13 points – but Wayne Daniel's return to Test cricket after seven years (replacing the injured Garner) made more of an impact. Although Roberts was injured and played only the last two Tests (his last two as it turned out), Winston Davis supplied useful back-up, even if his final average of over 40 pushed his rating down to just 302.

All of which proved rather challenging for the shellshocked – and ever changing – Indian batting line-up. Of the mainline batsmen, only Gavaskar and Gaekwad (who failed to score a fifty) played all six Tests. Yashpal Sharma was tried for one, Malhotra had three, and Navjot Singh (later to become better known as N.S. Sidhu – if you don't at first succeed, try, try, try again under a different name) was given two. Patil was finally dropped after yet more low scores, while Amarnath, hero of the previous winter, had a shocking run – in five Tests that season (two against Pakistan, three against West Indies), he scored just 12 runs, and his rating plunged more than 250 points.

It was left, as one might expect, to Gavaskar and Vengsarkar to introduce some sanity and indeed some runs to this sagging order. Both averaged over 50, and Gavaskar's two centuries, the second a match-saving 236 in the final Test, finally edged him past Sir Donald Bradman's Test record of 29. No such heroics could dignify India's bowling, however. Besides Kapil Dev, whose 29 wickets set another new record for the series, the bowling was at best unpenetrating and at worst positively amiable. All the usual bits-and-pieces players were drafted in, and indeed Binny and Madan Lal both scored useful runs, but wickets were conspicuous by their absence. But at least Maninder Singh improved his rating – from 40 to 151.

Their failures were all the more feeble for the poor form that some of the West Indian batsmen were clearly suffering. Haynes averaged just 17, while neither Gomes nor Richards made as many runs as expected/feared. Richards, indeed, dropped from 2nd in the world to 13th, his lowest position yet. Logie, whose rating remained in only the high 200s, was deemed by *Wisden* to be 'rather wanting in temperament'.

Once again, though, Lloyd scored loads and loads of runs, time and again putting the game beyond India's reach when the West Indies had started poorly. His 496 runs at 82.66 put his rating up to 890, displacing Javed Miandad at the top of the world list. Dujon and Greenidge also averaged over 50, and with Marshall and Holding on top form, India never had a chance.

AUSTRALIA vs PAKISTAN

First Test (Perth, 11–14 November) Australia won by an innings and 9 runs
Australia 1st Innings: 436 for 9 declared (Phillips 159, Yallop 141, Azeem Hafeez 5–100, Abdul Qadir 3–121)
Pakistan 1st Innings: 129 (Qasim Omar 48, Rackemann 5–32, Hogg 3–20)
Pakistan 2nd Innings: 298 (Qasim Omar 65, Javed Miandad 46, Rackemann 6–86)

Second Test (Brisbane, 25–29 November) Match Drawn
Pakistan 1st Innings: 156 (Zaheer Abbas 56, Lawson 5–49, Rackemann 3–28)
Australia 1st Innings: 509 for 7 declared (Chappell 150 not out, Border 118, Lawson 49, Phillips 46, Rashid Khan 3–129, Azeem Hafeez 3–152)
Pakistan 2nd Innings: 82 for 3

Third Test (Adelaide, 9–13 December) Match Drawn
Australia 1st Innings: 465 (Wessels 179, Border 117 not out, Yallop 68, Azeem Hafeez 6–167, Sarfraz Nawaz 3–105)
Pakistan 1st Innings: 624 (Mohsin Khan 149, Javed Miandad 131, Qasim Omar 113, Salim Malik 77, Zaheer Abbas 46, Mudassar Nazar 44, Lillee 6–171)
Australia 2nd Innings: 310 for 7 (K.J. Hughes 106, Border 66, Phillips 54)

Fourth Test (Melbourne, 26–30 December) Match Drawn
Pakistan 1st Innings: 470 (Mohsin Khan 152, Imran Khan 83, Abdul

Qadir 45, Zaheer Abbas 44, Maguire 3–111)
Australia 1st Innings: 555 (Yallop 268, K.J. Hughes 94, G.R.J. Matthews 75, Abdul Qadir 5–166, Azeem Hafeez 3–115)
Pakistan 2nd Innings: 238 for 7 (Imran Khan 72 not out, Zaheer Abbas 50, Lillee 3–71)

Fifth Test (Sydney, 2–6 January) Australia won by 10 wickets
Pakistan 1st Innings: 278 (Mudassar Nazar 84, Zaheer Abbas 61, Salim Malik 54, Lawson 5–59, Lillee 4–65)
Australia 1st Innings: 454 for 6 declared (Chappell 182, K.J. Hughes 76, Border 64, Mudassar Nazar 3–81)
Pakistan 2nd Innings: 210 (Javed Miandad 60, Lawson 4–48, Lillee 4–88)
Australia 2nd Innings: 35 for no wicket

Captains: Australia – K.J. Hughes
Pakistan – Zaheer Abbas (1st–3rd Tests), Imran Khan (4th & 5th Tests)

Débuts: Australia – W.B. Phillips (1st Test), J.N. Maguire, G.R.J. Matthews (4th Test)

Rising Stars: Australia – W.B. Phillips (+252 batting)
Pakistan – Azeem Hafeez (+171 bowling)

The difference between playing Tests at home and away can be enormous. Pakistan at home, for instance, are amongst the hardest teams to beat, for reasons that would no doubt induce a libel suit should I attempt to explain them in detail. Away, though, they remain strangely prone to batting collapses, ineffective bowling and, their speciality, internecine arguments. All three factors contributed to what turned out to be, for them, a disappointing tour to Australia in 1983–84.

The trouble began with the captaincy. Although Zaheer was again appointed in Imran's absence, the chairman of the Pakistani board overruled his selectors (indeed he fired them too) and instituted Imran as captain. The aristocratic one helped to choose the team, but was still not fit, at least to bowl, when they arrived in Australia so, no doubt to his chagrin, Zaheer took over again, but with a team he had had no part in selecting. Furthermore, Sarfraz Nawaz, who was still in 'disagreement' with the board, had said so in public and had been swiftly banned from international cricket for six months, as well as slapped on the hand. When the tour started disastrously, this ban was naturally lifted without delay and Sarfraz arrived in time for the third Test.

Such politicking was perhaps not the best preparation for Pakistan's first full five-Test series in Australia, especially when the home team were at full strength once again, with Chappell, Lillee and Marsh back in harness. And indeed the Australians proved much too strong. Their fast bowlers, Lawson, Lillee, Hogg and, before he was injured, Rackemann, consistently rolled over the suddenly fragile Pakistani batting. Why? How? Whatever the reasons, the effect was clear. Batsmen like Javed, Zaheer and Mudassar were made to look ordinary, and ratings plummeted. But there were successes. The new boy Qasim Omar, who averaged marginally over 40, moved up from 61 to 532 in the ratings, while Salim Malik, summoned from home at the same time as Sarfraz, finally broke 400, if not by much.

The real problem, though, was the lack of bowling. Mudassar was almost completely ineffectual (3 wickets at 96), while Sarfraz, when he did turn up, was little better. Abdul Qadir, with six left-handers to face in Australia's top eight, averaged over 60. It was left to the young Azeem Hafeez to take the actual wickets, and a rating of 571 was his reward. The Australian batsmen had much more fun. All the top six made centuries, and Yallop's 268 was the seventh highest Australian score in Test cricket.

In fact, after the crushing victory of the fifth Test, Australian cricket had rarely been at a higher ebb. Six batsmen in the top twenty with Border at third and Chappell at fifth, and the best bowler in the world (Geoff Lawson once more, with a startling 905): what more could they want? What they got, in fact, was the retirements of Chappell, Lillee and Marsh, together with an imminent tour of the West Indies. The Australians had about six weeks to cheer and celebrate before everything started to go horribly wrong again.

NEW ZEALAND vs ENGLAND

First Test (Wellington, 20–24 January) Match Drawn
New Zealand 1st Innings: 219 (J.J. Crowe, 52, Botham 5–59, Willis 3–37)
England 1st Innings: 463 (Randall 164, Botham 138, Cairns 7–143)
New Zealand 2nd Innings: 537 (Coney 174 not out, M.D. Crowe 100, Cairns 64, N.G.B. Cook 3–153)
England 2nd Innings: 69 for no wicket

Second Test (Christchurch, 3–5 February) New Zealand won by an innings and 132 runs
New Zealand 1st Innings: 307 (Hadlee 99, J.J. Crowe 47, Coney 41, Willis 4–51, Cowans 3–52)
England 1st Innings: 82 (Chatfield 3–10, Hadlee 3–16, Cairns 3–35)
England 2nd Innings: 93 (Hadlee 5–28, Boock 3–25)

The unsung Crowe brother, J.J., sorting out the spinners.

Third Test (Auckland, 10–15 February) Match Drawn
New Zealand 1st Innings: 496 for 9 declared (Wright 130, J.J. Crowe 128, I.D.S. Smith 113 not out, Willis 3–109, Marks 3–115)
England 1st Innings: 439 (Randall 104, C.L. Smith 91, Botham 70, Lamb 49, Boock 3–103)
New Zealand 2nd Innings: 16 for no wicket

Captains: New Zealand – G.P. Howarth
England – R.G.D. Willis

Débuts: England – A.C.S. Pigott (2nd Test)

Rising Stars: New Zealand – J.J. Crowe (+116 batting)
England – D.W. Randall (+60 batting)

And so England lost their first ever series in New Zealand, at the same time contriving to be bowled out for under 100 twice – something no other England side had managed this century. England's bowling in that Test was described by captain Bob Willis as among the worst he had ever seen at international level, and much of it came from

Botham, who in 17 overs took 1 for 88 – 6 more runs than England managed in the whole of their first innings.

One has to look hard here for silver linings, although Randall's form was certainly one. With two chanceless centuries, he was top scorer in each Test (reaching 25 in the second innings at Christchurch), and reached his career-best rating 660, just six Tests before that career came to an end. Chris Smith too enhanced his reputation, especially by not playing at Christchurch. Both averaged in the seventies. Gower, Gatting, Fowler and Tavaré, though, all averaged under 20, and Lamb only managed 20.5. This of course had nothing to do with allegations in the *Mail on Sunday* that members of Willis' team had availed themselves of recreational pharmaceuticals in their off-duty moments; although all no doubt reacted to their failures in a suitably mellow manner.

The bowling was no less incompetent. Although New Zealand managed to get themselves out for just 219 in the first Test, only Willis, with 12 wickets at 25.5, ended the tour with figures on the respectable side of mediocre. The three other bowlers most used, Cook, Botham and Foster, respectively averaged 49, 50 and 57, as opposed to the New Zealand quartet, Hadlee, the left-arm spinner Boock, and the two seamers Cairns and Chatfield (19, 20, 20 and 31). New Zealand's batting and bowling ratings flourished appropriately. Martin Crowe rose 100 to 376, Jeff Crowe added a stupendous 346 to his, while wicketkeeper Ian Smith, averaging 99, passed 400 for the first time. With Edgar failing, Coney took over as New Zealand's top batsman, at 11th in the world. At 10th was Gower, down from 2nd. (Randall, for the first and last time, crept into the top twenty at 18th.)

A couple of days after the last one-day international, England were off again, first to Fiji for a couple of up-country knockabouts, and then to Pakistan, and straight into another Test. If it's Tuesday, it must be Karachi.

PAKISTAN vs ENGLAND

First Test (Karachi, 2–6 March) Pakistan won by 3 wickets
England 1st Innings: 182 (Gower 58, Abdul Qadir 5–74, Sarfraz Nawaz 4–42)
Pakistan 1st Innings: 277 (Salim Malik 74, Mohsin Khan 54, Abdul Qadir 40, N.G.B. Cook 6–65)
England 2nd Innings: 159 (Gower 57, Tauseef Ahmed 3–37, Abdul Qadir 3–59, Wasim Raja 2–2)
Pakistan 2nd Innings: 66 for 7 (N.G.B. Cook 5–18)

Second Test (Faisalabad, 12–17 March) Match Drawn

Pakistan 1st Innings: 449 for 8 declared (Salim Malik 116, Wasim Raja 112, Zaheer Abbas 68, Abdul Qadir 50, Dilley 3–101)
England 1st Innings: 546 for 8 declared (Gower 152, Marks 83, Gatting 75, C.L. Smith 66, Randall 65, Fowler 57, Sarfraz Nawaz 3–129)
Pakistan 2nd Innings: 137 for 4 (Salim Malik 76)

Third Test (Lahore, 19–24 March) Match Drawn
England 1st Innings: 241 (Marks 74, Fowler 58, Abdul Qadir 5–84, Sarfraz Nawaz 4–49)
Pakistan 1st Innings: 343 (Sarfraz Nawaz 90, Zaheer Abbas 82 not out, Qasim Omar 73, Foster 5–67)
England 2nd Innings: 344 for 9 declared (Gower 173 not out, Marks 55, Gatting 53, Abdul Qadir 5–110)
Pakistan 2nd Innings: 217 for 6 (Mohsin Khan 104, Shoaib Mohammad 80, Cowans 5–42)

Captains: Pakistan – Zaheer Abbas
England – R.G.D. Willis (1st Test), D.I. Gower (2nd & 3rd Tests)

Débuts: Pakistan – Anil Dalpat, Ramiz Raja (1st Test), Mohsin Kamal (3rd Test)

Rising Stars: Pakistan – Salim Malik (+189 batting)
England – D.I. Gower (+153 batting)

Again, Pakistan may have been abject in Australia, but they knew a struggling England side when they saw one. It can't be easy to play your first Test match of a tour within sixty hours of touching down, but England's rigorously abbreviated tour itinerary allowed no games to acclimatize, and Abdul Qadir exploited a bouncy turner to the full. Cook also bowled well in that first Test, as Pakistan quickly declined to 138 for 6, but another expensive spell from Botham removed the pressure, and that was essentially the end of the series. The victory sewn up, wickets miraculously became more conducive to Javed Miandad batting and less conducive to England winning.

A pity, really, because when Willis and Botham, both injured, were forced to fly back to England after the first Test, a new resolve and toughness appeared in England's play. Captained by David Gower, the team suddenly started doing all the things it was supposed to do – score runs, take wickets, that sort of thing. Pakistan had, after all, been thoroughly wallpapered by Australia a short time before – could this not be taken advantage of?

In the end the runs of Gower (449 at 112.5), Chris Smith and Marks, and the wickets of Cowans, Dilley and Foster, didn't prove particularly conclusive, but at least they restored some confidence to the team and cheer to its gloomy supporters. Gower returned to 2nd in the world batting list, while Nick Cook and Cowans appeared in the top twenty bowlers' list for the first time. As for the Pakistanis, still under Zaheer's captaincy, they looked rather more settled than they had of late, not least because Imran and Javed, for various reasons, were out of the picture. Instead, new faces were tried out – relatives of the famous like Ramiz Raja (brother of Wasim) and Shoaib Mohammad (son of Hanif), who had played twice against India. Twenty-year-old wicketkeeper Anil Dalpat was preferred to Wasim Bari, while Qasim Omar and the now flourishing Salim Malik were given longer runs in the side. Their side's series victory was, like New Zealand's, their first such at home against England.

WEST INDIES vs AUSTRALIA

First Test (Georgetown, Guyana, 2–7 March) Match Drawn
Australia 1st Innings: 279 (Ritchie 78, Hogg 52, Hogan 42 not out, Garner 6–75, Harper 4–56)
West Indies 1st Innings: 230 (Haynes 60, Hogan 4–56, Lawson 3–59)
Australia 2nd Innings: 273 for 9 declared (Phillips 76, Border 54, Garner 3–67, Daniel 3–86)
West Indies 2nd Innings: 250 for no wicket (Greenidge 120 not out, Haynes 103 not out)

Second Test (Port-of-Spain, Trinidad, 16–21 March) Match Drawn
Australia 1st Innings: 255 (Border 98 not out, Jones 48, Garner 6–60, Daniel 3–40)
West Indies 1st Innings: 468 for 8 declared (Dujon 130, Logie 97, Richards 76, Haynes 53)
Australia 2nd Innings: 299 for 9 (Border 100 not out)

Third Test (Bridgetown, Barbados, 30 March – 4 April) West Indies won by 10 wickets
Australia 1st Innings: 429 (Phillips 120, Wood 68, Ritchie 57, Hogan 40, Garner 3–110)
West Indies 1st Innings: 509 (Haynes 145, Richardson 131 not out, Lloyd 76, Greenidge 64, Hogg 6–77)
Australia 2nd Innings: 97 (Marshall 5–42, Holding 4–24)
West Indies 2nd Innings: 21 for no wicket

Fourth Test (St John's, Antigua, 7–11 April) West Indies won by an innings and 36 runs
Australia 1st Innings: 262 (Border 98, Hookes 51, Holding 3–42, Baptiste 3–42)
West Indies 1st Innings: 498 (Richards 178, Richardson 154,

Rackemann 5–160, Maguire 3–122)
Australia 2nd Innings: 200 (Garner 5–63, Marshall 3–51)

Fifth Test (Kingston, Jamaica, 28 April–2 May) West Indies won by 10 wickets
Australia 1st Innings: 199 (Border 41, Marshall 3–37, Garner 3–42)
West Indies 1st Innings: 305 (Greenidge 127, Haynes 60, Maguire 4–57, Lawson 3–91)
Australia 2nd Innings: 160 (Border 60 not out, Marshall 5–51)
West Indies 2nd Innings: 55 for no wicket

Captains: West Indies – C.H. Lloyd (1st Test), I.V.A. Richards (2nd Test), C.H. Lloyd (3rd–5th Tests)
Australia – K.J. Hughes

Débuts: West Indies – M.A. Small (2nd Test)
Australia – S.B. Smith (1st Test), D.M. Jones (2nd Test)

Rising Stars: West Indies – D.L. Haynes (+226 batting)
Australia – A.R. Border (+84 batting)

In which Australia's young hopefuls – replacing the gnarled crusty old faithfuls who, by amazing coincidence, had chosen to retire just before the series – were appropriately crushed by the rampaging West Indies, as strong, perhaps, as they ever had been. As well as Chappell, Marsh and Lillee, Australia were without Graham Yallop, their top scorer in the Pakistan series, who had a dodgy knee, and during the series injuries were sustained by Kepler Wessels (out after the second Test), Graeme Wood (out after the third), Carl Rackemann (who played only one Test), Hogg and Lawson, who played but were consistently below full fitness.

Poor old Kim Hughes. He also had a grim series with the bat, averaging 21. Only one batsman, in fact, averaged over 26 – Allan Border, whose 521 runs at 74.4 (he was top scorer in half of his ten Test innings) pushed him to the top of the world heap once again. Most of the younger batsmen had a dreadful time.

The bowlers had fun, though, or at least the West Indians did. Garner's 31 wickets pushed his rating back up to 800 after, for him, a relatively lean period. Malcolm Marshall (21 wickets) and Michael Holding (13 wickets) also seemed fully refreshed and hugely enthusiastic about taking Australian wickets, while the twenty-one-year-old off-spinner Roger Harper, playing in four Tests, provided the first instance of variety seen in the West Indian attack for some years. (His 10 wickets gave him an end-of-series rating of 216.) But a top seven batting line-up whose ratings, in order, are 838, 712, 598, 764, 590, 860 and 699 doesn't exactly give the opposition an awful lot of hope, especially when, in addition, three of the side's four bowlers (each in the world top five) have bowling ratings over 800. Compare that to the Australian attack in the final Test: Lawson (792 and falling), Hogg (552), Maguire (292), Hogan (252) and Greg Matthews (174). Who could begrudge Hughes a little blub?

SRI LANKA vs NEW ZEALAND

First Test (Kandy, 9–14 March) New Zealand won by 165 runs
New Zealand 1st Innings: 276 (Howarth 62, Wright 45, John 5–86)
Sri Lanka 1st Innings: 215 (Hadlee 4–35)
New Zealand 2nd Innings: 201 for 8 declared (Howarth 60, D.S. de Silva 3–59, John 3–73)
Sri Lanka 2nd Innings: 97 (Ranatunga 51, Boock 5–28, Hadlee 4–8)

Second Test (Colombo, 16–21 March) Match Drawn
Sri Lanka 1st Innings: 174 (Madugalle 44 not out, Cairns 4–47)
New Zealand 1st Innings: 198 (J.J. Crowe 50, R.J. Ratnayake 5–42, John 3–89)
Sri Lanka 2nd Innings: 289 for 9 declared (Dias 108, Wettimuny 65, Chatfield 4–78, Hadlee 3–58)
New Zealand 2nd Innings: 123 for 4 (Wright 48)

Third Test (Colombo, 24–29 March) New Zealand won by an innings and 61 runs
Sri Lanka 1st Innings: 256 (Madugalle 89 not out, Chatfield 5–63, Hadlee 5–73)
New Zealand 1st Innings: 459 (Reid 180, Coney 92, M.D. Crowe 45, I.D.S. Smith 42, John 3–99, J.R. Ratnayeke 3–128)
Sri Lanka 2nd Innings: 142 (Ranatunga 50, Hadlee 5–29, Boock 3–32)

Captains: Sri Lanka – L.R.D. Mendis
New Zealand – G.P. Howarth

Débuts: Sri Lanka – M.J.G. Amerasinghe, S.M.S. Kaluperuma (1st Test)

Rising Stars: Sri Lanka – R.S. Madugalle (+161 batting)
New Zealand – R.J. Hadlee (+64 bowling)

One of Test cricket's less gripping rubbers, during which New Zealand proved that Sri Lanka were still very much the novices of Test cricket. Presumably New Zealand were chosen as the first team to go there for a fully fledged series because they were deemed the weakest potential opposition – although by that token England should currently be booking their passage to the Maldive Islands, so that can't have been the reason.

But thanks to more consistent batting, and Richard Hadlee's world-class bowling – 23 wickets at 10.00 in three Tests – New Zealand recorded their best ever overseas result. Chatfield, with 10 wickets, finally crossed the 400 threshold (after nearly a year in the 300s), while John Reid, playing for the first time since 1980–81, notched up the highest innings against Sri Lanka so far (although it took him over eleven hours to do so). Coney's consistency did his rating no harm, either. Of the home side, the gloriously pronounceable John saw his rating leap up, while Madugalle and Dias entered the world top twenty for the first time. No-one, though, could have been hungrier, for runs or wickets, than Richard Hadlee.

WORLD TOP TWENTY AFTER 1983–84

BATTING

(12)	1.	A.R. Border (Australia)	884 (+143)
(4)	2.	D.I. Gower (England)	872 (+52)
(5)	3.	C.H. Lloyd (West Indies)	860 (+48)
(15)	4.	C.G. Greenidge (West Indies)	838 (+138)
(3)	5.	Zaheer Abbas (Pakistan)	778 (−93)
(1)	6.	I.V.A. Richards (West Indies)	764 (−114)
(22)	7.	J.V. Coney (New Zealand)	757 (+150)
(13)	8.	G.S. Chappell (Australia)	757 (+17)
(19)	9.	S.M. Gavaskar (India)	751 (+98)
(2)	10.	Javed Miandad (Pakistan)	745 (−131)
(20)	11.	D.L. Haynes (West Indies)	712 (+61)
(17)	12.	P.J.L. Dujon (West Indies)	699 (+1)
NE	13.	J.F. Reid (New Zealand)	685
(10)	14.	Mohsin Khan (Pakistan)	657 (−85)
(43)	15.	G.N. Yallop (Australia)	645 (+135)
(46)	16.	R.S. Madugalle (Sri Lanka)	644 (+161)
(18)	17.	I.T. Botham (England)	642 (−39)
(8)	18.	B.A. Edgar (New Zealand)	637 (−125)
(27)	19.	R.L. Dias (Sri Lanka)	632 (+46)
(30)	20.	D.B. Vengsarkar (India)	627 (+52)

BOWLING

(7)	1.	R.J. Hadlee (New Zealand)	856 (+107)
(1)	2.	Imran Khan (Pakistan)	835 (−80)
(10)	3.	M.D. Marshall (West Indies)	832 (+158)
(9)	4.	Kapil Dev (India)	831 (+152)

(4)	5.	M.A. Holding (West Indies)	818 (+26)
(8)	6.	J. Garner (West Indies)	800 (+60)
(3)	7.	R.G.D. Willis (England)	792 (−41)
(2)	8.	G.F. Lawson (Australia)	792 (−89)
(5)	9.	D.K. Lillee (Australia)	709 (−57)
NE	10.	C.G. Rackemann (Australia)	678
(6)	11.	A.M.E. Roberts (West Indies)	663 (−89)
(11)	12.	N.G.B. Cook (England)	608 (−32)
(17)	13.	B.L. Cairns (New Zealand)	598 (+18)
(13)	14.	D.R. Doshi (India)	566 (−54)
(34)	15.	N.G. Cowans (England)	558 (+171)
(19)	16.	R.M. Hogg (Australia)	552 (+16)
(23)	17.	R.J. Shastri (India)	550 (+60)
(12)	18.	Iqbal Qasim (Pakistan)	544 (−80)
(14)	19.	B. Yardley (Australia)	540 (−57)
(18)	20.	Sarfraz Nawaz (Pakistan)	539 (−21)

Another chart showing enormous changes in fortune – at least for the batsmen. An indifferent season for Viv Richards (it would have been perfectly acceptable for most other players) deprived him of the top batting spot, which first Clive Lloyd and then Allan Border nipped in to claim. David Gower's successes in Pakistan pushed him up to 872 and second, while Greenidge's burst of brilliant form propelled him into the top ten for the first time in the decade, remarkably enough. But it's also good to see Jeremy Coney up there as well, a player much underrated in his prime, and a batsman whose solidity was the basis of New Zealand's most prosperous period in Test cricket. John Reid was straight in as well, while Madugalle and Dias became Sri Lanka's first representatives in the twenty. Overall, in fact, it was an extremely competitive chart. Between 21st (Kim Hughes) and 30th (Derek Randall), there was a gap of just 23 points, which may help to explain the apparent volatility of the whole. Out of the twenty from the end of 1983 went Hughes (down 96), Mudassar (from 9th to 22nd, down 162 points), Gomes (14th to 28th, down 144), Lamb (11th to 31st, down 183 – exactly the same number of points he had risen during the previous season), Amarnath (6th to 33rd), and the biggest drop of all, Kepler Wessels – 7th to 36th, down 243 points.

The bowling ratings too were much changed, although at the very top the same old lags remained – Hadlee, Kapil Dev, Imran, Holding and Garner, and Bob 'Laughs' Willis. On his way to taking over the world, though, was Malcolm Marshall, who had been a new entry a year earlier. This year it was Carl Rackemann's turn – playing just one Test in the West Indies proved as good a career move as Yallop's knee injury. And back for a rerun, 'Flash' Cowans (where is he now?). Dropping out of the top flight: Abdul Qadir (whose achievements, at least at this stage, somehow never quite matched up to his terrifying reputation), Jeff Thomson (out of favour), and Ian Botham (out to lunch).

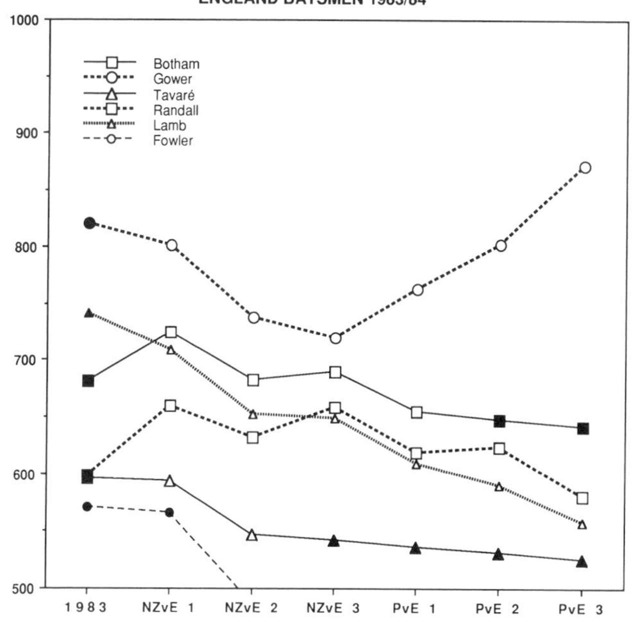
ENGLAND BATSMEN 1983/84
1000
900
800
700
600
500
Botham
Gower
Tavaré
Randall
Lamb
Fowler
1983
NZvE 1
NZvE 2
NZvE 3
PvE 1
PvE 2
PvE 3

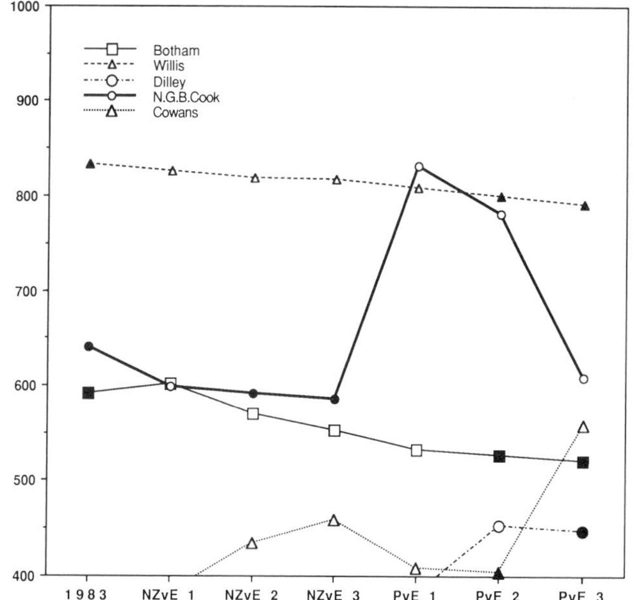
ENGLAND BOWLERS 1983/84
1000
900
800
700
600
500
400
Botham
Willis
Dilley
N.G.B.Cook
Cowans
1983
NZvE 1
NZvE 2
NZvE 3
PvE 1
PvE 2
PvE 3

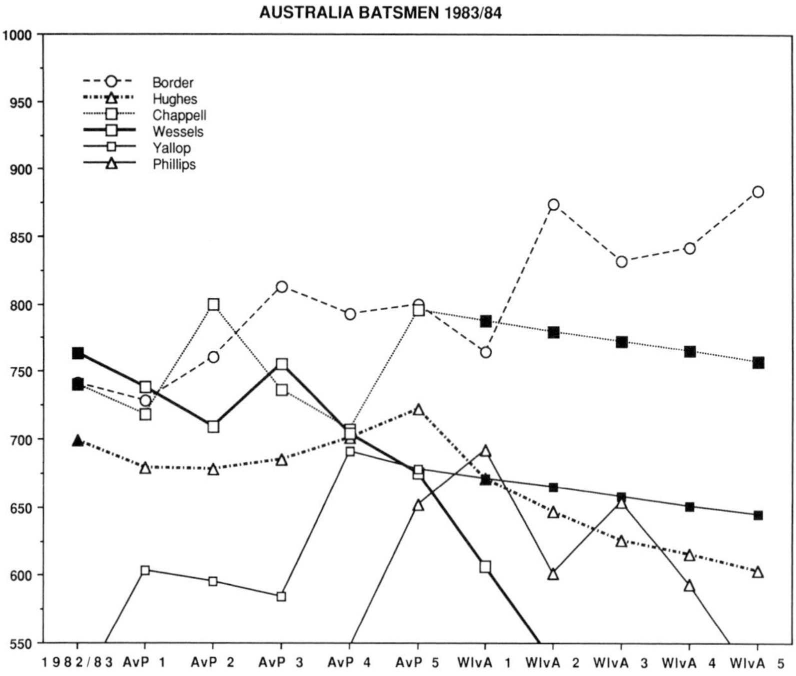

AUSTRALIA BATSMEN 1983/84
1000
950
900
850
800
750
700
650
600
550
Border
Hughes
Chappell
Wessels
Yallop
Phillips
1982/83
AvP 1
AvP 2
AvP 3
AvP 4
AvP 5
WIvA 1
WIvA 2
WIvA 3
WIvA 4
WIvA 5

AUSTRALIA BOWLERS 1983/84
1000
900
800
700
600
500
400
Lillee
Alderman
Lawson
Hogg
Rackemann
1982/83
AvP 1
AvP 2
AvP 3
AvP 4
AvP 5
WIvA 1
WIvA 2
WIvA 3
WIvA 4
WIvA 5

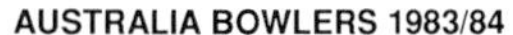

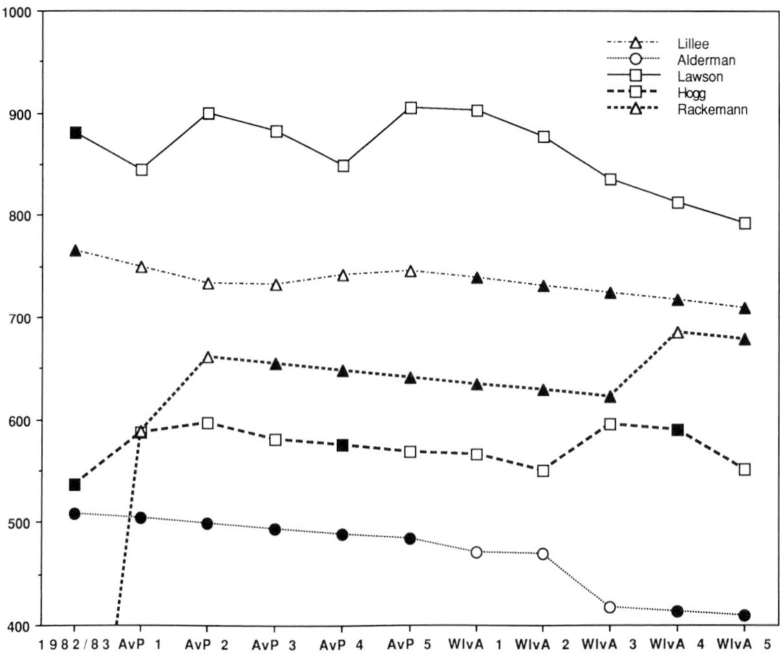

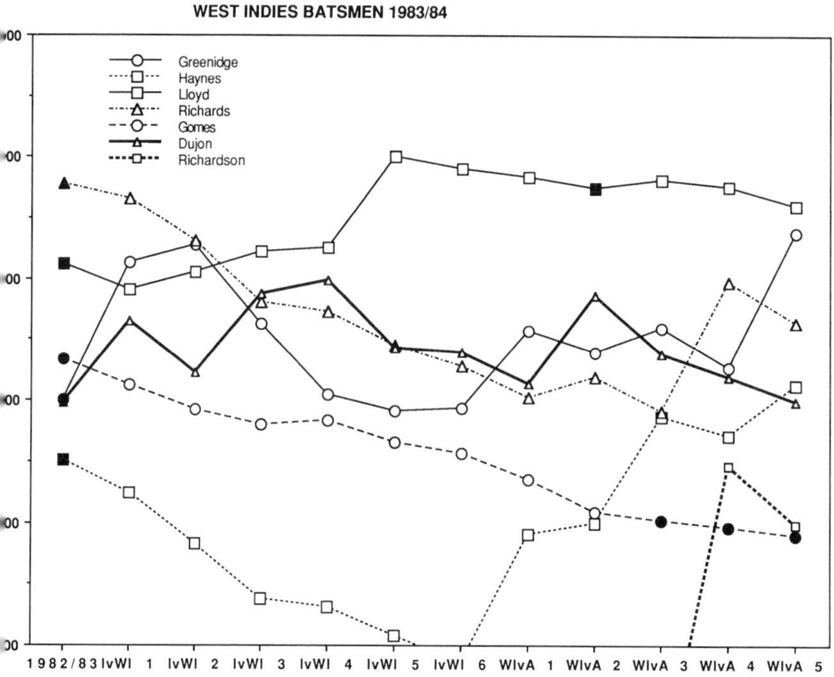

WEST INDIES BATSMEN 1983/84

Greenidge
Haynes
Lloyd
Richards
Gomes
Dujon
Richardson

1982/83 IvWI 1 IvWI 2 IvWI 3 IvWI 4 IvWI 5 IvWI 6 WIvA 1 WIvA 2 WIvA 3 WIvA 4 WIvA 5

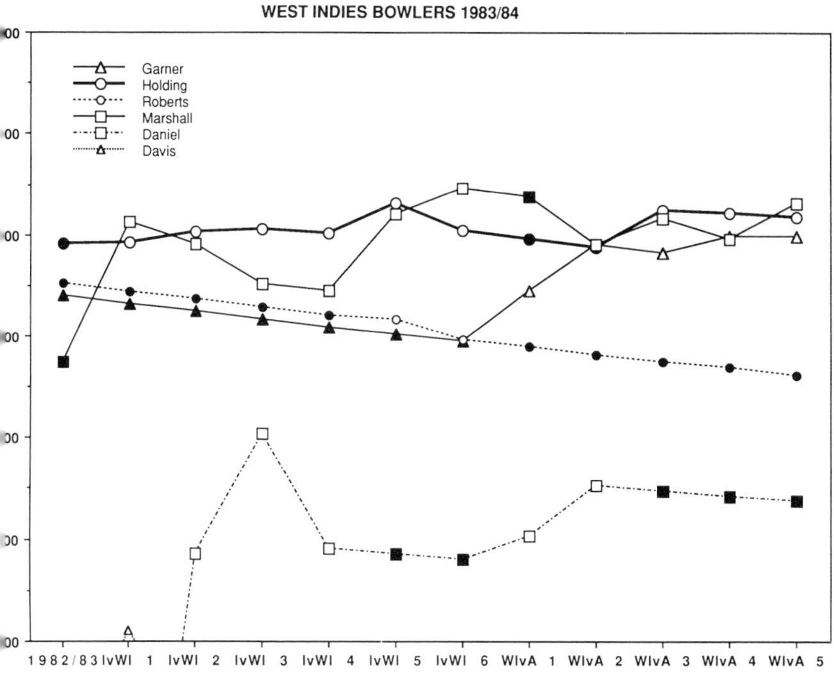

WEST INDIES BOWLERS 1983/84

Garner
Holding
Roberts
Marshall
Daniel
Davis

1982/83 IvWI 1 IvWI 2 IvWI 3 IvWI 4 IvWI 5 IvWI 6 WIvA 1 WIvA 2 WIvA 3 WIvA 4 WIvA 5

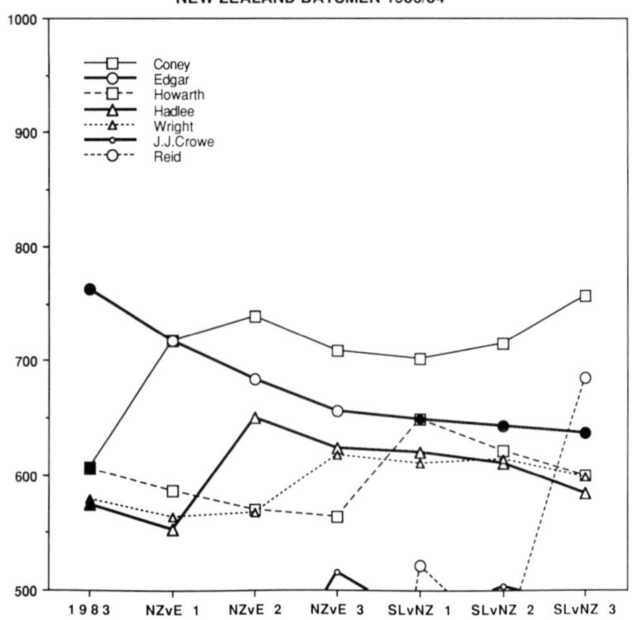
NEW ZEALAND BATSMEN 1983/84
1000
900
800
700
600
500
Coney
Edgar
Howarth
Hadlee
Wright
J.J.Crowe
Reid
1983
NZvE 1
NZvE 2
NZvE 3
SLvNZ 1
SLvNZ 2
SLvNZ 3

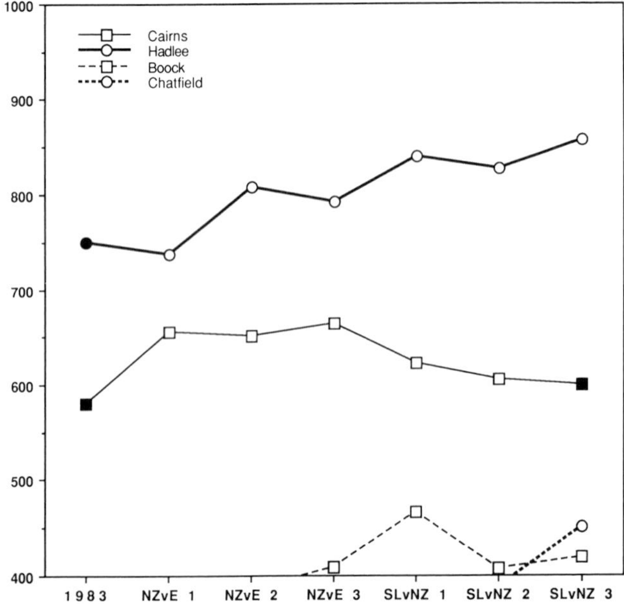
NEW ZEALAND BOWLERS 1983/84
1000
900
800
700
600
500
400
Cairns
Hadlee
Boock
Chatfield
1983
NZvE 1
NZvE 2
NZvE 3
SLvNZ 1
SLvNZ 2
SLvNZ 3

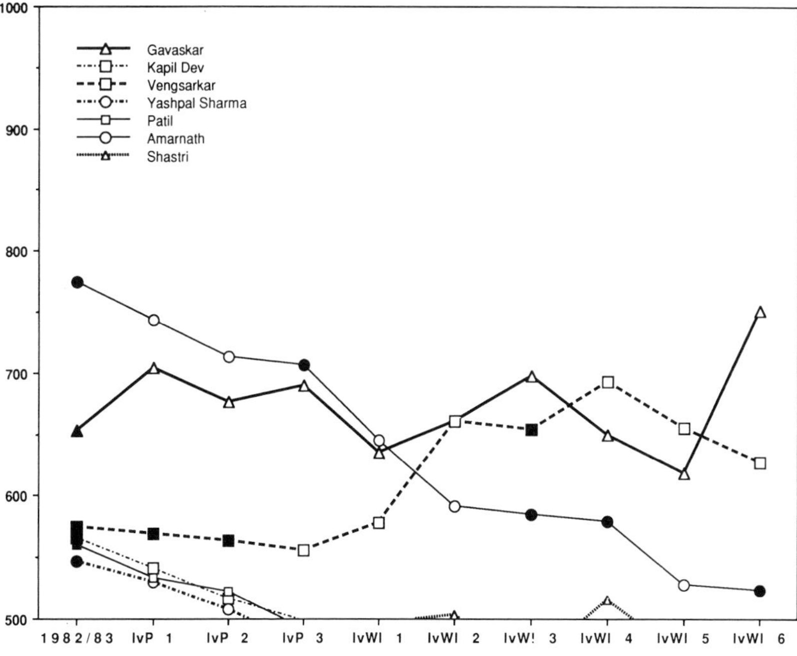
INDIA BATSMEN 1983/84
Gavaskar
Kapil Dev
Vengsarkar
Yashpal Sharma
Patil
Amarnath
Shastri
1000
900
800
700
600
500
1982/83
IvP 1
IvP 2
IvP 3
IvWI 1
IvWI 2
IvW! 3
IvWI 4
IvWI 5
IvWI 6

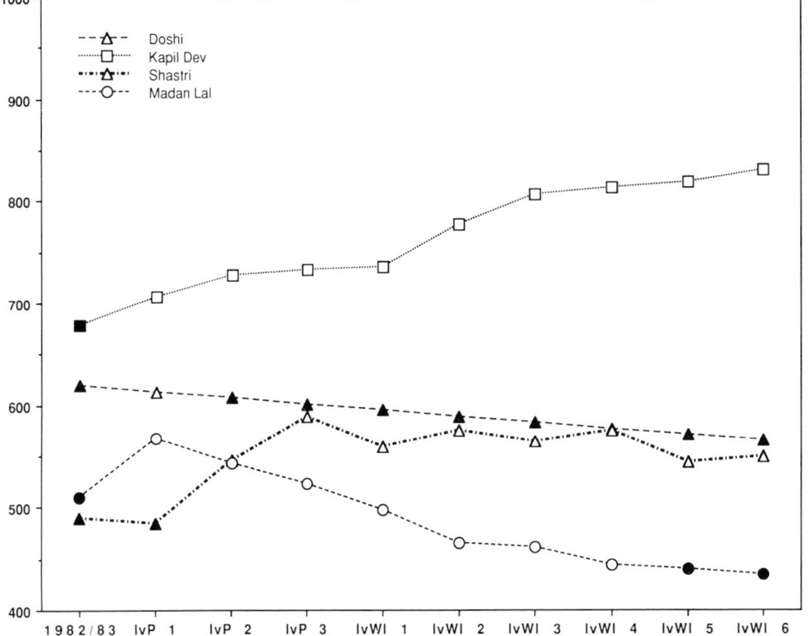
INDIA BOWLERS 1983/84
Doshi
Kapil Dev
Shastri
Madan Lal
1000
900
800
700
600
500
400
1982/83
IvP 1
IvP 2
IvP 3
IvWI 1
IvWI 2
IvWI 3
IvWI 4
IvWI 5
IvWI 6

PAKISTAN BATSMEN 1983/84

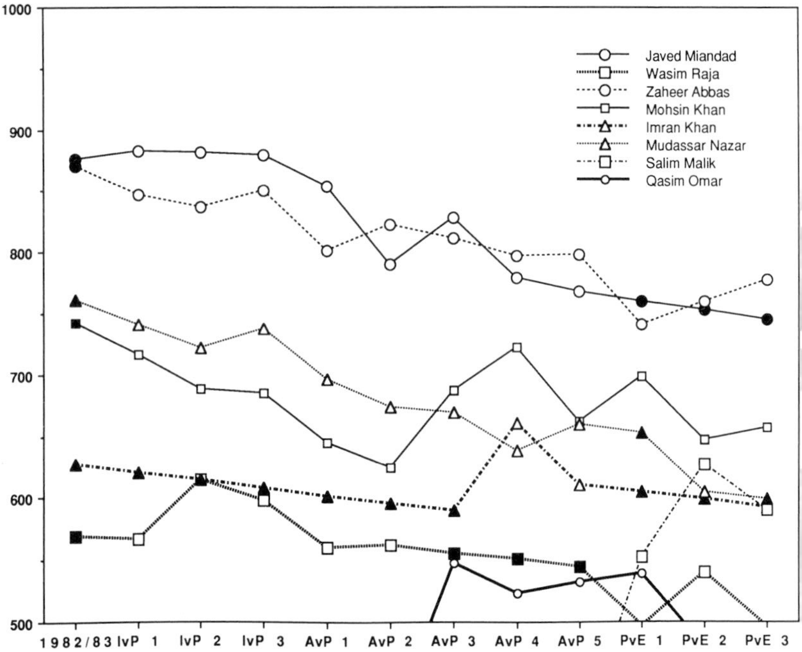

1000
900
800
700
600
500

Javed Miandad
Wasim Raja
Zaheer Abbas
Mohsin Khan
Imran Khan
Mudassar Nazar
Salim Malik
Qasim Omar

1982/83 IvP 1 IvP 2 IvP 3 AvP 1 AvP 2 AvP 3 AvP 4 AvP 5 PvE 1 PvE 2 PvE 3

PAKISTAN BOWLERS 1983/84
(above 450)

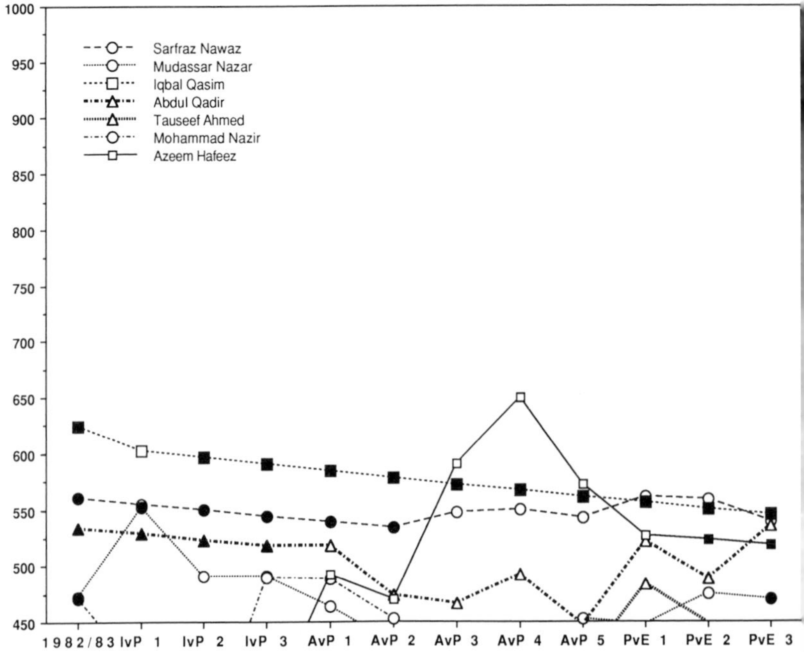

1000
950
900
850
800
750
700
650
600
550
500
450

Sarfraz Nawaz
Mudassar Nazar
Iqbal Qasim
Abdul Qadir
Tauseef Ahmed
Mohammad Nazir
Azeem Hafeez

1982/83 IvP 1 IvP 2 IvP 3 AvP 1 AvP 2 AvP 3 AvP 4 AvP 5 PvE 1 PvE 2 PvE 3

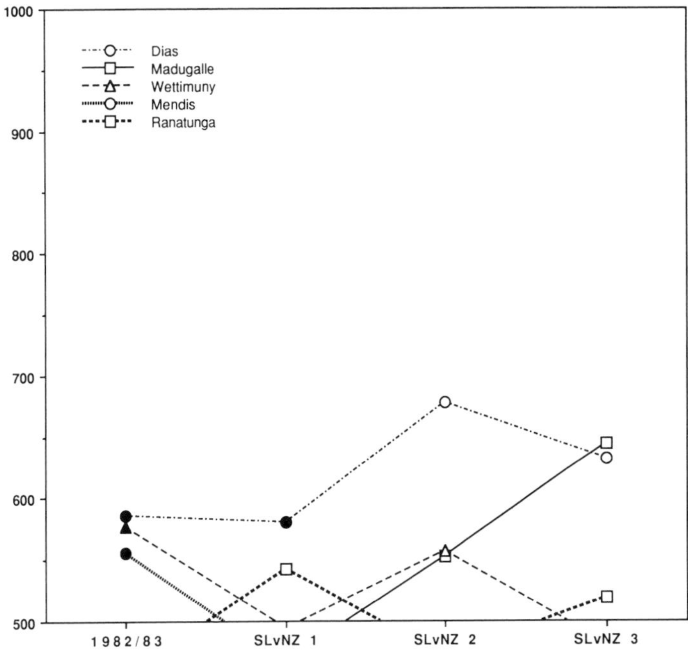
SRI LANKA BATSMEN 1983/84
1000
900
800
700
600
500
Dias
Madugalle
Wettimuny
Mendis
Ranatunga
1982/83
SLvNZ 1
SLvNZ 2
SLvNZ 3

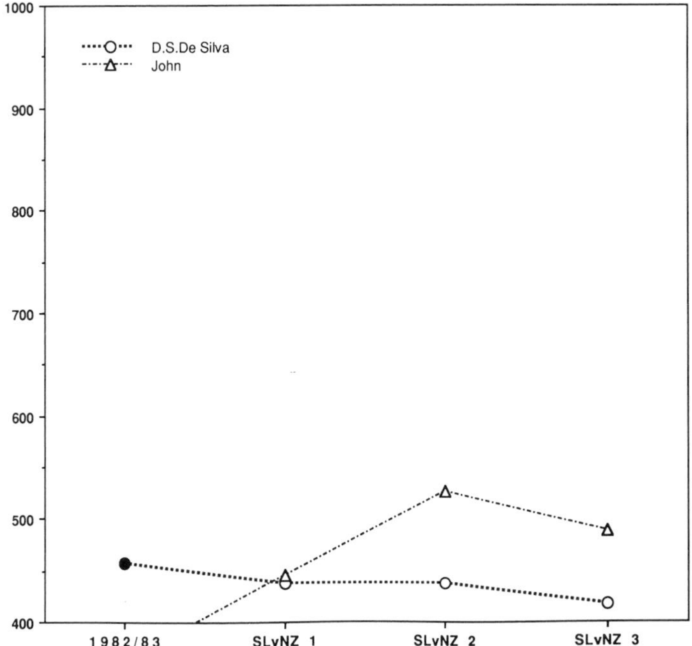
SRI LANKA BOWLERS 1983/84
1000
900
800
700
600
500
400
D.S.De Silva
John
1982/83
SLvNZ 1
SLvNZ 2
SLvNZ 3

1984

ENGLAND vs WEST INDIES

First Test (Edgbaston, 14–18 June) West Indies won by an innings and 180 runs
England 1st Innings: 191 (Botham 64, Garner 4–53)
West Indies 1st Innings: 606 (Gomes 143, Richards 117, Baptiste 87 not out, Lloyd 71, Holding 69, Pringle 5–108)
England 2nd Innings: 235 (Downton 56, Pringle 46 not out, Garner 5–55)

Second Test (Lord's, 28 June–3 July) West Indies won by 9 wickets
England 1st Innings: 286 (Fowler 106, Broad 55, Marshall 6–85)
West Indies 1st Innings: 245 (Richards 72, Baptiste 44, Botham 8–103)
England 2nd Innings: 300 for 9 declared (Lamb 110, Botham 81, Small 3–40, Garner 3–91)
West Indies 2nd Innings: 344 for 1 (Greenidge 214 not out, Gomes 92 not out)

Third Test (Headingley, 12–16 July) West Indies won by 8 wickets
England 1st Innings: 270 (Lamb 100, Botham 45, Holding 4–70, Harper 3–47)
West Indies 1st Innings: 302 (Gomes 104 not out, Holding 59, Lloyd 48, Allott 6–61)
England 2nd Innings: 159 (Fowler 50, Lamb 43, Marshall 7–53)
West Indies 2nd Innings: 131 for 2 (Greenidge 49, Haynes 43)

Fourth Test (Old Trafford, 26–31 July) West Indies won by an innings and 64 runs
West Indies 1st Innings: 500 (Greenidge 223, Dujon 101, Davis 77, Pocock 4–121, Allott 3–76)
England 1st Innings: 280 (Lamb 100 not out, Broad 42, Garner 4–51, Baptiste 3–31)
England 2nd Innings: 156 (Gower 57 not out, Harper 6–57)

Fifth Test (The Oval, 9–14 August) West Indies won by 172 runs
West Indies 1st Innings: 190 (Lloyd 60 not out, Botham 5–72, Allott 3–25)
England 1st Innings: 162 (Marshall 5–35)

An edged drive from Lamb during his unbeaten century at Old Trafford.

West Indies 2nd Innings: 346 (Haynes 125, Dujon 49, Ellison 3–60, Botham 3–103)
England 2nd Innings: 202 (Botham 54, Tavaré 49, Holding 5–43, Garner 4–51)

Captains: England – D.I. Gower
West Indies – C.H. Lloyd

Débuts: England – T.A. Lloyd (1st Test), B.C. Broad (2nd Test), V.P. Terry (3rd Test), J.P. Agnew, R.M. Ellison (5th Test)

Rising Stars: England – A.J. Lamb (+64 batting)
West Indies – H.A. Gomes (+133 batting)

Oh yes, that series. At 5–0 it represented the first time any team had ever won every Test of a rubber in England, and only the fifth time anywhere (the sixth was to follow eighteen months later, when the two sides met again in the Caribbean). Essentially, the West Indians were just a bit too good, and with Botham and Willis in seemingly irreversible decline, England didn't have the bowling to challenge them. Only two bowlers seemed to make any impact at all – Ellison, whose 5 good wickets at the Oval earned him a tour place to India and an immediate rating of 356, and Allott, who finally improved on his unsuccessful (if unlucky) early appearances for England (rating before recall: 47) to finish with 14 wickets at just over 20 from the last three Tests and a 370 rating.

Willis, though, ended his Test career on a rather downbeat note – 6 wickets at 61.16 was perhaps not how he would wish to be remembered. Botham's bowling was, in true Botham fashion, full of variety – was it a half volley or a long hop coming next? Oh, it was a full toss. In the second Test, when Greenidge scored his masterly double century, Botham conceded 117 runs off 20.1 hilarious overs.

The batting, Lamb aside, did not fare well. Some Test careers began, but more ended. Andy Lloyd was hospitalized in the first Test, his début, while Paul Terry broke his arm in the fourth. Gatting came, padded up twice, and went. Gower scored one fifty and averaged 19. It made for grim viewing.

The wickets, in the main, fell to Garner – on top form with 29 at 18.62 – and Marshall (24 at 18.21), who by the end of the series had taken 99 wickets in four series, all within eighteen months. Holding (15 wickets) and Harper (13 wickets) also cashed in.

So was the West Indies team that finally won the best in ratings history? Here are the figures (all those above 100, at least):

C.G. Greenidge	891 batting	
D.L. Haynes	675 batting	
H.A. Gomes	723 batting	
I.V.A. Richards	737 batting	149 bowling
P.J. Dujon	666 batting	
C.H. Lloyd	870 batting	
M.D. Marshall	250 batting	845 bowling
E.A.E. Baptiste	365 batting	394 bowling
R.A. Harper	211 batting	445 bowling
M.A. Holding	295 batting	802 bowling
J. Garner	180 batting	833 bowling

So, taking the best seven batsmen and best four bowlers, these average out at 703 batting and 731 bowling – remarkable figures. (Compare them to the next best thing – the West Indies just after they had crushed Australia the previous series, when the figures were 680 and 666 respectively). The corresponding figures for the England team were 537 and 373 – and that was *after* Pringle had been dropped.

England almost got off lightly.

ENGLAND vs SRI LANKA

Only Test (Lord's, 23–28 August) Match Drawn
Sri Lanka 1st Innings: 491 for 7 declared (Wettimuny 190, Mendis 111, Ranatunga 84)

England 1st Innings: 370 (Lamb 107, Broad 86, Gower 55, Ellison 41, John 4–98, de Mel 4–110)
Sri Lanka 2nd Innings: 294 for 7 (S.A.R. Silva 102, Mendis 94, Botham 6–90)

Captains: England – D.I. Gower
Sri Lanka – L.R.D. Mendis

Débuts: Sri Lanka – P.A. de Silva

This first home Test against the Sri Lankans must have been the last thing the England team felt like after facing the fusillade of the West Indies' fast bowlers. The Sri Lankans, after all, had much to gain, while England had to beat them convincingly or look pretty silly. England fans, on the other hand, didn't quite see it like this – here at last was a team we could stuff. It wasn't to be, though England were one of only two first-class sides Sri Lanka managed to bowl out in their entire tour (it was, of course, one of the few not to include a West Indian fast bowler), and they never came closer to winning a first-class game on the tour than this one. Wettimuny's 190 remains the highest score by anyone playing his first Test in England, while Amal Silva's 102 was his maiden first-class century, and he was the other opener.

More lastingly, this was the match that ended Chris Tavaré's Test career. Recalled for the final Test against the West Indies, he now scored 14 in not much less than a week, an innings that cost him the vice-captaincy on the tour to India. Broad's 86 was no faster, and he too was dropped, though not permanently.

Sadly the Sri Lankan ratings did not flourish as much as they might have expected in the circumstances – but then they were playing England.

WORLD TOP TWENTY AFTER 1984

BATTING

(4)	1.	C.G. Greenidge (West Indies)	891 (+53)
(1)	2.	A.R. Border (Australia)	884
(3)	3.	C.H. Lloyd (West Indies)	870 (+10)
(5)	4.	Zaheer Abbas (Pakistan)	778
(7)	5.	J.V. Coney (New Zealand)	757
(8)	6.	G.S. Chappell (Australia)	757
(9)	7.	S.M. Gavaskar (India)	751
(10)	8.	Javed Miandad (Pakistan)	745
(6)	9.	I.V.A. Richards (West Indies)	737 (−37)
(28)	10.	H.A. Gomes (West Indies)	723 (+133)
(2)	11.	D.I. Gower (England)	700 (−172)

(13)	12.	J.F. Reid (New Zealand)	685
(11)	13.	D.L. Haynes (West Indies)	675 (−37)
(12)	14.	P.J.L. Dujon (West Indies)	666 (−33)
(14)	15.	Mohsin Khan (Pakistan)	657
(31)	16.	A.J. Lamb (England)	653 (+95)
(15)	17.	G.N. Yallop (Australia)	645
(18)	18.	B.A. Edgar (New Zealand)	637
(20)	19.	D.B. Vengsarkar (India)	627
(17)	20.	I.T. Botham (England)	624 (−18)

BOWLING

(1)	1.	R.J. Hadlee (New Zealand)	856
(3)	2.	M.D. Marshall (West Indies)	845 (+13)
(2)	3.	Imran Khan (Pakistan)	835
(6)	4.	J. Garner (West Indies)	833 (+33)
(4)	5.	Kapil Dev (India)	831
(5)	6.	M.A. Holding (West Indies)	802 (−16)
(8)	7.	G.F. Lawson (Australia)	792
(9)	8.	D.K. Lillee (Australia)	709
(7)	9.	R.G.D. Willis (England)	707 (−85)
(10)	10.	C.G. Rackemann (Australia)	678
(11)	11.	A.M.E. Roberts (West Indies)	630 (−33)
(13)	12.	B.L. Cairns (New Zealand)	598
(24)	13.	I.T. Botham (England)	592 (+71)
(26)	14.	V.B. John (Sri Lanka)	582 (+93)
(12)	15.	N.G.B. Cook (England)	567 (−31)
(14)	16.	D.R. Doshi (India)	566
(16)	17.	R.M. Hogg (Australia)	552
(17)	18.	R.J. Shastri (India)	550
(18)	19.	Iqbal Qasim (Pakistan)	544
(20)	20.	Sarfraz Nawaz (Pakistan)	539

There's nothing like a Test series in England for making everyone else's ratings look good – whether they are playing or not. Jeremy Coney, for instance, rose effortlessly to the top five for the first time, and there were similarly easy jumps for Javed Miandad, Gavaskar and Greenidge (and he was playing). Lamb's four centuries might have served him better had he scored the odd run in between them. The only two to lose their places in the batsmen's élite were the Sri Lankans, Dias and Madugalle, down to 26th and 29th respectively.

Marshall, meanwhile, continued to stalk Richard Hadlee, while Garner gained on Imran. Willis finished his career in the top ten, as Botham somehow managed to sneak back into the twenty. John was Sri Lanka's first bowler to get in. Out was Cowans once again – he played only in the fourth Test but didn't get a wicket – plus Bruce Yardley, who had retired.

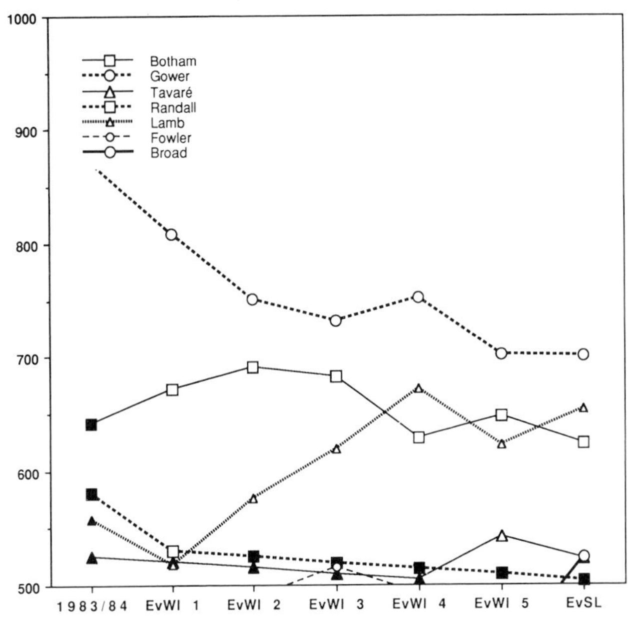
ENGLAND BATSMEN 1984
1000
900
800
700
600
500
Botham
Gower
Tavaré
Randall
Lamb
Fowler
Broad
1983/84
EvWI 1
EvWI 2
EvWI 3
EvWI 4
EvWI 5
EvSL

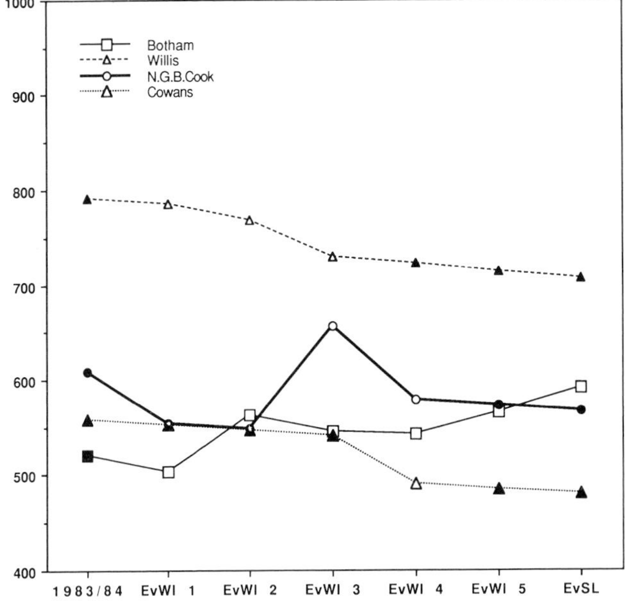
ENGLAND BOWLERS 1984
1000
900
800
700
600
500
400
Botham
Willis
N.G.B.Cook
Cowans
1983/84
EvWI 1
EvWI 2
EvWI 3
EvWI 4
EvWI 5
EvSL

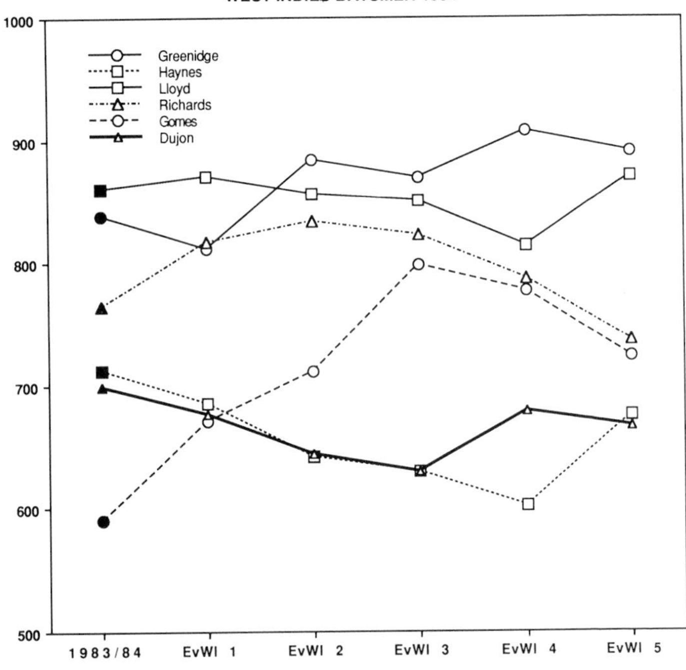
WEST INDIES BATSMEN 1984
1000
900
800
700
600
500
Greenidge
Haynes
Lloyd
Richards
Gomes
Dujon
1983/84
EvWI 1
EvWI 2
EvWI 3
EvWI 4
EvWI 5

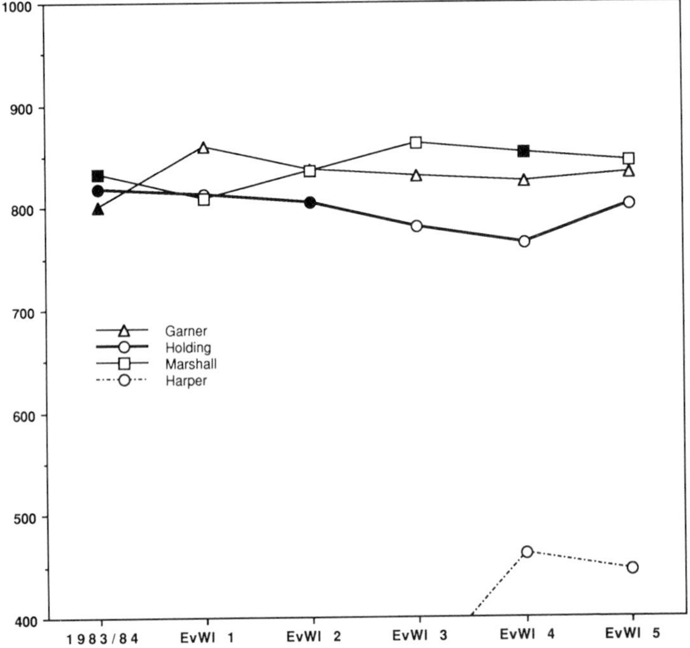
WEST INDIES BOWLERS 1984
1000
900
800
700
600
500
400
Garner
Holding
Marshall
Harper
1983/84
EvWI 1
EvWI 2
EvWI 3
EvWI 4
EvWI 5

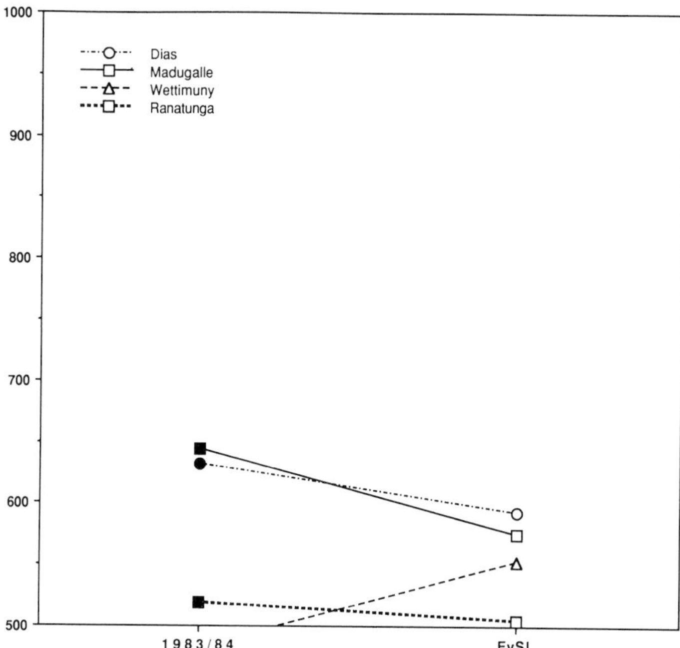
SRI LANKA BATSMEN 1984
1000
900
800
700
600
500
Dias
Madugalle
Wettimuny
Ranatunga
1983/84
EvSL

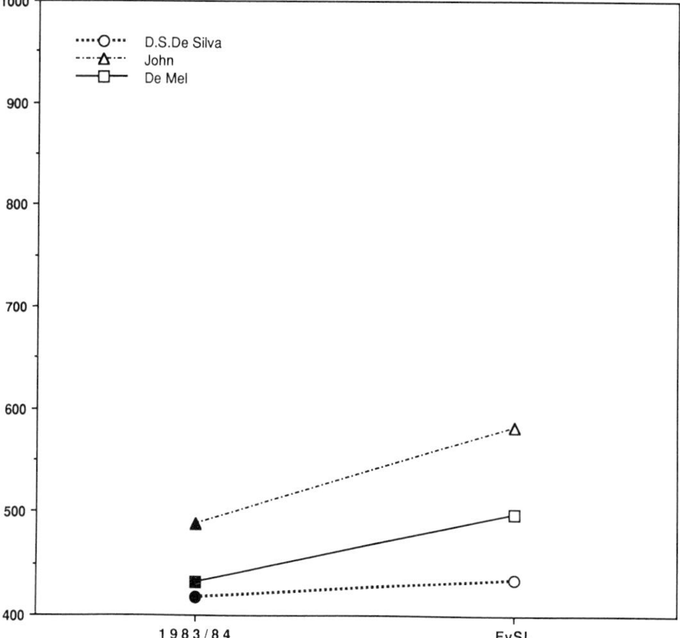
SRI LANKA BOWLERS 1984
1000
900
800
700
600
500
400
D.S.De Silva
John
De Mel
1983/84
EvSL

1984–85

PAKISTAN vs INDIA

First Test (Lahore, 17–22 October) Match Drawn
Pakistan 1st Innings: 428 for 9 declared (Zaheer Abbas 168 not out, Ashraf Ali 65, Qasim Omar 46, Salim Malik 45, Shastri 3–90, Chetan Sharma 3–94)
India 1st Innings: 156 (Gavaskar 48, Vengsarkar 41, Azeem Hafeez 6–46)
India 2nd Innings: 371 for 6 (Amarnath 101 not out, Shastri 71, Gaekwad 60)

Second Test (Faisalabad, 24–29 October) Match Drawn
India 1st Innings: 500 (Shastri 139, Patil 127, Gaekwad 74, Abdul Qadir 4–104, Azeem Hafeez 4–137)
Pakistan 1st Innings: 674 for 6 (Qasim Omar 210, Mudassar Nazar 199, Salim Malik 102 not out, Mohsin Khan 59)

Captains: Pakistan – Zaheer Abbas
India – S.M. Gavaskar

Débuts: Pakistan – Manzoor Elahi (2nd Test)
India – Chetan Sharma (1st Test)

One of Test cricket's less conclusive rubbers, even before Mrs Gandhi's assasination caused the cancellation of the third and final match. Played as ever in the spirit of fair play and good spirit that characterizes Test cricket in the sub-continent, it featured some umpiring decisions that *Wisden* described, not without irony, as 'unsatisfactory'. The Indian captain Gavaskar (reinstated in place of Kapil Dev) went further and congratulated his team on drawing the first Test 'despite the best efforts of the Pakistan umpires' (of whom one was Mr Shakoor Rana). The Pakistan batsmen somehow didn't have quite the same problems, and increased their ratings accordingly on the usual docile wickets. Gavaskar's appearance at Lahore was his hundredth in all, and Zaheer's unbeaten 168 there was his twelfth Test century, equalling Hanif's record, while Azeem's 6 wickets pushed him into the world top twenty (at 11th) for the first time. But it all made for heartbreakingly dreary cricket.

AUSTRALIA vs WEST INDIES

First Test (Perth, 9–12 November) West Indies won by an innings and 112 runs
West Indies 1st Innings: 416 (Dujon 139, Gomes 127, Haynes 56, Alderman 6–128, Hogg 4–101)
Australia 1st Innings: 76 (Holding 6–21, Garner 2–24, Marshall 2–25)
Australia 2nd Innings: 228 (Wood 56, Marshall 4–68, Garner 3–52)

Second Test (Brisbane, 23–26 November) West Indies won by 8 wickets
Australia 1st Innings: 175 (Phillips 44)
West Indies 1st Innings: 424 (Richardson 138, Lloyd 114, Marshall 57, Greenidge 44, Lawson 5–116, Alderman 3–107)
Australia 2nd Innings: 271 (Wessels 61, Phillips 54, Boon 51, Marshall 5–82, Holding 4–92)
West Indies 2nd Innings: 26 for 2

Third Test (Adelaide, 7–11 December) West Indies won by 191 runs
West Indies 1st Innings: 356 (Greenidge 95, Lloyd 78, Dujon 77,

Was this man really a newsagent? Kepler Wessels, the part-time Australian.

Gomes 60, Lawson 8–112)
Australia 1st Innings: 284 (Wessels 98, Lawson 49, Wood 41, Marshall 5–69)
West Indies 2nd Innings: 292 for 7 declared (Gomes 120 not out, Haynes 50, Richards 42, Lawson 3–69, Hogg 3–77)
Australia 2nd Innings: 173 (Wessels 70, Marshall 5–38, Harper 4–43)

Fourth Test (Melbourne, 22–27 December) Match Drawn
West Indies 1st Innings: 479 (Richards 208, Gomes 68, Marshall 55, Richardson 51, Lawson 3–108, McDermott 3–118)
Australia 1st Innings: 296 (Wessels 90, Hilditch 70, Marshall 5–86)
West Indies 2nd Innings: 186 for 5 declared (Haynes 63, Dujon 49 not out, McDermott 3–65)
Australia 2nd Innings: 198 for 8 (Hilditch 113, Border 41, Garner 3–49)

Fifth Test (Sydney, 30 December–2 January) Australia won by an innings and 55 runs
Australia 1st Innings: 471 for 9 declared (Wessels 173, Border 69, Boon 49, Wood 45, Holding 3–74)
West Indies 1st Innings: 163 (Holland 6–54)
West Indies 2nd Innings: 253 (Lloyd 72, Richards 58, Holland 4–90, Bennett 3–79)

Captains: Australia – K.J. Hughes (1st & 2nd Tests), A.R. Border (3rd–5th Tests)
West Indies – C.H. Lloyd

Débuts: Australia – D.C. Boon, R.G. Holland (2nd Test), M.J. Bennett, C.J. McDermott (4th Test)
West Indies – C.A. Walsh (1st Test)

Rising Stars: Australia – K.C. Wessels (+304 batting)
West Indies – H.A. Gomes (+133 batting)

Another glorious series victory for the rampaging West Indies, although they let the side down rather in Sydney, when they neglected to include Harper on a wicket that had been turning all season and were comprehensively spun out by Bob Holland and Murray Bennett. That, though, was the only consolation for Australia in what was a difficult and mostly unrewarding rubber. Only four players – Wessels, Wood, Border and Lawson – took part in all five Tests, and nineteen were used overall. Kim Hughes, after heavy defeats in the first two Tests, resigned the captaincy because of the 'constant criticism' and was dropped after the fourth Test (averaging 10.12 for the series). Border took over and had one of his less prodigious series with the bat.

Wessels, though, recovered from a poor start and began scoring serious runs, culminating with his fourth Test century in the victory at Sydney. Lawson's 23 wickets at 23 put him behind only Hadlee in the world list, while McDermott (10 wickets in two Tests at 27) looked a good find.

The West Indians, meanwhile, were as consistent as ever, although Clive Lloyd's tardy declaration at Melbourne – allowing Australia to squeeze a draw they hardly deserved – deprived his team of their twelfth successive Test match victory. Holding, Garner and Marshall were this time assisted by Courtney Walsh, who had bowled more consistently than Davis in the early state matches and played in all five Tests, reaching a 270 rating. Harper deputized for the injured Holding in two Tests, but otherwise the side was unchanged throughout the season, as the consistent batting of Gomes, who moved up to 3rd in the world, was once again the basis of some very large scores. By the end of the series the West Indies had five of the world's top batsmen. Lloyd, second in his team's averages (to Gomes) with 50.85, maintained his rating as Greenridge and Border dropped, and so took over at the top of the batting list once again – a fine way to mark his retirement from international cricket.

What no-one knew, of course, was that before the series, on the way back from a one-day tournament in India, many of the Australians had dropped off in Singapore, for 'conversations' with the South African Cricket Union. Four months after the tour ended, we found out why.

PAKISTAN vs NEW ZEALAND

First Test (Lahore, 16–20 November) Pakistan won by 6 wickets
New Zealand 1st Innings: 157 (M.D. Crowe 55, I.D.S. Smith 41, Iqbal Qasim 4–41, Mudassar Nazar 3–8)
Pakistan 1st Innings: 221 (Mohsin Khan 58, Zaheer Abbas 43, Chatfield 3–57)
New Zealand 2nd Innings: 241 (Wright 65, J.J. Crowe 43, Iqbal Qasim 4–65, Abdul Qadir 3–82)
Pakistan 2nd Innings: 181 for 4 (Javed Miandad 48 not out)

Second Test (Hyderabad, 25–29 November) Pakistan won by 7 wickets
New Zealand 1st Innings: 267 (Reid 106, Abdul Qadir 5–108)
Pakistan 1st Innings: 230 (Javed Miandad 104, Qasim Omar 45, Boock 7–87, Bracewell 3–44)
New Zealand 2nd Innings: 189 (J.J. Crowe 57, Iqbal Qasim 5–79, Abdul Qadir 3–59)
Pakistan 2nd Innings: 230 for 3 (Mudassar Nazar 106, Javed Miandad 103 not out)

Third Test (Karachi, 10–15 December) Match Drawn
Pakistan 1st Innings: 328 (Anil Dalpat 52, Wasim Raja 51, Salim Malik 50, Qasim Omar 45, Boock 4–83, Stirling 4–88)
New Zealand 1st Innings: 426 (Wright 107, Reid 97, J.J. Crowe 62, M.D. Crowe 45, McEwan 40 not out, Azeem Hafeez 4–132, Iqbal Qasim 4–133)
Pakistan 2nd Innings: 308 for 5 (Salim Malik 119 not out, Wasim Raja 60 not out, Javed Miandad 58)

Captains: Pakistan – Zaheer Abbas
New Zealand – J.V. Coney

Débuts: New Zealand – D.A. Stirling (1st Test)

Rising Stars: Pakistan – Javed Miandad (+114 batting)
New Zealand – S.L. Boock (+158 bowling)

Without Hadlee and Howarth (both 'unavailable'), the New Zealanders found it hard going on their fifth tour of Pakistan, and went down 2–0, both Tests lost by considerable margins. Although Boock bowled well, to take 17 wickets at 25.35, the wickets were perfectly geared to Pakistan's spinners, who took full advantage. Iqbal Qasim, who despite his consistently high rating had still been unable to command a regular place, was the star, with 18 wickets at 22, but Abdul Qadir backed him up well. He had to, for without Imran (still injured) and Sarfraz (retired again, this time for good), Pakistan's 'pace' bowling was reduced to Azeem and the ultimate trundler Mudassar, who found himself transformed into a quiz question when he opened the bowling and the batting in all three Tests. Still, these four bowlers were enough to make New Zealand look quite silly in the first two Tests. John Reid, as ever, provided most of the backbone, but few other reputations were enhanced. New Zealand's one opportunity to make amends came in the final Test, when they reduced Pakistan to 130 for 5 in the second innings, before Wasim Raja and Salim Malik (scoring his fifth Test century) tidied things up.

Possibly the most interesting moment of the tour, though, occurred in that same third Test, when umpire Shakoor Rana failed to give out Javed Miandad caught behind. The New Zealanders were so furious that they walked halfway off the field, and Jeremy Coney needed some persuasion to continue the game.

INDIA vs ENGLAND

First Test (Bombay, 28 November–3 December) India won by 8 wickets
England 1st Innings: 195 (Edmonds 48, Sivaramakrishnan 6–64)

India 1st Innings: 465 for 8 declared (Shastri 142, Kirmani 102, Amarnath 49, Kapil Dev 42, Pocock 3–133)
England 2nd Innings: 317 (Gatting 136, Downton 62, Fowler 55, Sivaramakrishnan 6–117)
India 2nd Innings: 51 for 2

Second Test (Delhi, 12–17 December) England won by 8 wickets
India 1st Innings: 307 (Kapil Dev 60, Amarnath 42, Ellison 4–66, Pocock 3–70)
England 1st Innings: 418 (Robinson 160, Downton 74, Lamb 52, Sivaramakrishnan 6–99)
India 2nd Innings: 235 (Gavaskar 65, Amarnath 64, Patil 41, Edmonds 4–60, Pocock 4–93)
England 2nd Innings: 127 for 2 (Lamb 37 not out)

Third Test (Calcutta, 31 December–5 January) Match Drawn
India 1st Innings: 437 for 7 declared (Shastri 111, Azharuddin 110, Vengsarkar 48, Amarnath 42, Edmonds 3–72, Cowans 3–103)

England 1st Innings: 276 (Lamb 67, Fowler 49, Gatting 48, Chetan Sharma 4–38, Yadav 4–86)
India 2nd Innings: 29 for 1

Fourth Test (Madras, 13–18 January) England won by 9 wickets
India 1st Innings: 272 (Amarnath 78, Kapil Dev 53, Azharuddin 48, Foster 6–104)
England 1st Innings: 652 for 7 declared (Gatting 207, Fowler 201, Robinson 74, Lamb 62)
India 2nd Innings: 412 (Azharuddin 105, Amarnath 95, Kirmani 75, Kapil Dev 49, Foster 5–59)
England 2nd Innings: 35 for 1

Fifth Test (Kanpur, 31 January–5 February) Match Drawn
India 1st Innings: 553 for 8 (Vengsarkar 137, Azharuddin 122, Srikkanth 84, Shastri 59, Kapil Dev 42, Foster 3–123)
England 1st Innings: 417 (Robinson 96, Gower 78, Fowler 69, Gatting 62, Edmonds 49, Kapil Dev 4–81, Shastri 3–52, Gopal Sharma 3–115)
India 2nd Innings: 97 for 1 declared (Azharuddin 54 not out, Srikkanth 41 not out)
England 2nd Innings: 91 for no wicket (Gatting 41 not out)

Captains: India – S.M. Gavaskar
England – D.I. Gower

Débuts: India – M. Prabhakar (2nd Test), M. Azharuddin (3rd Test), Gopal Sharma (5th Test)
England – R.T. Robinson, C.S. Cowdrey (1st Test)

Rising Stars: India – M. Azharuddin (+177 batting)
England – R.T. Robinson (+295 batting)

A remarkable start to England's *annus mirabilis,* as they became the first side ever to win a series in India coming from behind, and broke sundry other records in the process. Even so, the tour had started dismally, with England beaten first by an Under-25 XI, then by India and their new seventeen-year-old leg-spinner, Laxman Sivaramakrishnan (also known as Siva) in the first Test. It needed a huge century from Tim Robinson and, in India's second innings, some high-class spin bowling from Edmonds and Pocock to even the score.

But it was the fourth Test at Madras that really asserted England's surprising superiority. No sooner had Neil Foster bowled India out for a modest 272, than Graeme Fowler and Mike Gatting scored, respectively, the first and largest double centuries by Englishmen in a Test in India. Both their ratings leapt mightily in the process, and suddenly England had their strongest and most consistent-looking batting order for some years. Bowling ratings were more modest. Edmonds (whose final series average of 41.71 was described by *Wisden* as 'a travesty of justice') remained in the 300s (ending on 373), and Pocock finished on just 295. But then even the ratings don't get it right every time.

Perhaps the main disappointment was the form of all-rounder Chris Cowdrey, who played in all five Tests but achieved ratings of only 190 (batting) and 123 (bowling). But Foster broke through at last, and Robinson's 695 points made him England's top batsman.

Indian ratings, by contrast, did not flourish to the same degree. Siva, after his spectacular start, dropped back below 400 after the final Test, while Chetan Sharma made no sort of impact at all, ending on 177. Gavaskar, who had broken Sir Donald Bradman's Test centuries record the previous year when he scored his thirtieth, was held to be lacking in motivation, and indeed only averaged 17.5. In a generally high-scoring series, Shastri's 383 runs at 54.7 gave him, in the end, just 9 extra rating points.

Azharuddin's three centuries in his first three Tests, though, did make a difference – with a 570 rating, and a Test average of 109.75, the Rising Star award was his by a mile. For England, Robinson only just beat Gatting, who in jumping 243 points to 648 also added 8 runs to his career average. It was the beginning of an excellent year for England.

NEW ZEALAND vs PAKISTAN

First Test (Wellington, 18–22 January) Match Drawn
New Zealand 1st Innings: 492 (Reid 148, Hadlee 89, I.D.S. Smith 65,

Coney 48, Azeem Hafeez 5–127)
Pakistan 1st Innings: 322 (Salim Malik 66, Abdul Qadir 54, Mohsin Khan 40, Boock 5–117)
New Zealand 2nd Innings: 103 for 4

Second Test (Auckland, 25–28 January) New Zealand won by an innings and 99 runs
Pakistan 1st Innings: 169 (Salim Malik 41 not out, Hadlee 4–60, Cairns 3–73)
New Zealand 1st Innings: 451 for 9 declared (Reid 158 not out, M.D. Crowe 84, Wright 66, Azeem Hafeez 3–157)
Pakistan 2nd Innings: 183 (Mudassar Nazar 89, Cairns 4–49, Chatfield 3–47)

Third Test (Dunedin, 9–14 February) New Zealand won by 2 wickets
Pakistan 1st Innings: 274 (Qasim Omar 96, Javed Miandad 79, Hadlee 6–51)
New Zealand 1st Innings: 220 (M.D. Crowe 57, Wasim Akram 5–56)
Pakistan 2nd Innings: 223 (Qasim Omar 89, Chatfield 3–65)
New Zealand 2nd Innings: 278 for 8 (Coney 111 not out, M.D. Crowe 84, Wasim Akram 5–72)

Captains: New Zealand – G.P. Howarth
Pakistan – Javed Miandad

Débuts: Pakistan – Wasim Akram (2nd Test)

Rising Stars: New Zealand – M.D. Crowe (+194 batting)
Pakistan – Wasim Akram (+117 bowling)

Once again Pakistan, almost invincible at home, were heavily beaten away – sustaining, in fact, their first ever defeat in New Zealand as they lost the three-match series 2–0. Javed Miandad was back in charge, and the old arguments swelled up again. Abdul Qadir, ineffective in the first two Tests (2–212), was sent home before the third for 'disciplinary reasons', while Zaheer was only available for the second and third (he failed too). Imran was again badly missed, although Wasim Akram's 12 wickets at a shade under 20 portended well. Azeem and Mudassar were rather more expensive. The batting too looked more brittle than it had only a few weeks before against the same opposition, but then Richard Hadlee was back, and his 16 wickets, also at just below 20, made more than a small difference. Boock, Chatfield and Cairns again provided useful back-up. The New Zealand batting, lacking an out-of-form Edgar, relied once more on John Reid, who passed 1,000 Test runs more quickly than any New Zealander before him – twelve matches, twenty innings. His 833 points left him 2nd in the world, also a record for his country. Martin

Crowe's consistency and Coney's indefatigibility when his side was in trouble – his innings won the third Test – were also hugely valuable. Only Qasim Omar of the visitors matched their resolution.

WEST INDIES vs NEW ZEALAND

First Test (Port-of-Spain, Trinidad, 29 March–3 April) Match Drawn
West Indies 1st Innings: 307 (Greenidge 100, Richardson 78, Richards 57, Chatfield 4–51, Hadlee 4–82)
New Zealand 1st Innings: 262 (J.J. Crowe 64, Howarth 45, Wright 40, Holding 4–79)
West Indies 2nd Innings: 261 for 8 declared (Haynes 78, Richards 78, Logie 42, Chatfield 6–73)
New Zealand 2nd Innings: 187 for 6 (Coney 44, Marshall 4–65)

Second Test (Georgetown, Guyana, 6–11 April) Match Drawn
West Indies 1st Innings: 511 for 6 declared (Richardson 185 not out, Haynes 90, Dujon 60 not out, Gomes 53, Logie 52, Richards 40)
New Zealand 1st Innings: 440 (M.D. Crowe 188, Coney 73, I.D.S. Smith 53, Marshall 4–110, Holding 3–89)
West Indies 2nd Innings: 268 for 6 (Greenidge 69, Richardson 60, Logie 41 not out)

Third Test (Bridgetown, Barbados, 26 April–1 May) West Indies won by 10 wickets
New Zealand 1st Innings: 94 (Marshall 4–40, Davis 3–28)
West Indies 1st Innings: 336 (Richards 105, Marshall 63, Haynes 62, Hadlee 3–86)
New Zealand 2nd Innings: 248 (Coney 83, Wright 64, Marshall 7–80, Davis 3–66)
West Indies 2nd Innings: 10 for no wicket

Fourth Test (Kingston, Jamaica, 4–8 May) West Indies won by 10 wickets
West Indies 1st Innings: 363 (Haynes 76, Dujon 70, Greenidge 46, Gomes 45, Hadlee 4–53)
New Zealand 1st Innings: 138 (Wright 53, Davis 4–19)
New Zealand 2nd Innings: 283 (J.J. Crowe 112, Howarth 84, Marshall 4–66)
West Indies 2nd Innings: 59 for no wicket

Captains: West Indies – I.V.A. Richards
New Zealand – G.P. Howarth

Débuts: West Indies – C.G. Butts (2nd Test)
New Zealand – K.R. Rutherford (1st Test)

Rising Stars: West Indies – R.B. Richardson (+116 batting)
New Zealand – J.J. Crowe (+77 batting)

No sooner had they polished off the warring Pakistanis than New Zealand left for a brisk seven-week thrashing by the West Indies. 2–0 was the final result, with the first Test won by the weather, and the second played on such a lifeless pitch that the West Indian bowlers were for once powerless to stop runs being scored in considerable quantities. Most of all New Zealand missed John Reid, who declined to tour because of teaching commitments: his replacement, nineteen-year-old Ken Rutherford, made a pair in the first Test, and in all four Tests, scored just 12 runs, finishing with a relatively flattering rating of 14. Howarth too was in less than top form, and although the Crowes each scored a century, neither got round to scoring very much else. Hadlee's usual haul of wickets (15 at 27.26) often delayed the inevitable, but with only Chatfield providing any sort of support, the New Zealand bowling was on the thin side. Cairns didn't do a great deal, and Boock took just 2 wickets for 339 runs. The West Indian batting was solid rather than spectacular, but then it didn't need to be spectacular, with Malcolm Marshall taking 27 wickets and moving to the top of the world bowlers' list for the first time. (He's been up there ever since.) Winston Davis reclaimed his place to great effect, moving up from 257 to 419 in the final two Tests. Richards, in his first series as captain, had much to be pleased about.

WORLD TOP TWENTY AFTER 1984–85

BATTING

(3)	1.	C.H. Lloyd (West Indies)	843 (−27)
(36)	2.	K.C. Wessels (Australia)	824 (+304)
(9)	3.	I.V.A. Richards (West Indies)	808 (+71)
(12)	4.	J.F. Reid (New Zealand)	800 (+115)
(2)	5.	A.R. Border (Australia)	798 (−86)
(1)	6.	C.G. Greenidge (West Indies)	791 (−100)
(5)	7.	J.V. Coney (New Zealand)	756 (−1)
(8)	8.	Javed Miandad (Pakistan)	746 (+1)
(10)	9.	H.A. Gomes (West Indies)	728 (+5)
(13)	10.	D.L. Haynes (West Indies)	723 (+48)
(6)	11.	G.S. Chappell (Australia)	720 (−37)
NE	12.	R.T. Robinson (England)	695
(14)	13.	P.J.L. Dujon (West Indies)	688 (+22)
(30)	14.	R.B. Richardson (West Indies)	659 (+90)
(53)	15.	M.W. Gatting (England)	648 (+243)
(16)	16.	A.J. Lamb (England)	634 (−19)
(27)	17.	Salim Malik (Pakistan)	633 (+43)

(44)	18.	Qasim Omar (Pakistan)	620 (+132)
(4)	19.	Zaheer Abbas (Pakistan)	617 (−171)
(11)	20.	D.I. Gower (England)	616 (−84)

BOWLING

(2)	1.	M.D. Marshall (West Indies)	879 (+34)
(1)	2.	R.J. Hadlee (New Zealand)	870 (+14)
(7)	3.	G.F. Lawson (Australia)	851 (+59)
(6)	4.	M.A. Holding (West Indies)	827 (+25)
(3)	5.	Imran Khan (Pakistan)	771 (−64)
(5)	6.	Kapil Dev (India)	749 (−82)
(4)	7.	J. Garner (West Indies)	705 (−128)
(8)	8.	D.K. Lillee (Australia)	675 (−34)
(9)	9.	R.G.D. Willis (England)	673 (−34)
(19)	10.	Iqbal Qasim (Pakistan)	583 (+39)
(14)	11.	V.B. John (Sri Lanka)	582
(22)	12.	Azeem Hafeez (Pakistan)	581 (+63)
(11)	13.	A.M.E. Roberts (West Indies)	576 (−54)
(13)	14.	I.T. Botham (England)	563 (−29)
NE	15.	R.G. Holland (Australia)	550
(12)	16.	B.L. Cairns (New Zealand)	544 (−54)
NE	17.	C.J. McDermott (Australia)	543
(15)	18.	N.G.B. Cook (England)	540 (−27)
(16)	19.	D.R. Doshi (India)	527 (−29)
(27)	20.	E.J. Chatfield (New Zealand)	524 (+73)

There's nothing a batsman's rating likes more than a few runs against the West Indies. At least, so the South African 'Australian' Kepler Wessels found, for his 505 brave runs in what was otherwise a drastically unsuccessful series for Australia sent him hurtling up the world list to 2nd, behind Clive Lloyd, who had the distinction of retiring as the top batsman in the world.

As always, the West Indies were very much in charge, with five of the top ten batsmen. John Reid, though, forged ahead, as did Qasim Omar, and to a lesser extent, Salim Malik. Dropping out of the twenty: Ian Botham (absent from India, down from 20th to 22nd), Mohsin Khan (down from 15th to 30th), Graham Yallop (17th to 31st), Gavaskar (plummeting from 7th to 34th), Vengsarkar (19th to 38th) and Edgar of New Zealand (18th to 42nd).

Marshall, meanwhile, took over the bowling top spot from Richard Hadlee, with only Iqbal Qasim disturbing the Top Ten club. Azeem, up from 22nd at the end of 1984, had actually reached 8th before the second New Zealand series, but dropped back. Losing their places completely were Shastri (down from 18th to 21st), Hogg (17th to 29th), Sarfraz (20th to 30th) and the meteoric Rackemann – in at 10th last time, now back down to 31st.

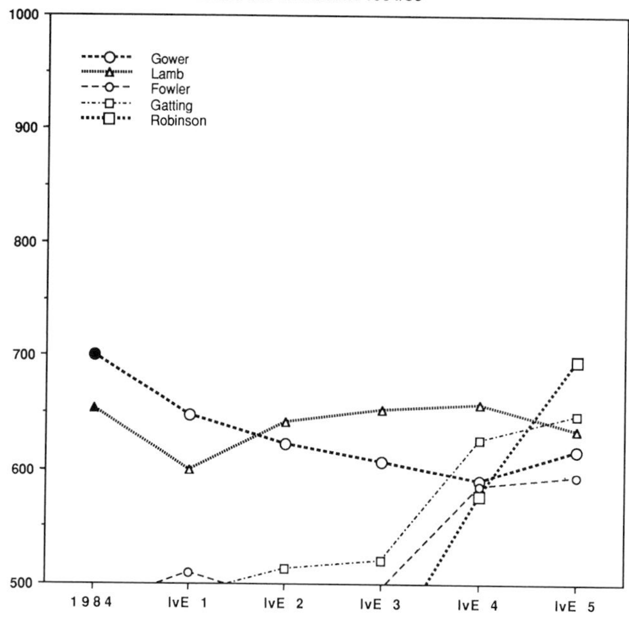

ENGLAND BOWLERS 1984/85

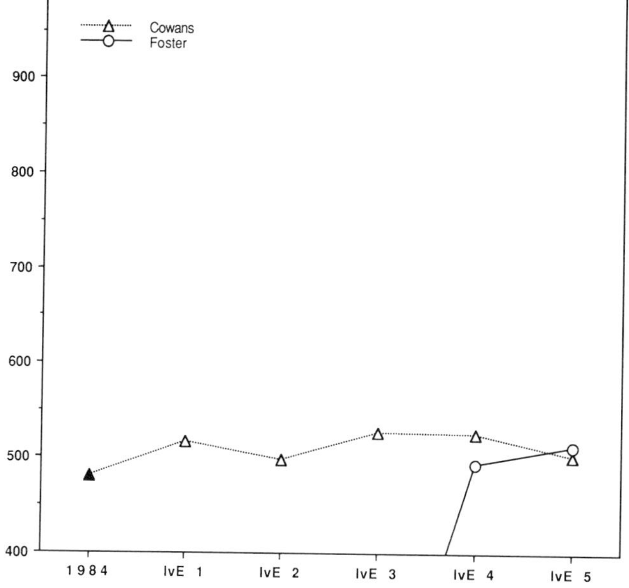

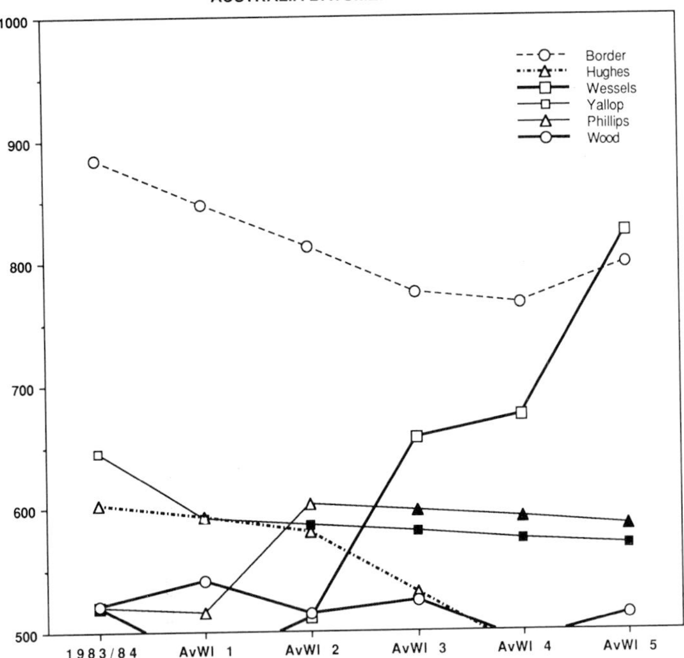
AUSTRALIA BATSMEN 1984/85
1000
900
800
700
600
500
Border
Hughes
Wessels
Yallop
Phillips
Wood
1983/84
AvWI 1
AvWI 2
AvWI 3
AvWI 4
AvWI 5

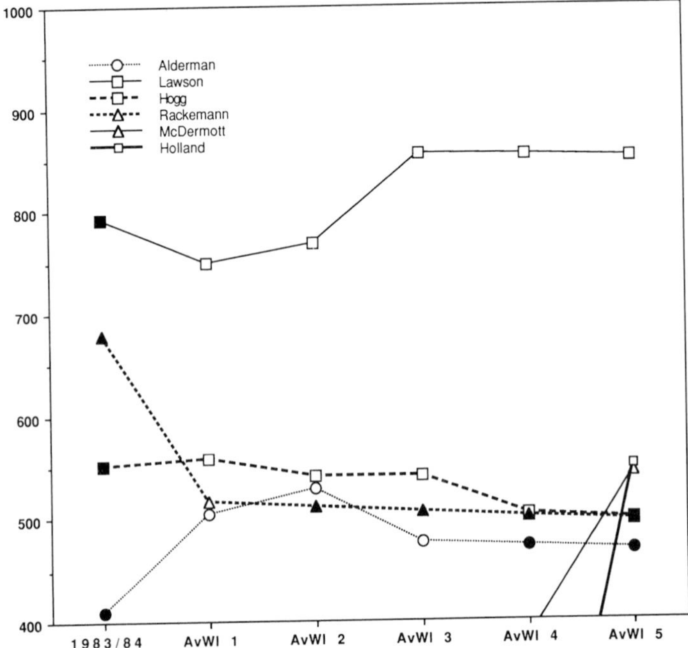
AUSTRALIA BOWLERS 1984/85
1000
900
800
700
600
500
400
Alderman
Lawson
Hogg
Rackemann
McDermott
Holland
1983/84
AvWI 1
AvWI 2
AvWI 3
AvWI 4
AvWI 5

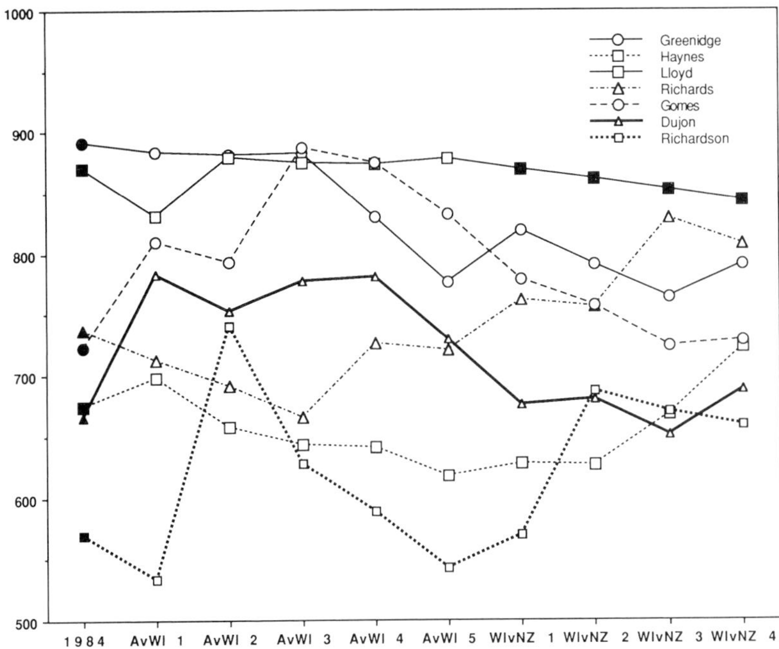
WEST INDIES BATSMEN 1984/85
1000
900
800
700
600
500
Greenidge
Haynes
Lloyd
Richards
Gomes
Dujon
Richardson
1984
AvWI 1
AvWI 2
AvWI 3
AvWI 4
AvWI 5
WIvNZ 1
WIvNZ 2
WIvNZ 3
WIvNZ 4

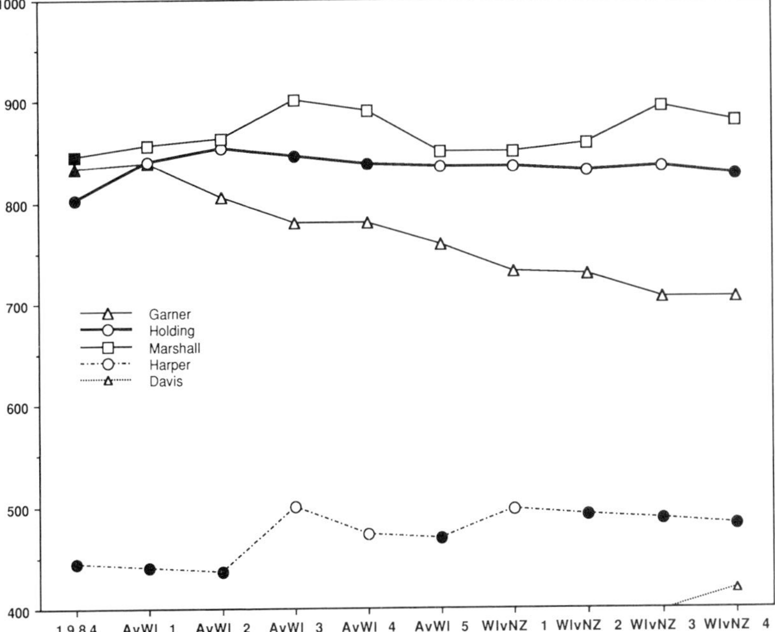
WEST INDIES BOWLERS 1984/85
1000
900
800
700
600
500
400
Garner
Holding
Marshall
Harper
Davis
1984
AvWI 1
AvWI 2
AvWI 3
AvWI 4
AvWI 5
WIvNZ 1
WIvNZ 2
WIvNZ 3
WIvNZ 4

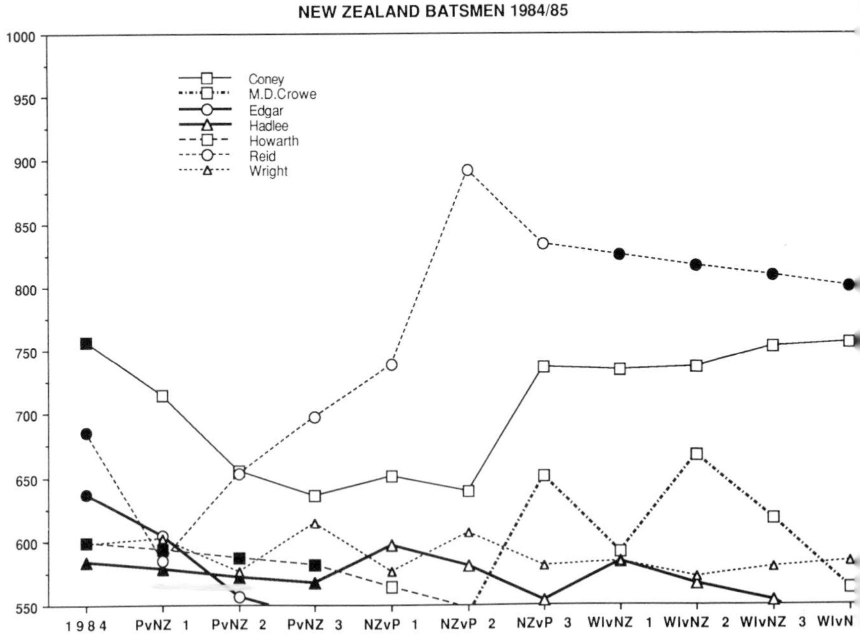
NEW ZEALAND BATSMEN 1984/85
Coney
M.D.Crowe
Edgar
Hadlee
Howarth
Reid
Wright
1000
950
900
850
800
750
700
650
600
550
1984
PvNZ 1
PvNZ 2
PvNZ 3
NZvP 1
NZvP 2
NZvP 3
WIvNZ 1
WIvNZ 2
WIvNZ 3
WIvN

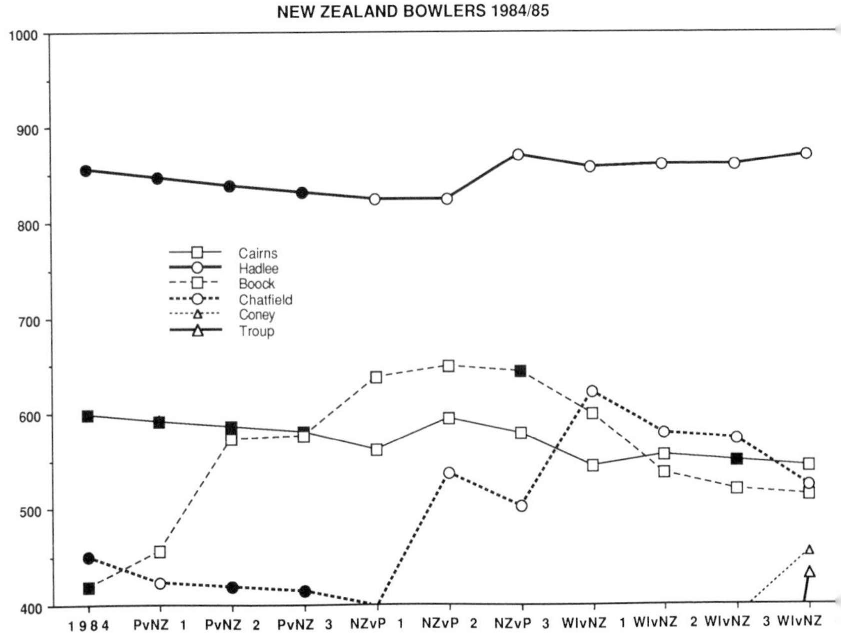
NEW ZEALAND BOWLERS 1984/85
Cairns
Hadlee
Boock
Chatfield
Coney
Troup
1000
900
800
700
600
500
400
1984
PvNZ 1
PvNZ 2
PvNZ 3
NZvP 1
NZvP 2
NZvP 3
WIvNZ 1
WIvNZ 2
WIvNZ 3
WIvNZ

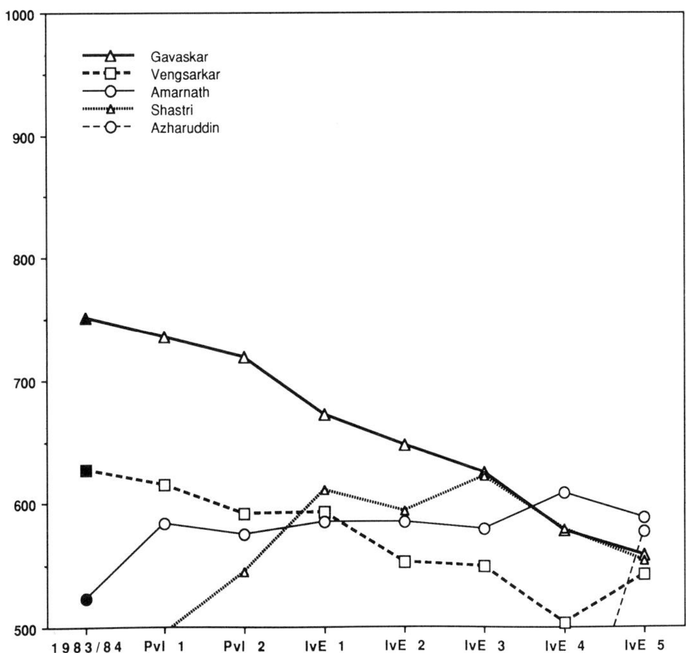
INDIA BATSMEN 1984/85
1000
900
800
700
600
500
Gavaskar
Vengsarkar
Amarnath
Shastri
Azharuddin
1983/84
Pvl 1
Pvl 2
IvE 1
IvE 2
IvE 3
IvE 4
IvE 5

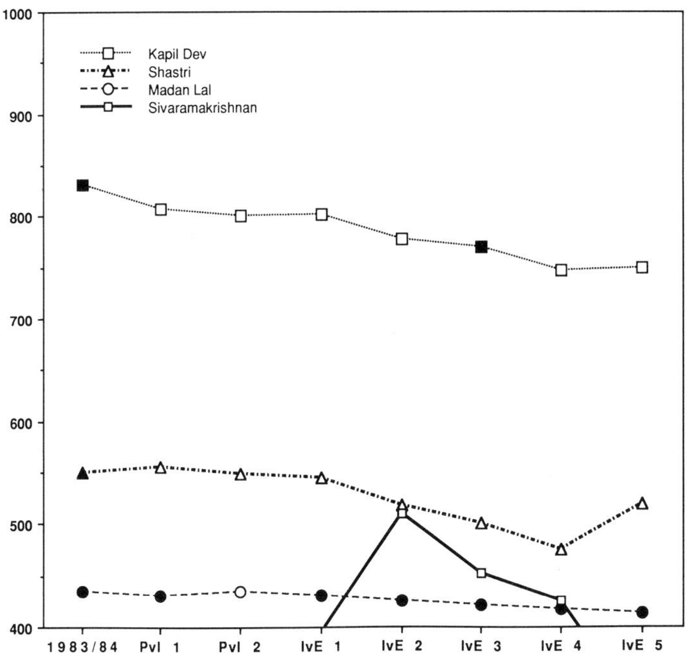
INDIA BOWLERS 1984/85
1000
900
800
700
600
500
400
Kapil Dev
Shastri
Madan Lal
Sivaramakrishnan
1983/84
Pvl 1
Pvl 2
IvE 1
IvE 2
IvE 3
IvE 4
IvE 5

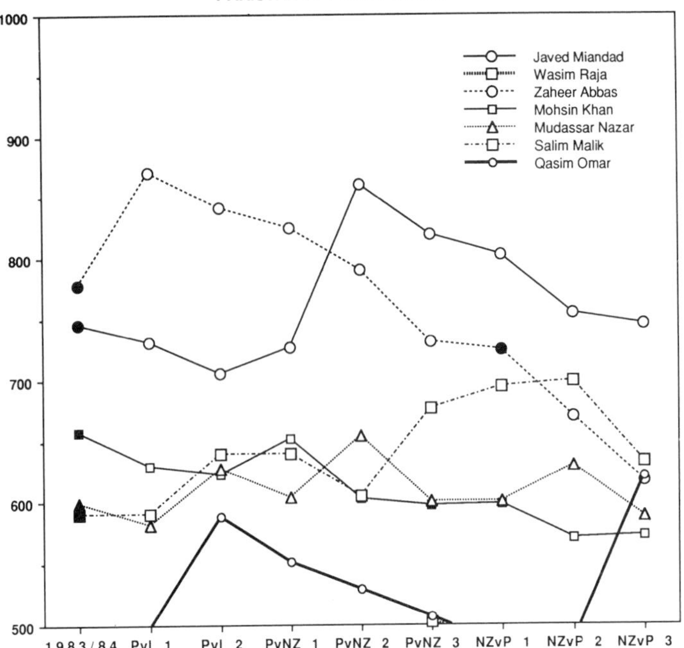
PAKISTAN BATSMEN 1984/85
1000
900
800
700
600
500
Javed Miandad
Wasim Raja
Zaheer Abbas
Mohsin Khan
Mudassar Nazar
Salim Malik
Qasim Omar
1983/84
PvI 1
PvI 2
PvNZ 1
PvNZ 2
PvNZ 3
NZvP 1
NZvP 2
NZvP 3

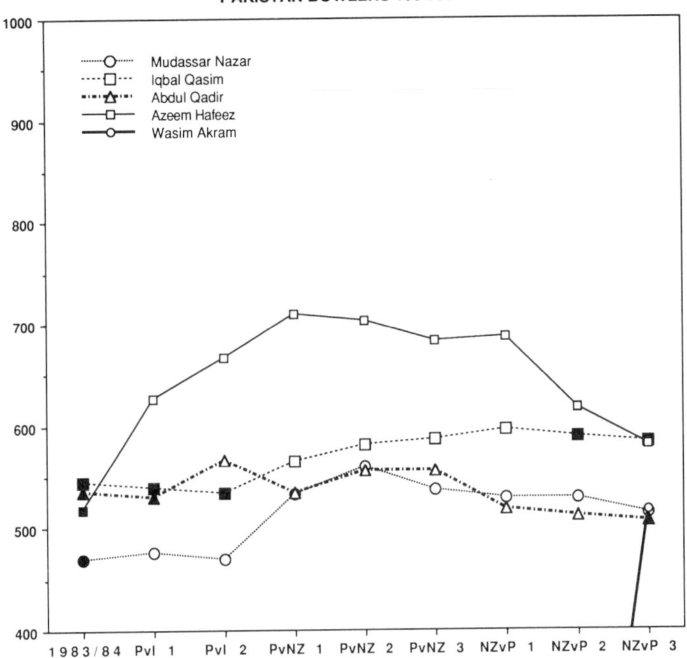
PAKISTAN BOWLERS 1984/85
1000
900
800
700
600
500
400
Mudassar Nazar
Iqbal Qasim
Abdul Qadir
Azeem Hafeez
Wasim Akram
1983/84
PvI 1
PvI 2
PvNZ 1
PvNZ 2
PvNZ 3
NZvP 1
NZvP 2
NZvP 3

1985

ENGLAND vs AUSTRALIA

First Test (Headingley, 13–18 June) England won by 5 wickets
Australia 1st Innings: 331 (Hilditch 119, Ritchie 46, Botham 3–86)
England 1st Innings: 533 (Robinson 175, Botham 60, Downton 54, Gatting 53, McDermott 4–134, Lawson 3–117)
Australia 2nd Innings: 324 (Phillips 91, Hilditch 80, Wessels 64, Emburey 5–82, Botham 4–107)
England 2nd Innings: 123 for 5 (O'Donnell 3–37)

Second Test (Lord's, 27 June–2 July) Australia won by 4 wickets
England 1st Innings: 290 (Gower 86, Lamb 47, McDermott 6–70, Lawson 3–91)
Australia 1st Innings: 425 (Border 196, Ritchie 94, O'Donnell 48, Botham 5–109)
England 2nd Innings: 261 (Botham 85, Gatting 75 not out, Holland 5–68, Lawson 3–86)
Australia 2nd Innings: 127 for 6 (Border 41 not out)

Third Test (Trent Bridge, 11–16 July) Match Drawn
England 1st Innings: 456 (Gower 166, Gatting 74, Gooch 70, Lawson 5–103)
Australia 1st Innings: 539 (Wood 172, Ritchie 146, Hilditch 47, O'Donnell 46, Botham 3–107, Emburey 3–129)
England 2nd Innings: 196 for 2 (Robinson 77 not out, Gooch 48)

Fourth Test (Old Trafford, 1–6 August) Match Drawn
Australia 1st Innings: 257 (Boon 61, Hilditch 49, O'Donnell 45, Edmonds 4–40, Botham 4–79)
England 1st Innings: 482 for 9 declared (Gatting 160, Gooch 74, Lamb 67, Gower 47, McDermott 8–141)
Australia 2nd Innings: 340 for 5 (Border 146 not out, Wessels 50, Hilditch 40, Emburey 4–99)

Fifth Test (Edgbaston, 15–20 August) England won by an innings and 118 runs
Australia 1st Innings: 335 (Wessels 83, Lawson 53, Border 45, Ellison 6–77)
England 1st Innings: 595 for 5 declared (Gower 215, Robinson 148, Gatting 100 not out, Lamb 46)
Australia 2nd Innings: 142 (Phillips 59, Ellison 4–27, Botham 3–52)

Sixth Test (The Oval, 29 August–2 September) England won by an innings and 94 runs
England 1st Innings: 464 (Gooch 196, Gower 157, Lawson 4–101, McDermott 4–108)
Australia 1st Innings: 241 (Ritchie 64 not out, Botham 3–64)
Australia 2nd Innings: 129 (Border 58, Ellison 5–46, Botham 3–44)

Captains: England – D.I. Gower
Australia – A.R. Border

Débuts: England – A. Sidebottom (3rd Test), L.B. Taylor (5th Test)
Australia – S.P. O'Donnell (1st Test), D.R. Gilbert (6th Test)

Rising Stars: England – D.I. Gower (+260 batting)
Australia – C.J. McDermott (+327 bowling)

Another remarkable Ashes series, with England's superiority suddenly manifesting itself in the final two Tests, which were won by an innings. Australia were considerably weakened by the announcement in April of a rebel tour to South Africa, which deprived them of some of their better players, Terry Alderman, Carl Rackemann, John Dyson and Rodney Hogg among them. What made things worse was the unseemly haggling that followed the announcement, which resulted in Graeme Wood, Wayne Phillips and Dirk Wellham changing their minds and going to England instead, while Kim Hughes and Graeme Yallop, both unaccountably omitted from the official touring team, decamped to South Africa. All this toing and froing not surprisingly affected morale, and as England had just returned from a triumphant tour of India, the essentially slender differences between the two sides were magnified beyond all proportion.

That said, this was the series in which England's highly rated but hitherto underperforming batting order finally came into its own. with the exception of Allan Lamb, who merely trod water, and a strangely subdued Ian Botham (a hilarious six-ball 18 notwithstanding), all the major batsmen scored piles of runs, assisted all too often by wayward Australian bowling. Gatting and Robinson both averaged over 80, and Gower's three centuries, including a career-best 215 at the Oval, pushed him up to the top of the world ratings. Gooch's return after his three-year ban was hardly less productive.

It was the Australian bowling that suffered most strongly from the defections to South Africa. Bob Holland, the thirty-eight-year-old legspinner, took 5 wickets at Lord's but only took one more in the next three Tests, and was dropped for the Oval. Geoff Lawson had fitness problems, while Jeff Thomson was clearly past his best, and even his quite good. Only the twenty-year-old Craig McDermott, with 30 wickets at just over 30 runs each, consistently posed problems, although he too found the going tough when the England batsmen were at their most aggressive.

In fact, the difference between the two sides in the final Tests can be summed up in two words: Richard Ellison. Taking 17 wickets at under 11 runs each and swinging the ball viciously, he appeared almost unplayable at times, and improved spectacularly on England's otherwise mediocre bowling record earlier in the series. Botham as ever had led the attack with 31 wickets at 27.5, and Emburey and Edmonds had both been steady, but the sundry other seamers tried – Cowans, Allott, Sidebottom, Les Taylor, Agnew and Foster – had achieved little. Only when Ellison appeared did the Australians finally crack.

Border's wicket, of course, was still the one everyone prized. His 597 runs were all scored when it mattered, and his 196 at Lord's won the match. His was one of only two Australian batting ratings to rise, the other being that of Greg Ritchie, who climbed from 342 to 448 and, at Trent Bridge, scored his maiden Test century. The weaknesses of Wessels and Hilditch, though, were relentlessly probed – much as Allan Border undermined the England batsmen's confidence four years later – and their form disintegrated. David Boon, on his first tour, had a terrible time – his rating dropped from 293 to 277 and he was dropped after the fourth Test.

WORLD TOP TWENTY AFTER 1985

BATTING

(20)	1.	D.I. Gower (England)	876 (+260)
(15)	2.	M.W. Gatting (England)	847 (+199)
(1)	3.	C.H. Lloyd (West Indies)	843
(12)	4.	R.T. Robinson (England)	838 (+143)
(5)	5.	A.R. Border (Australia)	828 (+30)
(3)	6.	I.V.A. Richards (West Indies)	808
(4)	7.	J.F. Reid (New Zealand)	800
(6)	8.	C.G. Greenidge (West Indies)	791
(7)	9.	J.V. Coney (New Zealand)	756
(8)	10.	Javed Miandad (Pakistan)	746
(9)	11.	H.A. Gomes (West Indies)	728
(10)	12.	D.L. Haynes (West Indies)	723
(13)	13.	P.J.L. Dujon (West Indies)	688
(14)	14.	R.B. Richardson (West Indies)	659
RE	15.	G.A. Gooch (England)	659
(17)	16.	Salim Malik (Pakistan)	633
(16)	17.	A.J. Lamb (England)	622 (−12)
(2)	18.	K.C. Wessels (Australia)	620 (−204)
(18)	19.	Qasim Omar (Pakistan)	620
(19)	20.	Zaheer Abbas (Pakistan)	617

BOWLING

(1)	1.	M.D. Marshall (West Indies)	879
(17)	2.	C.J. McDermott (Australia)	870 (+327)
(2)	3.	R.J. Hadlee (New Zealand)	870
(4)	4.	M.A. Holding (West Indies)	827
(3)	5.	G.F. Lawson (Australia)	786 (−65)
(6)	6.	Kapil Dev (India)	749
(70)	7.	R.M. Ellison (England)	722 (+525)
(7)	8.	J. Garner (West Indies)	705
(9)	9.	R.G.D. Willis (England)	633 (−40)
(14)	10.	I.T. Botham (England)	612 (+49)
(10)	11.	Iqbal Qasim (Pakistan)	583
(11)	12.	V.B. John (Sri Lanka)	582
(12)	13.	Azeem Hafeez (Pakistan)	581
(16)	14.	B.L. Cairns (New Zealand)	544
(20)	15.	E.J. Chatfield (New Zealand)	524
(21)	16.	R.J. Shastri (India)	519
(22)	17.	Wasim Akram (Pakistan)	517
(23)	18.	S.L. Boock (New Zealand)	514
(24)	19.	Mudassar Nazar (Pakistan)	514
(18)	20.	N.G.B. Cook (England)	508 (−32)

Rarely can England have dominated the batting ratings as they did after their 1985 Ashes success. In the Eighties, at least, the operative word is 'never'. This was it: a few months later, England were being blackwashed by the West Indies again and all was back to normal.

Gooch's return at only 15th shows how low his rating had sunk over those three years away from Test cricket, while Wessel's drop was almost as large as his rise the previous season. The next highest Australian batsmen were Yallop (36th and unavailable) and Phillips (38th). Out of the twenty altogether was Greg Chappell, whose retirement the previous year had finally filtered through.

The bowling ratings, for once, were considerably livelier than their batting equivalents, with three whole changes in the top ten – McDermott and Ellison bursting in from nowhere and Botham oozing in again. Lillee (retired), Roberts (ditto), Imran (injured) and Doshi (forgotten) all dropped out of the twenty on the 18-month rule, to be replaced by numbers 16 to 19, the last of whom, Mudassar, became only the second player to appear in both top twenties at the same time, after I.T. Botham. Also out, poor Bob Holland, who no doubt would have loved to bowl on that bouncy Oval pitch.

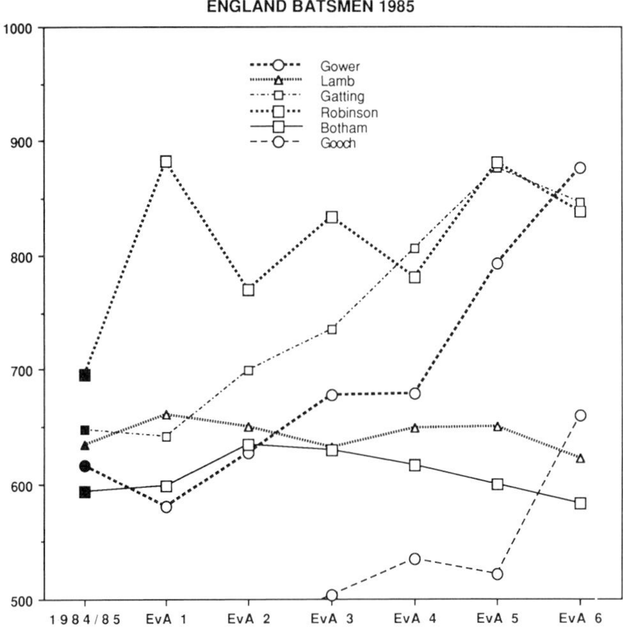
ENGLAND BATSMEN 1985
1000
900
800
700
600
500
Gower
Lamb
Gatting
Robinson
Botham
Gooch
1984/85
EvA 1
EvA 2
EvA 3
EvA 4
EvA 5
EvA 6

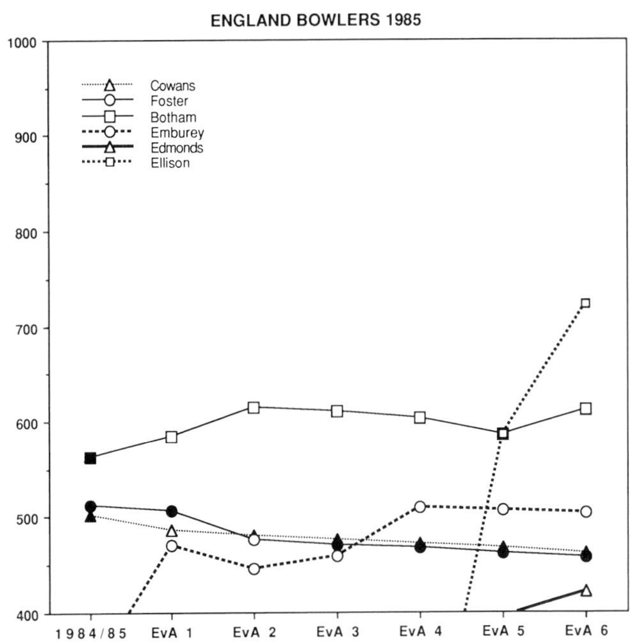
ENGLAND BOWLERS 1985
1000
900
800
700
600
500
400
Cowans
Foster
Botham
Emburey
Edmonds
Ellison
1984/85
EvA 1
EvA 2
EvA 3
EvA 4
EvA 5
EvA 6

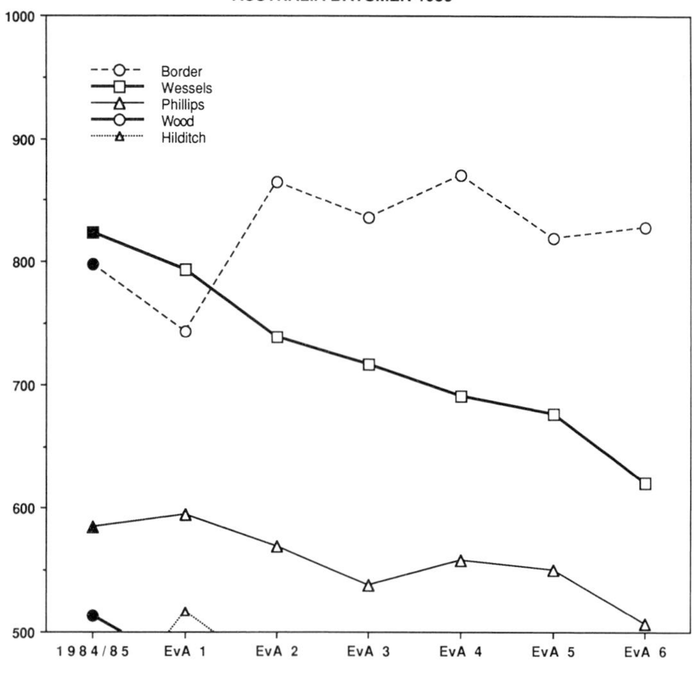
AUSTRALIA BATSMEN 1985
1000
900
800
700
600
500
Border
Wessels
Phillips
Wood
Hilditch
1984/85
EvA 1
EvA 2
EvA 3
EvA 4
EvA 5
EvA 6

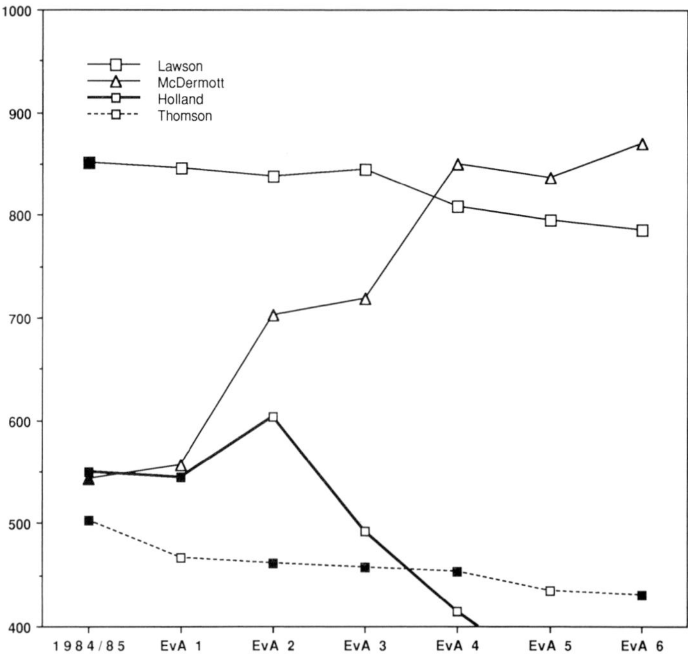
AUSTRALIA BOWLERS 1985
1000
900
800
700
600
500
400
Lawson
McDermott
Holland
Thomson
1984/85
EvA 1
EvA 2
EvA 3
EvA 4
EvA 5
EvA 6

1985–86

SRI LANKA vs INDIA

First Test (Colombo, 30 August–4 September) Match Drawn
India 1st Innings: 218 (Gavaskar 51, de Mel 5–64)
Sri Lanka 1st Innings: 347 (Ranatunga 111, Madugalle 103, Mendis 51, Kapil Dev 3–74, Chetan Sharma 3–81)
India 2nd Innings: 251 (Vengsarkar 98 not out, Rajput 61, Shastri 40, R.J. Ratnayake 6–85, Ahangama 3–49)
Sri Lanka 2nd Innings: 61 for 4

Second Test (Colombo, 6–11 September) Sri Lanka won by 149 runs
Sri Lanka 1st Innings: 385 (Silva 111, Dias 95, Madugalle 54, Mendis 51, Chetan Sharma 5–118, Shastri 3–74)
India 1st Innings: 244 (Srikkanth 64, Amarnath 60, Gavaskar 52, R.J. Ratnayake 4–76, Ahangama 3–59)
Sri Lanka 2nd Innings: 206 for 3 declared (P.A. de Silva 75, Dias 60 not out)
India 2nd Innings: 198 (Kapil Dev 78, R.J. Ratnayake 5–49, de Mel 3–64)

Third Test (Kandy, 14–19 September) Match Drawn
India 1st Innings: 249 (Vengsarkar 62, Gavaskar 49, Srikkanth 40, Ahangama 5–52)
Sri Lanka 1st Innings: 198 (Mendis 53, Maninder Singh 4–31)
India 2nd Innings: 325 for 5 declared (Amarnath 116 not out, Shastri 81, Srikkanth 47, Azharuddin 43, Ahangama 3–72)
Sri Lanka 2nd Innings: 307 for 7 (Mendis 124, Dias 106, Chetan Sharma 3–65, Kapil Dev 3–74)

Captains: Sri Lanka – L.R.D. Mendis
India – Kapil Dev

Débuts: Sri Lanka – F.S. Ahangama, E.A.R. de Silva (1st Test), C.D.U.S. Weerasinghe (2nd Test), B.R. Jurangpathy (3rd Test)
India – L.S. Rajput, S. Viswanath (1st Test)

Rising Stars: Sri Lanka – F.S. Ahangama (+156 bowling)
India – M. Amarnath (+52 bowling)

Sri Lanka's first victory in Test cricket, in only their fourteenth Test, was achieved against an Indian side both woefully out of practice and, one suspects, a mite over-confident. Yet the home side almost won the first Test as well – Vengsarkar's stalwart rearguard action gave them just eleven overs to score the required 123, a task that only just proved beyond them. And with Sri Lanka holding on in the final Test against a rather more purposeful performance by the Indians, they also won their first ever series. A public holiday was immediately declared.

The series was especially a triumph for Sri Lanka's old lags, who had played throughout their country's early tentative forays in Test cricket. Mendis, Madugalle and Dias all scored centuries, the latter roaring back into the world top twenty in the process. The wickets, though, were shared by two relative newcomers – R.J. Ratnayake (not to be confused with J.R. Ratnayeke) and the débutant Ahangama, who took 18 good wickets at 19.33 and shot up the ratings. Amal Silva also had a good series, with nine dismissals and a century in the second Test, a combination no wicketkeeper of any nationality had ever managed before.

India, as so often, were hampered by inconsistent batting, not helped by Gavaskar's decision to drop down the order. Their bowling, with Kapil Dev not firing on all cylinders and Siva injured, also let them down, although Chetan Sharma's advance – 14 wickets at 27, pushing his rating up from 177 to 435 – was at least encouraging. But Sri Lanka's achievement overshadowed all else. India's first victory, incidentally, came in their twenty-fifth Test, while New Zealand had to wait until their forty-fifth for theirs. It had taken the Sri Lankans just three and a half years.

PAKISTAN vs SRI LANKA

First Test (Faisalabad, 16–21 October) Match Drawn
Sri Lanka 1st Innings: 479 (P.A. de Silva 122, Ranatunga 79, R.J. Ratnayake 56, Wettimuny 52, Dias 48, Imran Khan 3–112, Abdul Qadir 3–132)
Pakistan 1st Innings: 555 for 3 (Qasim Omar 206, Javed Miandad 203 not out, Mudassar Nazar 78)

Second Test (Sialkot, 27–31 October) Pakistan won by 8 wickets
Sri Lanka 1st Innings: 157 (Wettimuny 45, Imran Khan 4–55, Mohsin Kamal 3–50)
Pakistan 1st Innings: 259 (Mudassar Nazar 78, Mohsin Khan 50, Javed Miandad 40, J.R. Ratnayeke 8–83)
Sri Lanka 2nd Innings: 200 (Madugalle 65, Imran Khan 5–40)
Pakistan 2nd Innings: 100 for 2 (Mohsin Khan 44)

Third Test (Karachi, 7–11 November) Pakistan won by 10 wickets
Sri Lanka 1st Innings: 162 (Abdul Qadir 5–44)

Pakistan 1st Innings: 295 (Javed Miandad 63, Imran Khan 63, Ramiz Raja 52, de Mel 6–109)
Sri Lanka 2nd Innings: 230 (P.A. de Silva 105, Tauseef Ahmed 5–54)
Pakistan 2nd Innings: 98 for no wicket (Mudassar Nazar 57 not out)

Captains: Pakistan – Javed Miandad
Sri Lanka – L.R.D. Mendis

Débuts: Sri Lanka – A.P. Gurusinha (3rd Test)

Rising Stars: Pakistan – Mudassar Nazar (+73 batting)
Sri Lanka – P.A. de Silva (+142 batting)

Still hugely chuffed by their series win over India, Sri Lanka found their visit to Pakistan a month later rather more arduous. After the dullest of dull draws in the first Test, they lost the subsequent two by considerable margins, as their batsmen lost form and the Pakistan bowlers pressed home their advantage. That advantage, of course, was Imran Khan, back from injury and full of beans. 17 wickets were his reward, at an average of under 16. The Sri Lankans' most successful bowler, by contrast, was J.R. Ratnayeke (not to be confused with R.J. Ratnayake), whose 10 wickets at 29.7 included his country's best ever return (in the second Test). Otherwise their bowling was unimpressive, and the Pakistan batsmen, Miandad in particular, tucked into it will ill-disguised glee.

Announced during the second Test was the retirement of Zaheer Abbas, after seventy-eight Tests, 5,062 runs and twelve centuries. Although selected for the final Test, he withdrew and so denied himself an appropriately rousing send-off. Javed Miandad, meanwhile, resigned the captaincy after the series – Imran Khan, no doubt to the relief of many, took over.

AUSTRALIA vs NEW ZEALAND

First Test (Brisbane, 8–12 November) New Zealand won by an innings and 41 runs
Australia 1st Innings: 179 (Wessels 70, Hadlee 9–52)
New Zealand 1st Innings: 553 for 7 (M.D. Crowe 188, J.F. Reid 108, Hadlee 54, Wright 46, G.R.J. Matthews 3–110)
Australia 2nd Innings: 333 (Border 152 not out, G.R.J. Matthews 115, Hadlee 6–71, Chatfield 3–75)

Second Test (Sydney, 22–26 November) Australia won by 4 wickets
New Zealand 1st Innings: 293 (J.G. Bracewell 83 not out, Edgar 50, Holland 6–106)

Australia 1st Innings: 227 (Ritchie 89, G.R.J. Matthews 50, Hadlee 5–65)
New Zealand 2nd Innings: 193 (Edgar 52, Wright 43, Holland 4–68, Bright 3–39)
Australia 2nd Innings: 260 for 6 (Boon 81, Phillips 63, J.G. Bracewell 3–91)

Third Test (Perth, 30 November–4 December) New Zealand won by 6 wickets
Australia 1st Innings: 203 (Hadlee 5–65, Chatfield 3–33)
New Zealand 1st Innings: 299 (Edgar 74, M.D. Crowe 71, Lawson 4–79, Holland 3–63)
Australia 2nd Innings: 259 (Border 83, Boon 50, Ritchie 44, Hadlee 6–90)
New Zealand 2nd Innings: 164 for 4 (M.D. Crowe 42 not out, Gilbert 3–48)

Captains: Australia – A.R. Border
New Zealand – J.V. Coney

Débuts: Australia – R.B. Kerr (2nd Test)
New Zealand – V.R. Brown (1st Test)

Rising Stars: Australia – R.G. Holland (+127 bowling)
New Zealand – M.D. Crowe (+135 batting)

The underdog bites back. After Sri Lanka's triumph over India, it was New Zealand's turn to cause an upset, although with their opponents at such a low ebb, they must have been cross not to win all three Tests. Jeremy Coney's team (Howarth had been dropped) did, after all, contain the one world-class bowler on either side, Richard Hadlee, and it was in this series that he hit the peak of his form. Amongst his 33 wickets (at 12.15) were 9 (for 52) in the first innings of the first Test, which just happened to be the fourth best return in Test history. The Australians, perhaps trying to kill with kindness, had thoughtfully prepared most of the pitches to suit Hadlee's devilish medium-fast stuff, and he did not waste the opportunity. The only exception was, not surprisingly, the traditional turner at Sydney, for which New Zealand opened their bowling with Hadlee and a no doubt bemused Martin Crowe, before turning to their three specialist spinners. (Hadlee still took 7 wickets in the match.)

The poor form of the Australian batsmen continued, as their flaws in technique were skilfully probed and exploited by Hadlee. Hilditch and Wessels were dropped, Hookes and Robbie Kerr (in his only two Tests) did no better, and although Boon finally passed 400 after two half-centuries, he still averaged less than 30 in the three Tests. Only Border (of course) and the off-spinning all-rounder Greg Matthews prospered to any degree, averaging 55 and 41 respectively.

With Hadlee taking all the wickets, there wasn't much room for any other bowler to shine, but Chatfield and Bracewell backed him up admirably. Bracewell, indeed, won the Man of the Match award at Sydney, although that was more for his unbeaten 83 – part of a record tenth wicket stand (against Australia) of 124 with Stephen Boock (35) – than for any bowling heroics. As it is, New Zealand were well placed to win that Test while Wright and Edgar were compiling a 100 partnership in the second innings – but their innings collapsed and Australia stormed home.

That occasion aside, though, the New Zealand batting was confident and composed, with Martin Crowe (309 runs at 77.25) causing particular damage. Wright and Edgar were also at their steadiest, and Reid's 108 was as watchful as ever. Holland caused them major problems at Sydney (and jumped from 286 to 522 in the process), but he was the only bowler to do so. Coney's popular and proficient side deserved their success.

AUSTRALIA vs INDIA

First Test (Adelaide, 13–16 December) Match Drawn
Australia 1st Innings: 381 (Ritchie 128, Boon 123, Border 49, Kapil Dev 8–106)
India 1st Innings: 520 (Gavaskar 166 not out, Chetan Sharma 54, Srikkanth 51, Shastri 42, Reid 4–113, McDermott 3–131)
Australia 2nd Innings: 17 for no wicket

Second Test (Melbourne, 26–30 December) Match Drawn
Australia 1st Innings: 262 (G.R.J. Matthews 100 not out, Hookes 42, Shastri 4–87, Yadav 3–64)
India 1st Innings: 445 (Srikkanth 86, Vengsarkar 75, Kapil Dev 55, Shastri 49, Amarnath 45, Reid 4–100)
Australia 2nd Innings: 308 (Border 163, Shastri 4–92, Yadav 3–84)
India 2nd Innings: 59 for 2.

Third Test (Sydney 2–6 January) Match Drawn
India 1st Innings: 600 for 4 declared (Gavaskar 172, Amarnath 138, Srikkanth 116, Azharuddin 59 not out, Kapil Dev 42)
Australia 1st Innings: 396 (Boon 131, G.R. Marsh 92, Border 71, G.R.J. Matthews 40, Yadav 5–99, Shastri 4–101)
Australia 2nd Innings: 119 for 6 (Yadav 3–19)

Captains: Australia – A.R. Border
India – Kapil Dev

Débuts: Australia – G.R. Marsh, M.G. Hughes, B.A. Reid (1st Test), S.R. Waugh (2nd Test)

1985–86

Rising Stars: Australia – D.C. Boon (+98 batting)
India – K. Srikkanth (+84 batting)

With India recently knocked aside by Sri Lanka, and Australia made to look second rate by Richard Hadlee, international cricket's wooden spoon was now generally considered to be at stake. And indeed, neither team was what you might describe as 'much cop'. Although India were unbeaten in first-class matches in Australia for the first time, they still didn't manage to win any Test matches, so the three-match series ended grippingly at 0–0.

India's batsmen scored runs by the bucketful. Trouble was, Srikkanth aside, they didn't score them very quickly. Clearly under the impression that timeless Tests had been reinstated, India had almost all of the play after lunch on the last day of the second Test to score 126, with rain forecast. When it finally arrived after tea, they had chugged along to just 59 for 2. On the second day of the last Test, with India on 334 for 1, Gavaskar and Amarnath scored just 64 before lunch. So excessively cautious were they that Kapil Dev promoted himself in the order for a necessary swish.

But India's bowling once again let them down. Other than a swift burst from Kapil Dev, the bulk of the work fell to the off-spinner Yadav and the left-armer Shastri. Chetan Sharma didn't take a wicket – his rating declined to 350 – and Siva's form and confidence had now apparently deserted him for good. Even so, the Australian batsmen, their line-up still changing with every Test, were never on top. Phillips' experimental period as an opener, partially successful against New Zealand, came to an end as he averaged 13 and scuttled back down the order. Hookes, unimpressive in the first two Tests, was dropped. Ritchie, after his century in the first Test, fractured some toes and was ruled out of the second.

It's around now, however, that the nucleus of the successful Australian team of 1989 began to be formed. In the first Test, Geoff Marsh appeared at number 3, although it wasn't until he was promoted to open in the final Test that he really got going. Enter, too, Steve Waugh – initially unimpressive (after two Tests, his batting and bowling ratings were 60 and 85) but full of potential. And, for one brief appearance in the first Test, replacing the injured Dave 'Where Are They Now?' Gilbert, one Merv Hughes, who took 1 for 123 in that match.

The other successes were David Boon, promoted to open with Phillips but with more satisfactory results (323 runs at 64.6 with two centuries), and Bruce Reid, the six foot eight inch left-arm pace bowler who was the only Australian bowler to take more than 4 wickets (11 at just under 30), ending with a rating of 387 after three Tests. Two careers ended right here – David Hookes, after 23 Tests, and the leg-spinner Bob Holland (11 Tests), who, picked for Sydney as always, took just 1–113.

NEW ZEALAND vs AUSTRALIA

First Test (Wellington, 21–25 February) Match Drawn
Australia 1st Innings: 435 (G.R.J. Matthews 130, Ritchie 92, Boon 70, G.R. Marsh 43, Coney 3–47, Hadlee 3–116)
New Zealand 1st Innings: 379 for 6 (Coney 101 not out, Hadlee 72 not out, Rutherford 65, Reid 3–104)

Second Test (Christchurch, 28 February–4 March) Match Drawn
Australia 1st Innings: 364 (Border 140, Waugh 74, Hadlee 7–116)
New Zealand 1st Innings: 339 (M.D. Crowe 137, Coney 98, Waugh 4–56, Reid 4–90)
Australia 2nd Innings: 219 for 7 declared (Border 114 not out, J.G. Bracewell 4–77)
New Zealand 2nd Innings: 16 for 1

Third Test (Auckland, 13–17 March) New Zealand won by 8 wickets
Australia 1st Innings: 314 (G.R. Marsh 118, Phillips 62, Ritchie 56, J.G. Bracewell 4–74, Hadlee 3–60)
New Zealand 1st Innings: 258 (Coney 93, Wright 56, G.R.J. Matthews 4–61)
Australia 2nd Innings: 103 (Boon 58 not out, J.G. Bracewell 6–32, Chatfield 3–19)
New Zealand 2nd Innings: 160 for 2 (Wright 59, Rutherford 50 not out)

Captains: New Zealand – J.V. Coney
Australia – A.R. Border

Débuts: New Zealand – S.R. Gillespie (1st Test), G.K. Robertson (3rd Test)
Australia – T.J. Zoehrer, S.P. Davis (1st Test)

Rising Stars: New Zealand – J.V. Coney (+124 batting)
Australia – G.R. Marsh (+106 batting)

It's odd to think that until 1973–74, when regular tours began, Australia and New Zealand had played each other just four times. That's two fewer, in fact, than the number of times they played each other between 8 November 1985 and 17 March 1986 – and in each of those two three-match series, New Zealand won.

This time, though, it wasn't Richard Hadlee who clinched the victory, but John Bracewell, an off-spinner who, after fifteen Tests, still had a rating of just 364. But his 10 wickets on a rampantly spinning wicket in Auckland – one that his Australian counterparts

Bright and Matthews were incapable of exploiting – reduced the visiting team to 103 in their second innings, by 59 the lowest score they had ever recorded against New Zealand. In doing so Bracewell became the first New Zealand spinner to take 10 wickets in a Test, and his rating leapt to 519.

The Australians remained in the doldrums. Boon and Marsh were beginning to make a name for themselves as an opening pair – Marsh notched up his first century in only his fourth Test, while Boon, in that horrific collapse at Auckland, became the tenth Australian to carry his bat in a completed innings – but the middle order retained its self-destructive streak. Phillips, a reluctant wicketkeeper at the best of times, handed his gloves over to Tim Zoehrer to concentrate on his batting, but he still didn't make many runs; while Greg Matthews, after his lively 130, scored only 18 runs in his next four innings. Allan Border, inevitably, stood out from his charges, with 290 runs at 72.5 and two match-saving centuries at Christchurch.

And the bowling was still a problem. No-one took many wickets: Gilbert, Bright and McDermott were particularly ineffective. Matthews and Reid did the most bowling, but they were steady rather than penetrative. The New Zealand batsmen didn't mind too much, especially Jeremy Coney, whose three innings were 101 not out, 98 and 93, while Martin Crowe's 137 at Christchurch was a superb attacking innings, the last 86 of which he scored after he had mishooked a ball from Reid into his jaw and sustained ten stitches.

The New Zealand bowling, after Cairns' retirement, was even thinner than usual, but Bracewell's success took some of the pressure off Hadlee, who nevertheless maintained his Olympian rating with 16 inexpensive wickets. Gillespie, Troup (yet again) and Robertson were tried out as Cairns' replacements – but none held onto his place. But it had been a good season for the New Zealand crocks, one that *Wisden* described, with unseemly relish, as 'a late flowering, and a full one, of their somewhat elderly team.'

WEST INDIES vs ENGLAND

First Test (Kingston, Jamaica 21–23 February) West Indies won by 10 wickets
England 1st Innings: 159 (Gooch 51, Lamb 49, Patterson 4–30)
West Indies 1st Innings: 307 (Greenidge 58, Gomes 56, Dujon 54, Ellison 5–78)
England 2nd Innings: 152 (Willey 71, Garner 3–22, Marshall 3–29, Patterson 3–44)
West Indies 2nd Innings: 5 for no wicket

Second Test (Port-of-Spain, Trinidad 7–12 March) West Indies won by 7 wickets

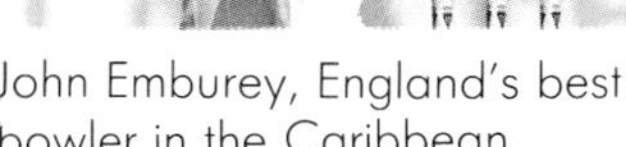

John Emburey, England's best bowler in the Caribbean.

Duleep Mendis, Sri Lanka's sturdily built skipper.

England 1st Innings: 176 (Gower 66, Lamb 62, Marshall 4–38, Garner 3–45)
West Indies 1st Innings: 399 (Richardson 102, Haynes 67, Marshall 62 not out, Emburey 5–78)
England 2nd Innings: 315 (Gower 47, Gooch 43, Lamb 40, Walsh 4–74, Marshall 4–94)
West Indies 2nd Innings: 95 for 3 (Greenidge 45)

Third Test (Bridgetown, Barbados 21–25 March) West Indies won by an innings and 30 runs
West Indies 1st Innings: 418 (Richardson 160, Haynes 84, Richards 51, Thomas 4–70, Foster 3–76)
England 1st Innings: 189 (Gower 66, Gooch 53, Marshall 4–42, Patterson 3–54)
England 2nd Innings: 199 (Robinson 43, Garner 4–69, Patterson 3–28, Holding 3–47)

Fourth Test (Port-of-Spain, Trinidad 3–5 April) West Indies won by 10 wickets
England 1st Innings: 200 (D.M. Smith 47, Garner 4–43, Holding 3–52)
West Indies 1st Innings: 312 (Richards 87, Gomes 48, Greenidge 42, Botham 5–71, Emburey 3–62)
England 2nd Innings: 150 (Garner 3–15, Marshall 3–42)
West Indies 2nd Innings: 39 for no wicket

Fifth Test (St John's, Antigua 11–16 April) West Indies won by 240 runs
West Indies 1st Innings: 474 (Haynes 131, Marshall 76, Holding 73, Harper 60)

England 1st Innings: 310 (Gower 90, Slack 52, Gooch 51, Garner 4–67, Marshall 3–64)
West Indies 2nd Innings: 246 for 2 declared (Richards 110 not out, Haynes 70)
England 2nd Innings: 170 (Gooch 51, Harper 3–10)

Captains: West Indies – I.V.A. Richards
England – D.I. Gower

Débuts: West Indies – C.A. Best, B.P. Patterson (1st Test), T.R.O. Payne (2nd Test)
England – D.M. Smith, J.G. Thomas (1st Test), W.N. Slack (2nd Test)

Rising Stars: West Indies – D.L. Haynes (+153 batting)
England – J.E. Emburey (+84 bowling)

Although perhaps we should have been used to it by now, the second successive 5–0 blackwash was a dispiriting experience for England supporters. 3–0 we could have coped with. Even 4–0 would have been a little encouraging. But England lost the lot, beaten by the relentless pace and accuracy of the West Indies and some fearsomely bad pitches.

Of England's large and relatively well-chosen squad – a spare opening batsman would have been nice, but never mind – only Gower and Emburey came even close to enhancing their reputations. Gower's average of 37 was nearly ten higher than the next man's (Gooch's), while Emburey, although he averaged only 32, removed Richardson six times on the trot. The rest had an awful time. Robinson, 4th in the world after Australia, averaged 9. Gooch, provoked by politicians for his part in the 1982 rebel tour to South Africa, succumbed to moody silence and low scores. Gatting, the only man in form, had his nose flattened by Marshall, and returned home for three weeks. When he returned, he immediately broke a thumb. Willey and Lamb started well but declined. David Smith top-scored at Port-of-Spain but then his back went. Downton's batting rating fell to 319, but still Bruce French did not get a game. Edmonds took few wickets but scored useful later order runs; ironically he was omitted after the third Test in favour of a batsman. Slack replaced Gatting, but by the time he found form at St John's, it was all a bit too late.

At the centre of this, two players: Ian Botham, who had an abysmal tour with bat and ball, and David Gower, whose style of captaincy did not prove equal to the demands made of it. Motivation was lax, practice non-existent, but the beaches were apparently in excellent shape.

In these conditions, Viv Richards' fifty-six-ball century in the final Test – the fastest ever in terms of balls received – was almost inevitable, so defeated and resigned had England become by then. In the meantime his bowlers had harvested their usual crop of wickets, 5 of them – Marshall, Garner, Patterson and Holding, plus Walsh who played in the second Test – averaging in the low 20s or below. Patrick Patterson was a new name, whose exploits in the Shell Shield had forced him into the side for the first Test, in which he took 7 wickets and set the tone for the series. Marshall and Garner each took 27 wickets in the five matches.

The batsmen too prospered: Haynes averaged 78, Richards 66, Richardson 55 and Harper in his two Tests a creditable 50. But then they were the better side and conditions were very much in their favour. At Kingston one of the sightscreens did not adequately frame the hands of bowlers more than six feet tall, i.e. all the West Indian bowlers. The England team management complained. The Jamaica Cricket Association said it couldn't be raised, as to do so would block the view of 200 spectators who had already bought their tickets. England lost by 10 wickets, and Patterson took all his 7 from that end.

SRI LANKA vs PAKISTAN

First Test (Kandy, 23–27 February) Pakistan won by an innings and 20 runs
Sri Lanka 1st Innings: 109 (Imran Khan 3–20, Abdul Qadir 3–29, Tauseef Ahmed 3–32)
Pakistan 1st Innings: 230 (Mudassar Nazar 81, Salim Malik 54, de Mel 3–50, R.J. Ratnayake 3–57)
Sri Lanka 2nd Innings: 101 (Tauseef Ahmed 6–45)

Second Test (Colombo, 14–18 March) Sri Lanka won by 8 wickets
Pakistan 1st Innings: 132 (Salim Malik 42, Kuruppuarachchi 5–44, de Mel 3–39)
Sri Lanka 1st Innings: 273 (Ranatunga 77, Wasim Akram 4–55)
Pakistan 2nd Innings: 172 (Qasim Omar 52, J.R. Ratnayeke 5–37, de Mel 3–79)
Sri Lanka 2nd Innings: 32 for 2

Third Test (Colombo, 22–27 March) Match Drawn
Sri Lanka 1st Innings: 281 (Mendis 58, Ranatunga 53, Mahanama 41, Imran Khan 4–69, Zakir Khan 3–80)
Pakistan 1st Innings: 318 (Ramiz Raja 122, J.R. Ratnayeke 4–116, Amalean 3–59)
Sri Lanka 2nd Innings: 323 for 3 (Ranatunga 135 not out, Gurusinha 116 not out)

Captains: Sri Lanka – L.R.D. Mendis
Pakistan – Imran Khan

Débuts: Sri Lanka – K.P.J. Warnaweera (1st Test), R.S. Mahanama, S.D. Anurasiri, A.K. Kuruppuarachchi (2nd Test), K.N. Amalean (3rd Test)
Pakistan – Zulqarnain (1st Test), Zakir Khan (3rd Test)

Rising Stars: Sri Lanka – A. Ranatunga (+217 batting)
Pakistan – Salim Malik (+42 batting)

First India, now Pakistan – it really had been a splendid season for Sri Lanka. Their victory in the second Test was marred, however, by the usual umpiring problems – the Pakistani team even considered doing a runner in protest, but in *Wisden*'s sage words, 'good sense prevailed'. Men in white coats aside, the main contributors were: the two Sri Lankan left-handed batsmen, Ranatunga (average 79) and Gurusinha (average 93.5); all those dodgy old seamers Sri Lanka always pick; Ramiz Raja, scorer of Pakistan's only century (and his first); and the tourists' strike bowlers, Imran Khan and Wasim Akram. Ranatunga indeed was so successful that he jumped into the world top ten, while Gurusinha's rating rose from 81 to 472. Untold numbers of one-day games were played between each Test.

WORLD TOP TWENTY AFTER 1985–86

BATTING

(6)	1.	I.V.A. Richards (West Indies)	881 (+73)
(12)	2.	D.L. Haynes (West Indies)	876 (+153)
(5)	3.	A.R. Border (Australia)	844 (+16)
(1)	4.	D.I. Gower (England)	834 (−42)
(3)	5.	C.H. Lloyd (West Indies)	802 (−41)
(9)	6.	J.V. Coney (New Zealand)	769 (+13)
(14)	7.	R.B. Richardson (West Indies)	764 (+105)
(39)	8.	A. Ranatunga (Sri Lanka)	763 (+259)
(8)	9.	C.G. Greenidge (West Indies)	758 (−33)
(2)	10.	M.W. Gatting (England)	750 (−97)
(29)	11.	M.D. Crowe (New Zealand)	723 (+160)
(10)	12.	Javed Miandad (Pakistan)	714 (−32)
(11)	13.	H.A. Gomes (West Indies)	696 (−32)
(22)	14.	M. Amarnath (India)	661 (+73)
(7)	15.	J.F. Reid (New Zealand)	645 (−155)
(23)	16.	Mudassar Nazar (Pakistan)	638 (+50)

(32)	17.	S.M. Gavaskar (India)	638 (+80)
(13)	18.	P.J.L. Dujon (West Indies)	637 (−51)
(16)	19.	Salim Malik (Pakistan)	632 (−1)
(15)	20.	G.A. Gooch (England)	632 (−27)

BOWLING

(1)	1.	M.D. Marshall (West Indies)	901 (+22)
(3)	2.	R.J. Hadlee (New Zealand)	900 (+30)
(8)	3.	J. Garner (West Indies)	811 (+106)
RE	4.	Imran Khan (Pakistan)	789
(4)	5.	M.A. Holding (West Indies)	786 (−41)
(6)	6.	Kapil Dev (India)	707 (−42)
(5)	7.	G.F. Lawson (Australia)	703 (−83)
(7)	8.	R.M. Ellison (England)	678 (−44)
(2)	9.	C.J. McDermott (Australia)	636 (−234)
(22)	10.	J.E. Emburey (England)	587 (+84)
(51)	11.	J.R. Ratnayeke (Sri Lanka)	586 (+309)
(24)	12.	R.A. Harper (West Indies)	576 (+94)
(10)	13.	I.T. Botham (England)	559 (−53)
(15)	14.	E.J. Chatfield (New Zealand)	556 (−32)
(11)	15.	Iqbal Qasim (Pakistan)	549 (−34)
(13)	16.	Azeem Hafeez (Pakistan)	547 (−34)
(43)	17.	Tauseef Ahmed (Pakistan)	542 (+207)
NE	18.	F.S. Ahangama (Sri Lanka)	523
(48)	19.	J.G. Bracewell (New Zealand)	519 (+329)
(19)	20.	Mudassar Nazar (Pakistan)	516 (+2)

England's tour of the West Indies had a dire effect on their ratings. Gower and Gatting retained their places in the top ten – although in Gatting's case, only just – while Tim Robinson, 4th after the 1985 season, dropped to 27th. (Lamb too dropped out of the twenty, to 25th.) Richards and Haynes took their places at the front of the grid, while Richie Richardson (Emburey notwithstanding) climbed to his highest position yet. Perhaps the biggest surprise of the season, though, was the progress of Ranatunga, whose runs against Pakistan when it mattered sent him hurtling up to 8th. Dropping out were Zaheer Abbas (20th to 23rd), Wessels (18th to 24th) and Qasim Omar (19th to 31st).

The bowling ratings, in the meantime, had the return of Imran Khan to worry about, as he steamed back in at 4th. Sri Lanka were represented for the first time by Ahangama and J.R. Ratnayeke (not to be confused with R.J. Ratnayake), while an unprecedented seven bowlers trickled out of the chart: Willis, Nick Cook and John of Sri Lanka (all under the 18-month rule), Wasim Akram (17th to 23rd), Shastri (16th to 26th), the retired Cairns (14th to 28th) and New Zealand's Boock (18th to 31st).

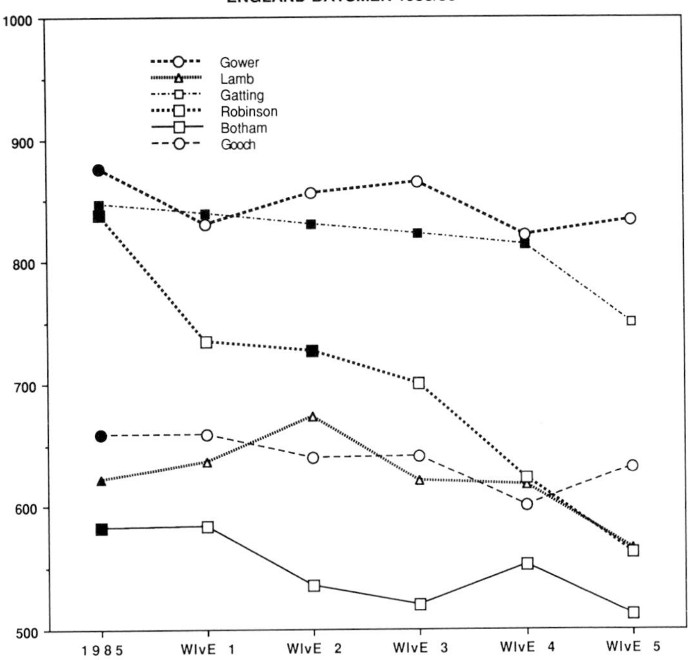
ENGLAND BATSMEN 1985/86
1000
900
800
700
600
500
Gower
Lamb
Gatting
Robinson
Botham
Gooch
1985
WIvE 1
WIvE 2
WIvE 3
WIvE 4
WIvE 5

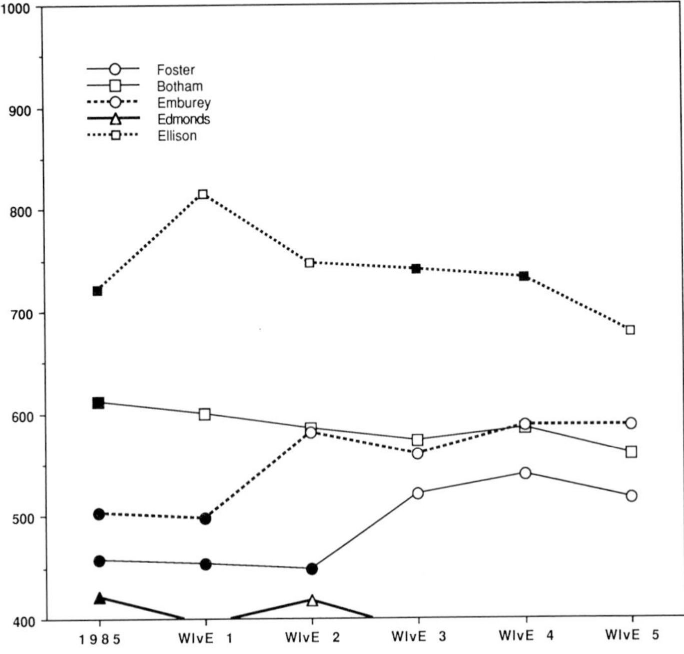
ENGLAND BOWLERS 1985/86
1000
900
800
700
600
500
400
Foster
Botham
Emburey
Edmonds
Ellison
1985
WIvE 1
WIvE 2
WIvE 3
WIvE 4
WIvE 5

AUSTRALIA BATSMEN 1985/86

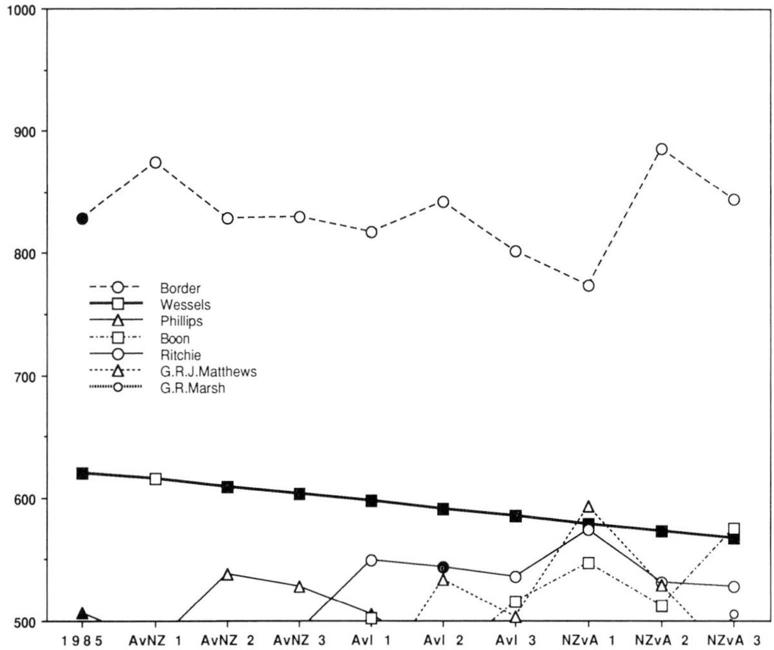

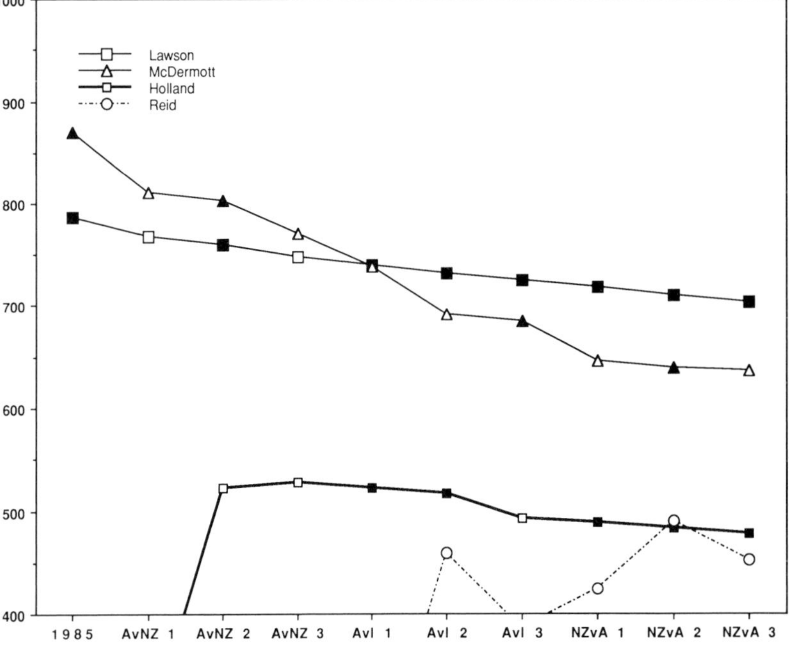

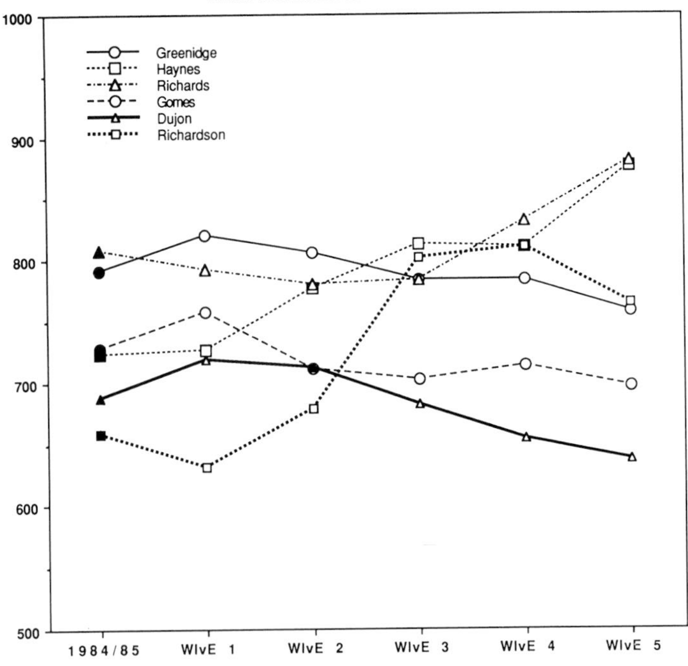
WEST INDIES BATSMEN 1985/86
Greenidge
Haynes
Richards
Gomes
Dujon
Richardson
1000
900
800
700
600
500
1984/85
WIvE 1
WIvE 2
WIvE 3
WIvE 4
WIvE 5

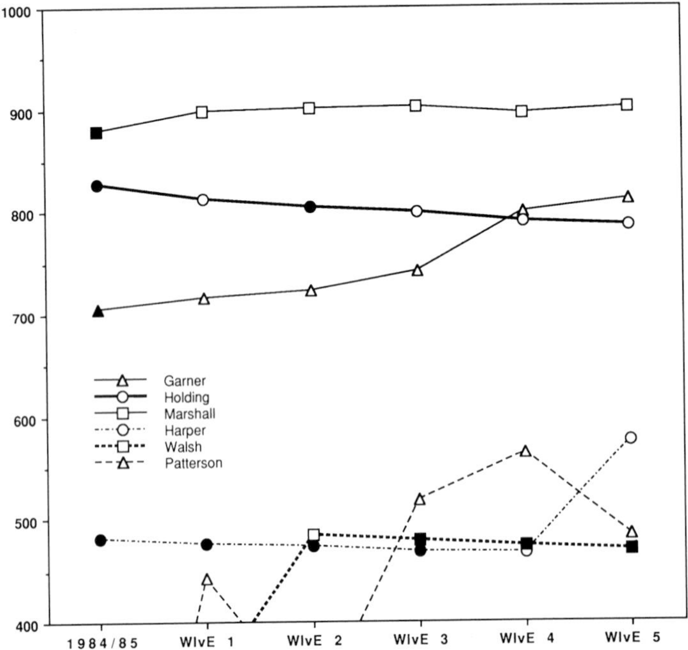
WEST INDIES BOWLERS 1985/86
Garner
Holding
Marshall
Harper
Walsh
Patterson
1000
900
800
700
600
500
400
1984/85
WIvE 1
WIvE 2
WIvE 3
WIvE 4
WIvE 5

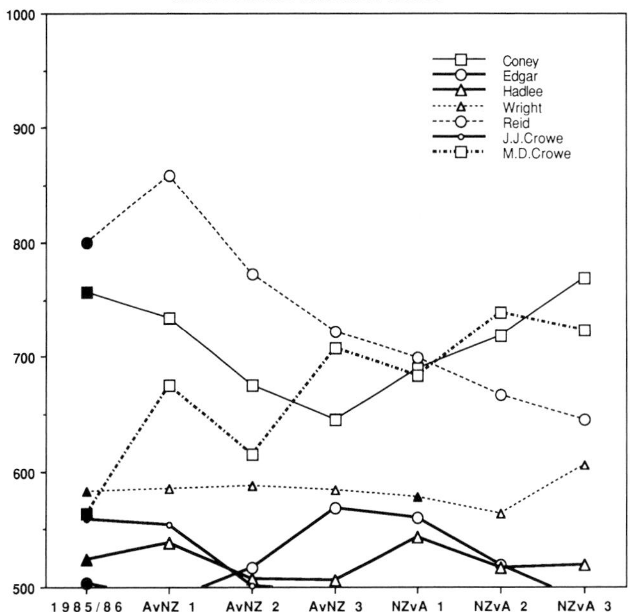

NEW ZEALAND BOWLERS 1985/86

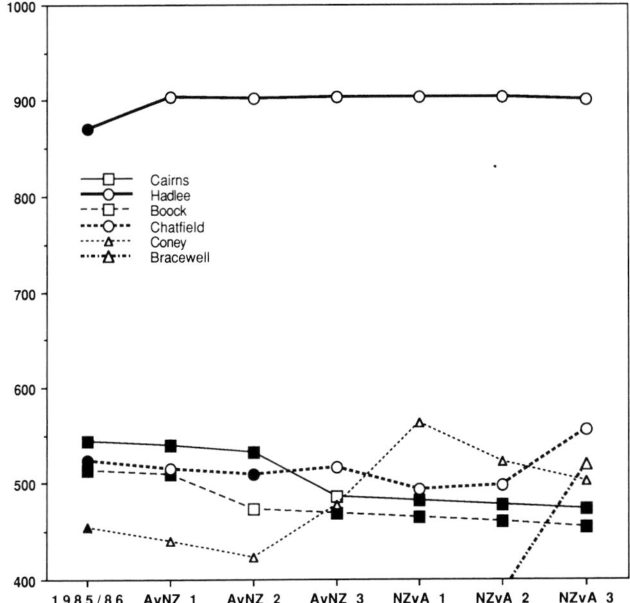

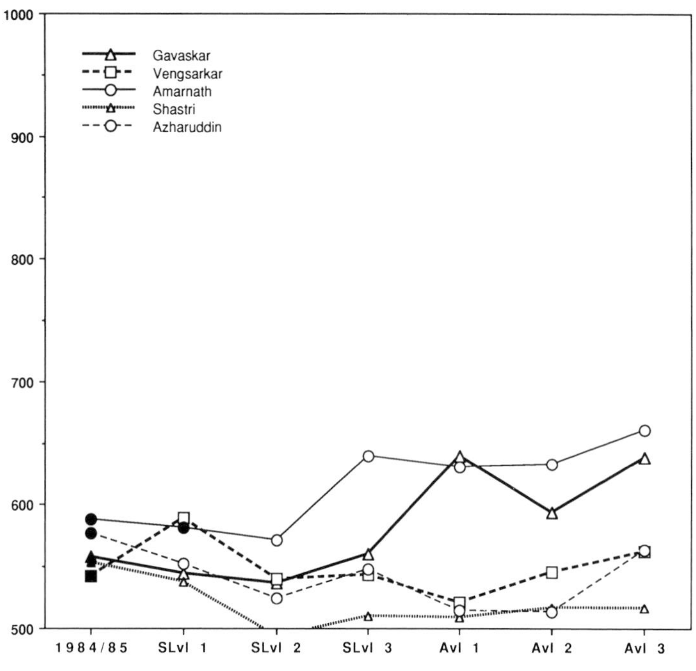
INDIA BATSMEN 1985/86
1000
900
800
700
600
500
Gavaskar
Vengsarkar
Amarnath
Shastri
Azharuddin
1984/85
SLvI 1
SLvI 2
SLvI 3
AvI 1
AvI 2
AvI 3

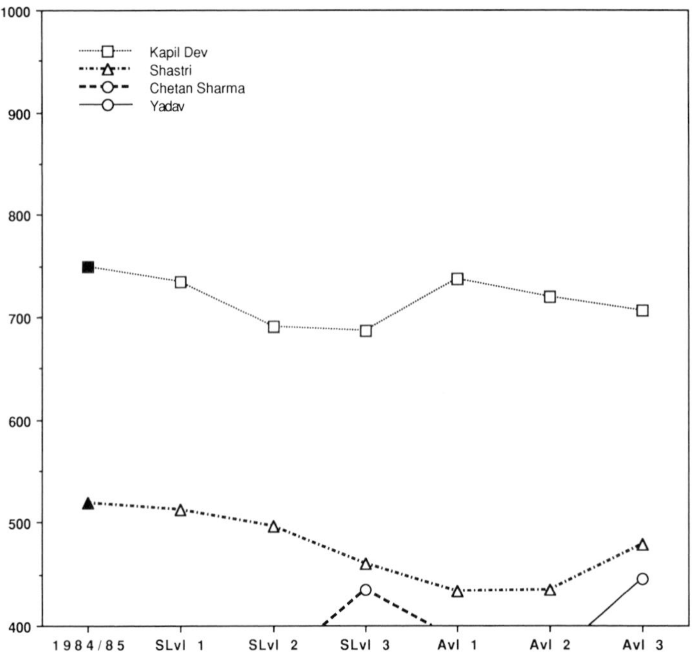
INDIA BOWLERS 1985/86
1000
900
800
700
600
500
400
Kapil Dev
Shastri
Chetan Sharma
Yadav
1984/85
SLvI 1
SLvI 2
SLvI 3
AvI 1
AvI 2
AvI 3

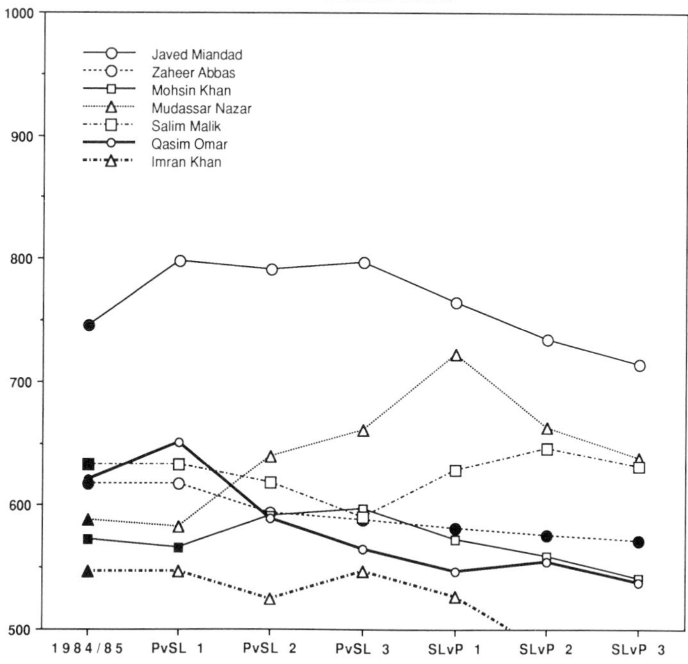
PAKISTAN BATSMEN 1985/86
1000
900
800
700
600
500
Javed Miandad
Zaheer Abbas
Mohsin Khan
Mudassar Nazar
Salim Malik
Qasim Omar
Imran Khan
1984/85
PvSL 1
PvSL 2
PvSL 3
SLvP 1
SLvP 2
SLvP 3

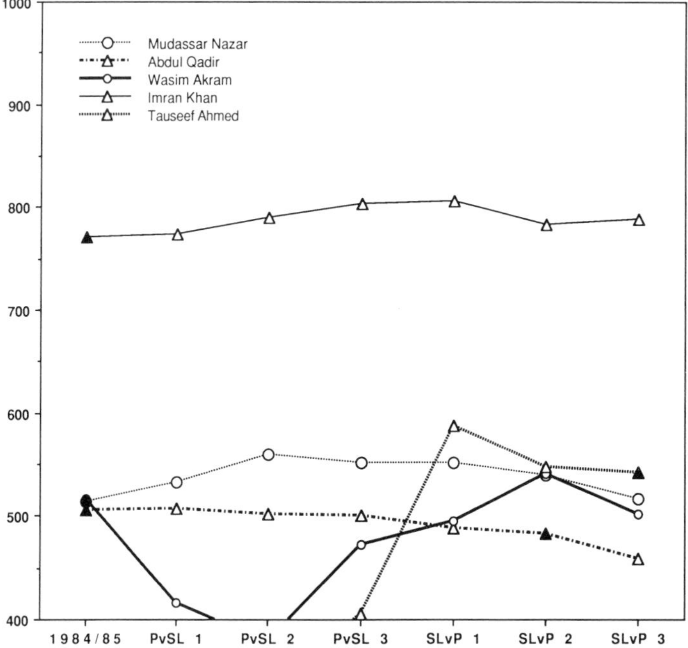
PAKISTAN BOWLERS 1985/86
1000
900
800
700
600
500
400
Mudassar Nazar
Abdul Qadir
Wasim Akram
Imran Khan
Tauseef Ahmed
1984/85
PvSL 1
PvSL 2
PvSL 3
SLvP 1
SLvP 2
SLvP 3

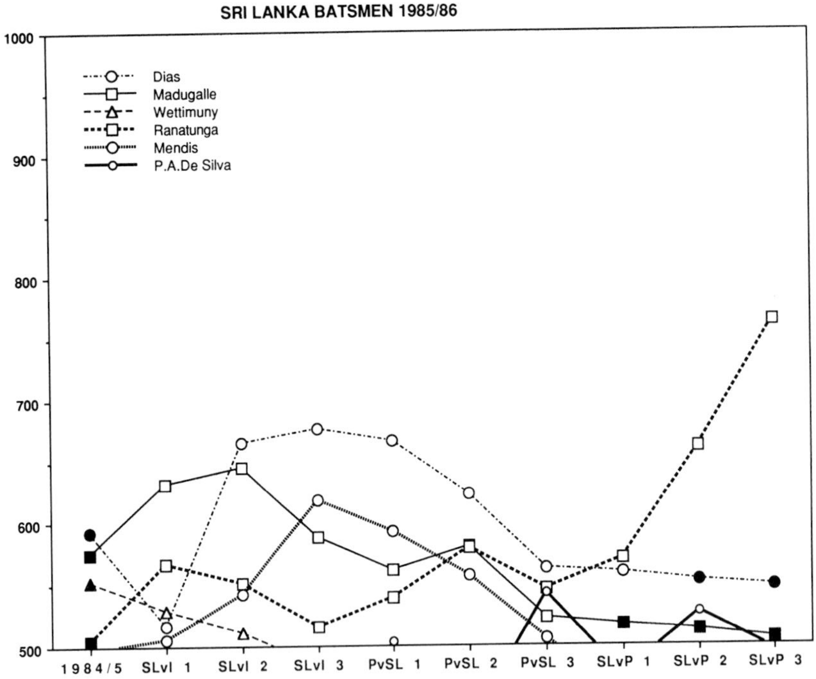

SRI LANKA BATSMEN 1985/86

Dias
Madugalle
Wettimuny
Ranatunga
Mendis
P.A.De Silva

1000
900
800
700
600
500

1984/5 SLvI 1 SLvI 2 SLvI 3 PvSL 1 PvSL 2 PvSL 3 SLvP 1 SLvP 2 SLvP 3

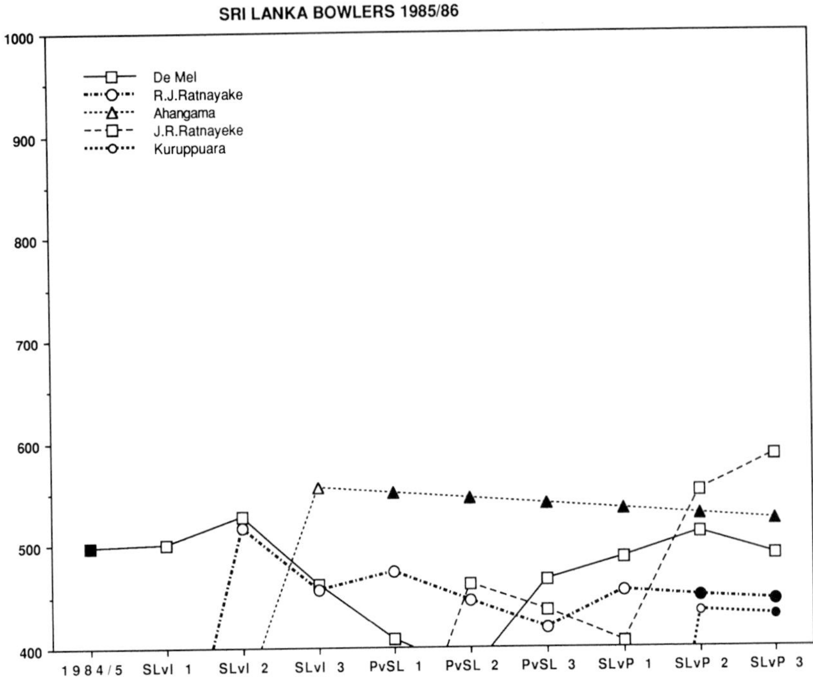

SRI LANKA BOWLERS 1985/86

De Mel
R.J.Ratnayake
Ahangama
J.R.Ratnayeke
Kuruppuara

1000
900
800
700
600
500
400

1984/5 SLvI 1 SLvI 2 SLvI 3 PvSL 1 PvSL 2 PvSL 3 SLvP 1 SLvP 2 SLvP 3

1986

ENGLAND vs INDIA

First Test (Lord's, 5–10 June) India won by 5 wickets
England 1st Innings: 294 (Gooch 114, Pringle 63, Chetan Sharma 5–64, Binny 3–55)
India 1st Innings: 341 (Vengsarkar 126 not out, Amarnath 69, Dilley 4–146, Pringle 3–58)
England 2nd Innings: 180 (Gatting 40, Kapil Dev 4–52, Maninder Singh 3–9)
India 2nd Innings: 136 for 5

Second Test (Headingley, 19–23 June) India won by 279 runs
India 1st Innings: 272 (Vengsarkar 61, Pringle 3–47, Dilley 3–54)
England 1st Innings: 102 (Binny 5–40, Madan Lal 3–18)
India 2nd Innings: 237 (Vengsarkar 102 not out, Lever 4–64, Pringle 4–73)
England 2nd Innings: 128 (Maninder Singh 4–26)

Third Test (Edgbaston, 3–8 July) Match Drawn
England 1st Innings: 390 (Gatting 183 not out, Gower 49, Pringle 44, Chetan Sharma 4–130)
India 1st Innings: 390 (Amarnath 79, Azharuddin 64, More 48, Binny 40, Foster 3–93)
England 2nd Innings: 235 (Gooch 40, Chetan Sharma 6–58)
India 2nd Innings: 174 for 5 (Gavaskar 54, Edmonds 4–31)

Captains: England – D.I. Gower (1st Test), M.W. Gatting (2nd & 3rd Tests)
India – Kapil Dev

Débuts: England – B.N. French (2nd Test), M.R. Benson, N.V. Radford (3rd Test)
India – K.S. More (1st Test), C.S. Pandit (2nd Test)

Rising Stars: England – M.W. Gatting (+68 batting)
India – Chetan Sharma (+296 bowling)

The series that saw the end of Gower's first captaincy tenure was another clear-cut disaster for England – their first series defeat to

India at home, and by a whopping 2–0 to boot. Gower was finally fired after the first Test, during which England's inability to dismiss India's tail (their last 2 wickets put on 77) and general batting ineptitude (Maninder's 3 for 9 was off 20.4 overs) gave Kapil Dev his first victory in twenty-one Tests as captain, and only India's second in England. They soon got their third, on a dismal pitch at Headingley, when for the first time since 1978 England took the pitch without Gower or Botham in the side. Gower's absence was due to injury, while Botham had been banned from all first-class cricket for two months after admitting he had ingested 'wacky baccy' at various points in his career.

India, though, did play very well. With Maninder (invariably referred to by Ray Illingworth on TV as 'Minander') and Chetan Sharma in the wickets, the bowling for once did not rely almost entirely on Kapil Dev. Sharma's rating rose from 350 to 696, while Maninder's 12 wickets at under 16 gave him only a 286 rating – but then the highest rated batsman he dismissed was Derek Pringle (258).

The star batsman was Dilip Vengsarkar, who scored two centuries and averaged 90, the highest by any Indian batsman on an England tour. Both at Lord's and Headingley, he passed three figures only when accompanied by the number 11 batsman. And his Lord's century was his third successive three-figure score there, a unique achievement.

The rest of the batting was prone to collapse, but not anywhere near as much as England's was. Amarnath, who missed the second Test through injury, was the next highest in the averages (43.00) but Azharuddin, Srikkanth and especially Shastri were less successful. Gavaskar was rather friskier than usual, apparently happier with a sprightly 45 than a laborious 145, but with Vengsarkar in such solid form, his unexpected change of approach did not weaken the batting.

Indeed, what really counted in the end was the sheer depth of India's batting. The wicketkeeper, Kiran More, batting at number 10, averaged 50, and even Maninder at number 11 wasn't completely hopeless. England, on the other hand, had Derek Pringle at number 6, which says it all, really. With only five batsmen, England had to rely on their established middle-order of Gower, Gatting and Lamb, with Gooch and 'A.N. Other' opening the innings. All except Gatting had a poor series. Gooch looked good at Lord's but faded, while his opening partner changed by the match – first the shell-shocked Robinson, then the out-of-form Wilf Slack, then, for one match only, the unfortunate Mark Benson. As the selectors vacillated, the team became more and more despondent, and only Gatting's brilliant unbeaten 183 at Edgbaston provided any respite – nudging him up to 4th in the world list in the process. The bowling too was chopped and changed – Ellison, Lever, Foster and Radford all played one Test each, and the top wicket-taker (13 at 23) was the generally steady Pringle. *Wisden* talked of 'the fear of failure' that appeared to have gripped the

Mike Gatting, the former captain, in typically pugnacious form.

team: with nineteen players chosen for the three Tests, it was hard to blame them.

ENGLAND vs NEW ZEALAND

First Test (Lord's, 24–29 July) Match Drawn
England 1st Innings: 307 (Moxon 74, Gower 62, Athey 44, Willey 44, Hadlee 6–80)

New Zealand 1st Innings: 342 (M.D. Crowe 106, Edgar 83, Coney 51, Dilley 4–82, Edmonds 4–97)
England 2nd Innings: 295 for 6 declared (Gooch 183, Willey 42, Gray 3–83)
New Zealand 2nd Innings: 41 for 2

Second Test (Trent Bridge, 7–12 August) New Zealand won by 8 wickets
England 1st Innings: 256 (Gower 71, Athey 55, Hadlee 6–80)
New Zealand 1st Innings: 413 (J.G. Bracewell 110, Hadlee 68, Wright 58, Gray 50, Small 3–88)
England 2nd Innings: 230 (Emburey 75, Hadlee 4–60, J.G. Bracewell 3–29)
New Zealand 2nd Innings: 77 for 2 (M.D. Crowe 48 not out)

Third Test (The Oval, 21–26 August) Match Drawn
New Zealand 1st Innings: 287 (Wright 119, Dilley 4–92, Botham 3–75)
England 1st Innings: 388 for 5 declared (Gower 131, Gatting 121, Botham 59 not out, Chatfield 3–73)
New Zealand 2nd Innings: 7 for no wicket

Captains: England – M.W. Gatting
New Zealand – J.V. Coney

Débuts: England – M.D. Moxon (1st Test), G.C. Small (2nd Test)
New Zealand – W. Watson (1st Test), T.E. Blain (3rd Test)

Rising Stars: England – G.R. Dilley (+45 bowling)
New Zealand – J.G. Bracewell (+31 bowling)

Still Botham-free, England continued on their losing ways. It was noticeable that when the all-rounder was eventually picked, for the third Test at the Oval, England's side was the most balanced and successful they had had all summer – indeed, it proved the basis for the successful touring side in Australia. By that time, the usual trillions of changes had been made – Benson shamefully dropped after scoring 21 and 30 in his only Test against India, Moxon given a couple of Tests and then abandoned, Radford and Foster found wanting, Willey and Greg Thomas briefly recalled, and Lamb brought back apparently for good. Athey, meanwhile, clung on by the skin of his teeth, and only injury at the Oval prevented Pringle from playing all six Tests in the summer – dark days for England indeed.

New Zealand, on the other hand, were a settled if ageing side, generally considered to be a year or two past their prime. With Hadlee and Chatfield both thirty-six, the former's commitment to his benefit year and the latter's injury problems enabled the New Zealand selectors to try out some possible replacements – but both Derek Stirling (a 146 rating after the third Test) and Willie Watson (a mere 34) were unimpressive. As a result the New Zealand seam bowling veered violently between the world-class (i.e. when Hadlee was bowling) and the pedestrian (when he wasn't). Nor were the spinners Gray and Bracewell exactly terrifying.

Both, though, were notably successful with the bat. Bracewell's 110 at Trent Bridge was his first century in Tests, and only his third in first-class cricket as a whole, his second having been the previous week. Although the side was again without Reid, who had chosen not to tour, Coney and Wright played well, and for the second time that summer, England had a world-class batsman in full flow to cope with, in the shape of Martin Crowe. Elegant and correct, he averaged 68 and looked even better.

For New Zealand, though, the tour's highlight was the victory at Trent Bridge, which helped them to their first ever series victory in England, 1–0. For this, the inspired (and inspirational) bowling of Hadlee was without doubt primarily responsible. His 19 wickets at 20.5 took him past Bob Willis in the all-time wicket-takers' table to 334, with only Lillee and Botham (who overtook Lillee at the Oval) in his sights. His rating, at around 900, barely faltered.

WORLD TOP TWENTY AFTER 1986

BATTING

(1)	1.	I.V.A. Richards (West Indies)	881
(2)	2.	D.L. Haynes (West Indies)	876
(3)	3.	A.R. Border (Australia)	844
(4)	4.	D.I. Gower (England)	772 (−62)
(7)	5.	R.B. Richardson (West Indies)	764
(8)	6.	A. Ranatunga (Sri Lanka)	763
(9)	7.	C.G. Greenidge (West Indies)	758
(10)	8.	M.W. Gatting (England)	748 (−2)
(11)	9.	M.D. Crowe (New Zealand)	743 (+20)
(6)	10.	J.V. Coney (New Zealand)	742 (−27)
(28)	11.	D.B. Vengsarkar (India)	717 (+155)
(12)	12.	Javed Miandad (Pakistan)	714
(13)	13.	H.A. Gomes (West Indies)	696
(14)	14.	M. Amarnath (India)	645 (−16)
(16)	15.	Mudassar Nazar (Pakistan)	638
(18)	16.	P.J.L. Dujon (West Indies)	637
(19)	17.	Salim Malik (Pakistan)	632

(15)	18.	J.F. Reid (New Zealand)	626 (−19)
(20)	19.	G.A. Gooch (England)	612 (−20)
(21)	20.	J.G. Wright (New Zealand)	593 (−17)

BOWLING

(1)	1.	M.D. Marshall (West Indies)	901
(2)	2.	R.J. Hadlee (New Zealand)	900 (−)
(3)	3.	J. Garner (West Indies)	811
(4)	4.	Imran Khan (Pakistan)	789
(5)	5.	M.A. Holding (West Indies)	786
(7)	6.	G.F. Lawson (Australia)	703
(46)	7.	Chetan Sharma (India)	696 (+346)
(6)	8.	Kapil Dev (India)	676 (−31)
(9)	9.	C.J. McDermott (Australia)	636
(8)	10.	R.M. Ellison (England)	590 (−88)
(11)	11.	J.R. Ratnayeke (Sri Lanka)	586
(14)	12.	E.J. Chatfield (New Zealand)	582 (+26)
(12)	13.	R.A. Harper (West Indies)	576
(19)	14.	J.G. Bracewell (New Zealand)	550 (+31)
(13)	15.	I.T. Botham (England)	548 (−11)
(10)	16.	J.E. Emburey (England)	545 (−42)
(17)	17.	Tauseef Ahmed (Pakistan)	542
(18)	18.	F.S. Ahangama (Sri Lanka)	523
(20)	19.	Mudassar Nazar (Pakistan)	516
(23)	20.	Wasim Akram (Pakistan)	502

The changes at the top of the batting list, or rather lack of them, do not really reflect the up-and-down turmoil of England's leading batsmen. After his 183 not out against India, Mike Gatting had been 4th with 818, with Gower down at 9th. One series later, they had virtually swapped positions. Most batting scores over the summer, though, showed a slow dribble downwards – only Vengsarkar showed any real improvement, reaching his highest score and position yet. Out of the chart: Gavaskar, who lost 52 rating points and fell from 17th to 21st, and the retired Clive Lloyd.

The bowling chart was more volatile, with Chetan Sharma's consistent performance paying substantial dividends and another new entry in Wasim Akram (who hadn't bowled a ball). Out, on the 18-month rule, were Iqbal Qasim and Azeem Hafeez, two Pakistani bowlers who had found themselves overshadowed by the more charismatic duo of Abdul Qadir and Imran Khan. Hadlee was unlucky, considering his immaculate bowling against England, to stay in only 2nd place. Ellison's slight drop concealed a catastrophic loss of form that had followed the disastrous West Indies tour – he was discarded after just one Test against India.

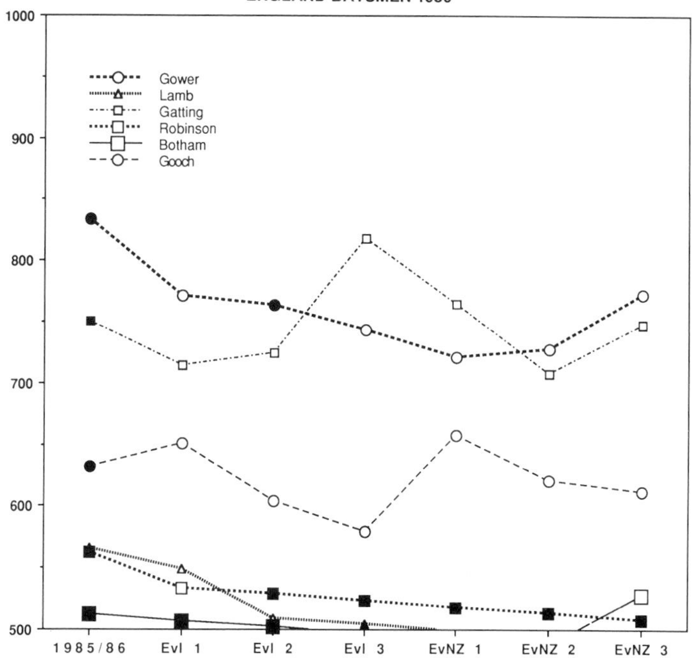
ENGLAND BATSMEN 1986
1000
900
800
700
600
500
Gower
Lamb
Gatting
Robinson
Botham
Gooch
1985/86
EvI 1
EvI 2
EvI 3
EvNZ 1
EvNZ 2
EvNZ 3

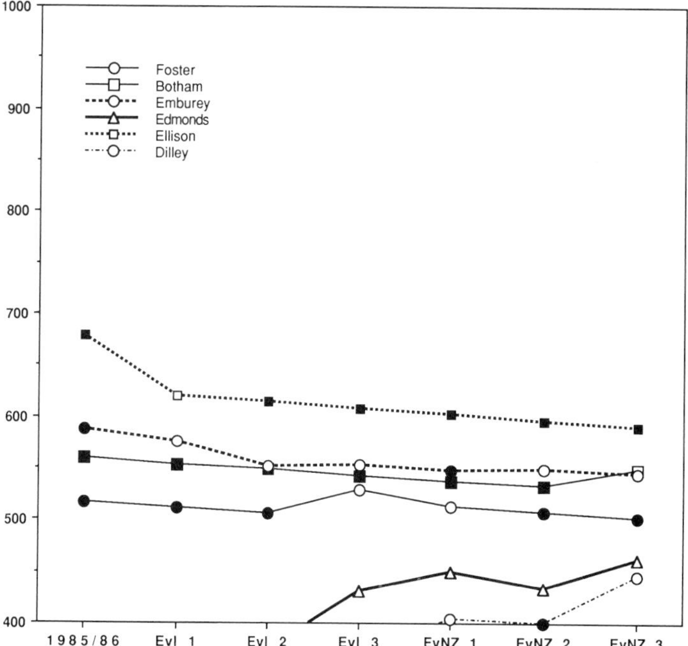
ENGLAND BOWLERS 1986
1000
900
800
700
600
500
400
Foster
Botham
Emburey
Edmonds
Ellison
Dilley
1985/86
EvI 1
EvI 2
EvI 3
EvNZ 1
EvNZ 2
EvNZ 3

NEW ZEALAND BATSMEN 1986

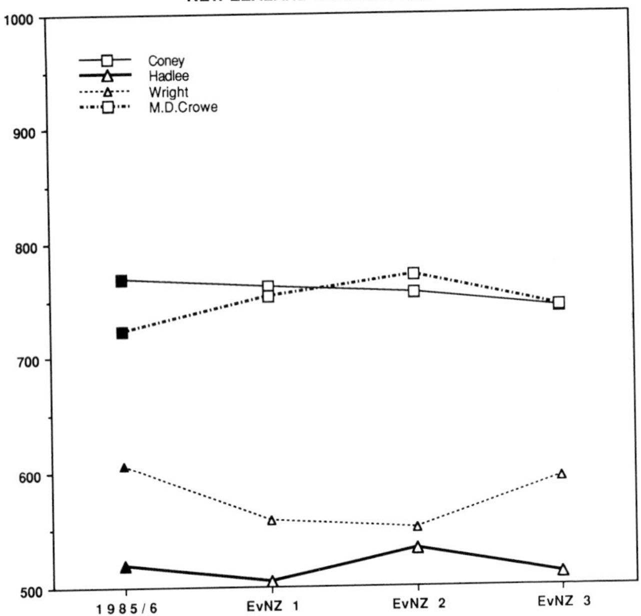
Coney
Hadlee
Wright
M.D.Crowe
1000
900
800
700
600
500
1985/6
EvNZ 1
EvNZ 2
EvNZ 3

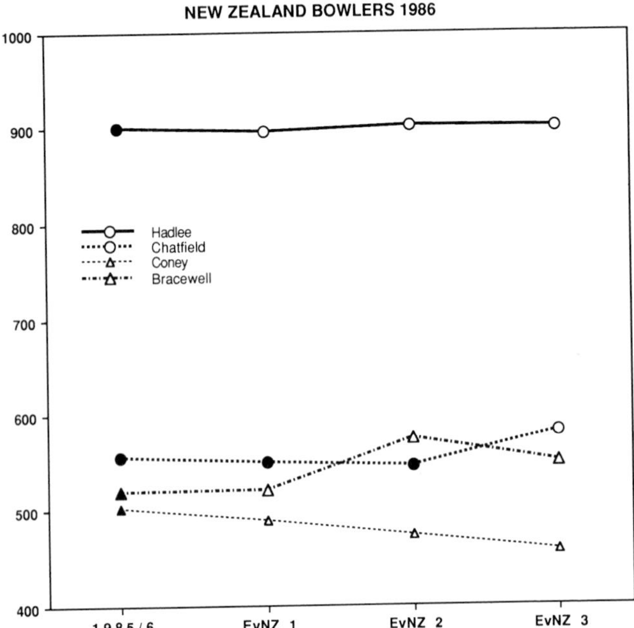
NEW ZEALAND BOWLERS 1986
Hadlee
Chatfield
Coney
Bracewell
1000
900
800
700
600
500
400
1985/6
EvNZ 1
EvNZ 2
EvNZ 3

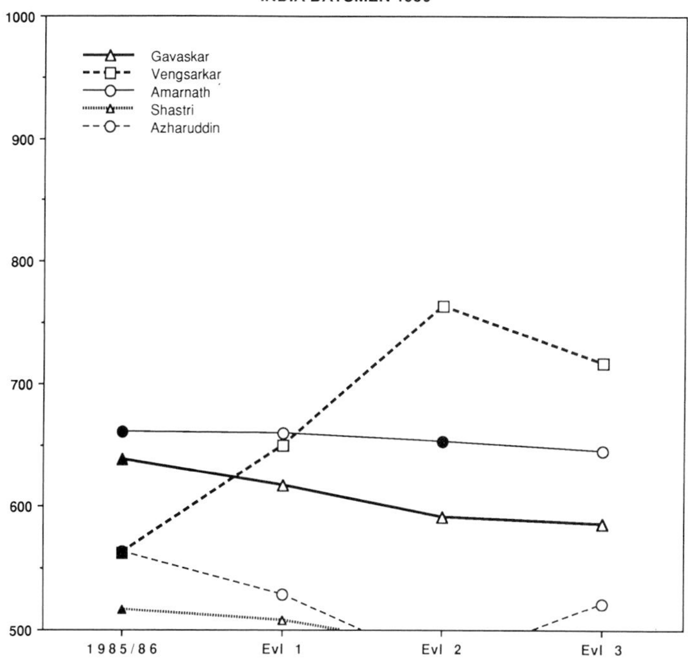
INDIA BATSMEN 1986
1000
900
800
700
600
500
Gavaskar
Vengsarkar
Amarnath
Shastri
Azharuddin
1985/86
Evl 1
Evl 2
Evl 3

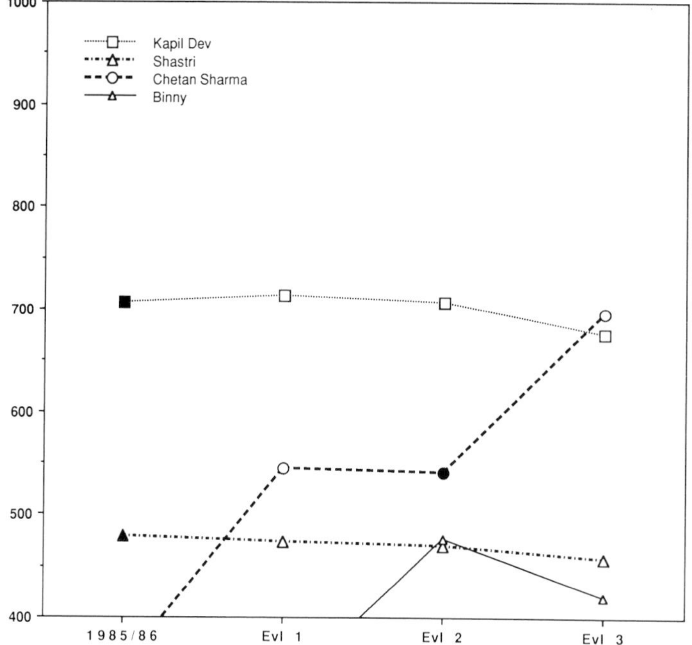
INDIA BOWLERS 1986
1000
900
800
700
600
500
400
Kapil Dev
Shastri
Chetan Sharma
Binny
1985/86
Evl 1
Evl 2
Evl 3

1986–87

INDIA vs AUSTRALIA

First Test (Madras, 18–22 September) Match Tied
Australia 1st Innings: 574 for 7 declared (Jones 210, Boon 122, Border 106, G.R.J. Matthews 44, Yadav 4–142)
India 1st Innings: 397 (Kapil Dev 119, Shastri 62, Srikkanth 53, Azharuddin 50, G.R.J. Matthews 5–103)
Australia 2nd Innings: 170 for 5 declared (Boon 49, Maninder Singh 3–60)
India 2nd Innings: 347 (Gavaskar 90, Amarnath 51, Shastri 48 not out, Azharuddin 42, Bright 5–94, G.R.J. Matthews 5–146)

Second Test (Delhi, 26–30 September) Match Drawn
Australia 1st Innings: 207 for 3 declared (Boon 67, Zoehrer 52 not out)
India 1st Innings: 107 for 3

Third Test (Bombay, 15–19 October) Match Drawn
Australia 1st Innings: 345 (G.R. Marsh 101, Boon 47, Border 46, Yadav 4–84, Kulkarni 3–85)
India 1st Innings: 517 for 5 declared (Vengsarkar 164 not out, Shastri 121 not out, Gavaskar 103, G.R.J. Matthews 4–158)
Australia 2nd Innings: 216 for 2 (Jones 73 not out, Border 66 not out, Boon 40)

Captains: India – Kapil Dev
Australia – A.R. Border

Débuts: India – R. R. Kulkarni (3rd Test)

Rising Stars: India – R. J. Shastri (+99 batting)
Australia – G.R.J. Matthews (+177 bowling)

What had been intended as a mere warm-up series for the Ashes produced one of the most gripping Test matches of all time, when India, presented with 348 to win in a minimum of eighty-seven overs, contrived to be all out for 347 to the penultimate ball of the match. It was only the second tied Test in history: the first, between Australia and West Indies at the 'Gabba, had come twenty-six years and 554 Tests before.

Unlike that famously enthralling result, though, the possibility of a close result only emerged in the match's later stages. Australia had dominated the first three days' play, with Dean Jones celebrating his return to Test cricket with 210, his first Test century, Boon scoring his third (all against India) and Border his nineteeth. At the end of the second day India were 270 for 7, 105 away for from saving the follow-on, and with Kapil Dev (33 not out) and Chetan Sharma (14 not out) at the wicket. But after Kapil's match-saving century and some swift pre-declaration hefting from the Australians, India were given that tempting target. After a 103-run stand for the second wicket between Gavaskar (in his 100th consecutive Test appearance) and Amarnath, India came into tea at 190 for 2 – 158 needed off thirty overs. But wickets fell, and when Yadav was bowled by Bright, they needed 4 runs off eight balls, with just one wicket remaining, and Shastri and Maninder (probably still being described as 'Minander' by Ray Illingworth) at the crease. Shastri got 3 of them, but with three balls left, Maninder faced Greg Matthews (who had been bowling unchanged since the ninth over) and the second one he missed.

Heart-stopping stuff indeed, and Australian ratings improved accordingly. Jones' three-year absence from Tests had brought his rating down to 139, but it immediately jumped above 400, and it has never since dropped below. Matthews, whose first and second 5-wicket returns these were, climbed from 396 to 538, and his batting rating improved too.

After this, of course, the final two Tests were always going to be anti-climactic, although no-one perhaps foresaw quite how much. For the second Test it rained, while the last, potentially interesting Test, drifted off into a draw as the pitch became easier and easier – only 2 wickets fell on the fourth day and none on the fifth. Vengsarkar and Shastri's no doubt thrilling (and unbeaten) sixth-wicket stand of 298 was a record for any stand against Australia, and for the sixth wicket against anyone. Only its sublime irrelevance stopped it from pushing their ratings through the roof.

PAKISTAN vs WEST INDIES

First Test (Faisalabad, 24–29 October) Pakistan won by 186 runs
Pakistan 1st Innings: 159 (Imran Khan 61, Gray 4–39, Marshall 3–48)
West Indies 1st Innings: 248 (Richardson 54, Haynes 40, Wasim Akram 6–91)
Pakistan 2nd Innings: 328 (Wasim Akram 66, Salim Yousuf 61, Qasim Omar 48, Mohsin Khan 40, Walsh 3–49)
West Indies 2nd Innings: 53 (Abdul Qadir 6–16, Imran Khan 4–30)

Second Test (Lahore, 7–9 November) West Indies won by an innings and 10 runs
Pakistan 1st Innings: 131 (Javed Miandad 46, Marshall 5–33, Walsh 3–56)
West Indies 1st Innings: 218 (Greenidge 75, Richards 44, Imran Khan 5–59, Abdul Qadir 4–96)
Pakistan 2nd Innings: 77 (Walsh 4–21, Gray 3–20)

Third Test (Karachi, 20–25 November) Match Drawn
West Indies 1st Innings: 240 (Richards 70, Richardson 44, Abdul Qadir 4–107)
Pakistan 1st Innings: 239 (Javed Miandad 76, Ramiz Raja 62, Butts 4–73, Gray 3–40)
West Indies 2nd Innings: 211 (Haynes 88 not out, Imran Khan 6–46, Abdul Qadir 3–84)
Pakistan 2nd Innings: 125 for 7 (Marshall 3–31)

Captains: Pakistan – Imran Khan
West Indies – I.V.A. Richards

Débuts: Pakistan – Asif Mujtaba (2nd Test), Saleem Jaffer (3rd Test)
West Indies – A.H. Gray (1st Test)

Rising Stars: Pakistan – Abdul Qadir (+113 bowling)
West Indies – C.A. Walsh (+116 bowling)

So which was the best team in the world? The two leading contenders, Pakistan and West Indies, met in a close-fought series that didn't really provide any answers. Injury, illness and the absence of Garner and Holding, who were not available to tour, meant that neither side was ever at full strength, and some dodgy Pakistan pitches made batting far harder than it should have been. No-one on either side made a century, and only two batsmen – Haynes and Richards – averaged over 30. The bowlers, though, had a field day. Imran Khan and Abdul Qadir took 18 wickets each (at 11.05 and 20.05 respectively) and Wasim Akram, until injured just before Karachi, supported them well with 6 equally cheap wickets. For the tourists, Marshall was pre-eminent as ever, with 16 wickets at 16.62. Tony Gray, in his first three Tests, was no less hostile, with 14 wickets at 16.21 (and a rating of 452), and even the off-spinner Clyde Butts was given a good bowl, coming away from Karachi with match figures of 6 for 95.

Pakistan, though, did well to draw the series, especially after Salim Malik had had his arm broken in the first Test by a Courtney Walsh lifter. Throughout the Tests and one-day internationals they experimented with different opening line-ups, although it was no surprise when they eventually settled on the old firm of Mohsin and Mudassar. Qasim Omar and Ramiz Raja were quite out of form (although

Ramiz's 62 at Karachi bumped up his rating by 141 points), but it's bowling that wins matches, and Pakistan were indebted to the brilliance of Qadir and Imran for their victory at Faisalabad. The West Indies took their revenge at Lahore, the only pitch that assisted their quickies.

AUSTRALIA vs ENGLAND

First Test (Brisbane, 14–19 November) England won by 7 wickets
England 1st Innings: 456 (Botham 138, Athey 76, Gatting 61, Gower 51, Lamb 40, DeFreitas 40, Waugh 3–76, C.D. Matthews 3–95, M.G. Hughes 3–134)
Australia 1st Innings: 248 (G.R.J. Matthews 56 not out, G.R. Marsh 56, Ritchie 41, Dilley 5–68)
Australia 2nd Innings: 282 (G.R. Marsh 110, Ritchie 45, Emburey 5–80, DeFreitas 3–62)
England 2nd Innings: 77 for 3

Second Test (Perth, 28 November–3 December) Match Drawn
England 1st Innings: 592 for 8 declared (Broad 162, Gower 136, Richards 133, Athey 96, Reid 4–115, C.D. Matthews 3–112)
Australia 1st Innings: 401 (Border 125, Waugh 71, G.R.J. Matthews 45, Dilley 4–79)
England 2nd Innings: 199 for 8 declared (Gatting 70, Gower 48, Waugh 5–69, Reid 3–58)
Australia 2nd Innings: 197 for 4 (Jones 69, G.R. Marsh 49)

Third Test (Adelaide, 12–16 December) Match Drawn
Australia 1st Innings: 514 for 5 declared (Boon 103, Jones 93, Waugh 79 not out, G.R.J. Matthews 73 not out, Border 70, G.R. Marsh 43)
England 1st Innings: 455 (Broad 116, Gatting 100, Athey 55, Emburey 49, Reid 4–64, Sleep 4–132)
Australia 2nd Innings: 201 for 3 declared (Border 100 not out, G.R.J. Matthews 46 not out, G.R. Marsh 41)
England 2nd Innings: 39 for 2

Fourth Test (Melbourne, 26–28 December) England won by an innings and 14 runs
Australia 1st Innings: 141 (Jones 59, Botham 5–41, Small 5–48)
England 1st Innings: 349 (Broad 112, Lamb 43, Gatting 40, Reid 4–78, McDermott 4–83)
Australia 2nd Innings: 194 (G.R. Marsh 60, Waugh 49, Edmonds 3–45)

Fifth Test (Sydney, 10–15 January) Australia won by 55 runs
Australia 1st Innings: 343 (Jones 184 not out, Small 5–75, Edmonds 3–79)
England 1st Innings: 275 (Gower 72, Emburey 69, Richards 46, P.L. Taylor 6–78)
Australia 2nd Innings: 251 (Waugh 73, Border 49, P.L. Taylor 42, Emburey 7–78)
England 2nd Innings: 264 (Gatting 96, Sleep 5–72)

Captains: Australia – A.R. Border
England – M.W. Gatting

Débuts: Australia – C.D. Matthews (1st Test), G.C. Dyer (3rd Test), P.L. Taylor (5th Test)
England – P.A.J. DeFreitas, C.J. Richards (1st Test), J.J. Whitaker (3rd Test)

Rising Stars: Australia – D.M. Jones (+212 batting)
England – B.C. Broad (+233 batting)

At this point, it's hard not to feel sorry for Allan Border. Diligently attempting to rebuild his decimated Australian team, even he must have felt confident when faced with an England side that hadn't won a Test for eighteen months, were without their best batsman, Graham Gooch, and were captained by a relative novice whose first few months in the job – three Tests drawn, and two lost, one to India, one to New Zealand – had hardly been auspicious.

Once again, though, Border's luck turned against him, and England retained the Ashes 2–1 with some style. Central to their success was the fast bowling of Small, DeFreitas and Dilley, and the makeshift opening partnership of Athey and Broad – a match hardly made in heaven, but far more effective than anyone could have dared hope. Athey averaged just 33 (and his rating rose to a still modest 347) but he played an important subsidiary role while the left-handed Broad scored all the runs. With three successive centuries in the series (something only Hobbs and Hammond had achieved before), he was named International Player of the Season, an award he fully deserved. While pugnacious in the extreme, he hadn't yet developed the stump-smashing and umpire-glaring habits that were, in the end, to abbreviate his Test career.

Not that he was the only batsmen to thrive. Gower too hit form after an unconvincing start (he was out for a pair in the first state game), and eventually finished second in the Test averages (57) to Broad (69). Even so, had he not been dropped for 0 in the first innings of the first Test, the series may well have panned out rather differently. England would have been 198 for 5, and the 456 they did finally reach – a winning score on the pitch – would probably have been beyond them. But their victory there was not least due to Ian Botham's powerful and controlled 138 (off 174 balls), his first century for twenty-two Test matches (and probably his last). If he didn't do much in the series after that, he proved an invaluable team member throughout (particularly in the encouragement of the youthful DeFreitas) and played more than usefully in England's one-day successes later in the season.

DeFreitas, after a good start (5 wickets and a bowling rating of 340 in his first match at Brisbane), drifted off a little, and ended with batting and bowling ratings of 219 and 150 respectively. Small, injured at the start of the series and then kept out by Dilley and DeFreitas, took advantage of his opportunity in the last two Tests and headed the averages, with 12 wickets at 15. Edmonds and Emburey bowled more overs than anyone, conceding between them a mere 2.08 runs per over.

It wasn't a successful tour for everyone, though. Allan Lamb played every Test, failed to score a fifty, averaged just 18, and saw his rating drop to 396, its lowest level since 1982. Wilf Slack and Neil Foster did not play at all, while James Whitaker replaced the injured Botham for one Test only. Bruce French, on his first tour as England's first-choice wicketkeeper, found himself displaced for all five Tests by his deputy, Jack Richards, whose century (and average of 37.71) gave him a series' end rating of 327.

The Australians were let down by the inexperience of their bowling attack. When Lawson (strangely out of favour after his recovery from injury) was left out of the eleven at Brisbane, the three pace bowlers chosen – Reid, Merv Hughes and Chris Matthews – had played just nine Tests between them. McDermott was not considered – conflicting coaching advice had inevitably led to a loss of form – and only Reid during the series made any real advance, taking 20 wickets at 26.35 and jumping in the ratings from 317 to 575. The all-rounder Waugh, with a more modest set of figures, also rose through the ranks, from 307 to 502. But by the series' end Hughes had reached only 203, and Chris Matthews (241) had been dropped.

The team's batting had rather more substance. Geoff Marsh was at his most determined, while Dean Jones scored another of his huge imperious centuries in the victory at Sydney, to move up to 11th in the world. Jones, Greg Matthews and Border all averaged over 50, while Waugh (whose rating again rose substantially, from 235 to 432) was just behind. Only Boon, his century apart, was less successful, scoring just 41 runs in his other seven innings.

For the home team, though, the performance of the summer was that of Peter Taylor, an unknown thirty-year-old off-spinner who had only ever played six times for his state New South Wales. Assumed by everyone except the selectors to be a misprint for the NSW opener Mark Taylor (who was eventually picked two years later), he took 6 for 76 in his first match at Sydney, and also scored a valuable 42 –

fairytale stuff, to be sure. In a disappointing season for Australian supporters, his remarkable match-winning début was a glorious consolation.

INDIA vs SRI LANKA

First Test (Kanpur, 17–22 December) Match Drawn
Sri Lanka 1st Innings: 420 (J.R. Ratnayeke 93, Wettimuny 79, Ranatunga 52, Dias 50, Arun 3–76)
India 1st Innings: 676 for 7 (Azharuddin 199, Gavaskar 176, Kapil Dev 163, Vengsarkar 57, J.R. Ratnayeke 4–132)

Second Test (Nagpur, 27–31 December) India won by an innings and 106 runs
Sri Lanka 1st Innings: 204 (Ranatunga 59, Yadav 5–76, Maninder Singh 3–56)
India 1st Innings: 451 for 6 declared (Vengsarkar 153, Amarnath 131, Gavaskar 74, Lamba 53)
Sri Lanka 2nd Innings: 141 (J.R. Ratnayeke 54, Maninder Singh 7–51)

Third Test (Cuttack, 4–7 January) India won by an innings and 67 runs
India 1st Innings: 400 (Vengsarkar 166, Kapil Dev 60, Srikkanth 40, J.R. Ratnayeke 5–85, Anurasiri 4–71)
Sri Lanka 1st Innings: 191 (Dias 49, Gurusinha 40, Maninder Singh 4–41, Kapil Dev 4–69)
Sri Lanka 2nd Innings: 142 (Shastri 4–11, Yadav 3–32)

Captains: India – Kapil Dev
Sri Lanka – L.R.D. Mendis

Débuts: India – R. Lamba, B. Arun (1st Test)
Sri Lanka – G.F. Labrooy (1st Test)

Rising Stars: India – Maninder Singh (+143 bowling)
Sri Lanka – J.R. Ratnayeke (+9 bowling)

Sri Lanka's Rising Star award here says it all. After their splendid victory at home to India the previous season, they played away and were solidly trounced. Their batting fell apart, their bowling was innocuous, and the Indians had two players, Vengsarkar and Maninder Singh, at the very peak of form. Indeed, Vengsarkar's 376 runs at an average of a mere 125.33 (no not outs) gave him the number one spot on the world list, a position he was to retain for the best part of two years.

India's secret weapon, as so often, was their pitches – a 'sporting' one at Nagpur and a disgraceful one at Cuttack suited the home side's spin attack very nicely, thank you, and the Sri Lankans lost their wickets, their confidence and finally their nerve. Kapil Dev's decline as a strike bowler, increasingly evident in the previous year, became irrelevant. The accurate and attacking spin bowling of Yadav and Maninder, who finally crossed that elusive 400 threshold, proved rather more significant.

INDIA vs PAKISTAN

First Test (Madras, 3–8 February) Match Drawn
Pakistan 1st Innings: 487 for 9 declared (Imran Khan 135 not out, Shoaib Mohammad 101, Javed Miandad 94, Wasim Akram 62, Maninder Singh 5–135)
India 1st Innings: 527 for 9 declared (Srikkanth 123, Vengsarkar 96, Gavaskar 91, Amarnath 89, Shastri 41, Tauseef Ahmed 3–189)
Pakistan 2nd Innings: 182 for 3 (Rizwan-uz-Zaman 54 not out, Javed Miandad 54, Shoaib Mohammad 45)

Second Test (Calcutta, 11–16 February) Match Drawn
India 1st Innings: 403 (Azharuddin 141, Kapil Dev 66, Binny 52 not out, Arun Lal 52, Wasim Akram 5–96)
Pakistan 1st Innings: 229 (Ramiz Raja 69, Rizwan-uz-Zaman 60, Binny 6–56)
India 2nd Innings: 181 for 3 declared (Arun Lal 70, Vengsarkar 41 not out)
Pakistan 2nd Innings: 179 for 5 (Javed Miandad 63 not out, Salim Yousuf 43)

Third Test (Jaipur, 21–26 February) Match Drawn
India 1st Innings: 465 for 8 declared (Shastri 125, Azharuddin 110, Kapil Dev 50, Amarnath 49, Srikkanth 45)
Pakistan 1st Innings: 341 (Ramiz Raja 114, Imran Khan 66, Javed Miandad 50, Gopal Sharma 4–88)
India 2nd Innings: 114 for 2 (Srikkanth 51)

Fourth Test (Ahmedabad, 4–9 March) Match Drawn
Pakistan 1st Innings: 395 (Ijaz Faqih 105, Imran Khan 72, Manzoor Elahi 52, Ramiz Raja 41, Younis Ahmed 40, Yadav 4–109, Kapil Dev 3–46)
India 1st Innings: 323 (Vengsarkar 109, Gavaskar 63, Kapil Dev 50 not out, Wasim Akram 4–60)
Pakistan 2nd Innings: 136 for 2 (Rizwan-uz-Zaman 58)

Fifth Test (Bangalore, 13–17 March) Pakistan won by 16 runs
Pakistan 1st Innings: 116 (Maninder Singh 7–27)
India 1st Innings: 145 (Vengsarkar 50, Iqbal Qasim 5–48, Tauseef Ahmed 5–54)
Pakistan 2nd Innings: 249 (Ramiz Raja 47, Salim Yousuf 41 not out, Shastri 4–69, Maninder Singh 3–99)
India 2nd Innings: 204 (Gavaskar 96, Iqbal Qasim 4–73, Tauseef Ahmed 4–85)

Captains: India – Kapil Dev
Pakistan – Imran Khan

Débuts: Pakistan – Ijaz Ahmed (1st Test)

Rising Stars: India – R.M.H. Binny (+95 bowling)
Pakistan – Ramiz Raja (+77 bowling)

One of those interminable series that gives modern Test cricket a bad name. These five Tests, played virtually back to back, produced just one positive result, when an underprepared pitch was ordered at Bangalore to sort the sheep from the goats (both of which species no doubt having acted as assistant groundsmen). Before that, the four successive draws had brought the current run between the countries to 11, as batsmen on both sides scored mightily and bowlers toiled on easy-paced wickets. With Kapil Dev now in seemingly permanent decline – his 11 wickets cost a smidgeon under 40 runs apiece – most Indian hopes lay with Maninder Singh, whose improvement fortunately continued. But although India built up strong positions in the second and fourth Tests, they were unable to force a win in either. Hence the 'result wicket' at Bangalore, where India's batting, hitherto so resolute, came unstuck. It was Pakistan's first series win in India.

Their victory was all the more impressive for the fact that none of their bowlers averaged under 30. No-one struggled more than Abdul Qadir, who took 4 for 242 in the series at an average of 60.5. The best Indian batting came from Srikkanth and Azharuddin, although Vengsarkar was again the highest scorer, averaging over 67, and Gavaskar, who ended his record sequence of 106 consecutive appearances when he withdrew for 'personal reasons' from the second Test, passed 10,000 Test runs at Ahmedabad. Pakistan's most prolific batsman was the rapidly improving opener Ramiz Raja, who with Rizwan-uz-Zaman was preferred to an out-of-form Mudassar. Imran was in good touch too, averaging 64.8, while Javed was his usual consistent self.

NEW ZEALAND vs WEST INDIES

First Test (Wellington, 20–24 February) Match Drawn
New Zealand 1st Innings: 228 (Wright 75, Garner 5–51)
West Indies 1st Innings: 345 (Haynes 121, Greenidge 78, Chatfield 4–102, Boock 3–76)
New Zealand 2nd Innings: 386 for 5 declared (Wright 138, M.D. Crowe 119)
West Indies 2nd Innings: 50 for 2

Second Test (Auckland, 27 February–3 March) West Indies won by 10 wickets
West Indies 1st Innings: 418 for 9 declared (Greenidge 213, Dujon 77, Richardson 41, Hadlee 6–105)
New Zealand 1st Innings: 157 (Smith 40 not out, Marshall 4–43, A.H. Gray 3–45)
New Zealand 2nd Innings: 273 (M.D. Crowe 104, J.G. Bracewell 43, Walsh 5–73)
West Indies 2nd Innings: 16 for no wicket

Third Test (Christchurch, 12–15 March) New Zealand won by 5 wickets
West Indies 1st Innings: 100 (Hadlee 6–50, Chatfield 4–30)
New Zealand 1st Innings: 332 for 9 declared (M.D. Crowe 83, J.G. Bracewell 66, J.J. Crowe 55, Garner 4–79)
West Indies 2nd Innings: 264 (Marshall 45, Snedden 5–68, Hadlee 3–101)
New Zealand 2nd Innings: 33 for 5 (Walsh 3–16)

Captains: New Zealand – J.V. Coney
West Indies – I.V.A. Richards

Débuts: New Zealand – D.N. Patel (1st Test), P.A. Horne (3rd Test)

Rising Stars: New Zealand – M.D. Crowe (+113 batting)
West Indies – A.H. Gray (+159 bowling)

The general consensus after this scrappy and slightly disappointing series was that both sides were well past their peak. New Zealand, still dominated by the same nucleus of ageing players, were more than a little creaky, while the good news for everyone else was that the West Indies were finally looking beatable. Indeed, the relative age of the teams was highlighted by the retirement of three players at various stages of the series. First Bruce Edgar, at only thirty, decided that he had had enough; then, after the first Test, Michael Holding (0–

99) also called it a day. Finally, the New Zealand captain, Jeremy Coney, honoured his pre-season pledge to retire at the end of the series.

The West Indians' fragility, though, was less to do with lack of ability than simple tiredness. After a hard-fought series in Pakistan and a more than averagely exhausting one-day jamboree in Australia, most of the senior players were severely pooped. The middle-order batting was especially snoozy, with both Richards and Gomes averaging under 20, and only the peerless batting of Greenidge held their side together. When he was dismissed for 2 and 16 in the third Test, New Zealand won convincingly.

Malcolm Marshall was also on less than top form, taking just 9 wickets at over 32. Instead Garner (who missed the second Test through illness), Gray and Walsh made the running, causing considerable problems for all the home batsmen. Rutherford failed yet again, while the former Worcestershire all-rounder Dipak Patel, who had abruptly changed allegiances (his wife was a New Zealander), averaged just 12. Only Martin Crowe rose above all this, averaging 65 with two centuries, and climbed to 2nd in the world (one place ahead of Greenidge). New Zealand's bowling once again revolved around Hadlee (17 wickets) and Chatfield (10) – Bracewell took just 1 wicket for 147 runs. Hadlee passed 350 wickets in the final Test, to creep up menacingly behind Botham in the all-time list. His rating, after dipping worryingly low to 890 after the first Test, swiftly returned to 901, and didn't look like moving back down again. He remained, needless to say, the world's best bowler.

SRI LANKA vs NEW ZEALAND

First Test (Colombo, 16–21 April) Match Drawn
Sri Lanka 1st Innings: 397 for 9 declared (Kuruppu 201 not out, Madugalle 60, Hadlee 4–102)
New Zealand 1st Innings: 406 for 5 (Hadlee 151 not out, J.J. Crowe 120 not out)

Captains: Sri Lanka – L.R.D. Mendis
New Zealand – J.J. Crowe

Débuts: Sri Lanka– D.S.B.P. Kuruppu
New Zealand – A.H. Jones

Arranged in something of a hurry, New Zealand's brief tour of Sri Lanka was conceived as a rebuilding exercise after the traumas of the West Indian tour, during which most of the incumbent batsmen had repeatedly failed. Quite how brief, of course, they had no way of knowing, for after the first Test had degenerated into the stalest of draws, political unrest caused the whole tour to be called off. In the meantime, Andrew Jones made his Test début, batting at number three, and Kuruppu became the first batsman with four initials to make a double century on his Test début (a quiz question that I hereby copyright). Hadlee's hundred was his second in Tests, and when he had Ratnayake caught by Bracewell, he equalled Lillee's career haul of 355 wickets. There was only Botham on the horizon now.

WORLD TOP TWENTY AFTER 1986–87

BATTING

(11)	1.	D.B. Vengsarkar (India)	887 (+160)
(7)	2.	C.G. Greenidge (West Indies)	831 (+73)
(9)	3.	M.D. Crowe (New Zealand)	828 (+85)
(2)	4.	D.L. Haynes (West Indies)	802 (−74)
(1)	5.	I.V.A. Richards (West Indies)	801 (−80)
(3)	6.	A.R. Border (Australia)	778 (−66)
(4)	7.	D.I. Gower (England)	754 (−18)
RE	8.	D.M. Jones (Australia)	735
(5)	9.	R.B. Richardson (West Indies)	725 (−39)
(12)	10.	Javed Miandad (Pakistan)	708 (−6)
(8)	11.	M.W. Gatting (England)	681 (−67)
(6)	12.	A. Ranatunga (Sri Lanka)	655 (−108)
(21)	13.	S.M. Gavaskar (India)	652 (+64)
RE	14.	B.C. Broad (England)	633
(10)	15.	J.V. Coney (New Zealand)	629 (−113)
(36)	16.	Imran Khan (Pakistan)	618 (+139)
(31)	17.	R.J. Hadlee (New Zealand)	601 (+90)
(30)	18.	M. Azharuddin (India)	601 (+80)
(18)	19.	J.F. Reid (New Zealand)	601 (−25)
(17)	20.	Salim Malik (Pakistan)	594 (−38)

BOWLING

(2)	1.	R.J. Hadlee (New Zealand)	903 (+3)
(1)	2.	M.D. Marshall (West Indies)	841 (−60)
(4)	3.	Imran Khan (Pakistan)	802 (+13)
(3)	4.	J. Garner (West Indies)	779 (−32)
(5)	5.	M.A. Holding (West Indies)	714 (−74)
(25)	6.	C.A. Walsh (West Indies)	652 (+182)
(12)	7.	E.J. Chatfield (New Zealand)	640 (+58)

(20)	8.	Wasim Akram (Pakistan)	622 (+120)
(17)	9.	Tauseef Ahmed (Pakistan)	619 (+77)
NE	10.	A.H. Gray (West Indies)	611
(11)	11.	J.R. Ratnayeke (Sri Lanka)	598 (+12)
(6)	12.	G.F. Lawson (Australia)	593 (−110)
(7)	13.	Chetan Sharma (India)	588 (−108)
(8)	14.	Kapil Dev (India)	582 (−94)
(45)	15.	Maninder Singh (India)	575 (+289)
(31)	16.	B.A. Reid (Australia)	575 (+122)
(10)	17.	R.M. Ellison (England)	561 (−29)
(9)	18.	C.J. McDermott (Australia)	549 (−87)
RE	19.	Iqbal Qasim (Pakistan)	541
(28)	20.	Abdul Qadir (Pakistan)	536 (+77)

And so Dilip Vengsarkar, after pots of runs against everyone in sight, moved triumphantly to the top of the pile. A fixture in the Indian team for the best part of a decade, this was nevertheless the first time he had scored consistently enough to merit a place in the top ten, let alone the top one. Even so, he was to hold on to the top place longer than any previous incumbent.

Greenidge and Crowe, by far their sides' most impressive batsmen in the recent series, took the following two places, while Dean Jones entered the top twenty for the first time after his sparkling Test comeback. Chris Broad's three successive centuries against Australia also had the desired effect. Imran Khan and Richard Hadlee became the third and fourth players to appear in both top twenties at the same time. On their way out: Wright of New Zealand (to 22nd), Gooch (19th to 23rd), Amarnath (14th to 24th), Mudassar (15th to 25th), Gomes (13th to 26th) and Dujon (16th to 27th).

With Hadlee now unequivocally the world's leading bowler, attention turned to the West Indies' replacements for Holding (retired) and Garner (not long to go), as Walsh and Gray stormed into the top ten. And with the Pakistan contingent also prospering, it was farewell to Botham (yet again – 15th to 21st), Harper (13th to 22nd), Mudassar (*not* a good season for him – 19th to 24th), Ahangama of Sri Lanka (18th to 25th), Bracewell (14th to 30th) and Emburey (16th to 33rd). That left just one English bowler in the twenty – Ellison, whose England place, it seems, was gone forever. And this was the side that had just retained the Ashes?

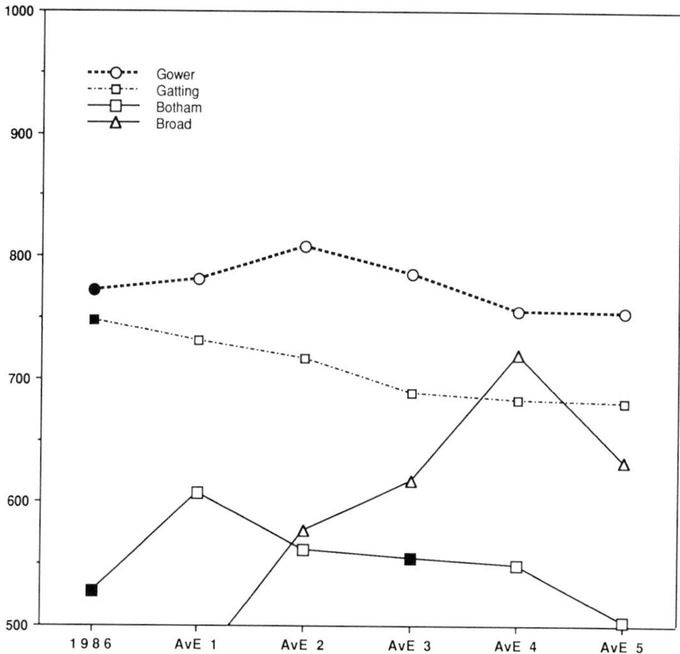
ENGLAND BATSMEN 1986/87
1000
900
800
700
600
500
Gower
Gatting
Botham
Broad
1986
AvE 1
AvE 2
AvE 3
AvE 4
AvE 5

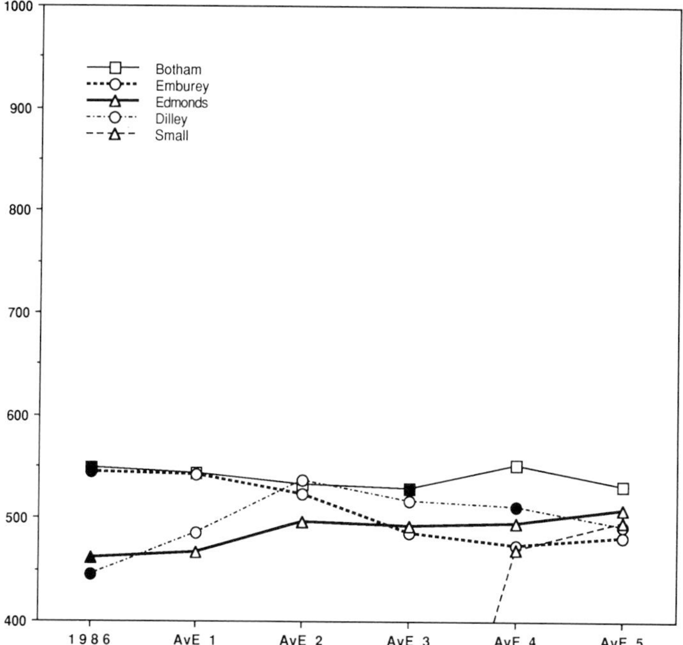
ENGLAND BOWLERS 1986/87
1000
900
800
700
600
500
400
Botham
Emburey
Edmonds
Dilley
Small
1986
AvE 1
AvE 2
AvE 3
AvE 4
AvE 5

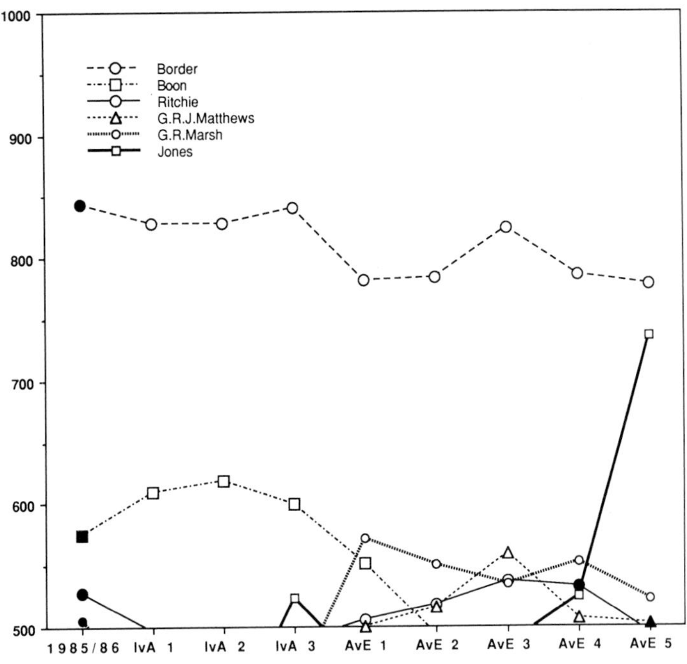
AUSTRALIA BATSMEN 1986/87
Border
Boon
Ritchie
G.R.J.Matthews
G.R.Marsh
Jones
1000
900
800
700
600
500
1985/86
IvA 1
IvA 2
IvA 3
AvE 1
AvE 2
AvE 3
AvE 4
AvE 5

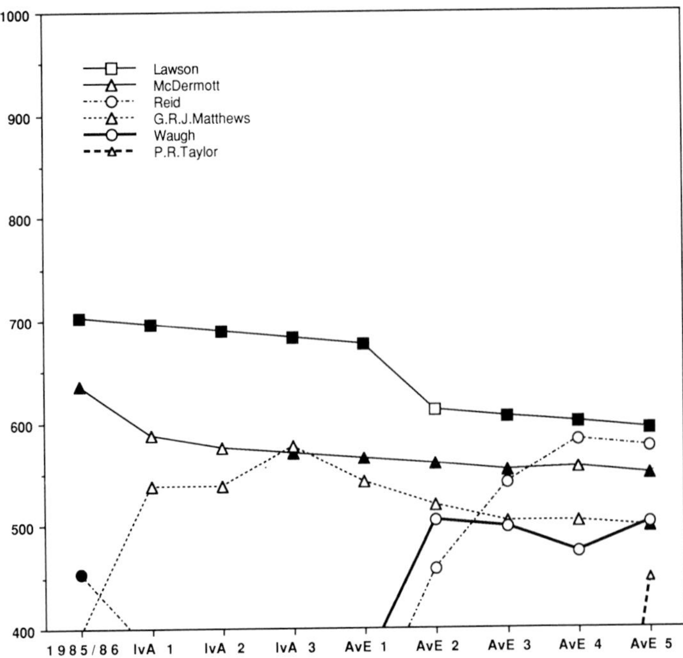
AUSTRALIA BOWLERS 1986/87
Lawson
McDermott
Reid
G.R.J.Matthews
Waugh
P.R.Taylor
1000
900
800
700
600
500
400
1985/86
IvA 1
IvA 2
IvA 3
AvE 1
AvE 2
AvE 3
AvE 4
AvE 5

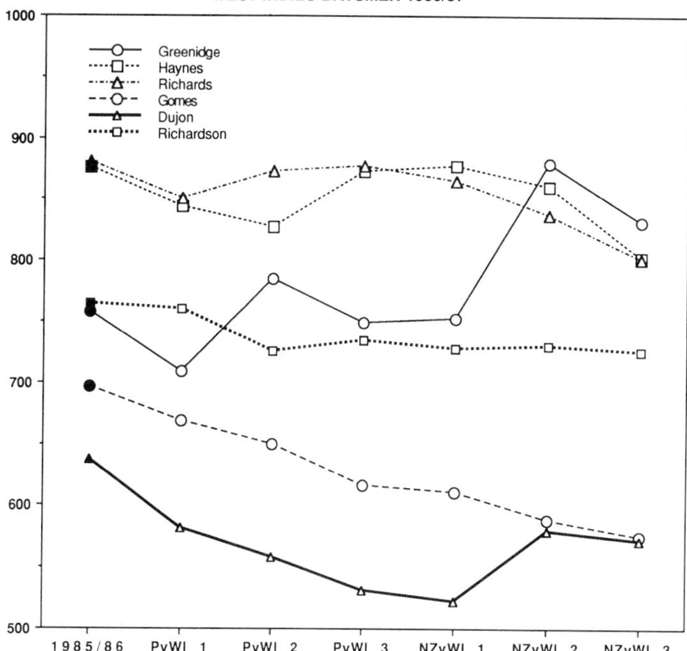
WEST INDIES BATSMEN 1986/87
1000
900
800
700
600
500
Greenidge
Haynes
Richards
Gomes
Dujon
Richardson
1985/86
PvWI 1
PvWI 2
PvWI 3
NZvWI 1
NZvWI 2
NZvWI 3

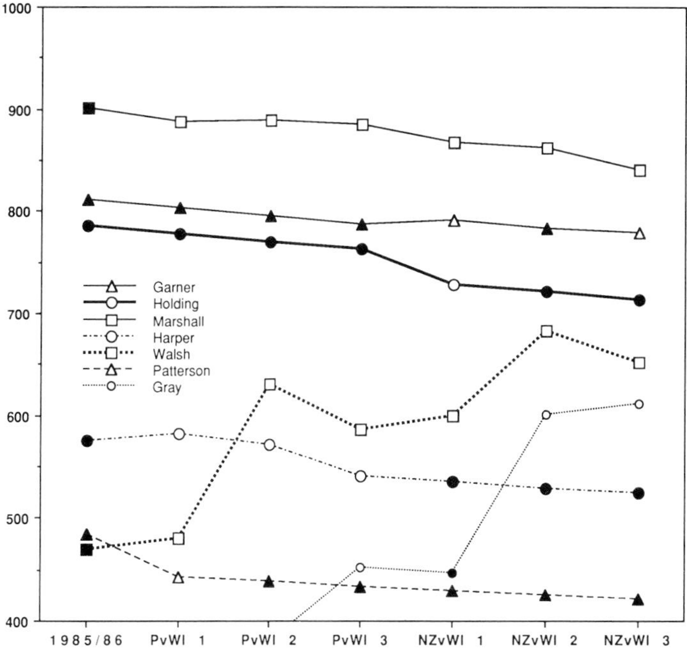
WEST INDIES BOWLERS 1986/87
1000
900
800
700
600
500
400
Garner
Holding
Marshall
Harper
Walsh
Patterson
Gray
1985/86
PvWI 1
PvWI 2
PvWI 3
NZvWI 1
NZvWI 2
NZvWI 3

NEW ZEALAND BATSMEN 1986/87

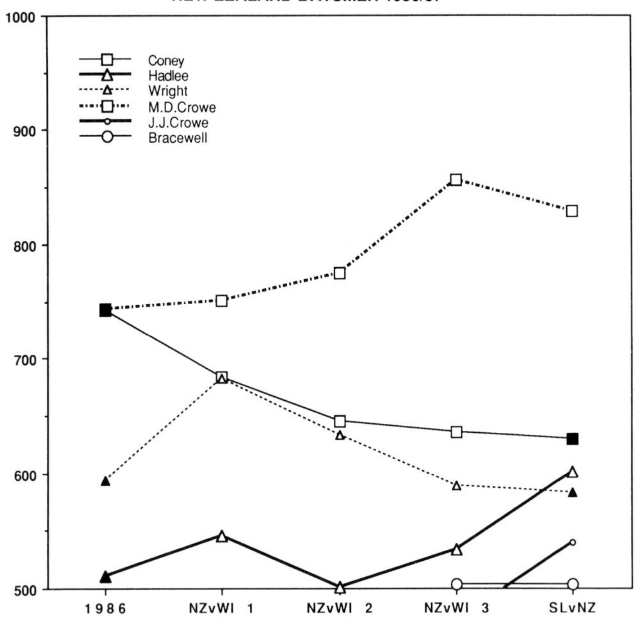
1000
900
800
700
600
500
Coney
Hadlee
Wright
M.D.Crowe
J.J.Crowe
Bracewell
1986
NZvWI 1
NZvWI 2
NZvWI 3
SLvNZ

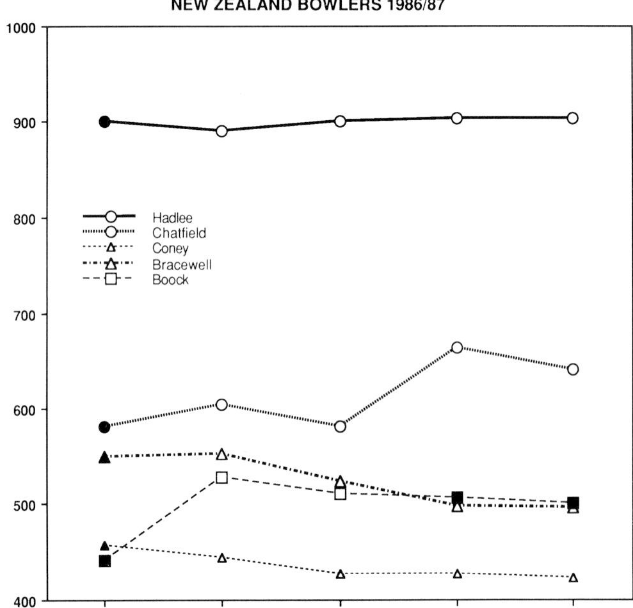
NEW ZEALAND BOWLERS 1986/87
1000
900
800
700
600
500
400
Hadlee
Chatfield
Coney
Bracewell
Boock
1986
NZvWI 1
NZvWI 2
NZvWI 3
SLvNZ

INDIA BATSMEN 1986/87

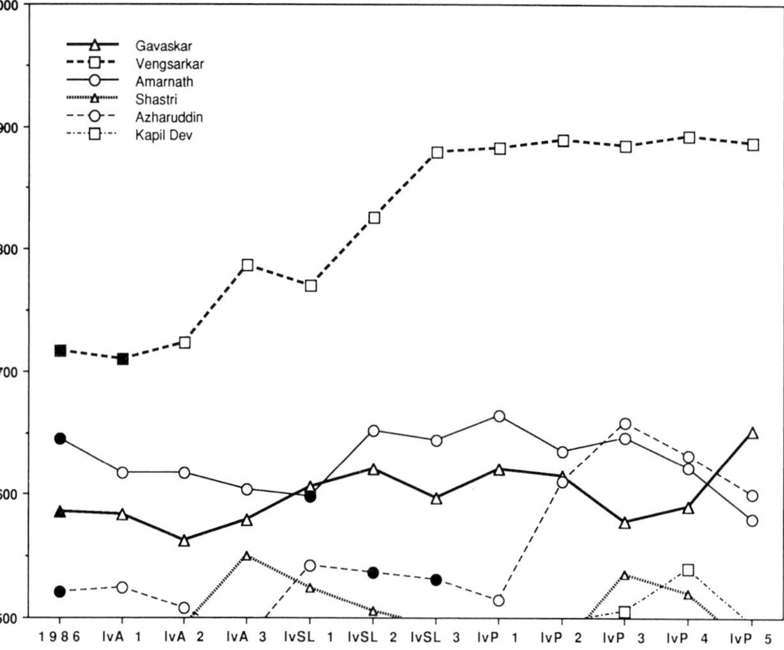
000
900
800
700
600
500
Gavaskar
Vengsarkar
Amarnath
Shastri
Azharuddin
Kapil Dev
1986
IvA 1
IvA 2
IvA 3
IvSL 1
IvSL 2
IvSL 3
IvP 1
IvP 2
IvP 3
IvP 4
IvP 5

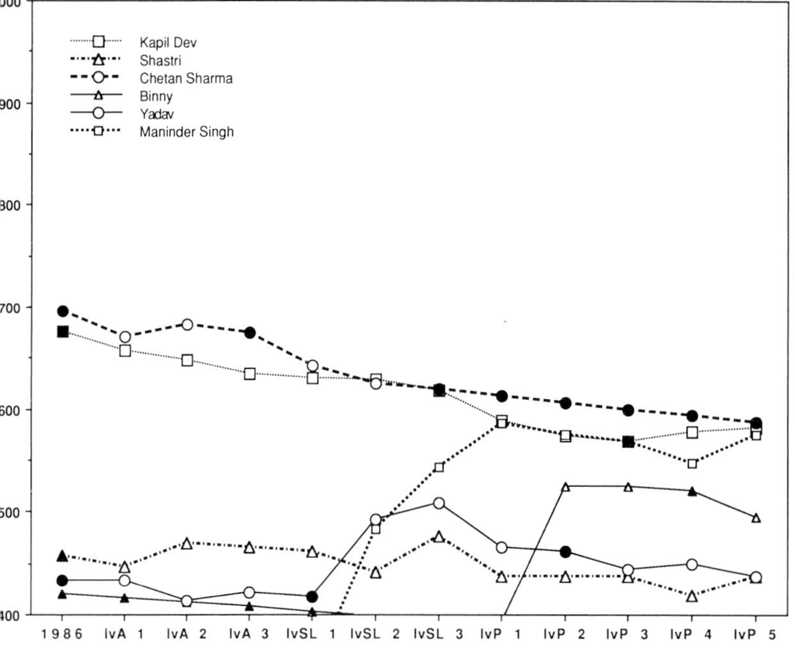
INDIA BOWLERS 1986/87
000
900
800
700
600
500
400
Kapil Dev
Shastri
Chetan Sharma
Binny
Yadav
Maninder Singh
1986
IvA 1
IvA 2
IvA 3
IvSL 1
IvSL 2
IvSL 3
IvP 1
IvP 2
IvP 3
IvP 4
IvP 5

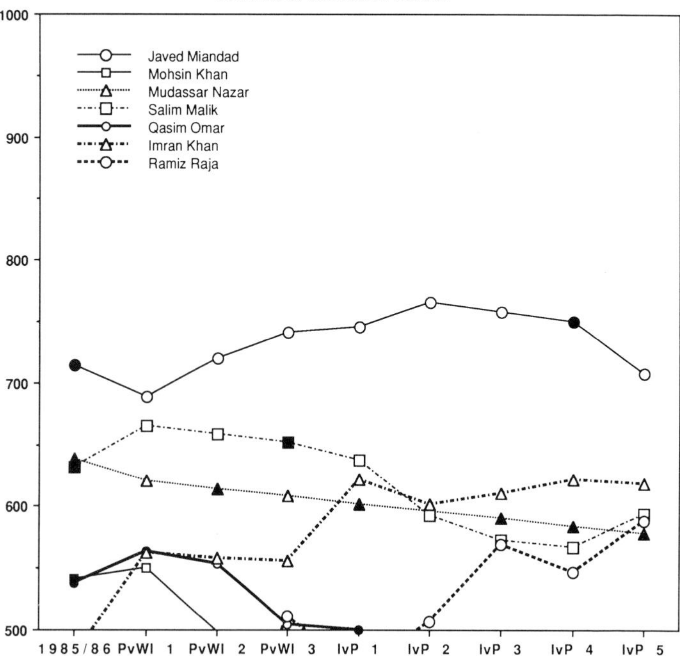
PAKISTAN BATSMEN 1986/87
1000
900
800
700
600
500
Javed Miandad
Mohsin Khan
Mudassar Nazar
Salim Malik
Qasim Omar
Imran Khan
Ramiz Raja
1985/86 PvWI 1 PvWI 2 PvWI 3 IvP 1 IvP 2 IvP 3 IvP 4 IvP 5

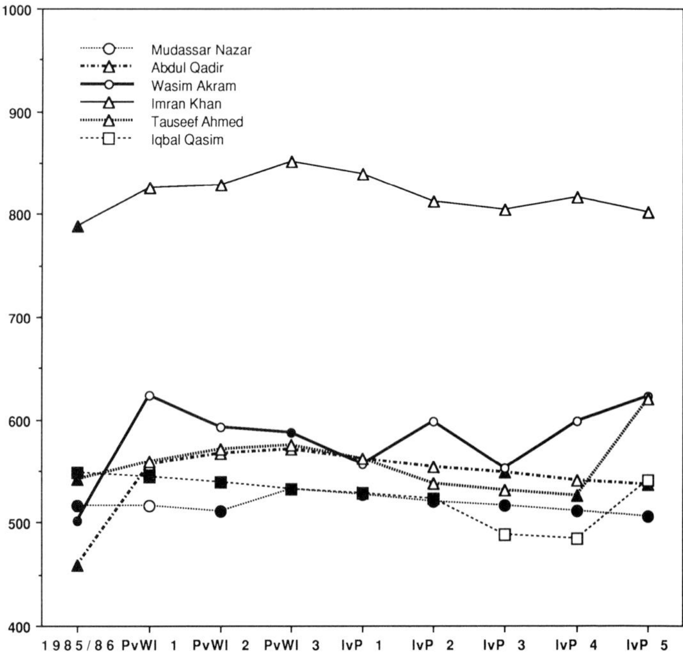
PAKISTAN BOWLERS 1986/87
1000
900
800
700
600
500
400
Mudassar Nazar
Abdul Qadir
Wasim Akram
Imran Khan
Tauseef Ahmed
Iqbal Qasim
1985/86 PvWI 1 PvWI 2 PvWI 3 IvP 1 IvP 2 IvP 3 IvP 4 IvP 5

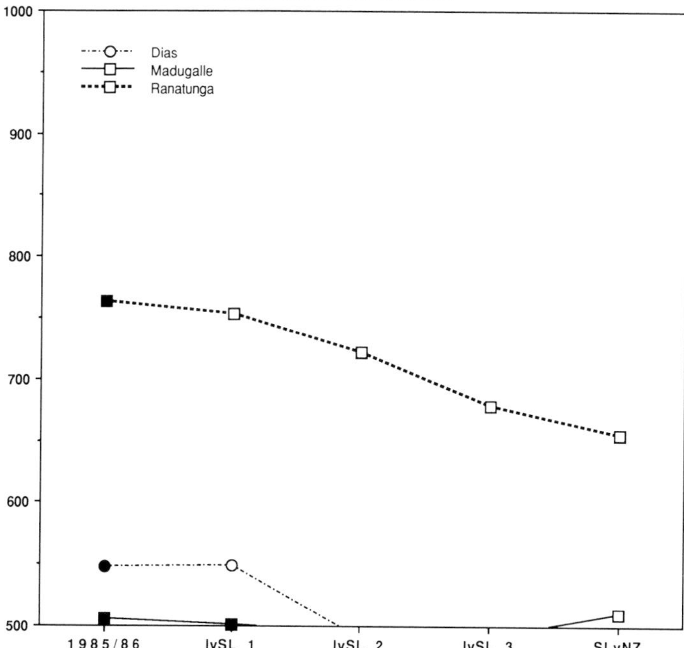
SRI LANKA BATSMEN 1986/87
Dias
Madugalle
Ranatunga
1000
900
800
700
600
500
1985/86
IvSL 1
IvSL 2
IvSL 3
SLvNZ

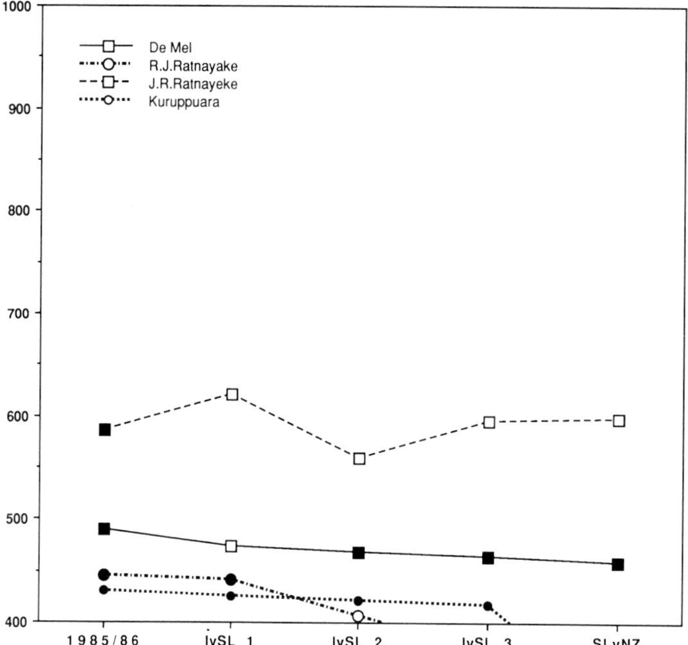
SRI LANKA BOWLERS 1986/87
De Mel
R.J.Ratnayake
J.R.Ratnayeke
Kuruppuara
1000
900
800
700
600
500
400
1985/86
IvSL 1
IvSL 2
IvSL 3
SLvNZ

1987

ENGLAND vs PAKISTAN

First Test (Old Trafford, 4–9 June) Match Drawn
England 1st Innings: 447 (Robinson 166, French 59, Botham 48, Gatting 42, Wasim Akram 4–111, Mohsin Kamal 4–127)
Pakistan 1st Innings: 140 for 5 (Mansoor Akhtar 75)

Second Test (Lord's, 18–23 June) Match Drawn
England 1st Innings: 368 (Athey 123, Broad 55, Gatting 43, French 42)

Third Test (Headingley, 2–6 July) Pakistan won by an innings and 18 runs
England 1st Innings: 136 (Capel 53, Mohsin Kamal 3–22, Wasim Akram 3–36, Imran Khan 3–37)
Pakistan 1st Innings: 353 (Salim Malik 99, Ijaz Ahmed 50, Wasim Akram 43, Foster 8–107)
England 2nd Innings: 199 (Gower 55, Imran Khan 7–40)

Fourth Test (Edgbaston, 23–28 July) Match Drawn
Pakistan 1st Innings: 439 (Mudassar 124, Salim Yousuf 91 not out, Javed Miandad 75, Dilley 5–92)
England 1st Innings: 521 (Gatting 124, Robinson 80, Gower 61, Emburey 58, Broad 54, Imran Khan 6–129, Wasim Akram 3–83)
Pakistan 2nd Innings: 205 (Shoaib Mohammad 50, Foster 4–59)
England 2nd Innings: 109 for 7

Fifth Test (The Oval, 6–11 August) Match Drawn
Pakistan 1st Innings: 708 (Javed Miandad 260, Imran Khan 118, Salim Malik 102, Dilley 6–154, Botham 3–217)
England 1st Innings: 232 (Gatting 61, Emburey 53, Abdul Qadir 7–96)
England 2nd Innings: 315 for 4 (Gatting 150 not out, Botham 51 not out, Broad 42, Abdul Qadir 3–115)

Captains: England – M.W. Gatting
Pakistan – Imran Khan

Débuts: England – N.H. Fairbrother (1st Test), D.J. Capel (3rd Test)

Rising Stars: England – N.A. Foster (+77 bowling)
Pakistan – Salim Yousuf (+80 batting)

England's third successive series defeat at home (this time by a comparatively modest 1–0) provoked the normal outcry, but Gatting and his troops were beaten as much by their own preconceptions as by the opposition. Their single defeat came, as so often before, at Headingley, where their paranoia made an admittedly substandard pitch look completely unplayable. Naturally things were a little different when the Pakistanis came in to bat: other than Foster, whose consistent accuracy earned him 8 wickets (including the first 6 to fall), the England bowling was ineffective. The home side's second innings was only marginally longer than the first, as Imran bowled beautifully, and when he dismissed Jack Richards (deputizing for the injured French), he passed 300 Test wickets.

This abject display aside, however, England could claim to have been unlucky. In the first Test, with Imran unable to bowl after a training injury, they had the Pakistanis in all sorts of trouble. It rained. In the second, Athey's first (and almost certainly last) Test century had put them in a strong position. It rained even harder. In the fourth Test, the rather bizarre scores conceal a stirring and close-fought match. With a draw seemingly on the cards after four days, Pakistan collapsed against Foster and Botham on the fifth, leaving England eighteen overs in which to score the 124 they needed to win. Only when Athey ('Slasher' Mackay's spiritual heir) appeared at number six did we realize that victory was but a forlorn hope. In the final Test, England desperately needed to bat first on a pitch packed full of runs. They lost the toss.

Unusually for a five-Test series, both sides were settled. Although England were without Gooch (out of form), Lamb (dropped) and Small (injured) for the entire summer, they retained most of the side from their successful tour of Australia. In addition Robinson made a comeback, and French re-established himself as England's number one 'keeper. But the batting, Gatting aside, was still inconsistent. Athey's century, which finally pushed him above 400 in the ratings, did not prevent him being dropped later in the series when runs dried up once more; Broad's form also declined; while Gower, though in great touch for his county, seemed out of sorts in Tests. Only the captain averaged above 40, but while his batting continued to prosper (his two centuries brought his tally to five in fourteen Tests and nine overall), his leadership came under constant criticism. His bowlers did not exactly help matters. Besides Foster, who finally established himself as his side's main strike bowler (with 15 wickets at 22.6) and to a lesser extent Dilley, the attack was toothless. Edmonds took 4 wickets at 54, Botham 4 at 61, and Emburey didn't actually take a wicket at all, although he conceded 222 runs. Capel played one match, but didn't impress. DeFreitas, his Australian achievements going to his head, lost both form and place.

The Pakistanis, on the other hand, had the guiding hand of Imran Khan to lead them, not to mention his 21 inexpensive wickets. Of the batsmen, Javed Miandad, Mudassar Nazar (restored to his opening position after Ramiz Raja's injury) and the rather excitable wicket-keeper-cum-appealer Salim 'One Hand One Bounce' Yousuf were most prolific, although perhaps more prominent was Salim Malik, who consistently played the right innings at the right time. His 99 at Headingley contributed as much as anything to his side's victory, and his century at the Oval (his sixth in all, but his first outside Pakistan) seemed a just reward. Shoaib, Ramiz and the recalled Mansoor Akhtar, back after four years in the wilderness, were less effective.

Pakistan's most entertaining player, though, never even took the field. Haseeb Ahsan, their manager (and player of twelve Tests in the early sixties), kept everyone hugely entertained with his glorious comic Angry Manager outbursts. Cross about this, livid about that, he had most commentators rolling in the aisles with his droll one-liners excoriating umpires, reviling England manager Mickey Stewart, and supporting the antics of 'One Hand One Bounce'. Trouble was, we all thought he was joking.

WORLD TOP TWENTY AFTER 1987

BATTING

(1)	1.	D.B. Vengsarkar (India)	887
(2)	2.	C.G. Greenidge (West Indies)	831
(3)	3.	M.D. Crowe (New Zealand)	828
(4)	4.	D.L. Haynes (West Indies)	802
(5)	5.	I.V.A. Richards (West Indies)	801
(6)	6.	A.R. Border (Australia)	778
(11)	7.	M.W. Gatting (England)	745 (+64)
(8)	8.	D.M. Jones (Australia)	735
(10)	9.	Javed Miandad (Pakistan)	730 (+22)
(9)	10.	R.B. Richardson (West Indies)	725
(7)	11.	D.I. Gower (England)	671 (−83)
(12)	12.	A. Ranatunga (Sri Lanka)	655
(13)	13.	S.M. Gavaskar (India)	652
(15)	14.	J.V. Coney (New Zealand)	629
(20)	15.	Salim Malik (Pakistan)	615 (+21)
(16)	16.	Imran Khan (Pakistan)	612 (−6)
(17)	17.	R.J. Hadlee (New Zealand)	601
(18)	18.	M. Azharuddin (India)	601
(25)	19.	Mudassar Nazar (Pakistan)	601 (+23)
(22)	20.	J.G. Wright (New Zealand)	583

BOWLING

(1)	1.	R.J. Hadlee (New Zealand)	903
(2)	2.	M.D. Marshall (West Indies)	841
(3)	3.	Imran Khan (Pakistan)	838 (+36)
(4)	4.	J. Garner (West Indies)	779
(5)	5.	M.A. Holding (West Indies)	714
(6)	6.	C.A. Walsh (West Indies)	652
(7)	7.	E.J. Chatfield (New Zealand)	640
(8)	8.	Wasim Akram (Pakistan)	623 (+1)
(10)	9.	A.H. Gray (West Indies)	611
(11)	10.	J.R. Ratnayeke (Sri Lanka)	598
(12)	11.	G.F. Lawson (Australia)	593
(13)	12.	Chetan Sharma (India)	588
(14)	13.	Kapil Dev (India)	582
(9)	14.	Tauseef Ahmed (Pakistan)	575 (−44)
(15)	15.	Maninder Singh (India)	575
(16)	16.	B.A. Reid (Australia)	575
(34)	17.	N.A. Foster (England)	554 (+77)
(18)	18.	C.J. McDermott (Australia)	549
(32)	19.	G.R. Dilley (England)	542 (+49)
(17)	20.	R.M. Ellison (England)	533 (−28)

Gatting's series average of 63.57 ensured him a healthy rise in the ratings, while Gower moved the other way. In fact, for all the high scores and useful performances in the series, there were very few upward movements of any real note – Salim Malik's heroism earned him a jump of just five places, while for all his runs, Mudassar only edged back into the twenty. On their way out: Chris Broad (14th to 24th) and New Zealand's John Reid, on the 18-month rule.

In the bowling chart, Imran's wickets similarly could not push him ahead of Marshall or Hadlee. Foster and Dilley finally made it into the twenty, replacing Iqbal Qasim (who as assistant manager in the recent series, hadn't actually played) and, more surprisingly, Abdul Qadir, down from 20th to 23rd.

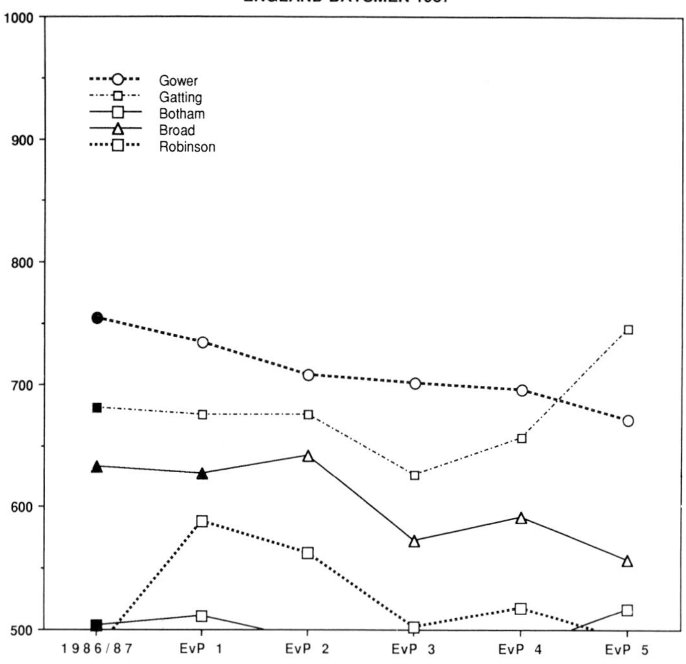
ENGLAND BATSMEN 1987
1000
900
800
700
600
500
Gower
Gatting
Botham
Broad
Robinson
1986/87
EvP 1
EvP 2
EvP 3
EvP 4
EvP 5

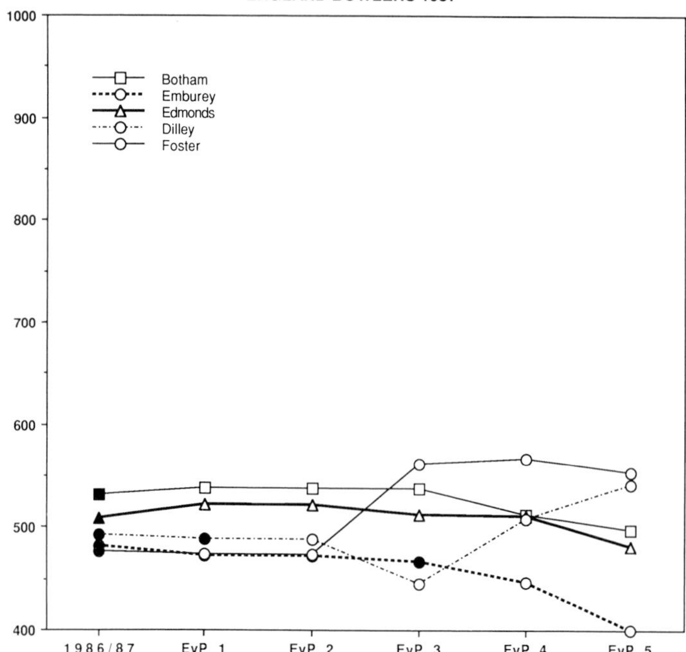
ENGLAND BOWLERS 1987
1000
900
800
700
600
500
400
Botham
Emburey
Edmonds
Dilley
Foster
1986/87
EvP 1
EvP 2
EvP 3
EvP 4
EvP 5

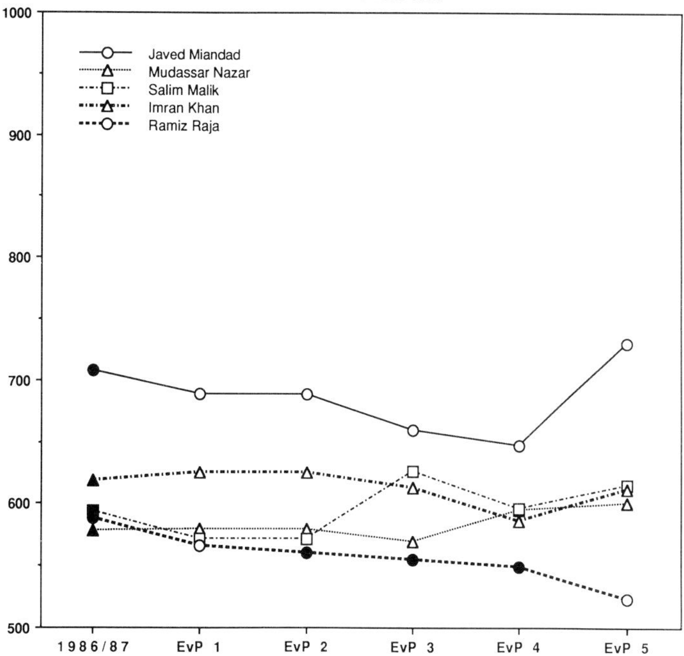
PAKISTAN BATSMEN 1987
1000
900
800
700
600
500
Javed Miandad
Mudassar Nazar
Salim Malik
Imran Khan
Ramiz Raja
1986/87
EvP 1
EvP 2
EvP 3
EvP 4
EvP 5

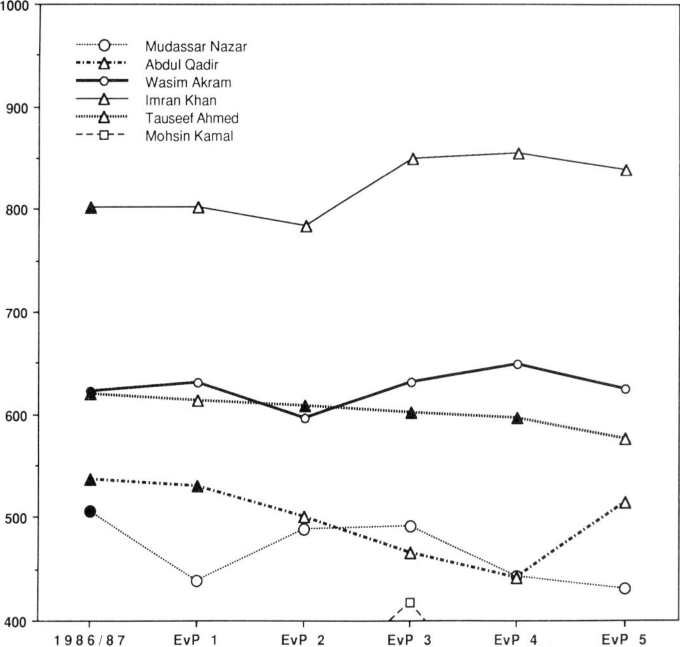
PAKISTAN BOWLERS 1987
1000
900
800
700
600
500
400
Mudassar Nazar
Abdul Qadir
Wasim Akram
Imran Khan
Tauseef Ahmed
Mohsin Kamal
1986/87
EvP 1
EvP 2
EvP 3
EvP 4
EvP 5

1987–88

PAKISTAN vs ENGLAND

First Test (Lahore, 25–28 November) Pakistan won by an innings and 87 runs
England 1st Innings: 175 (Broad 41, Abdul Qadir 9–56)
Pakistan 1st Innings: 392 (Mudassar 120, Javed Miandad 65, Ijaz Ahmed 44, Wasim Akram 40, N.G.B. Cook 3–87, Emburey 3–109)
England 2nd Innings: 130 (Abdul Qadir 4–45, Tauseef Ahmed 3–28, Iqbal Qasim 3–39)

Second Test (Faisalabad, 7–12 December) Match Drawn
England 1st Innings: 292 (Broad 116, Gatting 79, Iqbal Qasim 5–83, Abdul Qadir 4–105)
Pakistan 1st Innings: 191 (Salim Malik 60, Foster 4–42, Emburey 3–49)
England 2nd Innings: 137 for 6 declared (Gooch 65, Abdul Qadir 3–45)
Pakistan 2nd Innings: 51 for 1

Third Test (Karachi, 16–21 December) Match Drawn
England 1st Innings: 294 (Capel 98, Emburey 70, Abdul Qadir 5–88)
Pakistan 1st Innings: 353 (Aamer Malik 98 not out, Abdul Qadir 61, Salim Malik 55, Ramiz Raja 50, DeFreitas 5–86)
England 2nd Innings: 258 for 9 (Gooch 93, Emburey 74 not out, Abdul Qadir 5–98, Saleem Jaffer 3–79)

Captains: Pakistan – Javed Miandad
England – M.W. Gatting

Débuts: Pakistan – Aamer Malik (2nd Test)

Rising Stars: Pakistan – Abdul Qadir (+116 bowling)
England – J.E. Emburey (+97 batting)

One of the decade's more controversial series, as Pakistan finally revealed themselves as perhaps the most determined Test teams of all time. With everybody's chum Javed Miandad back as captain and Haseeb Ahsan as manager, England can't exactly have expected the series to be handed to them on a plate, but even they were surprised at the reception they received. After the first Test, the England

Salim Malik, indisputably the best of Pakistan's younger breed of batsmen.

players claimed that nine incorrect decisions had been given against them – whether through incompetence or simple downright cheating was a matter of strongly held opinion. The most well-known example was when Broad, himself one of cricket's more competitive characters, refused to walk after being given out caught at the wicket. A full minute elapsed before his partner Gooch persuaded him that the umpire was unlikely to change his mind. Then in the second Test, we had the famous 'argument', when Shakoor Rana allegedly called Gatting a '******* ****', which certainly made the England captain sit up and take notice. A day and a half's play was lost before the tiff was settled – it was of course purely coincidental that, before the delay, England were well on top in the game and could have won.

Two things became clear in the aftermath of the episode, (i) that Pakistan intended to win the series (especially after their pitiful defeat in the World Cup, which immediately preceded it), and they weren't bothered how they did it, and (ii) Gatting's career was all but over. A few months later he was famously 'barmaided' by the popular press, and his career never recovered.

Abdul Qadir's 30 wickets were, not surprisingly, rather overshadowed by all this bickering, although how many of them were wickets and how many were 'wickets' remains a moot point. Whichever the case, the England batsmen could not make head or tail of him, with the unlikely exception of Emburey, who outscored anyone on either side except Gooch, and topped the English averages with 69. Unfortunately he only took 7 wickets, a performance in keeping with the general level of the tourists' bowling throughout the series. The recalled Cook and Hemmings did no better (Edmonds had retired after Middlesex refused to let him continue as an 'amateur'), while Foster and DeFreitas found little help in the catatonic pitches. Capel's batting came on, but Gatting's unwillingness to let him bowl hardly bolstered his confidence. It was a sorry series for all concerned.

INDIA vs WEST INDIES

First Test (Delhi, 25–29 November) West Indies won by 5 wickets
India 1st Innings: 75 (Patterson 5–24, Davis 3–20)
West Indies 1st Innings: 127 (Haynes 45, Chetan Sharma 5–55, Kapil Dev 3–41)
India 2nd Innings: 327 for 9 declared (Vengsarkar 102, More 49, Kapil Dev 44, Arun Lal 40, Walsh 5–54, Patterson 3–100)
West Indies 2nd Innings: 276 for 5 (Richards 109 not out, Logie 46, Arshad Ayub 4–72)

Second Test (Bombay, 11–16 December) Match Drawn

India 1st Innings: 281 (Srikkanth 71, Vengsarkar 51, Kapil Dev 47, Walsh 5–54)
West Indies 1st Innings: 337 (Richardson 89, Haynes 58, Shastri 4–71, Chetan Sharma 3–64)
India 2nd Innings: 173 (Srikkanth 65, Vengsarkar 40 not out, Patterson 5–68, Walsh 4–40)
West Indies 2nd Innings: 4 for 1

Third Test (Calcutta, 26–31 December) Match Drawn
West Indies 1st Innings: 530 for 5 declared (Greenidge 141, Logie 101, Hooper 100 not out, Richards 68, Richardson 51, Dujon 40 not out)
India 1st Innings: 565 for 9 declared (Vengsarkar 102 not out, Arun Lal 93, Azharuddin 60, Arshad Ayub 57, Shastri 47, More 44, Amarnath 43, Walsh 4–136, Davis 3–84)
West Indies 2nd Innings: 157 for 2 (Greenidge 69, Haynes 47)

Fourth Test (Madras, 11–15 January) India won by 255 runs
India 1st Innings: 382 (Kapil Dev 109, Arun Lal 69, Azharuddin 47, Davis 4–76, Walsh 3–85)
West Indies 1st Innings: 184 (Richards 68, Hirwani 8–61)
India 2nd Innings: 217 for 8 declared (Raman 83, Walsh 4–55)
West Indies 2nd Innings: 160 (Logie 67, Hirwani 8–75)

Captains: D.B. Vengsarkar (1st–3rd Tests), R.J. Shastri (4th Test)
West Indies – I.V.A. Richards

Débuts: India – S.V. Manjrekar, Arshad Ayub (1st Test), W.V. Raman, Ajay Sharma, N.D. Hirwani (4th Test)
West Indies – W.K.M. Benjamin (1st Test), C.L. Hooper (2nd Test), P.V. Simmons (4th Test)

Rising Stars: India – N.D. Hirwani (+242 bowling)
West Indies – C.A. Walsh (+137 bowling)

Coming straight after the World Cup, which its hosts India and Pakistan had hyped to within an inch of its life, this series failed to capture the imagination of the Indian public, who avoided it in their millions. So undersubscribed were the Tests, in fact, that the second Test at Nagpur was cancelled after the tour had started, and swiftly transformed into two one-day internationals, all in the cause of large profits.

Such, though, is the way the game is moving in the sub-continent, those years of dreary draws having finally perhaps had an effect. Ironically, this series was rather more interesting than usual, not least because India, much the weaker side, managed to level it 1–1 in the final Test. They were assisted by a disgraceful pitch and an astonishing performance by an unknown nineteen-year-old leg-spinner, Narendra Hirwani.

With a match analysis of 16 for 136 (the third-best of all time and the best by a débutant), Hirwani recorded the highest first rating yet – 642. The West Indians' historic vulnerability to high-class spin bowling on a helpful pitch destroyed them yet again: only Richards in the first innings and Logie in the second held out for long.

Both sides had a rebuilt look about them. For India, Gavaskar had finally retired after 125 Tests, 10,122 runs and thirty-four centuries, to be replaced by Arun Lal, who after five previous Tests had yet to establish himself. West Indies, meanwhile, were without Gomes and Garner, who had retired, and Marshall, who declined to tour. But neither side really missed their absentees. Vengsarkar, the new captain, continued his fine form, with two centuries and another average over 100, although injury prevented him from playing at Madras. Curiously it was the brilliant century there by his predecessor, Kapil Dev, that set up the victory chance so skilfully taken by Hirwani. For the West Indies, Courtney Walsh bowled superbly throughout, all too often on pitches that gave him no help at all, and took 26 wickets at 16.8. Carl Hooper hit a maiden Test century in the coma-inducing third Test. Overall, though, West Indies must have felt that they were robbed.

AUSTRALIA vs NEW ZEALAND

First Test (Brisbane, 4–7 December) Australia won by 9 wickets
New Zealand 1st Innings: 186 (M.D. Crowe 67, McDermott 4–43, M.G. Hughes 3–40)
Australia 1st Innings: 305 (Boon 143, D.K. Morrison 4–86, Hadlee 3–95)
New Zealand 1st Innings: 212 (Patel 62, A.H. Jones 45, B.A. Reid 4–53, McDermott 3–79)
Australia 2nd Innings: 97 for 1

Second Test (Adelaide, 11–15 December) Match Drawn
New Zealand 1st Innings: 485 for 9 declared (A.H. Jones 150, M.D. Crowe 137, Wright 45, McDermott 4–135)
Australia 1st Innings: 496 (Border 205, Sleep 62, Waugh 61, Dyer 60, Hadlee 5–68)
New Zealand 2nd Innings: 182 for 7 (A.H. Jones 64, Patel 40, Sleep 3–61, May 3–68)

Third Test (Melbourne, 26–30 December) Match Drawn
New Zealand 1st Innings: 317 (Wright 99, M.D. Crowe 82, Smith 44, A.H. Jones 40, McDermott 5–97, Whitney 4–92)

Australia 1st Innings: 357 (Sleep 90, Waugh 55, Dodemaide 50, Hadlee 5–109)
New Zealand 2nd Innings: 286 (M.D. Crowe 79, Wright 43, Dodemaide 6–58, Sleep 3–107)
Australia 2nd Innings: 230 for 9 (Boon 54, Border 43, Hadlee 5–67)

Captains: Australia – A.R. Border
New Zealand – J.J. Crowe

Débuts: Australia – M.R.J. Veletta (1st Test), T.B.A. May (2nd Test), A.I.C. Dodemaide (3rd Test)
New Zealand – D.K. Morrison (1st Test)

Rising Stars: Australia – D.C. Boon (+122 batting)
New Zealand – A.H. Jones (+72 batting)

With both sides still attempting to rebuild – New Zealand because most of their players had collected their bus passes, and Australia because they just kept losing – there were many changes from the teams that had met just two years earlier. This time, though, Australia came out as winners in a no less hard-fought and, at times, fascinating series. True, the second Test was a monumentally boring draw, played on Adelaide's notoriously benign pitch, but the first Test saw Allan Border's side avenge their defeat on the same ground in 1985, while the third was a thriller. Australia needed just 247 to win with a whole day in which to do it, and at 176 for 4, with Waugh and Veletta well set and twenty-eight overs left, all looked rosy. But then Hadlee returned to the attack, and when the ninth wicket fell, at 227, he had equalled Botham's record of 373 Test wickets. The last two men, McDermott and Whitney, survived the last 4.5 overs to earn their side a draw and with it the series. When Whitney blocked out the final ball, Hadlee walked down the pitch to him, put his arm round his shoulder and shook his hand. And they say sportsmanship is dead.

The series' victory must have been especially sweet for Allan Border, even after his side's victory in the World Cup in India. He once again top-scored for his side, with an average of 72, followed by the recalled leg-spinner Peter Sleep, whose 211 runs at 52 did more for his long-term prospects than his 7 wickets at 48 (batting rating 351, bowling rating 235). David Boon began his *annus mirabilis* with a century at Brisbane, and an overall average of 47, but neither Marsh, Veletta (a 187 rating after three Tests) nor Dean Jones passed 40. Tony Dodemaide claimed the vacant all-rounder's position in the final Test with 7 wickets at 15.14 and a useful 50, while McDermott was the side's most consistent bowler with 17 wickets.

New Zealand's batting predictably relied principally on Martin Crowe (396 runs at 66), but Andrew Jones was equally consistent, scoring a 150 in just his third Test. Patel waxed and waned, while captain Jeff Crowe was hopelessly out of touch. Rutherford's innings, as ever, were entirely unfettered by runs. Top of the bowling averages? Well, Hadlee of course – 18 wickets at under 20, well ahead of Bracewell and Morrison. Chatfield was not at his best, and the rest weren't anywhere at all.

Most promisingly, the attendances were well up on New Zealand's last tour – despite, or possibly because of, the 589 one-day internationals that were played. Test cricket was regaining its old popularity, and Australia's recovery had a lot to do with it.

AUSTRALIA vs ENGLAND

Bicentennial Test (Sydney, 29 January–2 February) Match Drawn
England 1st Innings: 425 (Broad 139, French 47, Robinson 43, Moxon 40, P.L. Taylor 4–84, Waugh 3–51)
Australia 1st Innings: 214 (Jones 56, Sleep 41, Hemmings 3–53, Dilley 3–54)
Australia 2nd Innings: 328 for 2 (Boon 184 not out, G.R. Marsh 56, Border 48 not out)

Captains: Australia – A.R. Border
England – M.W. Gatting

Débuts: None

This may not have been the most gripping of Test matches, but it was hardly the dismal bore the Australian media dismissed it as at the time. Bursting with national pride after the World Cup success and their narrow defeat of New Zealand, Australian fans were disappointed when England – without Gooch, Gower and Botham – did not prove as hopelessly incompetent as they expected them to be. In amassing 425 in their first innings, with Broad scoring his fourth century in six Tests in Australia (all at different grounds, a feat matched only by J.H. Edrich), England denied their rather cross hosts any chance of victory, and looked to have a good chance of wrapping it up themselves when Australia were forced to follow on a day and a half later. But Boon, continuing his run of masterly form, was not to be moved, and hit his sixth Test hundred and highest score to date. England's bowling, though efficient, was never sufficiently penetrating to force the result. In the end, the match was remembered more for Broad's petulance when bowled – he knocked the leg stump out of the ground and probably had a damn good cry afterwards – than for any of the actual cricket.

AUSTRALIA vs SRI LANKA

Only Test (Perth, 12–15 February) Australia won by an innings and 108 runs
Australia 1st Innings: 455 (Jones 102, Border 88, Boon 64, G.R. Marsh 53, Amalean 4–97, Ratnayeke 4–98)
Sri Lanka 1st Innings: 194 (Ranatunga 55, Mahanama 41, Waugh 4–33, Dodemaide 3–40, McDermott 3–50)
Sri Lanka 2nd Innings: 153 (Ranatunga 45, M.G. Hughes 5–67, Dodemaide 4–58)

Captains: Australia – A.R. Border
Sri Lanka – R.S. Madugalle

Début: Sri Lanka – C.P.H. Ramanayake

In which Sri Lanka were made to look slightly foolish by the rampaging Australians, although luckily for them no-one was interested enough to watch: the total attendance for the four days was just 10,607 (the lowest in Australia since 1887–88) and only the first day was shown on TV. Sri Lanka were without Mendis, who was unavailable, Dias, Wettimuny, or John, and looked much weaker for it. Australia made light work of them.

NEW ZEALAND vs ENGLAND

First Test (Christchurch, 12–17 February) Match Drawn
England 1st Innings: 319 (Broad 114, Robinson 70, Emburey 42, D.K. Morrison 5–69, Chatfield 4–87)
New Zealand 1st Innings: 168 (Dilley 6–38)
England 2nd Innings: 152 (Chatfield 4–36, Snedden 4–45)
New Zealand 2nd Innings: 130 for 4 (Jones 54 not out)

Second Test (Auckland, 25–29 February) Match Drawn
New Zealand 1st Innings: 301 (Wright 103, Dilley 5–60)
England 1st Innings: 323 (Moxon 99, Robinson 54, Emburey 45, Gatting 42, Chatfield 4–37, J.G. Bracewell 3–88)
New Zealand 2nd Innings: 350 for 7 (Greatbatch 107 not out, Franklin 62, Wright 49)

Third Test (Wellington, 3–7 March) Match Drawn
New Zealand 1st Innings: 512 for 6 declared (M.D. Crowe 143, Rutherford 107 not out, Greatbatch 68, J.G. Bracewell 54, Vance 47)

England 1st Innings: 183 for 2 (Moxon 81 not out, Broad 61)

Captains: New Zealand – J.J. Crowe (1st & 2nd Tests), J.G. Wright (3rd Test)
England – M.W. Gatting

Débuts: New Zealand – M.J. Greatbatch (2nd Test), R.H. Vance (3rd Test)
England – P.W. Jarvis (1st Test)

Rising Stars: New Zealand – E.J. Chatfield (+52 bowling)
England – M.D. Moxon (+128 batting)

An excruciatingly dull series which lacked even the excitement of Hadlee overtaking Botham's tally of 373 Test wickets. After eighteen wicket-free overs in the first Test, the great all-rounder strained a calf muscle, and took no further part in the match or indeed the series. The New Zealand attack was thus reduced to the pedestrian, and so a good match for England's batting. Gooch had returned home after the Pakistani leg of the tour, Gower was taking a winter off, and Botham had retired from touring, so such charismatic big hitters as Athey, Robinson and Moxon had been drafted in to take their places. Moxon scored a few runs along the way, but the overall result was tedium of the highest level. Only the penetrative fast bowling of Graham Dilley (15 wickets at 14) perked things up to any extent, although Jarvis made a promising début. Foster had by this time returned home for treatment on an injured knee, while Emburey was still incapable of taking a wicket. Naturally enough, this did not render him ineligible for selection.

The New Zealanders, lacking Hadlee and Andrew Jones for all but the first Test, looked tired and unimaginative, and their captain Jeff Crowe finally lost his place after a dismal run of low scores. But after a rain-ruined first Test, the pitches for the other two were so easy-paced that even Ken Rutherford scored runs (although his rating was too far gone to rise more than marginally – 132 to 197). Only he and Moxon, who had really begun to hit his stride with the bat, could have been sorry when the series finally ended.

WEST INDIES vs PAKISTAN

First Test (Georgetown, Guyana, 2–6 April) Pakistan won by 9 wickets

West Indies 1st Innings: 292 (Logie 80, Richardson 75, Imran Khan 7–80)

Pakistan 1st Innings: 435 (Javed Miandad 114, Salim Yousuf 62, Shoaib Mohammad 46, Walsh 3–80, Patterson 3–82)
West Indies 2nd Innings: 172 (Greenidge 43, Imran Khan 4–41, Abdul Qadir 3–66)
Pakistan 2nd Innings: 32 for 1

Second Test (Port-of-Spain, Trinidad, 14–19 April) Match Drawn
West Indies 1st Innings: 174 (Richards 49, Richardson 42, Imran Khan 4–38, Abdul Qadir 4–83)
Pakistan 1st Innings: 194 (Salim Malik 66, Marshall 4–55, Benjamin 3–32)
West Indies 2nd Innings: 391 (Richards 123, Dujon 106 not out, Richardson 40, Imran Khan 5–115, Abdul Qadir 4–148)
Pakistan 2nd Innings: 341 for 9 (Javed Miandad 102, Ramiz Raja 44, Ijaz Ahmed 43, Benjamin 3–73)

Third Test (Bridgetown, Barbados, 22–27 April) West Indies won by 2 wickets
Pakistan 1st Innings: 309 (Ramiz Raja 54, Shoaib Mohammad 54, Marshall 4–79, Benjamin 3–52)
West Indies 1st Innings: 306 (Richards 67, Hooper 54, Marshall 48, Wasim Akram 3–88, Imran Khan 3–108)
Pakistan 2nd Innings: 262 (Shoaib Mohammad 64, Imran Khan 43 not out, Mudassar Nazar 41, Marshall 5–65)
West Indies 2nd Innings: 268 for 8 (Richardson 64, Ambrose 41 not out, Wasim Akram 4–73)

Captains: West Indies – C.G. Greenidge (1st Test), I.V.A. Richards (2nd & 3rd Tests)
Pakistan – Imran Khan

Début: West Indies – C.E.L. Ambrose (1st Test)

Rising Stars: West Indies – C.L. Hooper (+94 batting)
Pakistan – Salim Yousuf (+84 batting)

Another exciting series between these two, proving once again that if the West Indies were still pre-eminent in Test cricket, Pakistan were not far behind. In drawing 1–1, Pakistan became the first team not to lose a series in the islands since England's drawn rubber in 1973–74. Imran Khan, naturally enough, had much to do with this. In retirement since the end of the 1987 series, Imran gave in to popular pressure (and to President Zia, who asked him personally) and rejoined the fray. No captain before or since has so skilfully united the Pakistani team, although the leadership of Javed Miandad in the series against England may have had something to do with his brisk return. Imran's 'Mr Clean' persona – and low fast in-swinging yorkers – were just what his country needed.

Initially, things did not go Pakistan's way. With Imran, Wasim Akram and Abdul Qadir all out injured, the team lost the one-day series 5–0. But with all three back for the first Test, and Marshall and Richards now absent through injury from the West Indian team, Pakistan won in four days, recording the first victory by a visiting team since 1977–78. Javed Miandad's 114 was, although his seventeenth Test century, his first against the West Indies, and he followed it up with an equally valuable 102 in the tense draw at Port-of-Spain. Given 372, to win, Pakistan still needed 84 with twenty overs but only 3 wickets left. Marshall soon dismissed Wasim Akram, and the Pakistanis shut up shop, the draw being clinched with the last pair at the wicket and Abdul Qadir playing out the last five balls from Viv Richards. But West Indies finally squared the series in another even game in Bridgetown, when Abdul Qadir, cross after a series of disallowed appeals, biffed a heckler on the nose and had to pay him $1,000 in an out-of-court settlement. (His rating remained unaffected by the incident.)

For the West Indies, the batting was again dominated by Viv Richards, who averaged 69, but useful innings were also scored by Logie, Hooper and Dujon. Marshall and Benjamin carried the bowling – Curtly Ambrose, the new boy, had problems settling down, while Walsh, out of form, took just 4 wickets at 57.5. No bowler, though, made as much impact as Imran, whose 23 wickets at 18.08 were well ahead of anyone on either side.

WORLD TOP TWENTY AFTER 1987–88

BATTING

(1)	1.	D.B. Vengsarkar (India)	907 (+20)
(5)	2.	I.V.A. Richards (West Indies)	882 (+81)
(6)	3.	A.R. Border (Australia)	811 (+33)
(3)	4.	M.D. Crowe (New Zealand)	741 (−87)
(9)	5.	Javed Miandad (Pakistan)	732 (+2)
(10)	6.	R.B. Richardson (West Indies)	693 (−32)
(12)	7.	A. Ranatunga (Sri Lanka)	686 (+31)
(8)	8.	D.M. Jones (Australia)	659 (−76)
(2)	9.	C.G. Greenidge (West Indies)	658 (−173)
(24)	10.	B.C. Broad (England)	649 (+92)
(41)	11.	D.C. Boon (Australia)	641 (+195)
(13)	12.	S.M. Gavaskar (India)	626 (−26)
(11)	13.	D.I. Gower (England)	625 (−46)
(7)	14.	M.W. Gatting (England)	617 (−127)
(4)	15.	D.L. Haynes (West Indies)	603 (−199)

(14)	16. J.V. Coney (New Zealand)	592 (−37)
(15)	17. Salim Malik (Pakistan)	585 (−30)
(18)	18. M. Azharuddin (India)	585 (−16)
(23)	19. P.J. Dujon (West Indies)	585 (+14)
(20)	20. J.G. Wright (New Zealand)	570 (−13)

BOWLING

(1)	1. R.J. Hadlee (New Zealand)	882 (−21)
(3)	2. Imran Khan (Pakistan)	849 (+11)
(2)	3. M.D. Marshall (West Indies)	830 (−11)
(4)	4. J. Garner (West Indies)	726 (−53)
(6)	5. C.A. Walsh (West Indies)	686 (+34)
(5)	6. M.A. Holding (West Indies)	665 (−49)
(8)	7. Wasim Akram (Pakistan)	659 (+36)
(7)	8. E.J. Chatfield (New Zealand)	642 (+2)
NE	9. N. Hirwani (India)	642
(12)	10. Chetan Sharma (India)	638 (+50)
(10)	11. J.R. Ratnayeke (Sri Lanka)	614 (+16)
(16)	12. B.A. Reid (Australia)	605 (+30)
(19)	13. G.R. Dilley (England)	597 (+55)
(13)	14. Kapil Dev (India)	592 (+10)
(17)	15. N.A. Foster (England)	572 (+18)
(24)	16. S.R. Waugh (Australia)	570 (+68)
(9)	17. A.H. Gray (West Indies)	569 (−42)
(23)	18. Abdul Qadir (Pakistan)	567 (+53)
(18)	19. C.J. McDermott (Australia)	566 (+17)
(11)	20. G.F. Lawson (Australia)	564 (−29)

A solid assault by Viv Richards could not disturb Vengsarkar at the top of the heap, but there was much activity in the rest of the twenty. Broad made his now customary return to the top flight after a winter abroad (back in England he could barely score a run), while Boon, after a long apprenticeship, stormed in on the back of his spectacular recent form. Down and out: the two all-rounders, Imran Khan and Hadlee, down to 23rd and 25th respectively, and the yo-yo man Mudassar Nazar, down from 19th to 29th.

The bowling chart, meanwhile, welcomed the nineteen-year-old Indian leggie Hirwani – in at number nine after one Test. Finally showing more than 'potential for the future' (i.e. taking a few wickets) were Dilley and Foster, while Steve Waugh, yet to make his mark as a Test batsman, was well in there as a bowler. Moving out: Tauseef Ahmed (who returned home injured from the West Indies), down from 14th to 22nd; Maninder Singh (15th to 27th) whose form of the previous year had not held up, and Richard Ellison, out on the 18-month rule.

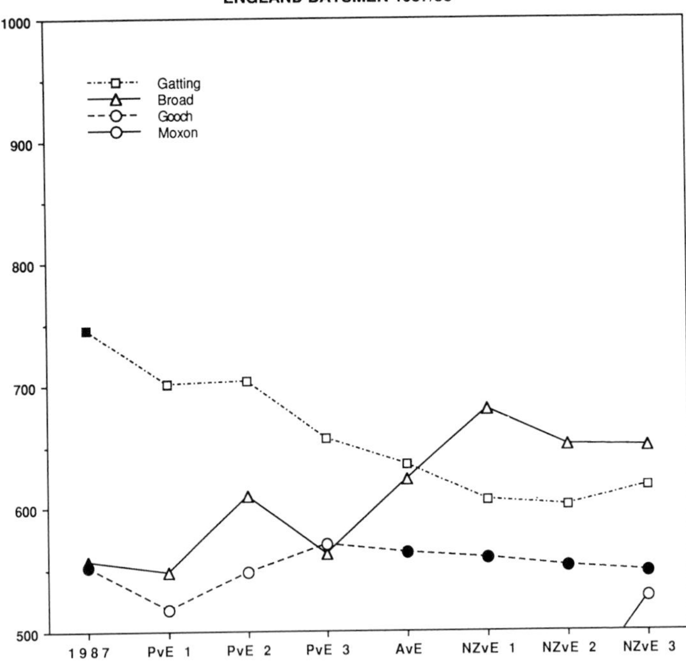
ENGLAND BATSMEN 1987/88
1000
900
800
700
600
500
Gatting
Broad
Gooch
Moxon
1987
PvE 1
PvE 2
PvE 3
AvE
NZvE 1
NZvE 2
NZvE 3

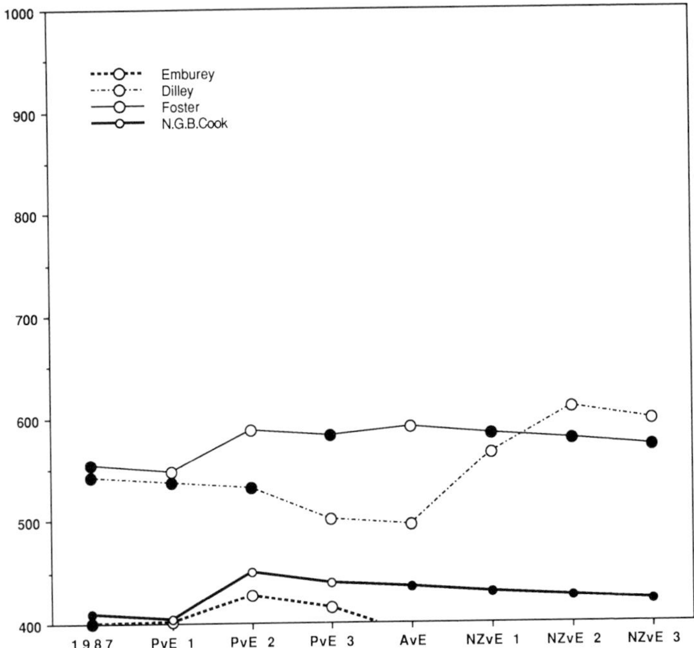
ENGLAND BOWLERS 1987/88
1000
900
800
700
600
500
400
Emburey
Dilley
Foster
N.G.B.Cook
1987
PvE 1
PvE 2
PvE 3
AvE
NZvE 1
NZvE 2
NZvE 3

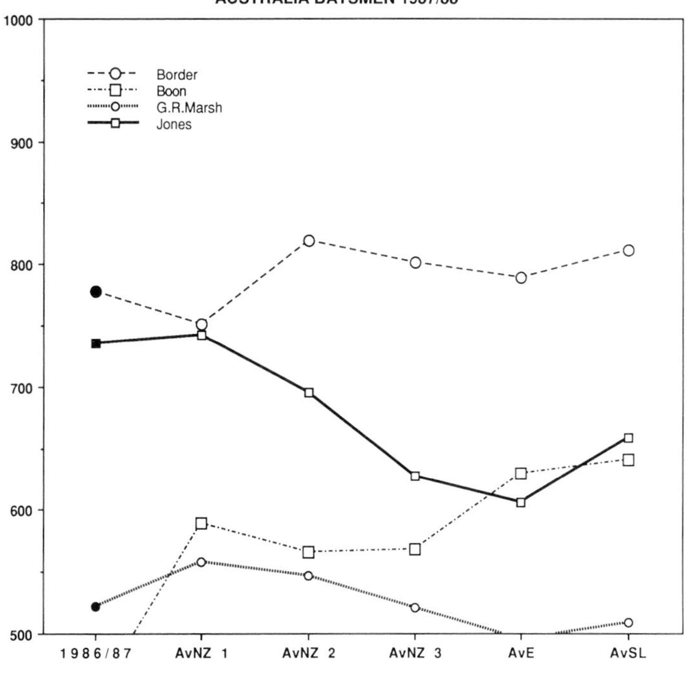
AUSTRALIA BATSMEN 1987/88
1000
900
800
700
600
500
Border
Boon
G.R.Marsh
Jones
1986/87
AvNZ 1
AvNZ 2
AvNZ 3
AvE
AvSL

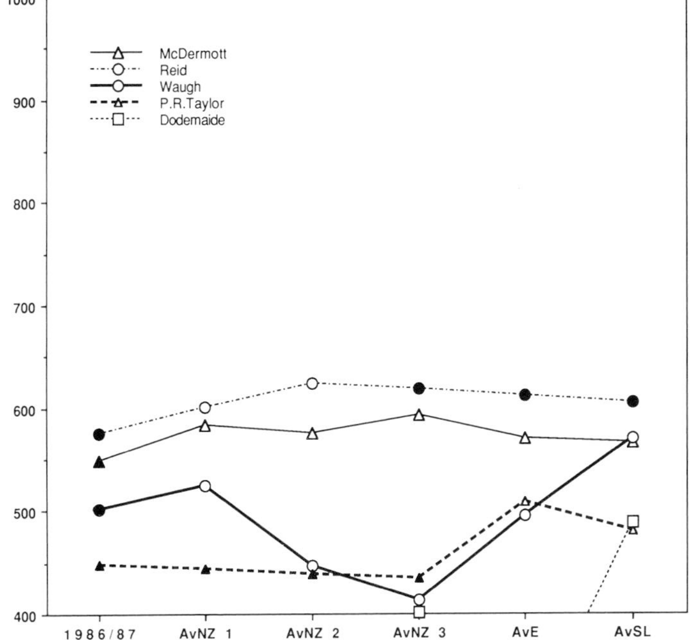
AUSTRALIA BOWLERS 1987/88
1000
900
800
700
600
500
400
McDermott
Reid
Waugh
P.R.Taylor
Dodemaide
1986/87
AvNZ 1
AvNZ 2
AvNZ 3
AvE
AvSL

WEST INDIES BATSMEN 1987/88

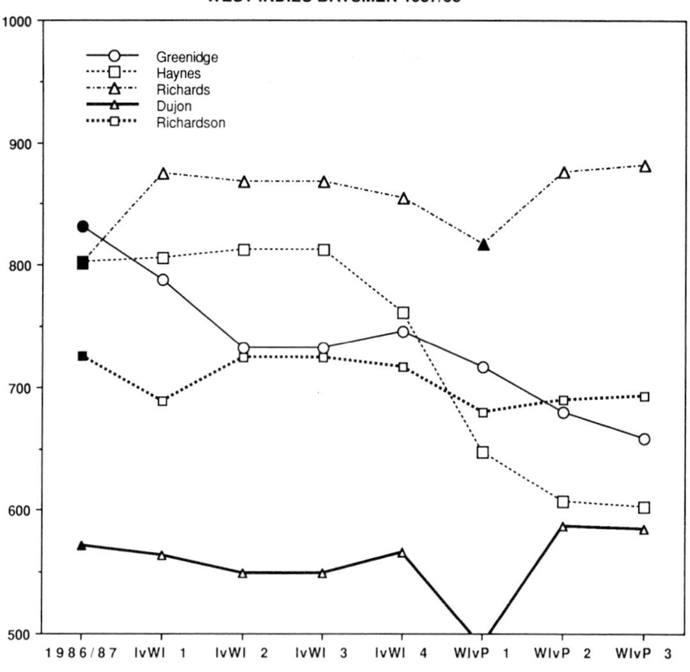

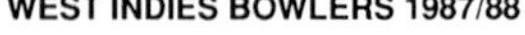

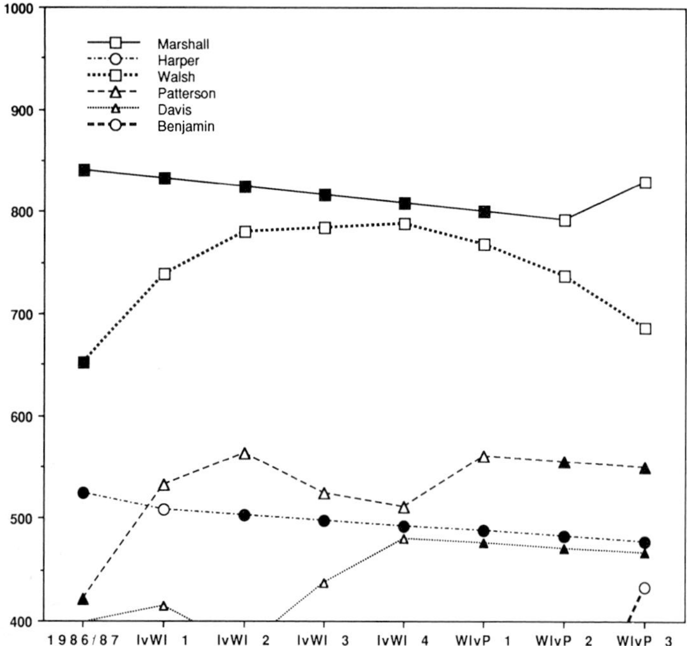

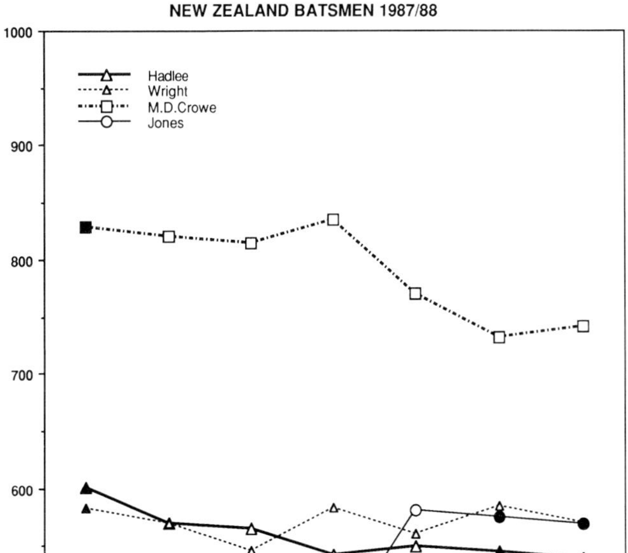
NEW ZEALAND BATSMEN 1987/88
Hadlee
Wright
M.D.Crowe
Jones
1000
900
800
700
600
500
1987
NZvA 1
NZvA 2
NZvA 3
NZvE 1
NZvE 2
NZvE 3

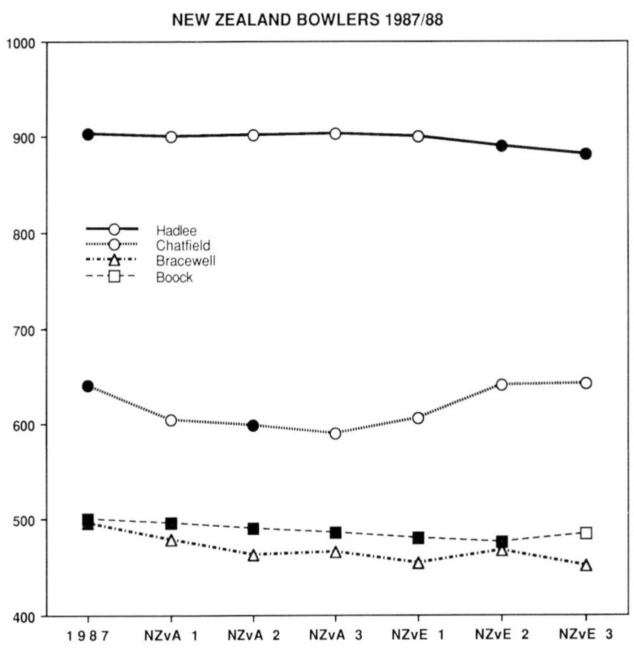
NEW ZEALAND BOWLERS 1987/88
Hadlee
Chatfield
Bracewell
Boock
1000
900
800
700
600
500
400
1987
NZvA 1
NZvA 2
NZvA 3
NZvE 1
NZvE 2
NZvE 3

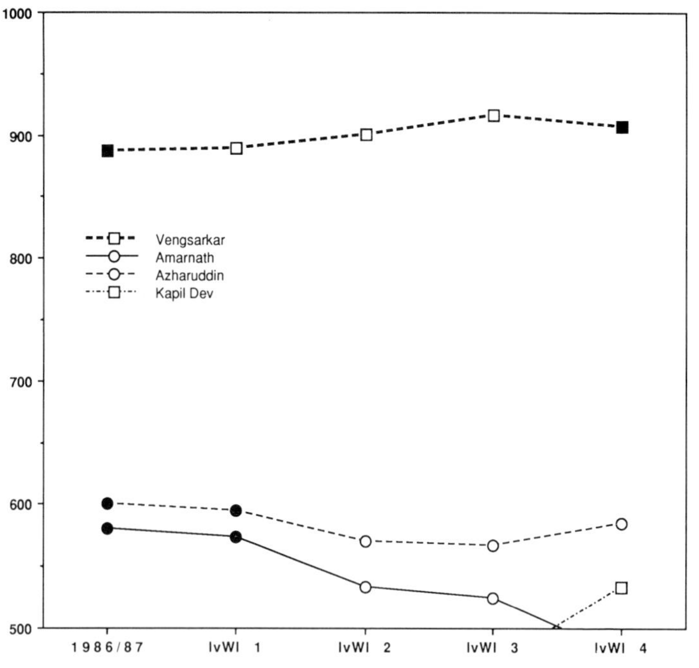
INDIA BATSMEN 1987/88
1000
900
800
700
600
500
Vengsarkar
Amarnath
Azharuddin
Kapil Dev
1986/87
IvWI 1
IvWI 2
IvWI 3
IvWI 4

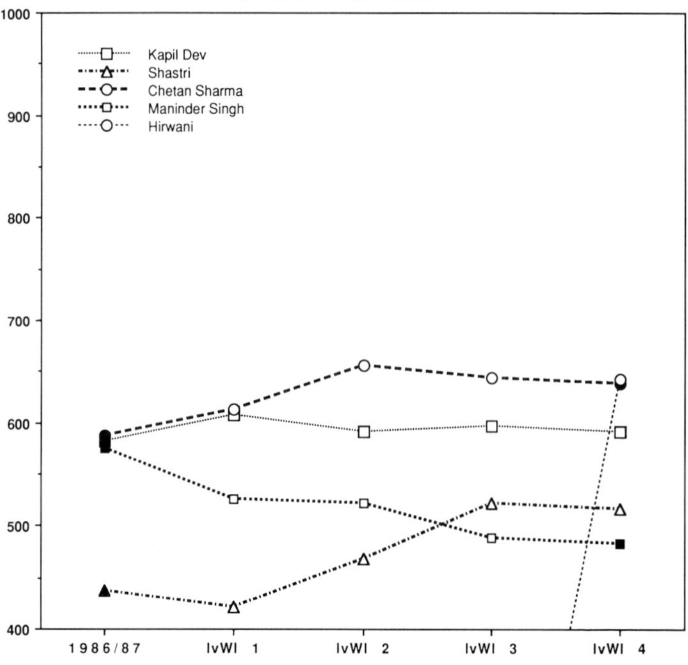
INDIA BOWLERS 1987/88
1000
900
800
700
600
500
400
Kapil Dev
Shastri
Chetan Sharma
Maninder Singh
Hirwani
1986/87
IvWI 1
IvWI 2
IvWI 3
IvWI 4

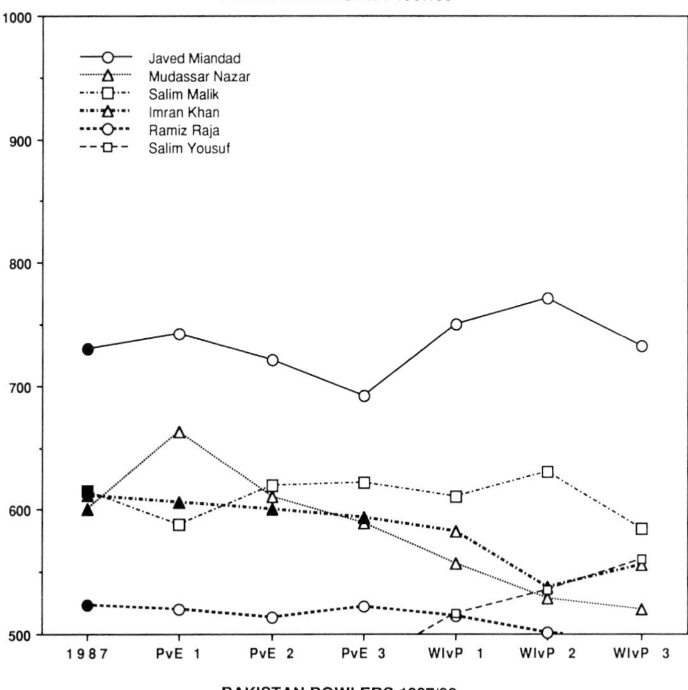
PAKISTAN BATSMEN 1987/88
Javed Miandad
Mudassar Nazar
Salim Malik
Imran Khan
Ramiz Raja
Salim Yousuf
1000
900
800
700
600
500
1987
PvE 1
PvE 2
PvE 3
WIvP 1
WIvP 2
WIvP 3

PAKISTAN BOWLERS 1987/88

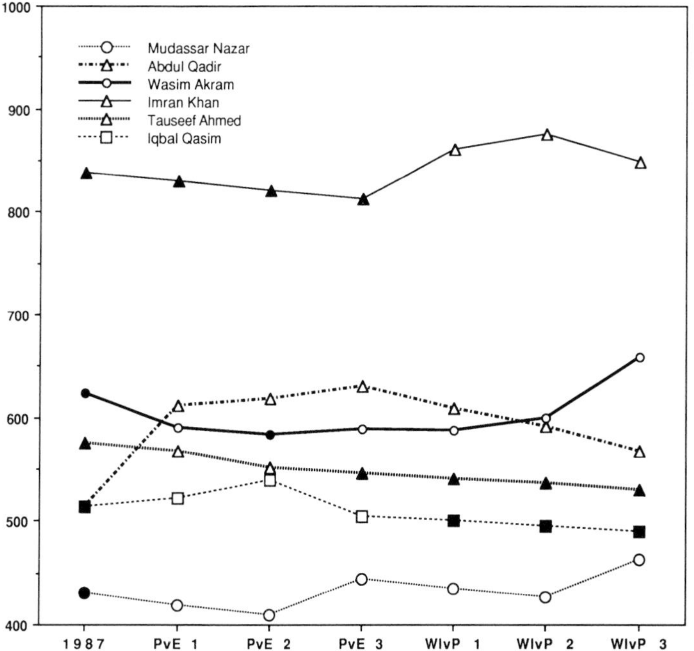
Mudassar Nazar
Abdul Qadir
Wasim Akram
Imran Khan
Tauseef Ahmed
Iqbal Qasim
1000
900
800
700
600
500
400
1987
PvE 1
PvE 2
PvE 3
WIvP 1
WIvP 2
WIvP 3

1988

ENGLAND vs WEST INDIES

First Test (Trent Bridge, 2–7 June) Match Drawn
England 1st Innings: 245 (Gooch 73, Broad 54, Marshall 6–69, Ambrose 4–53)
West Indies 1st Innings: 448 for 9 declared (Hooper 84, Richards 80, Marshall 72, Haynes 60, Ambrose 43 not out)
England 2nd Innings: 301 for 3 (Gooch 146, Gower 88 not out)

Second Test (Lord's, 16–21 June) West Indies won by 134 runs
West Indies 1st Innings: 209 (Logie 81, Dujon 53, Dilley 5–55, Small 4–64)
England 1st Innings:165 (Gower 46, Gooch 44, Marshall 6–32)
West Indies 2nd Innings: 397 (Greenidge 103, Logie 95 not out, Richards 72, Dujon 52, Dilley 4–73, Jarvis 4–107)
England 2nd Innings: 307 (Lamb 113, Marshall 4–60)

Third Test (Old Trafford, 30 June–5 July) West Indies won by an innings and 156 runs
England 1st Innings: 135 (Walsh 4–46)
West Indies 1st Innings: 384 for 7 declared (Harper 74, Dujon 67, Richards 47, Greenidge 45, Marshall 43 not out, Dilley 4–99)
England 2nd Innings: 93 (Marshall 7–22)

Fourth Test (Headingley, 21–26 July) West Indies won by 10 wickets
England 1st Innings: 201 (Lamb 64 retired hurt, Ambrose 4–58, Marshall 3–55)
West Indies 1st Innings: 275 (Harper 56, Haynes 54, Logie 44, Pringle 5–95, Foster 3–98)
England 2nd Innings: 138 (Gooch 50, Walsh 3–38, Ambrose 3–40)
West Indies 2nd Innings: 67 for no wicket (Dujon 40 not out)

Fifth Test (The Oval, 4–8 August) West Indies won by 8 wickets
England 1st Innings: 205 (R.A. Smith 57, Bailey 43, Ambrose 3–31, Harper 3–50, Marshall 3–64)
West Indies 1st Innings: 183 (Dujon 64, Logie 47, Foster 5–64, Pringle 3–45)
England 2nd Innings: 202 (Gooch 84, Benjamin 4–52)
West Indies 2nd Innings: 226 for 2 (Haynes 77 not out, Greenidge 77)

Captains: England – M.W. Gatting (1st Test), J.E. Emburey (2nd & 3rd Tests), C.S. Cowdrey (4th Test), G.A. Gooch (5th Test)
West Indies – I.V.A. Richards

Débuts: England – J.H. Childs (3rd Test), T.S. Curtis, R.A. Smith (4th Test), R.J. Bailey, M.P. Maynard (5th Test)
West Indies – K.L.T. Arthurton (4th Test)

Rising Stars: England – A.J. Lamb (+92 batting)
West Indies – W.K.M. Benjamin (+209 bowling)

In the year of the Four Captains, say Confucius, England get beaten. And so it was to be. Calling upon twenty-three players in the series, some of them not really very good at all, the selectors had another dreadful summer – so bad, in fact, that Peter May resigned as chairman soon afterwards. Starting out with a sturdy draw, thanks to splendid backs-to-the-wall stuff from Gooch and Gower, England lost their captain Gatting to the over-zealous attentions of the popular press, and thereafter lost all the Tests as well. From a settled, if not terribly successful side, they disintegrated into a constantly changing collection of very nervous individuals. Only Gooch played all five Tests (although Lamb and Dilley would have done so but for injury), while Gatting, after returning for one unhappy performance at Old Trafford (0 and 4), declared himself unavailable thereafter. Others on the merry-go-round included Broad (dropped after the second Test), Downton (after the third), Gower (after the fourth), Pringle (played all but the third), Capel (played the third and fifth), Small (played only the second, otherwise injured), Jack Richards (replaced Downton for the last two), DeFreitas (yo-yo impersonations), and indeed virtually every other player in county cricket. Even Athey was recalled at one point. After Gatting had been fired, Emburey took over as captain, but his inability to take wickets had finally been noticed on high, and he too received the heave-ho. Chris Cowdrey, May's godson, had one dismal Test in charge, and finally Gooch took over, after sixty-six Tests in the ranks.

All this ghastliness tended to detract from the brilliance of the West Indies, now guided back to form by Viv Richards. Malcolm Marshall was all but unplayable, taking a record 35 wickets at just 12.65, and Curtly Ambrose, whose first few Tests had promised much but delivered little, came quickly to prominence with 22 wickets (and a rating up from 102 to 444). Although Walsh and Patterson were less successful, Winston Benjamin nipped in with 12 useful and cheap wickets to win the Rising Star award. The batting, meanwhile, was dominated by Logie and Dujon, who time and again shored up the middle order after Foster or Dilley had taken some early wickets. Harper, Haynes and Greenidge (who scored the only century) all averaged just below 50, but Hooper, on his first tour, and Richardson found the going harder. Even so, by the end of the series, as the ratings show, the two teams were about as far apart as it's possible to be. Here was England's line-up after the final Test:

G.A. Gooch	batting rating: 636	bowling rating: 102
T.S. Curtis	batting rating: 187	
R.J. Bailey	batting rating: 210	
R.A. Smith	batting rating: 324	
M.P. Maynard	batting rating: 26	
D.J. Capel	batting rating: 268	bowling rating: 130
C.J. Richards	batting rating: 182	
D.R. Pringle	batting rating: 165	bowling rating: 338
P.A.J. DeFreitas	batting rating: 180	bowling rating: 219
N.A. Foster	batting rating: 185	bowling rating: 577
J.H. Childs	batting rating: 10	bowling rating: 41

Using our average (best seven batsmen, best four bowlers) that gives them team ratings of 284 (batting) and 316 (bowling) – as opposed to the West Indies' tallies of 593 and 646. No contest, and indeed, it wasn't one.

ENGLAND vs SRI LANKA

Only Test (Lord's, 25–30 August) England won by 7 wickets
Sri Lanka 1st Innings: 194 (J.R. Ratnayeke 59 not out, Kuruppu 46, Foster 3–51, Newport 3–77)
England 1st Innings: 429 (Russell 94, Gooch 75, Barnett 66, Lamb 63, Labrooy 4–119)
Sri Lanka 2nd Innings: 331 (Ranatunga 78, Samerasekera 57, Mendis 56, Newport 4–87)
England 2nd Innings: 100 for 3

Captains: England – G.A. Gooch
Sri Lanka – R.S. Madugalle

Débuts: England – R.C. Russell, K.J. Barnett, P.J. Newport, D.V. Lawrence
Sri Lanka – M.A.R. Samarasekera, A.W.R. Madurasinghe

A victory at last! The first in nineteen Tests! Admittedly it was against a distinctly rusty Sri Lankan team long accustomed to heavy defeat away from home (political unrest having ruled out Test cricket on their own turf). But the win was nonetheless an important morale-booster in a season that had seen England humiliated as rarely before, and Gooch's side carried it out efficiently and with few

The West Indies' strike force, Malcolm Marshall. There's none faster.

Neil Foster of Essex and England.

scrapes. All the débutants acquitted themselves well, especially Russell, who had long been kept out of the side because he supposedly couldn't bat. All four were picked for the winter tour to India, which was then cancelled, after government objections to half the side. (The touring party was as follows: Gooch (captain), Emburey (vice-captain), Bailey, Barnett, Childs, Dilley, Foster, Gower, Hemmings, Lamb, Lawrence, Newport, S.J. Rhodes, Robinson, Russell and R.A. Smith. Gatting had withdrawn from consideration.) The Sri Lankan Test match, meanwhile, did those English ratings no harm at all.

WORLD TOP TWENTY AFTER 1988

BATTING

(1)	1.	D.B. Vengsarkar (India)	907
(3)	2.	A.R. Border (Australia)	811
(2)	3.	I.V.A. Richards (West Indies)	803 (−79)
(4)	4.	M.D. Crowe (New Zealand)	741
(5)	5.	Javed Miandad (Pakistan)	732
(7)	6.	A. Ranatunga (Sri Lanka)	677 (−9)
(9)	7.	C.G. Greenidge (West Indies)	672 (+14)
(8)	8.	D.M. Jones (Australia)	659
(19)	9.	P.J. Dujon (West Indies)	658 (+73)
(24)	10.	G.A. Gooch (England)	646 (+98)

(11)	11.	D.C. Boon (Australia)	641
(15)	12.	D.L. Haynes (West Indies)	623 (+20)
(49)	13.	A.L. Logie (West Indies)	615 (+200)
(6)	14.	R.B. Richardson (West Indies)	604 (−89)
(18)	15.	M. Azharuddin (India)	585
(17)	16.	Salim Malik (Pakistan)	585
(13)	17.	D.I. Gower (England)	574 (−51)
(20)	18.	J.G. Wright (New Zealand)	570
(21)	19.	A.H. Jones (New Zealand)	568
(22)	20.	Salim Yousuf (Pakistan)	560

BOWLING

(3)	1.	M.D. Marshall (West Indies)	900 (+70)
(1)	2.	R.J. Hadlee (New Zealand)	882
(2)	3.	Imran Khan (Pakistan)	849
(7)	4.	Wasim Akram (Pakistan)	659
(39)	5.	W.K.M. Benjamin (West Indies)	643 (+209)
(8)	6.	E.J. Chatfield (New Zealand)	642
(9)	7.	N. Hirwani (India)	642
(10)	8.	Chetan Sharma (India)	638
(13)	9.	G.R. Dilley (England)	614 (+17)
(12)	10.	B.A. Reid (Australia)	605
(14)	11.	Kapil Dev (India)	592
(11)	12.	J.R. Ratnayeke (Sri Lanka)	578 (−36)
(5)	13.	C.A. Walsh (West Indies)	573 (−113)
(16)	14.	S.R. Waugh (Australia)	570
(15)	15.	N.A. Foster (England)	570 (−2)
(18)	16.	Abdul Qadir (Pakistan)	567
(19)	17.	C.J. McDermott (Australia)	566
(22)	18.	Tauseef Ahmed (Pakistan)	530
(23)	19.	R.J. Shastri (India)	516
(24)	20.	Iqbal Qasim (Pakistan)	490

In ratings terms, Gooch and Logie were the batting stars of the summer, while Richardson paid the penalty for his inability to cope with English conditions. With average ratings levels dropping slightly, Jones and Salim Yousuf found themselves in the top twenty for the first time, while two of England's failures, Broad and Gatting, found themselves well out, at 22nd and 26th respectively (down from 10th and 14th). Also missing, eighteen months after their retirements, were Gavaskar and Coney.

Marshall, meanwhile, took over Hadlee's spot at the top of the bowling chart, and Benjamin's position improved a touch as well. Again, three bowlers slithered in without bowling a ball, thanks to the 18-month rule which knocked out Garner and Holding (both retired), the out-of-favour Tony Gray, and the injured Geoff Lawson.

ENGLAND BATSMEN 1988

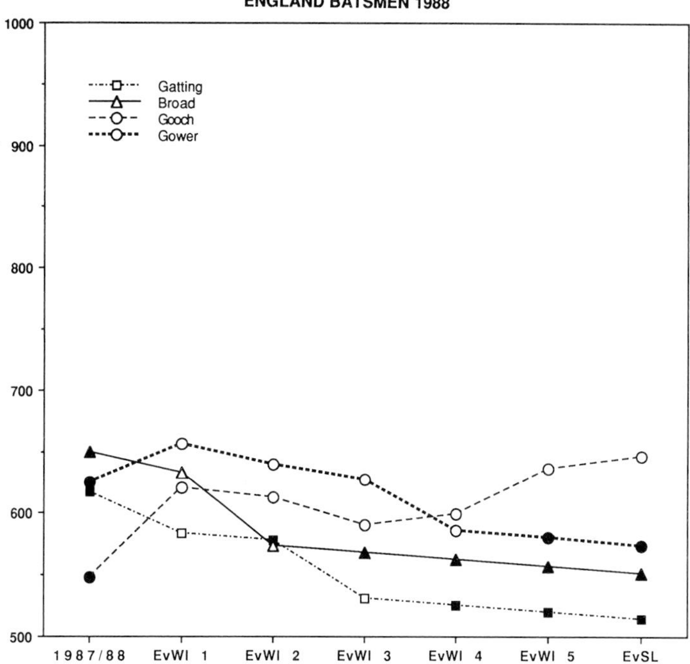
1000
900
800
700
600
500
Gatting
Broad
Gooch
Gower
1987/88
EvWI 1
EvWI 2
EvWI 3
EvWI 4
EvWI 5
EvSL

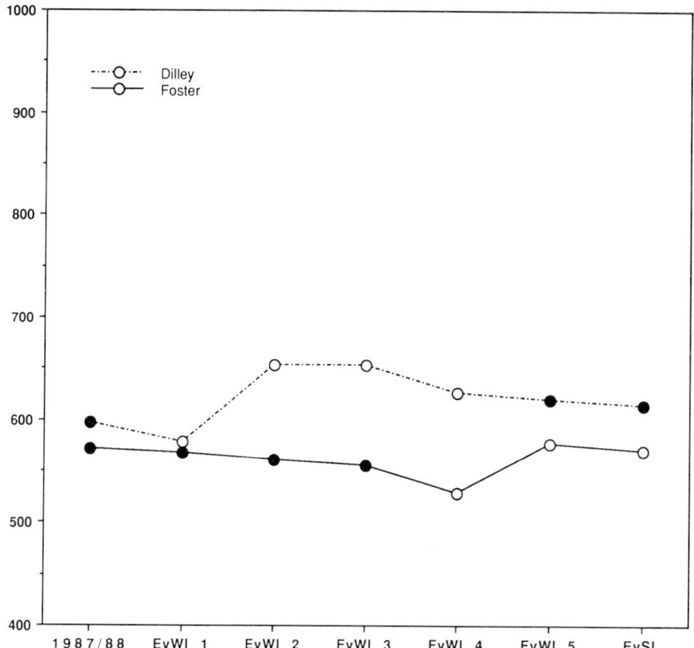
ENGLAND BOWLERS 1988
1000
900
800
700
600
500
400
Dilley
Foster
1987/88
EvWI 1
EvWI 2
EvWI 3
EvWI 4
EvWI 5
EvSL

WEST INDIES BATSMEN 1988

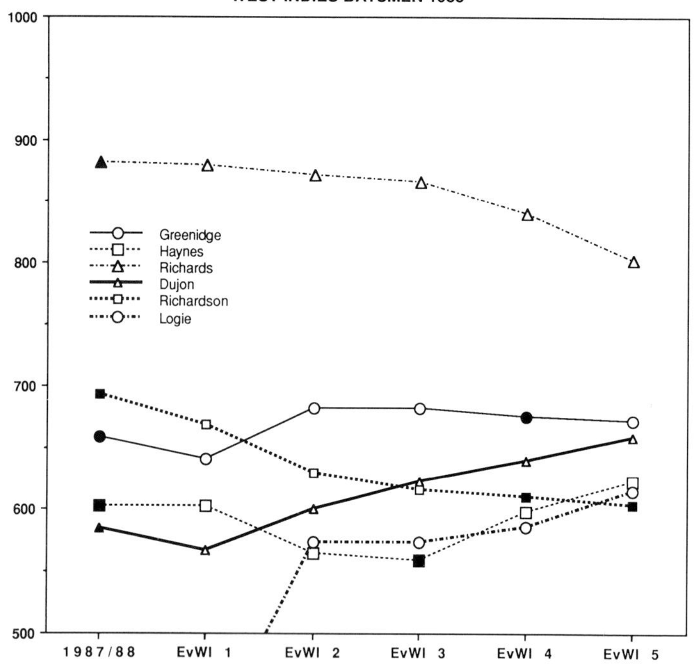
1000
900
800
700
600
500
Greenidge
Haynes
Richards
Dujon
Richardson
Logie
1987/88
EvWI 1
EvWI 2
EvWI 3
EvWI 4
EvWI 5

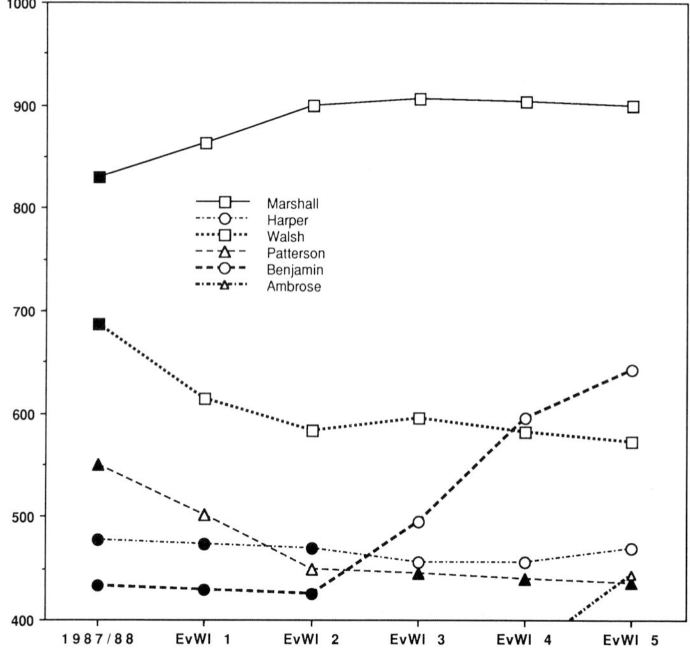
WEST INDIES BOWLERS 1988
1000
900
800
700
600
500
400
Marshall
Harper
Walsh
Patterson
Benjamin
Ambrose
1987/88
EvWI 1
EvWI 2
EvWI 3
EvWI 4
EvWI 5

SRI LANKA BATSMEN 1987/88 & 1988

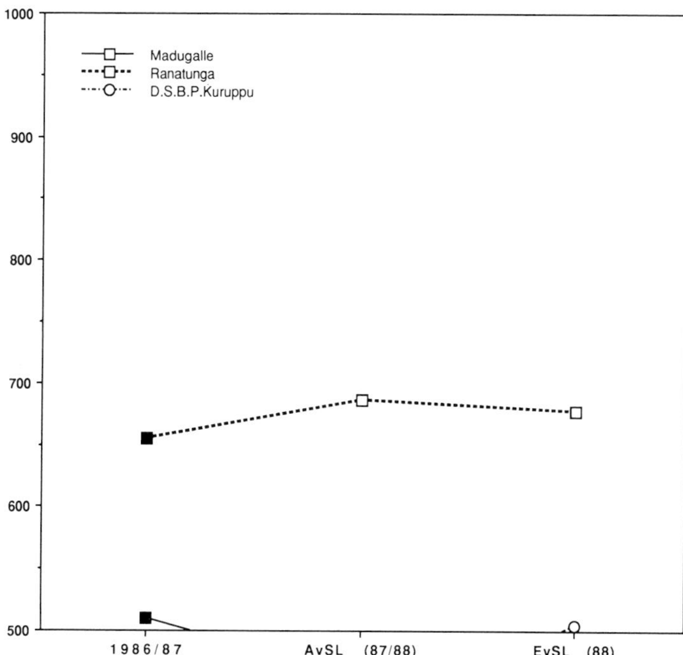
1000
900
800
700
600
500
Madugalle
Ranatunga
D.S.B.P.Kuruppu
1986/87
AvSL (87/88)
EvSL (88)

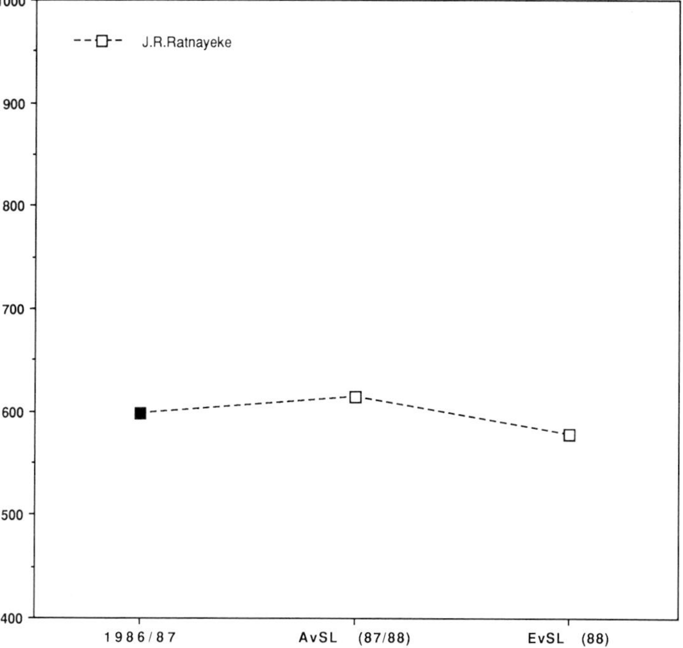
SRI LANKA BOWLERS 1987/88 & 1988
1000
900
800
700
600
500
400
J.R.Ratnayeke
1986/87
AvSL (87/88)
EvSL (88)

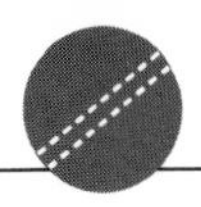

1988–89

PAKISTAN vs AUSTRALIA

First Test (Karachi, 15–20 September) Pakistan won by an innings and 188 runs
Pakistan 1st Innings: 469 (Javed Miandad 211, Shoaib Mohammad 94, Salim Malik 45, May 4–97, Reid 4–109)
Australia 1st Innings: 165 (P.L. Taylor 54 not out, Iqbal Qasim 5–35)
Australia 2nd Innings: 116 (Iqbal Qasim 4–49, Abdul Qadir 3–33)

Second Test (Faisalabad, 23–28 September) Match Drawn
Pakistan 1st Innings: 316 (Ijaz Ahmed 122, Salim Yousuf 62, Javed Miandad 43, Dodemaide 4–87, Reid 3–92)
Australia 1st Innings: 321 (Border 113 not out, G.R. Marsh 51, Tauseef Ahmed 3–73)
Pakistan 2nd Innings: 378 for 9 declared (Javed Miandad 107, Shoaib Mohammad 74, Salim Yousuf 66 not out, Reid 4–100, May 3–126)
Australia 2nd Innings: 67 for 3

Third Test (Lahore, 7–11 October) Match Drawn
Australia 1st Innings: 340 (Border 75, G.R. Marsh 64, Waugh 59, Tauseef Ahmed 3–86, Abdul Qadir 3–88)
Pakistan 1st Innings: 233 (Ramiz Raja 64, Reid 3–53, Dodemaide 3–56, May 3–73)
Australia 2nd Innings: 161 for 3 declared (G.R. Marsh 84 not out)
Pakistan 2nd Innings: 153 for 8 (Mudassar Nazar 49, Taylor 4–78, May 3–39)

Captains: Pakistan – Javed Miandad
Australia – A.R. Border

Début: Australia – I.A. Healy (1st Test)

Rising Stars: Pakistan – Javed Miandad (+102 batting)
Australia – B.A. Reid (+68 bowling)

With Imran Khan refusing to play because it was a bit early in the season for him, Pakistan came under the control of Javed Miandad once more, with all the inevitable consequences. The first Test, played on a dry, worn, grass-free pitch in the centre of a luscious

That's why Steve Waugh has a test average in the mid-forties.

green ground, provided the home side with their widest ever margin of victory, although many of the umpiring decisions were so 'controversial' that after the match the Australian team voted to fly home immediately. Miandad himself scored his usual double century, his fifth in Tests (all against different countries, curiously), having survived two confident lbw appeals from Tim May when on 15. Although relations did not deteriorate to the Gatting/Shakoor Rana level – or if they did, at least not so publicly – the Australians made no secret of their fury and frustration. Their ratings didn't look too happy, either. Of the major batsmen only Border (230 runs at 57.5) and Geoff Marsh (at his gritty best with 232 runs at 46.4) averaged over 20, although Peter Taylor's 110 runs at 55 improved his batting rating from 175 to 394. Dean Jones had a particularly grim series, averaging just 8.8s while Boon, Waugh and the recalled Graeme Wood fared only a little better. The bowlers were more successful – the final two Tests were, after all, quite well matched – with, surprisingly, the two swifter bowlers, Reid and Dodemaide, heading the averages. For Pakistan, deprived not only of Imran but of the injured Wasim Akram as well, the spinners took the honours and indeed most of the wickets, Iqbal Qasim returning to the fray with 12 wickets at 14.75. Javed Miandad, with a series average of over 80, once more dominated the mercurial Pakistani batting.

But a good tempered series it generally wasn't. Would there ever be such a thing in Pakistan again?

INDIA vs NEW ZEALAND

First Test (Bangalore, 14–17 November) India won by 172 runs
India 1st Innings: 384 for 9 declared (Sidhu 116, Vengsarkar 75, Shastri 54, More 46, Hadlee 5–65)

New Zealand 1st Innings: 189 (Jones 45, Arshad Ayub 4–51, Kapil Dev 3–24)
India 2nd Innings: 141 for 1 declared (Srikkanth 58 not out, Sidhu 43 not out)
New Zealand 2nd Innings: 164 (Wright 58, Hirwani 6–59, Arshad Ayub 4–53)

Second Test (Bombay, 24–29 November) New Zealand won by 136 runs
New Zealand 1st Innings: 236 (J.G. Bracewell 52, Greatbatch 46, Shastri 4–45, Hirwani 3–82)
India 1st Innings: 234 (Srikkanth 94, Hadlee 6–49)
New Zealand 2nd Innings: 279 (Jones 78, Smith 54, Arshad Ayub 5–50, Hirwani 4–93)
India 2nd Innings: 145 (Arun Lal 47, J.G. Bracewell 6–51, Hadlee 4–39)

Third Test (Hyderabad, 2–6 December) India won by 10 wickets
New Zealand 1st Innings: 254 (Greatbatch 90 not out, Smith 79, Arshad Ayub 4–55, Sanjeev Sharma 3–37)
India 1st Innings: 358 (Azharuddin 81, Srikkanth 69, Shastri 42, Kapil Dev 40, Snedden 4–69, Chatfield 3–82, Hadlee 3–99)
New Zealand 2nd Innings: 124 (Wright 62, Kapil Dev 3–21, Arshad Ayub 3–36, Hirwani 3–43)
India 2nd Innings: 22 for no wicket

Captains: India – D.B. Vengsarkar
New Zealand – J.G. Wright

Débuts: India – R.G. Patel (2nd Test), Sanjeer Sharma (3rd Test)
New Zealand – C.M. Kuggeleijn (1st Test)

Rising Stars: India – K. Srikkanth (+141 batting)
New Zealand – M.J. Greatbatch (+185 batting)

Another of those 'blink and you've missed it' series – three Tests in little over three weeks, with barely a pause for breath. In the meantime India won a well-matched series 2–1 and Richard Hadlee finally passed Botham's total of 373 Test wickets. Delhi belly and Narendra Hirwani on a dodgy pitch accounted for the visitors in the first Test, Hadlee and Bracewell won the second and the Indian spinners took command once more in the third. But the New Zealanders, under new leadership and in the absence of Martin Crowe, were never made to look second rate. Mark Greatbatch topped the averages with 39.2, which in a low-scoring series was enough to increase his rating from 213 to 585, while Hadlee kept up his terrifyingly high standards with 18 wickets at 14. Ken Rutherford failed yet again, and lost his place yet again, after the second Test, while the other great white hope, Andrew Jones, had a quiet series. Once again, though, the New Zealanders suffered through their lack of cover for Hadlee – the two young pretenders this time round, Danny Morrison and Chris Kuggeleijn, took just one wicket between them.

The Indians, with their highly proficient spin attack, were better placed to take advantage of the generally poor wickets – which may be why they were generally poor wickets. But both Ayub and Hirwani consolidated their immense promise with, respectively, 21 and 20 wickets. Ayub's rating shot up from 73 (shades of Maninder) to 518, while Hirwani's, already at 642 after one Test, saw his career bowling average climb from 8 to the ghastly heights of 14.61 and his rating to 739. Meanwhile, Srikkanth scored lots of runs – 280 at 60 – mostly in his inimitable crash-bang-wallop style, while Sidhu, recalled after five years and a name change (from Navjot Singh), also impressed with 198 runs at just under 50, and an early rating of 413. But it was the spin-bowling of Ayub and Hirwani, and New Zealand's inexperience against it, that turned the series.

AUSTRALIA vs WEST INDIES

First Test (Brisbane, 18–21 November) West Indies won by 9 wickets
Australia 1st Innings: 167 (Walsh 4–62, Ambrose 3–30)
West Indies 1st Innings: 394 (Richardson 81, Greenidge 80, Richards 68, Haynes 40, May 3–90, McDermott 3–99)
Australia 2nd Innings: 289 (Waugh 90, Border 41, Marshall 4–92, Walsh 3–61, Ambrose 3–78)
West Indies 2nd Innings: 63 for 1

Second Test (Perth, 2–6 December) West Indies won by 169 runs
West Indies 1st Innings: 449 (Richards 146, Logie 93, Richardson 66, Greenidge 40, M.G. Hughes 5–130, Lawson 3–97)
Australia 1st Innings: 395 for 8 declared (Wood 111, Waugh 91, Boon 80, Ambrose 5–72)
West Indies 2nd Innings: 349 for 9 declared (Haynes 100, Hooper 64, Richardson 48, M.G. Hughes 8–87)
Australia 2nd Innings: 234 (Healy 52, Wood 42, Ambrose 3–66)

Third Test (Melbourne, 24–29 December) West Indies won by 285 runs
West Indies 1st Innings: 280 (Greenidge 49, Ambrose 44, Alderman 4–68, McDermott 3–62, Waugh 3–77)
Australia 1st Innings: 242 (Waugh 42, Patterson 4–49, Ambrose 4–60)

West Indies 2nd Innings: 361 for 9 declared (Richardson 122, Richards 63, Dujon 46, Waugh 5–92, Alderman 3–78)
Australia 2nd Innings: 114 (Patterson 5–39)

Fourth Test (Sydney, 26–30 January) Australia won by 7 wickets
West Indies 1st Innings: 224 (Haynes 75, Greenidge 56, Border 7–46)
Australia 1st Innings: 401 (Boon 149, Border 75, Waugh 55 not out, Marshall 5–29)
West Indies 2nd Innings: 256 (Haynes 143, Border 4–50, Hohns 3–69)
Australia 2nd Innings: 82 for 3

Fifth Test (Adelaide, 3–7 February) Match Drawn
Australia 1st Innings: 515 (D.M. Jones 216, M.G. Hughes 72 not out, Border 64, Ambrose 3–93, Walsh 3–120)
West Indies 1st Innings: 369 (Richardson 106, Haynes 83, Richards 69, Whitney 7–89)
Australia 2nd Innings: 224 for 4 declared (G.R. Marsh 79, Boon 55 not out)
West Indies 2nd Innings: 233 for 4 (Greenidge 104, Richards 68 not out)

Captains: Australia – A.R. Border
West Indies – I.V.A. Richards

Débuts: Australia – T.V. Hohns, M.A. Taylor (4th Test)

Rising Stars: Australia – S.R. Waugh (+107 batting)
West Indies – C.E.L. Ambrose (+320 bowling)

Although West Indies took the series 3–1, it's probably the second figure in that scoreline that will be remembered longer than the first. For it was at Sydney, on the traditional spinners' wicket, that Allan Border, who had taken just one wicket in his preceding forty-nine Tests (David Gower in 1985–86), now claimed 11 from the West Indies, with judicious usage of the long hop and the full toss. Such an extraordinary performance from someone who would admit to being rather less than a frontline bowler had drastic effects on his bowling rating (up from 132 to 483), making him, by our criteria at least, a 'genuine' all-rounder. Had the world gone mad?

In the previous three Tests, of course, the West Indies had carried on as usual, winning by substantial margins. Marshall finally picked up his 300th Test wicket at Melbourne, in his sixty-first Test, while Ambrose's further advance – 26 wickets in the series at 21.46 – pushed his rating from 444 to 764, 4th in the world. With Walsh and Patterson no less hostile, the tourists' bowling was just too fast for most of the Australian batsmen. Veletta lost his place after the second Test, Graeme Wood after the third, while Marsh, with just one fifty, was also disappointing. But Waugh's two nineties, Jones' 216 (the first time he had passed fifty all season) and Boon's consistency under fire (he averaged 44) must have consoled Border during some difficult times, as indeed must the 243 no-balls the West Indian quicks bowled during the series. Border's 100th Test at Melbourne was, for him, less than memorable – his 0 was his first in 88 innings.

The Australian bowling, too, was not a roaring success. Dodemaide lasted just two Tests (his 4 wickets weren't enough), while Lawson, recalled after two years, had his jaw smashed to pieces by Ambrose. Alderman returned after his three-year ban, looked the part, but was injured just before the final Test. Merv Hughes, shorn of locks and beer belly, took 13 spectacular wickets at Perth (helping his rating up from 354 to 677 in the process), but took only one more in the rest of the series. McDermott, May and Peter Taylor all came and went.

The West Indian batsmen, when not facing Border, were more consistent than their opponents. Haynes, Richardson and Richards all averaged in the mid-fifties, with Greenidge not far behind. But Logie, after his prolific English summer, fell back into his old ways, as did his rating, down to 532 by the series' end. Carl Hooper, too, was finding it hard to settle down at the highest level – his rating briefly nudged above 400 and was gone again.

The resuscitation of Australia's fortunes – and consequently their confidence – was to prove valuable during their 1989 tour of England. But it wasn't a happy series. Umpiring decisions consistently upset the West Indies, while the excessive short pitched bowling certainly put the wind up the Aussies, as well as keeping the local hospitals busy. Both teams seemed relieved when this very long tour finally came to an end.

NEW ZEALAND vs PAKISTAN

First Test (Dunedin, 3–7 February) Match Abandoned

Second Test (Wellington, 10–14 February) Match Drawn
New Zealand 1st Innings: 447 (M.D. Crowe 174, Jones 86, Smith 40 not out, Imran Khan 3–75, Saleem Jaffer 3–94)
Pakistan 1st Innings: 438 for 7 declared (Shoaib Mohammad 163, Javed Miandad 118, Imran Khan 71, Hadlee 4–101)
New Zealand 2nd Innings: 186 for 8 (Vance 44, Saleem Jaffer 5–40, Imran Khan 3–34)

Third Test (Auckland, 24–28 February) Match Drawn
Pakistan 1st Innings: 616 for 5 declared (Javed Miandad 271, Shoaib

Mohammad 112, Salim Malik 80 not out, Imran Khan 69 not out, Aamer Malik 56)
New Zealand 1st Innings: 403 (M.D. Crowe 78, Greatbatch 76, Vance 68, Smith 58, Jones 47, Abdul Qadir 6–160)
New Zealand 2nd Innings: 99 for 3

Captains: New Zealand – J.G. Wright
Pakistan – Imran Khan

Débuts: Pakistan – Aaqib Javed (2nd Test)

Another gripping result-free series played on New Zealand's now notorious dead pitches. Well, at least the second and third Tests were; the first was washed out by rain, curiously only the third time a whole match has been lost in that way in Test history. With the brothers Crowe back in the side, and the unsuccessful Franklin and Rutherford replaced by Vance and Patel, the New Zealanders had a more solid look than they had had in India, but at Auckland, two long, lo-o-o-ong innings doomed the game to a draw days before it eventually ended. Shoaib's innings, the longest 150 of all time, was, at 720 minutes, the seventh longest anything of all time. He and Javed Miandad repeated their century-scoring trick in the final Test (which also saw Stephen Boock coaxed out of retirement) and, amidst Pakistani complaints about the umpiring (but of course), the game petered out once more. New Zealand had retained their unbeaten record at home – no Test lost since 1978–79 – and everyone had become very very bored indeed. Except of course, Shoaib (up to 603) and Miandad, who, with a rating of 903, returned to the top of the world pile for the first time since 1983. (Five batsmen, in fact, ended with averages over 100: Miandad (194.5), Imran (140), Shoaib (137.5), Ian Smith (127) and Salim Malik (118). A record?)

WEST INDIES vs INDIA

First Test (Georgetown, Guyana, 25–30 March) Match Drawn
West Indies 1st Innings: 437 (Richardson 194, Greenidge 82, Logie 46, Arshad Ayub 5–104)
India 1st Innings: 86 for 1 (Sidhu 42 not out)

Second Test (Bridgetown, Barbados 7–12 April) West Indies won by 8 wickets
India 1st Innings: 321 (Manjrekar 108, Azharuddin 61, Bishop 6–87)
West Indies 1st Innings: 377 (Greenidge 117, Richardson 93, Marshall 40 not out, Shastri 4–78)

India 2nd Innings: 251 (Shastri 107, More 50, Marshall 5–60, Ambrose 3–66)
West Indies 2nd Innings: 196 for 2 (Haynes 112 not out, Richardson 59)

Third Test (Port-of-Spain, Trinidad 15–20 April) West Indies won by 217 runs
West Indies 1st Innings: 314 (Logie 87, Haynes 65, Arshad Ayub 5–117)
India 1st Innings: 150 (Marshall 5–34, Walsh 4–37)
West Indies 2nd Innings: 266 (Richardson 99, Kapil Dev 5–58, Chetan Sharma 3–54)
India 2nd Innings: 213 (Vengsarkar 62, More 42, Marshall 6–55, Bishop 3–81)

Fourth Test (Kingston, Jamaica, 28 April–3 May) West Indies won by 7 wickets
India 1st Innings: 289 (Sidhu 116, Manjrekar 47, Walsh 6–62)
West Indies 1st Innings: 384 (Richardson 156, Richards 110, Kapil Dev 6–86)
India 2nd Innings: 152 (Manjrekar 41, Walsh 4–39, Bishop 4–61)
West Indies 2nd Innings: 60 for 3

Captains: West Indies – I.V.A. Richards
India – D.B. Vengsarkar

Débuts: West Indies – I.R. Bishop (1st Test)
India – M. Venkataramana (4th Test)

Rising Stars: West Indies – R.B. Richardson (+201 batting)
India – Arshad Ayub (+107 bowling)

It was India's turn to be rolled over next, and Dilip Vengsarkar's side played their roles to a T. The batsmen were all out cheaply, the bowlers didn't get many wickets, and the captain complained about the umpiring. Only three days of rain in the first Test saved India from the traditional blackwash.

Richie Richardson was the tourists' main bugbear. With 619 runs at over 88, he was a model of consistency, and his rating, already more than respectable at 690, shot up to 891 over the four Tests. Haynes, Logie and Greenidge were in the runs, too, while King Viv suffered an unusually barren patch before his 110 at Kingston wrapped up the series, and pushed him to fourth in the all-time run-scorers' list (until Border overtook him again a month or two later). The Indian batting, though, was rather less prolific. Without Srikkanth (who flew home early injured) and with Azharuddin troubled by a groin strain, it had a flimsy look about it. Manjrekar, perhaps surprisingly, was the only batsman to prosper to any extent, with a fine maiden century at Bridgetown, although his rating remained low at 191. By the series' end there were only two Indians with ratings over 500 – Vengsarkar, still riding high at 822, and Azharuddin.

The West Indies, on the other hand, had only two specialist batsmen below that figure – Dujon on 494 and the inexperienced Arthurton (231). The two sides' bowling attacks, though, were more balanced – at least in theory. But Ayub and Hirwani, so lethal at home, were not so tricky on foreign soil. Ayub's 14 wickets at 32 were at least respectable, but Hirwani's 6 at over 57 lost him his place for the final Test. Kapil Dev led the way, with 18 wickets at 21.44, and at Kingston became only the second bowler after Ian Botham to concede more than 10,000 runs in Tests. His performance at Kingston sent him hurtling back into the upper reaches of the bowling chart for the first time in some years. Curiously it was the same Test, in which he took just 2 wickets, that cost Marshall the leadership of the same chart. So what happened? Walsh and Bishop cleaned up instead.

WORLD TOP TWENTY AFTER 1988–89

BATTING

(5)	1.	Javed Miandad (Pakistan)	903 (+171)
(14)	2.	R.B. Richardson (West Indies)	891 (+287)
(1)	3.	D.B. Vengsarkar (India)	760 (−147)
(3)	4.	I.V.A. Richards (West Indies)	758 (−45)
(4)	5.	M.D. Crowe (New Zealand)	757 (+16)
(12)	6.	D.L. Haynes (West Indies)	745 (+122)
(2)	7.	A.R. Border (Australia)	730 (−81)
(6)	8.	A. Ranatunga (Sri Lanka)	677
(76)	9.	M.J. Greatbatch (New Zealand)	659 (+446)
(10)	10.	G.A. Gooch (England)	646
(7)	11.	C.G. Greenidge (West Indies)	629 (−43)
(11)	12.	D.C. Boon (Australia)	622 (−19)
(8)	13.	D.M. Jones (Australia)	621 (−38)
(13)	14.	A.L. Logie (West Indies)	605 (−10)
(47)	15.	Shoaib Mohammad (Pakistan)	603 (+217)
(15)	16.	M. Azharuddin (India)	595 (+10)
(21)	17.	Imran Khan (Pakistan)	593 (+37)
(32)	18.	K. Srikkanth (India)	576 (+117)
(16)	19.	Salim Malik (Pakistan)	576 (−9)
(17)	20.	D.I. Gower (England)	574

BOWLING

(2)	1.	R.J. Hadlee (New Zealand)	900 (+18)
(1)	2.	M.D. Marshall (West Indies)	883 (−17)
(3)	3.	Imran Khan (Pakistan)	815 (−34)
(11)	4.	Kapil Dev (India)	656 (+64)
(10)	5.	B.A. Reid (Australia)	640 (+35)
(13)	6.	C.A. Walsh (West Indies)	636 (+63)
(4)	7.	Wasim Akram (Pakistan)	627 (−32)
(63)	8.	Arshad Ayub (India)	625 (+552)
(29)	9.	C.E.L. Ambrose (West Indies)	619 (+175)
(9)	10.	G.R. Dilley (England)	614
NE	11.	I.R. Bishop (West Indies)	586
(8)	12.	Chetan Sharma (India)	584 (−54)
(12)	13.	J.R. Ratnayeke (Sri Lanka)	578
(15)	14.	N.A. Foster (England)	570
(6)	15.	E.J. Chatfield (New Zealand)	569 (−73)
(20)	16.	Iqbal Qasim (Pakistan)	563 (+73)
(5)	17.	W.K.M. Benjamin (West Indies)	562 (−71)
(7)	18.	N. Hirwani (India)	553 (−77)
(16)	19.	Abdul Qadir (Pakistan)	551 (−16)
RE	20.	G.F. Lawson (Australia)	542

Big changes in the chart reflected a busy season, for although neither England nor Sri Lanka had played a Test (the first because no-one would have them, the second because no-one would go near them), that didn't really affect the chart as such, for obvious reasons. Instead, ratings watchers were entertained by the re-emergence of Javed Miandad as the world's leading batsman, unseating Vengsarkar. Richie Richardson and Mark Greatbatch also leapt ahead, while the Pakistani selectors' inexplicable faith in Shoaib Mohammad finally paid off. Out of the twenty went Jones and Wright of New Zealand (to 21st and 22nd respectively), Salim Yousuf of Pakistan (to 24th), and Jeffrey Dujon, down from 9th to 29th.

As for the bowling, well, it was the West Indies' year. With their four first choice bowlers all in the top eleven, and Winston Benjamin only 24 points below, there could be little doubt that the West Indies were back in working order after some testing times. The Indians Ayub and Hirwani were the other main movers, the latter discovering the parlous consequences of going on tour to the West Indies. Moving out were Tauseef Ahmed (18th to 21st), McDermott and Waugh of Australia (down to 22nd and 26th respectively) and Shastri (19th to 23rd).

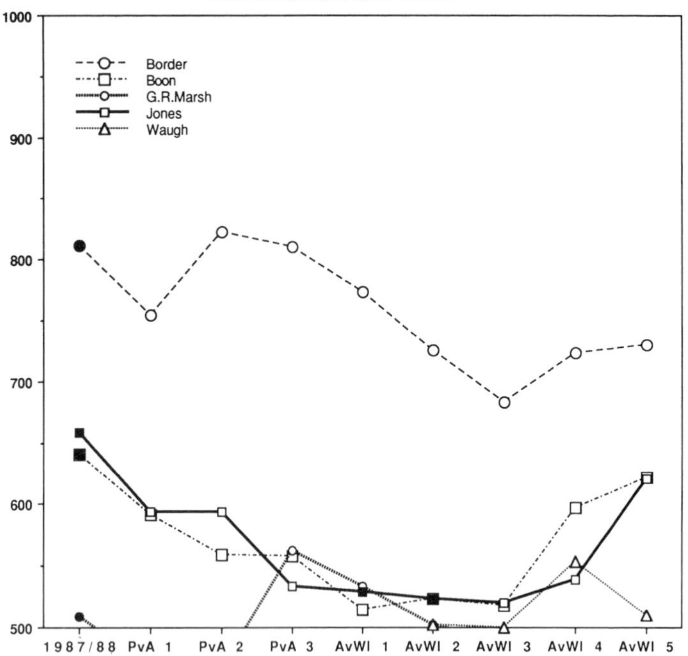
AUSTRALIA BATSMEN 1988/89
1000
900
800
700
600
500
Border
Boon
G.R.Marsh
Jones
Waugh
1987/88
PvA 1
PvA 2
PvA 3
AvWI 1
AvWI 2
AvWI 3
AvWI 4
AvWI 5

AUSTRALIA BOWLERS 1988/89

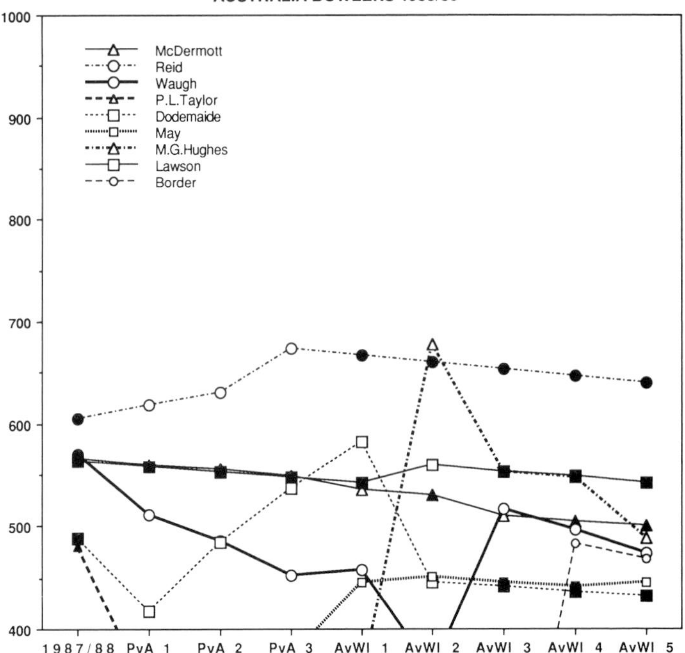
1000
900
800
700
600
500
400
McDermott
Reid
Waugh
P.L.Taylor
Dodemaide
May
M.G.Hughes
Lawson
Border
1987/88
PvA 1
PvA 2
PvA 3
AvWI 1
AvWI 2
AvWI 3
AvWI 4
AvWI 5

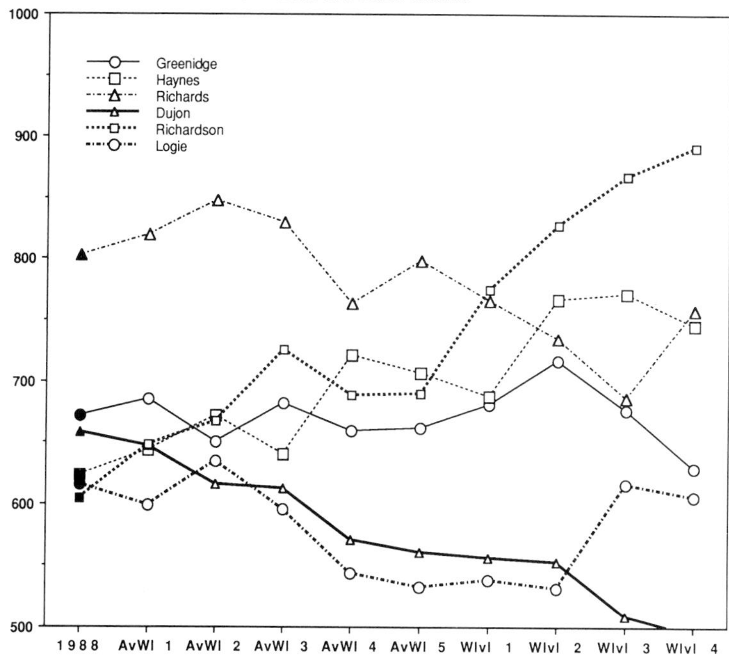
WEST INDIES BATSMEN 1988/89
Greenidge
Haynes
Richards
Dujon
Richardson
Logie
1000
900
800
700
600
500
1988 AvWI 1 AvWI 2 AvWI 3 AvWI 4 AvWI 5 WIvI 1 WIvI 2 WIvI 3 WIvI 4

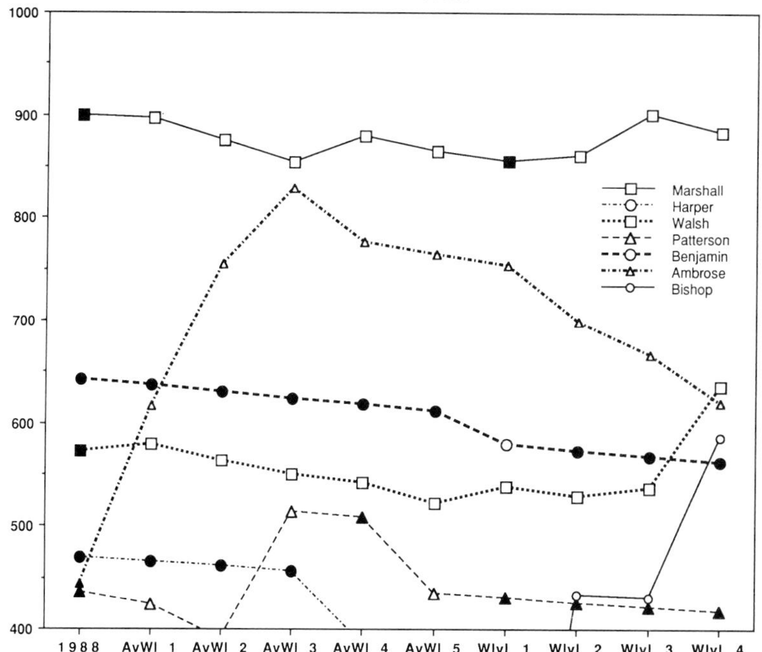
WEST INDIES BOWLERS 1988/89
Marshall
Harper
Walsh
Patterson
Benjamin
Ambrose
Bishop
1000
900
800
700
600
500
400
1988 AvWI 1 AvWI 2 AvWI 3 AvWI 4 AvWI 5 WIvI 1 WIvI 2 WIvI 3 WIvI 4

NEW ZEALAND BATSMEN 1988/89

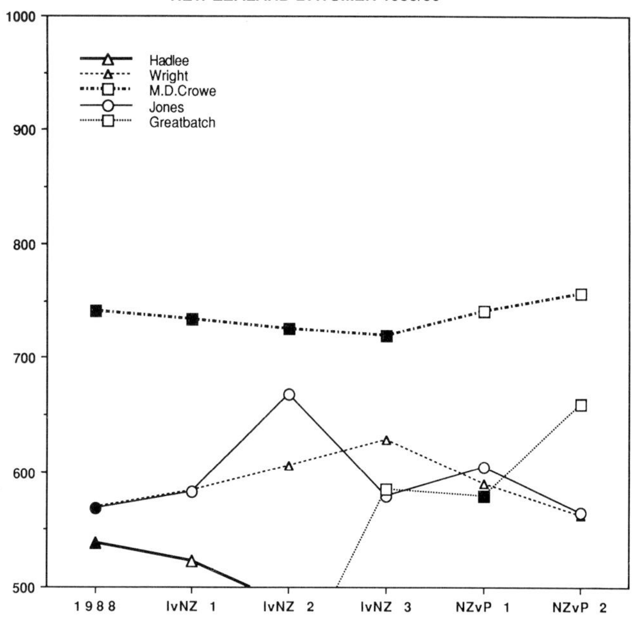

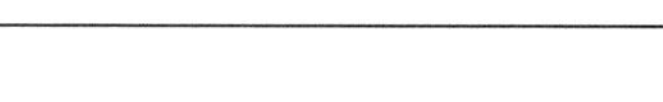
NEW ZEALAND BOWLERS 1988/89

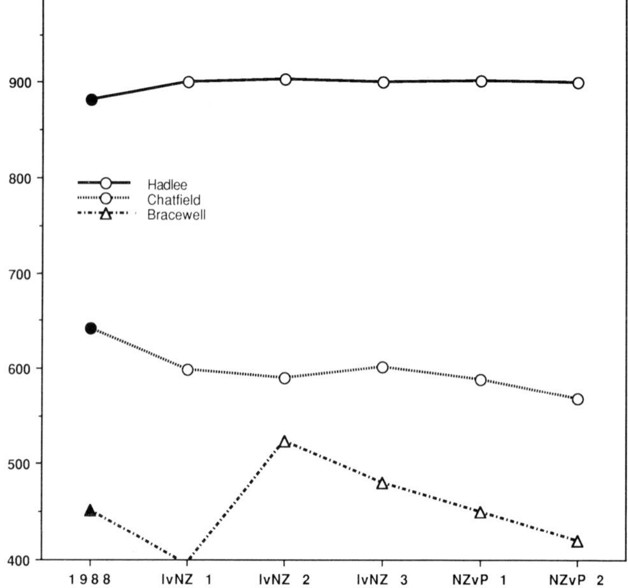

INDIA BATSMEN 1988/89

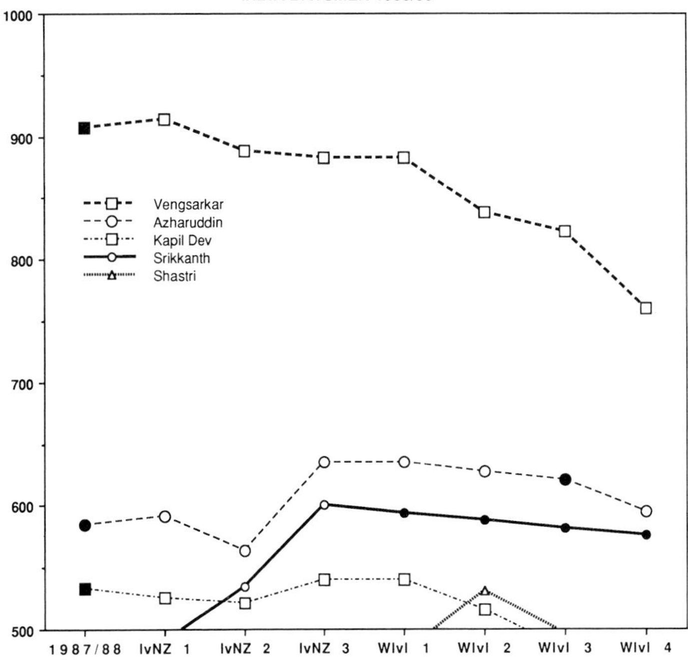

INDIA BOWLERS 1988/89

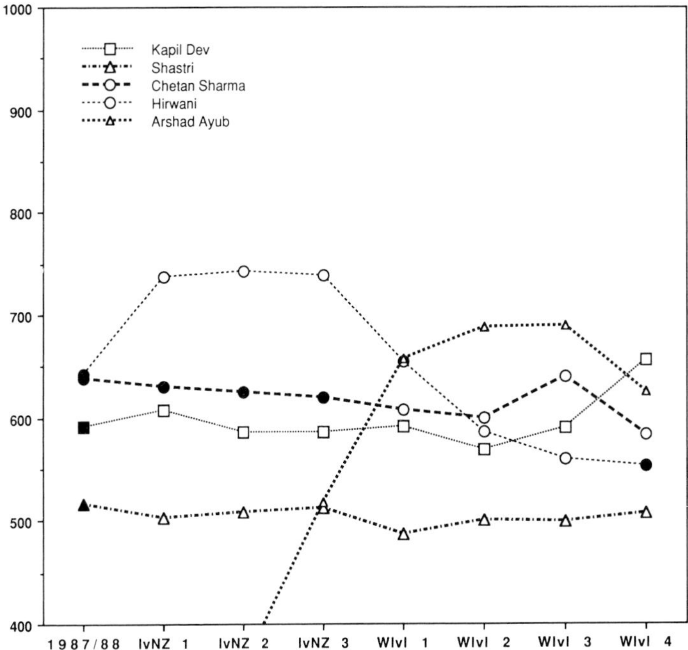

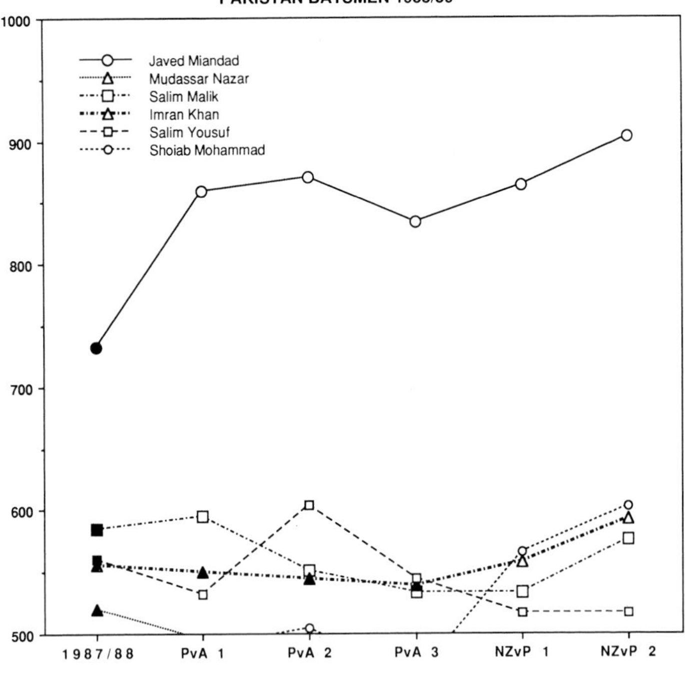
PAKISTAN BATSMEN 1988/89
1000
900
800
700
600
500
Javed Miandad
Mudassar Nazar
Salim Malik
Imran Khan
Salim Yousuf
Shoiab Mohammad
1987/88
PvA 1
PvA 2
PvA 3
NZvP 1
NZvP 2

PAKISTAN BOWLERS 1988/89

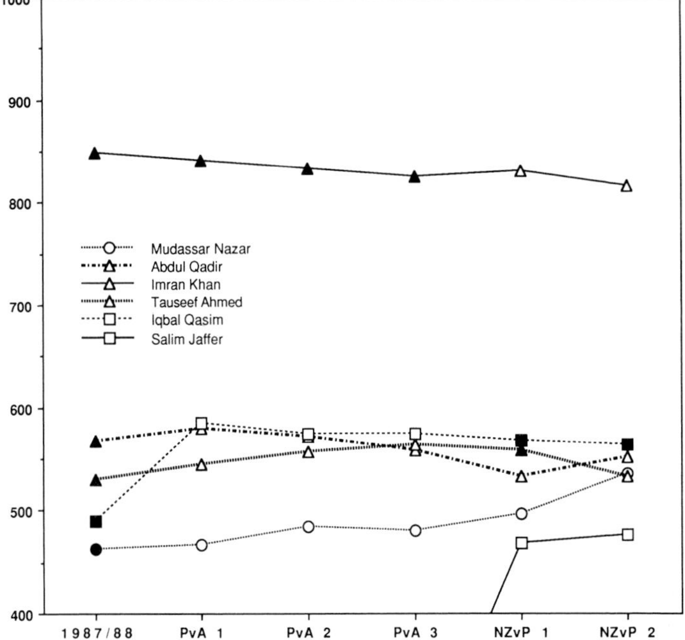
1000
900
800
700
600
500
400
Mudassar Nazar
Abdul Qadir
Imran Khan
Tauseef Ahmed
Iqbal Qasim
Salim Jaffer
1987/88
PvA 1
PvA 2
PvA 3
NZvP 1
NZvP 2

1989

ENGLAND vs AUSTRALIA

First Test (Headingley, 8–13 June) Australia won by 210 runs
Australia 1st Innings: 601 for 7 declared (Waugh 177 not out, M.A. Taylor 136, Jones 79, Hughes 71, Border 66, Foster 3–109)
England 1st Innings: 430 (Lamb 125, Barnett 80, R.A. Smith 66, Alderman 5–107, Lawson 3–105)
Australia 2nd Innings: 230 for 3 declared (Border 60 not out, M.A. Taylor 60, Boon 43, Jones 40 not out)
England 2nd Innings: 191 (Gooch 68, Alderman 5–44, Hughes 3–36)

Second Test (Lord's, 22–27 June) Australia won by 6 wickets
England 1st Innings: 286 (Russell 64 not out, Gooch 60, Gower 57, Hughes 4–71, Alderman 3–60)
Australia 1st Innings: 528 (Waugh 152 not out, Boon 94, Lawson 74, M.A. Taylor 62, Emburey 4–88, Foster 3–129)
England 2nd Innings: 359 (Gower 106, R.A. Smith 96, Alderman 6–128)
Australia 2nd Innings: 119 for 4 (Boon 58 not out, Foster 3–39)

Third Test (Edgbaston, 6–11 July) Match Drawn
Australia 1st Innings: 424 (Jones 157, M.A. Taylor 43, Waugh 43, G.R. Marsh 42, Hohns 40, Fraser 4–63)
England 1st Innings: 242 (Botham 46, Russell 42, Curtis 41, Alderman 3–61)
Australia 2nd Innings: 158 for 2 (M.A. Taylor 51, G.R. Marsh 42)

Fourth Test (Old Trafford, 27 July–1 August) Australia won by 9 wickets
England 1st Innings: 260 (R.A. Smith 143, Lawson 6–72, Hohns 3–59)
Australia 1st Innings: 447 (Waugh 92, M.A. Taylor 85, Border 80, Jones 69, G.R. Marsh 47, Fraser 3–95)
England 2nd Innings: 264 (Russell 126 not out, Emburey 64, Alderman 5–66, Lawson 3–81)
Australia 2nd Innings: 81 for 1

Fifth Test (Trent Bridge, 10–15 August) Australia won by an innings and 180 runs
Australia 1st Innings: 602 for 6 declared (M.A. Taylor 219, G.R. Marsh 138, Boon 73, Border 65 not out, N.G.B. Cook 3–91)

England 1st Innings: 255 (R.A. Smith 101, Alderman 5–69)
England 2nd Innings: 167 (Atherton 47, Hughes 3–46)

Sixth Test (The Oval, 24–29 August) Match Drawn
Australia 1st Innings: 468 (Jones 122, Border 76, M.A. Taylor 71, Boon 46, Healy 44, Pringle 4–70, Small 3–141)
England 1st Innings: 285 (Gower 79, Small 59, Alderman 5–66, Lawson 3–85)
Australia 2nd Innings: 219 for 4 declared (Border 51 not out, Jones 50, M.A. Taylor 48)
England 2nd Innings: 143 for 5 (R.A. Smith 77 not out)

Captains: England – D.I. Gower
Australia – A.R. Border

Débuts: England – A.R.C. Fraser (3rd Test), M.A. Atherton, D.E. Malcolm (5th Test), J.P. Stephenson, A.P. Igglesden (6th Test)
Australia – G.D. Campbell (1st Test)

Rising Stars: England – R.A. Smith (+321 batting)
Australia – M.A. Taylor (+357 batting)

There's nothing like saving the best till last. It all began when David Gower won the toss, surveyed Headingley's brown, well-tended surface, and decided to (i) leave out his only spinner, Emburey, and (ii) bowl. As cricket watchers around the country banged their heads against the wall with frustration, even the most pessimistic of them could not have guessed how the series would finally pan out over that long, hot summer. By the end of the season, Australia had inflicted their greatest humiliation on the old enemy in thirty years, most of England's first choice team had signed up for another tour of South Africa, and all of the rest were either injured or lbw b Alderman. It was a shambles.

Much of the problem was that Australia were really rather good. This clearly came as something of a shock to England and especially Gower, who was used to them being really rather bad. But with Border's bright and imaginative captaincy, coach Bobby Simpson's commitment to orthodoxy, and a certain amount of good fortune (Australian weather and virtually no injuries), they swiftly took charge of the series, and exploited the England team's (and particularly captain's) shortcomings ruthlessly.

The effect all this had on the ratings was startling. By the series' end, Australia had five of the world's top fifteen batsmen and two of the top six bowlers. England, on the other hand, had Robin Smith and that was it. Top of the averages with 553 runs at 61.44 – two hundreds and three fifties – Smith was by a long way England's best batsman.

Mark Taylor, during his 137 at Headingley.

Gower, as one of just three others to average more than 30, dropped only five places, but most of the others plunged out of sight. Wicketkeeper Jack Russell, with a final rating of 575, ended up just outside the world top twenty. These latter two were the only Englishmen to play all six Tests. Ten Australians saw the series through.

Among them was Mark Taylor, the tall, infinitely correct left-hander from New South Wales. In scoring 839 runs, average 83.9, he notched up the second highest aggregate in an Ashes series, and the third highest in any series. Even then he wasn't Man of the Series although he was winner of the Rising Star award. Terry Alderman's 41 wickets at 17.36 – only one less than he had picked up in the 1981 Ashes series – was judged to be the greater achievement. It certainly helped his rating, which rose 318 points. Australia's batting, though, was peerless – they were never out in a first innings for less than 400, a total England passed only once. David Boon, Steve Waugh and Dean Jones were respectively solid, masterly and imperious.

So did England gain anything from this dispiriting defeat? Smith and Russell, certainly, plus the certain knowledge that David Gower should no longer be captain, but something that didn't show up in the ratings was the advance of Angus Fraser, who played three Tests with varying luck. With Foster, Dilley and Jarvis all off to South Africa, he suddenly became England's fast bowling hope, the poor fellow. No doubt he will do better than 287 (43rd) in the future.

WORLD TOP TWENTY AFTER 1989

BATTING

(1)	1.	Javed Miandad (Pakistan)	903
(2)	2.	R.B. Richardson (West Indies)	891
(3)	3.	D.B. Vengsarkar (India)	760
(4)	4.	I.V.A. Richards (West Indies)	758
(5)	5.	M.D. Crowe (New Zealand)	757
(7)	6.	A.R. Border (Australia)	757 (+27)
NE	7.	M.A. Taylor (Australia)	757 (+599)
(41)	8.	R.A. Smith (England)	746 (+321)
(6)	9.	D.L. Haynes (West Indies)	745
(26)	10.	S.R. Waugh (Australia)	695 (+185)
(13)	11.	D.M. Jones (Australia)	677 (+56)
(8)	12.	A. Ranatunga (Sri Lanka)	677
(9)	13.	M.J. Greatbatch (New Zealand)	659
(12)	14.	D.C. Boon (Australia)	635 (+13)
(11)	15.	C.G. Greenidge (West Indies)	629
(14)	16.	A.L. Logie (West Indies)	605
(15)	17.	Shoaib Mohammad (Pakistan)	603
(16)	18.	M. Azharuddin (India)	595
(17)	19.	Imran Khan (Pakistan)	593
(18)	20.	K. Srikkanth (India)	576

BOWLING

(1)	1.	R.J. Hadlee (New Zealand)	900
(2)	2.	M.D. Marshall (West Indies)	883

(3)	3.	Imran Khan (Pakistan)	815
(34)	4.	T.M. Alderman (Australia)	694 (+318)
(4)	5.	Kapil Dev (India)	656
(20)	6.	G.F. Lawson (Australia)	647 (+105)
(6)	7.	C.A. Walsh (West Indies)	636
(8)	8.	Arshad Ayub (India)	625
(9)	9.	C.E.L. Ambrose (West Indies)	619
(5)	10.	B.A. Reid (Australia)	603 (−37)
(11)	11.	I.R. Bishop (West Indies)	586
(12)	12.	Chetan Sharma (India)	584
(13)	13.	J.R. Ratnayeke (Sri Lanka)	578
(15)	14.	E.J. Chatfield (New Zealand)	569
(16)	15.	Iqbal Qasim (Pakistan)	563
(17)	16.	W.K.M. Benjamin (West Indies)	562
(14)	17.	N.A. Foster (England)	560 (−10)
(18)	18.	N. Hirwani (India)	553
(19)	19.	Abdul Qadir (Pakistan)	551
(21)	20.	Mudassar Nazar (Pakistan)	535

Here then are the last charts of the Eighties. After a long period of relative underachievement languishing in the 700s, Javed Miandad is back at the top, with Richie Richardson not far behind him. Then a clutch of top-rate international cricketers, most of whom appear to be Australian. The Ashes team's achievements have already made an impact – the excellence of such players as Taylor and Waugh (and let's not forget Robin Smith here either) has boosted average ratings, and it will be interesting to see which, if any, of them moves further up the table to challenge the 850 boys. Moving out, though, are three players – Salim Malik (edged out through no fault of his own to 21st), Gower (down from 20th to 25th) and new captain Graham Gooch, who plummets from 10th to 28th after all those lbws.

The bowling chart, meanwhile, remains the outright property of Richard Hadlee and Malcolm Marshall, with Imran Khan in with a small stockholding. Alderman may be in at 4th, but he has a long way to go if he is to make the same long-term impact as these three. Lawson's return is counterbalanced to some extent by the eclipse of Bruce Reid, whose injury problems continued through 1989. Even so, it's odd to think that all of the top six bowlers in the world are well over thirty, with at least a couple staring retirement in the face. Fated now never to take their places, Foster and Dilley ended their Test careers with contrasting results, Foster dropping just 10 points (he was England's highest wicket-taker, with 12) and Dilley emulating Gooch with a drop of twelve places to 22nd. Also out goes Wasim Akram, after eighteen months on the sidelines.

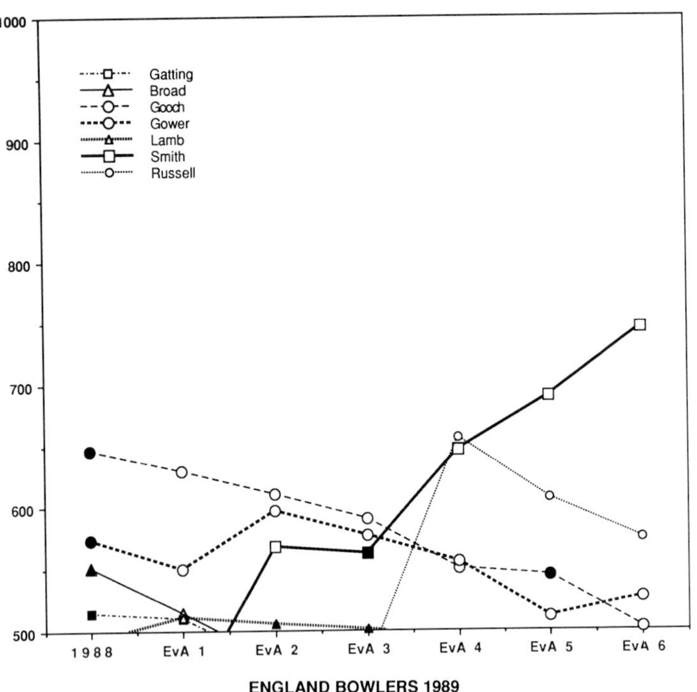
ENGLAND BATSMEN 1989
1000
900
800
700
600
500
Gatting
Broad
Gooch
Gower
Lamb
Smith
Russell
1988
EvA 1
EvA 2
EvA 3
EvA 4
EvA 5
EvA 6

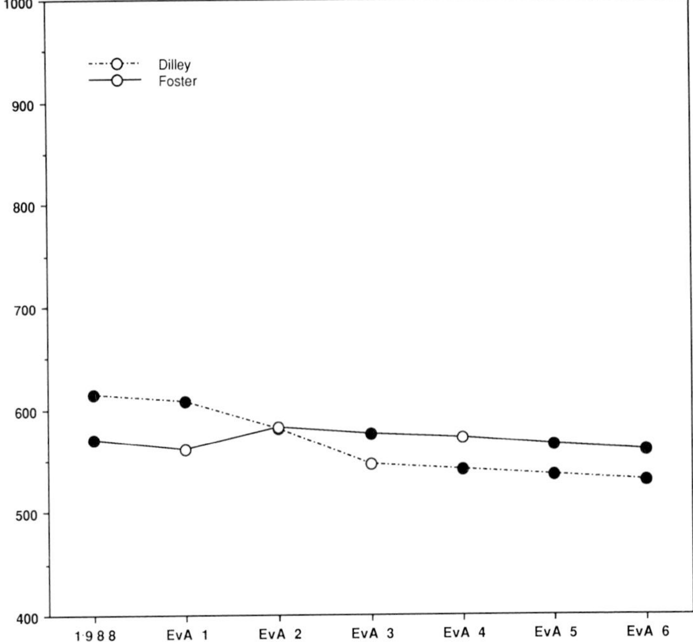
ENGLAND BOWLERS 1989
1000
900
800
700
600
500
400
Dilley
Foster
1988
EvA 1
EvA 2
EvA 3
EvA 4
EvA 5
EvA 6

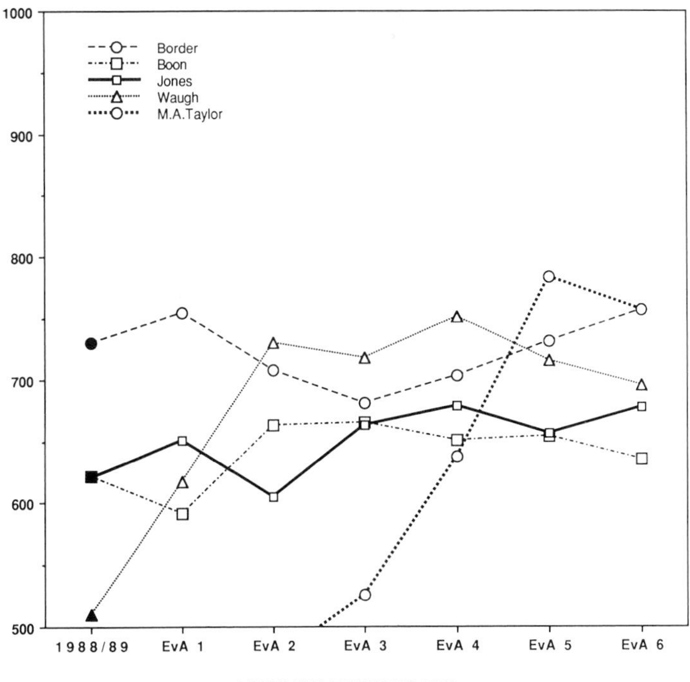
AUSTRALIA BATSMEN 1989
1000
900
800
700
600
500
Border
Boon
Jones
Waugh
M.A.Taylor
1988/89
EvA 1
EvA 2
EvA 3
EvA 4
EvA 5
EvA 6

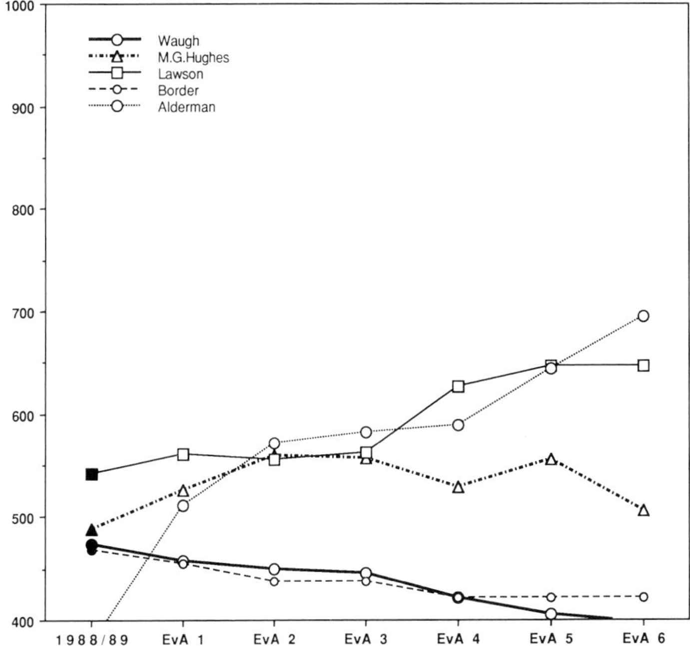
AUSTRALIA BOWLERS 1989
1000
900
800
700
600
500
400
Waugh
M.G.Hughes
Lawson
Border
Alderman
1988/89
EvA 1
EvA 2
EvA 3
EvA 4
EvA 5
EvA 6

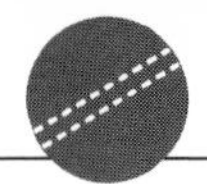

TEN YEARS OF RATINGS

Although that title is perhaps a misnomer – the ratings were, after all, only formulated in 1987 – backdating them to the beginning of the decade has proved very revealing. One interesting if odd phenomenon is that average ratings appear to have dropped slightly over the ten-year period. Taking a Test at random, the chart after the West Indies vs India series of 1982–83 (by which time any early inconsistencies in the ratings should have ironed themselves out) reveals four batsmen with ratings of over 800, nine bowlers with ratings over 700, and a rating of 651 for the 20th best batsman. This compares with the most recent chart, with just two batsmen over 800, three bowlers over 700, and a rating of 576 for the 20th best batsman. And that is after a series (England vs Australia) in which ratings at the top end of the scale generally climbed.

There are several possible explanations for this. When a player misses a match, his rating drops by 1 per cent – not a big deal if your rating was not very high in the first place, but noticeable if you are a major player missing an entire series, such as Greg Chappell when he decided not to tour England in 1981. There is also the damping effect on new players, with the result that, if there are lots of them around, their low ratings will eventually depress everyone else's.

Having thought about this for a while, though, I have come to the conclusion that there may be another simpler explanation: the players of the moment may not actually be as good as those of ten years ago. Look at the bowlers, for instance. The chart now is entirely controlled by Richard Hadlee, Malcolm Marshall and to a lesser extent Imran Khan. No-one has challenged their hold since Garner and Holding retired. But Alderman, at number 4, would have been no higher than 10th in the 1982–83 chart with his current 694 rating. If that seems a little unfair, that's partially because he had so demoralized England's batsmen by the end of the 1989 series that their ratings weren't high enough for him to benefit much from getting them out.

The great batsmen of the early Eighties, meanwhile, are also still around, but with the exception of Javed Miandad, are not making as many runs, or making them as convincingly, as they used to. With the ever-increasing quantity of one-day cricket, sides have also lost a certain stability of selection. England, of course, have suffered from this more than anyone, with thirty-seven different players selected in their last twelve Tests; but India, Pakistan and the West Indies are now chopping and changing far more than they used to. Only Australia, in recent times, have kept faith with the same players – with hugely successful results.

Australia's Terry Alderman, preparing to befuddle English batsmen, in 1981.

It's possible that the drop in ratings could be something far more prosaic – an unnoticed if minor computer bug, for instance – but I suspect not. It seems likelier that, if teams begin to settle down and new young talents assert themselves, ratings will climb again. There are players who can do it. Steve Waugh, Salim Malik, Robin Smith seem like good contenders for the top batting positions in a few years' time – and let's not forget the looming shadow of Graeme Hick. As for the bowlers, Ian Bishop, Curtly Ambrose and Wasim Akram look to be good bets. We'll just have to wait to find out . . . .

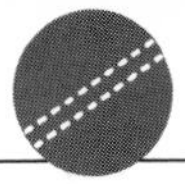

THE TOP BATSMEN

So who were the top batsmen of the decade? Which of the many hundreds of dashers, thumpers, nurdlers and stonewallers made their mark in the ratings? We've seen that it's not hard for any reasonably talented international batsman to secure a rating in the 500s and 600s and then hang on to it for as long as their knees and selectors will let them. Few, though, stay above 700 for long, and even fewer settle in the 800s. Indeed, only eighteen batsmen have ever reached 850, and most of those hit the mark in the earlier part of the decade, when higher ratings appear to have been more easily reached. In this section we will compare that list of eighteen (which includes four Englishmen, two Australians and six West Indians), to decide who, in ratings terms at least, were genuinely the batsmen of the Eighties.

THE EIGHTEEN

In order of highest ever ratings, they are:

1.	I.V.A. Richards (WI)	934	(1980–81, WI v E, 2nd & 3rd Tests)
2.	D.B. Vengsarkar (I)	916	(1987–88), I v WI, 3rd Test)
3.	G.S. Chappell (A)	908	(1980–81, A v I, 1st Test)
4.	C.G. Greenidge (WI)	907	(1984, E v WI, 4th Test)
5=	A.R. Border (A)	903	(1980, E v A, Centenary Test)
5=	Javed Miandad (P)	903	(1988–89, NZ v P, 2nd Test)
7.	C.H. Lloyd (WI)	901	(1983–84, I v WI, 5th Test)
8.	J.F. Reid (NZ)	892	(1984–85, NZ v P, 2nd Test)
9=	Zaheer Abbas (P)	891	(1982–83, P v I, 3rd Test)
9=	R.B. Richardson (WI)	891	(1988–89, WI v I, 4th Test)
11.	D.L. Haynes (WI)	890	(1980, E v WI, 2nd Test)
12.	H.A. Gomes (WI)	887	(1984–85, A v WI, 3rd Test)
13.	R.T. Robinson (E)	883	(1985, E v A, 1st Test)
14=	D.I. Gower (E)	876	(1985, E v A, 6th Test)
14=	M.W. Gatting (E)	876	(1985, E v A, 5th Test)
16.	I.T. Botham (E)	871	(1982, E v I, 3rd Test)
17.	S.M. Gavaskar (I)	862	(1981–82, I v E, 4th Test)
18.	M.D. Crowe (NZ)	856	(1986–87, NZ v WI, 3rd Test)

What instantly leaps out of the page is how many times these players recorded their highest rating when playing against England. In fact, India and England were the opposition five times each out of the eighteen, which you could read either as a coincidence or as a savage indictment of something or other. No less interesting (although perhaps more of a coincidence) is that two of the players, Javed Miandad and Richie Richardson, recorded their best scores in their last Test matches before this book's deadline, both at the end of the 1988–89 season.

What's perhaps more interesting in the long run, however, is not the highest rating reached, but how long each player stayed up there. Here the figures are rather less forgiving:

1.	I.V.A. Richards	35 matches above 850
2.	A.R. Border	19
3=	Javed Miandad	14
3=	C.H. Lloyd	14
5.	D.B. Vengsarkar	13
6.	C.G. Greenidge	8
7.	Zaheer Abbas	7
8=	D.L. Haynes	6
8=	G.S. Chappell	6
10.	D.I. Gower	4
11=	Richardson, Robinson, Gomes and Reid	2 each
15=	Botham, Gavaskar, Crowe and Gatting	1 each

In these terms, Viv Richards totally dominated the decade, while Botham and company at the bottom only just crept in. (The figures exclude games for which ratings stayed above 850 but the player didn't actually play. Not taking part is, of course, much the most foolproof method for keeping your rating high.) Individually, then:

I.V.A. RICHARDS

His thirty-five games include one stretch from the beginning of 1980 to the first Test in India in 1983–84 – twenty-two successive games above 850, incorporating sixteen successive games above 900. These are records that seem unlikely ever to be broken, and reflect the extraordinary form that Richards enjoyed during this period, when he averaged well above 60 (these days he's down to just the early 50s, poor chap). He reached his highest rating, 934, during West Indies' triumphant 1980–81 series against Botham's England, when he scored 182 not out at Bridgetown. A score of 114 at St John's, Antigua in the following Test kept his rating at the same level, before it dropped back to a relatively humiliating 930 after the final Test. His lowest rating, 665, came after the third Test in Australia in 1984–85, when he scored 0 and 42 (he averaged a mere 42 for the series). But during another golden patch, between 1985–86 and 1988, he returned to the 850 zone for another three spells, which have made him almost unassailable. He missed just one of his country's seventy-seven Tests in the Seventies (the 62nd), and his average rating throughout the decade was an extraordinary 829. Who will ever better that?

A.R. BORDER

The only batsman who can even hope to rival Richards' prodigious figures, Border has a few records of his own: the most spells above 850 (ten in all, with a maximum of four successive games at any one time), and he's also the only one of the eighteen who didn't miss a Test in ten years, playing eighty-two in all. Like Richards, his scores were better in the earlier part of the decade, when he and Greg Chappell were unquestionably their side's leading batsmen; and like Richards, he has only dipped below 700 four times. His nadir, 657, oddly enough came in one of his side's more successful series: the 1982–83 Ashes series against Bob Willis' team. He recorded his highest rating, no less oddly, in his first match of the decade, against England once again in the Centenary Test of 1980, when he scored 56 not out and 21 not out. His average rating in those eighty-two games was 810 – another indication of his importance to an often struggling side.

JAVED MIANDAD

The lovable scamp of Pakistan cricket, whose jolly antics and double centuries so cheered visiting teams throughout the decade, emerges as the third most successful batsman in ratings terms. No less consistent than Richards and Border – his batting average is higher than either's – his average rating was nevertheless a touch lower, thanks to Pakistan's featherbed pitches (if not their featherhead umpires). Missing just four Tests, he had five spells above 850, spread relatively evenly through the decade. His highest, 903, came not surprisingly after his masterly 271 against New Zealand at Auckland in 1988–89; his lowest, 647, was during the low-scoring series in England against M.W. Gatting's side in 1987. Indeed, four of the six Tests in which he dipped below 700 came in that series. Overall, though, he averaged 782. What a character.

C.H. LLOYD

Clive Lloyd's personal form, as he guided perhaps the most successful and fearsome Test side in history, started relatively modestly, but improved and improved as the decade went on. By 1984, with Viv Richards temporarily in abeyance, he had become his country's leading batsman once again. Indeed, when he retired after the tour of Australia in 1984–85, he was indisputably the world's leading batsman too. His 901 came during the previous year's tour of India, when he scored an unbeaten 161 out of 377 on a slow, unfriendly wicket, while his lowest rating, 581, was way back at the beginning of the decade, after the first Test in England in 1980. His average, 783, was one above Javed's.

D.B. VENGSARKAR

Perhaps the most surprising name in these lofty echelons, Dilip Vengsarkar has in fact provided the solidity in India's batting line-up ever since Gavaskar got bored and started spanking the ball around. Another virtual ever-present – he too missed just five games in ten years – Vengsarkar nevertheless had risen above 700 only once before the 1986 series in England. But at Lord's, when he scored 61 and 102 not out, he jumped from 650 to 763, and has never looked back, spending a record two years at the top of the batting ratings. It's rare enough for an established if unspectacular international batsman suddenly to emerge as a world-class performer; it's even rarer for someone to maintain that new status over a period of time. His high point, 916, came against West Indies in 1987–88, when he scored 102 (retired hurt) in the third Test and averaged the same in the whole series. His low point, 503, was against England at home in 1984–85. His average rating, dragged down by the first half of the decade, was 680.

C.G. GREENIDGE

The older and more prolific of West Indies' long-serving opening partnership had his best spell in 1984, first in England and later in Australia. His masterful 223 in the fourth Test at Manchester gave him his highest rating of 907, two Tests after his match-winning 214 not out at Lords (rating: 887). His lowest rating – not counting a 594 recorded when he missed an entire series against Pakistan in 1980–81 was 605, during the home series against England a few months later. But although he and Desmond Haynes have each had their off-series, they have remained the most effective opening partnership at Test level for many years. After the second Test in New Zealand in 1986–87, in fact, their ratings were respectively 880 and 860 – by far the highest aggregate for an opening pair. Missing just seven Tests out of seventy-seven, Greenidge's average rating was 733, the seventh highest.

ZAHEER ABBAS

As perhaps the most gifted member of that fine if mercurial Seventies Pakistan team, Zaheer also lasted the longest, weathering periods of poor form and the usual political upheavals to play seventy-eight Tests and score 5,062 runs (average 44.79). He had three spells over 850 in the Eighties – one can but wonder how his rating would have shaped up earlier in his career – but his best period was undoubtedly in the home series against India in 1982–83, when Pakistan won 3–0 in a six-match series. With 650 runs at 130, including three successive 150s, Zaheer was almost undismissible, and his rating soared well into the high 800s, the 891 occurring after the third Test, in which he scored 168. His low point came in his first series of the decade, at home to the West Indies, when he made 8 in the fourth Test and dropped to 529. His average, in thirty-eight Tests played up to his retirement in 1985–86, was 734 – one above Gordon Greenidge.

D.L. HAYNES

Although often overshadowed by his more fluent opening partner Greenidge, Desmond Haynes has scored consistently for West Indies over nearly as long a period. Missing just one Test in the entire decade (the third Test against England in 1988, thanks to a hamstring injury), he had two periods in the 850s: the 1980 series in England (after scoring his monumental 184 at Lord's), and in 1986–87, after some plucky innings in the low-scoring series in Pakistan. The Lord's century, in just the second Test of the decade, represents his apogee. He has also had runs of unusually poor form, even dropping below 500 in the final Test in India in 1983–84 (a series in which he averaged just 17.6). With an average rating of 691 throughout, though, he has remained a world-class opener throughout the decade – one can't help feeling that the West Indies will sorely miss his sterling solidity and Greenidge's intimations of genius when they both finally retire.

G.S. CHAPPELL

Unquestionably Australia's leading batsman before the Packer fracas, Chappell had a rival to deal with on his return: Allan Border. As the Eighties arrived, they were neck and neck at the top of the world lists, almost taking it in turns to take the lead. (They only drew level once, on 873, after the second Test against Pakistan in 1981–82. Viv Richards, needless to say, stayed well ahead of them both.) Chappell missed the 1981 tour of England (he was sated with international cricket), after which his form began to decline – although he nipped up above 850 briefly during the return visit by England eighteen months later (after 115 and 26 not out in the third Test). His lowest rating, 672, coincided with Australia's only defeat in the drawn 1981–82 series in New Zealand. His average, 787, was third only to Richards and Border.

D.I. GOWER

Gower's career has been a series of contrasts – of potential somehow never fully realized, and yet of consistency at international level in cricket's harshest era. No mug would have played more than 100 Tests by the age of thirty-one and scored more than 7,000 runs with an average comfortably in the forties. And yet. . . .

His rating, in fact, has been very steady, if it has rarely reached the sort of levels habitually enjoyed by the Borders and the Miandads.

David Gower, the last outpost of flair in English cricket.

Only in the past couple of years has it faltered, dropping below 700 in the 1987 home series against Pakistan, and below 600 a year later against the West Indies. His lowest ebb came in 1989 – 511 after the fifth Test. This is in interesting contrast to his highest recorded rating – 876 against Australia in 1985 after the sixth Test, in which he had scored a rip-roaring 157, his third century of the series. But with an average rating of 716 from his eighty-seven Tests (more than anyone else in the decade), he is undoubtedly England's top batsman of the Eighties. After all, he does hold the record for the most consecutive Test innings without a duck – 99.

R.B. RICHARDSON

The most recent graduate to the 850 club – he passed the figure at the very end of the 1988–89 season – Richie Richardson is one of the world's most promising batsmen, despite having a few problems with English conditions. His leap into the top flight was prompted by some masterly performances in the West Indies' home series against India – 194 in the first Test, 93 and 59 in the second, 15 and 99 in the third, and 156 and 3 in the fourth. Before this, he had mainly bobbed about between the 600s and 700s, having reached 647 in just his fifth appearance, after two successive centuries against Australia in 1983–84. His lowest rating since that breakthrough (it seems churlish to count the 44 he recorded after his first unsuccessful appearance) came in 1984–85 – 533 in Australia in the first Test match, but as he immediately leapt to 740 one Test later, after scoring 138, it seems unlikely that he loses too much sleep over it. Already forty-five Tests into his career, his average rating lies at 647 – not bad, but West Indian supporters may expect more. Whether his current position at the top of the chart (well, at second) is a one-off or a portent of things to come remains to be seen.

R.T. ROBINSON

Few cricket fans if asked to name the English batsman with the highest individual rating over the past ten years would instantly blurt out the name of Tim Robinson, but indeed he holds this considerable honour. Playing just twenty-nine Tests in an oddly unbalanced international career, the Nottinghamshire opener started spectacularly, with 444 runs at 63.42 in his first series in India in 1984–85 and another 490 at 61.25 against Australia the following summer, with three large centuries in those first eleven Tests. He passed 850 twice, in the first Test against Australia, when he scored 175 and his rating hit 883, and in the fifth, when his 148 pushed him up to 881. (His 883 coincided with his tenth innings, which gave him a full rating for the first time.)

Thereafter things began to go wrong. After a dismal series in the

West Indies and a failure in the first Test against India, he lost his place, and only really reclaimed it as a part-time replacement for the out-of-form Gooch in 1987 and 1987–88. After another recall and another failure in 1989 (when his rating dropped below 400 for the first time), he signed up for the South African rebels, which wrapped up his Test career there and then, with a batting average of 36.38, and an average rating of 574.

H.A. GOMES

Between his recall in 1980–81 and his retirement at the end of 1986–87, the left-handed Larry Gomes supplied the solidity in the West Indies' extravagantly talented but mercurial batting line-up, constantly called upon to shore up innings or to play the straight man as the others ran riot. Having exceeded 600 for the first time against England in 1980–81, he maintained a consistently high standard, losing his place only once (against Australia in 1983–84), and jumping above 850 for two Tests in his most successful series – away to Australia this time, in 1984–85. His average rating – 695 over forty-nine Tests (better than Desmond Haynes) – reflects this consistency. In fact the West Indies could rather do with it back . . . .

J.F. REID

New Zealand's most successful batsman of the mid-Eighties was an odd, unglamorous figure who made a speciality of compiling long, defensive centuries at important moments for his team. John Reid's late reintroduction to Test cricket (one match in 1978 had not proved fruitful) and a reluctance to tour (he was a schoolmaster by profession) limited his Test appearances to eighteen in the Eighties, but in those he twice rose above 850, his highest rating coming after an unbeaten 158 in New Zealand's innings win over Pakistan in 1984–85. His average rating of 640 is, perhaps, a little unflattering, but his batting average, 46.28, is not – it's the highest career average in New Zealand's history.

I.T. BOTHAM

An unlikely member of this select company – certainly his all-rounder contemporaries have never even got close to the 850 mark – Botham owes his place really to one series – no, not the Ashes of 1981, but England vs India a year later. Whereas previously his innings had owed as much to huge slices of good fortune as to his inimitable talent for the big hit, his form against India was unassailable. 67 in the first Test, 128 in the second, and finally a fearsome 208 in the third – at times he looked impossible to dismiss. At other times, of course, Botham's record has been patchy, although it's only since his 1989 comeback against the Australians that he has had to get used to a modest, even poor rating. Indeed, it was in his final Test of this book, the fifth, when he recorded his lowest rating, 401 – teetering on the edge of mediocrity. At other times he has been known to vary by up to 300 points within a calendar year. In his seventy-two Tests in the Eighties, he averaged 625 in the ratings – not bad at all, even if he hadn't bowled.

S.M. GAVASKAR

In many ways it's a surprise that Sunil Gavaskar has not dominated this book more than he has – his record tallies of Test appearances, runs and centuries seem likely to stand for some time (unless Allan Border decides to break them, of course). But we have caught him in

Sunil Gavaskar, fending off a Botham bouncer in the Jubilee Test of 1980–81.

very much his later, more carefree years, when he seemed to lose interest in those long, studied centuries and developed more of a taste for the one-day knockabout. The decline from top five to top twenty, from 750 ratings to 570s, was gradual, and perhaps more to do with motivation than anything else. His only nudge into 850 territory was against England in 1981–82, after 42 and a match-saving 83 not out in the fourth Test, while his lowest rating came four years later, 537 in Sri Lanka's first ever Test victory. With an average of 688 (eight above that of his compatriot Vengsarkar), he nevertheless remained consistent to the end, especially when there was a record in sight. After all, he did play 106 consecutive Tests – a record, of course.

M.D. CROWE

It has taken Martin Crowe a surprisingly long time to catch up with the rest of the 850 club – it is already seven years since he was first capped by his country and only recently has he confirmed his reputation as perhaps the world's most gifted young batsman. New Zealand generally do not have the luxury of easing their young prodigies slowly into Test cricket; theirs is by necessity a deep end policy, and once they have been chosen, their youngsters are expected to get on with it. Some, like Ken Rutherford, never seem to get over the shock, but M.D. Crowe, after a testing start, has flourished in the second half of the decade and looks set to dominate the next one. His single fleeting look at the top flight came in 1986–87, in the final Test against the West Indies, which New Zealand won to square the series (Crowe scored 83 and 9 not out). His lowest rating – 44 after his first Test – was lower than most. His average, 557, is therefore rather more modest than everyone else's – although at least that means we can expect it to rise with every Test match.

M.W. GATTING

The third of the three England batsmen who edged over 850 during the triumphant Ashes series of 1985 was Mike Gatting, Branston Pickle fan and owner of cricket's most famous beard. But while it took Tim Robinson just six Tests to pass the magic figure, Gatting's 876 came on his fortieth appearance. Although he inched above 500 briefly in 1981, he stayed in the 400s until his breakthrough on the India tour of 1984–85. From then on it was straight to the top, and his rating remained in the 700s and high 600s until Shakoor Rana entered the world stage. In the end, though, his average rating of 568 in 65 matches illustrates frustrating underachievement for a batsman of his exceptional gifts. For although his contemporary Gower is supposed to be the capricious, undisciplined one, it is he and not Gatting who has lasted the course, played 100 Tests, scored 7,000 runs and avoided going to South Africa. It will be interesting to see how cricket history judges him.

THE TOP BOWLERS

Eleven bowlers in all passed the magical 850 figure at some point in the Eighties; some of them, like Marshall and Hadlee, never seemed to drop below it again.

THE ELEVEN

In order of their personal highest ratings they are:

1.	Imran Khan (P)	915	(1982–83, P v I, 6th Test)
2=	I.T. Botham (E)	906	(1980, E v WI, 1st Test)
2=	G.F. Lawson (A)	906	(1982–83, A v E, 3rd Test)
2=	M.D. Marshall (WI)	906	(1988, E v WI, 3rd Test)
5.	R.J. Hadlee (NZ)	904	(1985–86, A v NZ, 3rd Test)
6.	J. Garner (WI)	901	(1980, E v WI, 2nd Test)
7.	D.K. Lillee (A)	900	(1981–82, A v P, 2nd Test)
8.	C.E.H. Croft (WI)	899	(1980–81, WI v E, 3rd Test)
9.	Kapil Dev (I)	880	(1980–81, A v I, 1st Test)
10.	C.J. McDermott (A)	870	(1985, E v A, 6th Test)
11.	M.A. Holding (WI)	865	(1981–82, A v WI, 3rd Test)

You will probably notice that they are all fast bowlers. (Indeed, only two spinners have ever passed 700, both of them Indian – D.R. Doshi, who reached 832 in 1981–82 against England, and N. Hirwani, who reached 743 against New Zealand in 1988–89.)

With such small differences between at least the first eight, it might be fair to say that it's not how far you get, it's how long you stay there that matters. And once again the figures are suitably revealing:

1.	M.D. Marshall	32 matches over 850
2.	R.J. Hadlee	28
3.	Imran Khan	13
4.	G.F. Lawson	12
5.	J. Garner	10
6.	D.K. Lillee	8
7.	I.T. Botham	7
8.	C.E.H. Croft	4
9.	Kapil Dev	3
10=	Holding and McDermott	2 each

The sheer consistency of Marshall and Hadlee almost beggars belief. Throughout the decade, it's almost eerie how rarely either of them goes through a Test match without at least 3 or 4 wickets, and 5-wicket innings seem to pop up every two or three Tests almost as of right. In the last five years there has been no-one to challenge them, although Imran Khan, when not injured or 'retired', has certainly made a valiant effort. Individually, then:

M.D. MARSHALL

After a slowish start – he had played three Tests against India in 1978–79 without much success, and it took him until 1982–83 to establish himself fully in the side – Malcolm Marshall has set the highest standards from the middle of the decade on. Since 1984 he has never dropped below 792, and after a relatively poor 1987–88 – owing more to the fact that he missed five Tests in a row than to any loss of form – he has returned to the 900 zone with a vengeance, recording his highest rating during perhaps his best tour, the 1988 dismemberment of England, when he took 35 wickets (a record, of course) at 12.65 each. His average rating over his sixty-three appearances between 1980 and 1989 was 757 – but, perhaps more pertinently, his average rating since 1983–84 (when he first hit 800) has been exactly 100 higher.

R.J. HADLEE

Marshall's chief rival for the top spot these past few years, and perhaps even more consistent a performer than the West Indian. With twenty-eight games over 850 overall, he hasn't dropped below that figure since 1984–85. Indeed, if we ignore two games he missed in 1987–88 through injury (the first time, incidentally, he had broken down in the entire decade), he has only dropped below 900 three times in his last twenty-two Tests – and then he plummeted only as far as 890. (Indeed, his twenty-one games with a rating of 900 or above compare well with Marshall's nine). Even before this remarkable run, he never dropped below 710, notching up that particular rating in his first Test of the Eighties, in Australia in 1980–81. In his fifty Tests in the Eighties (he missed just five – not bad for a bowler), he averaged 847: since 1985–86, he has actually averaged 901. What will New Zealand do when he has gone?

IMRAN KHAN

The world's sexiest man? And as well as being rich, good-looking and extremely bright, Imran is also an exceptionally gifted cricketer. It really isn't fair at all.

Imran Khan, master strategist and heart-throb, prepares to unleash another swift one.

As a bowler he has hit the 850 zone five times, with undoubtedly his most successful period in 1982–83, during the long six-Tester against India, when he took 40 wickets at just under 14, as Pakistan won 3–0. Earlier in the season Pakistan had whitewashed a visiting Australian team 3–0, and Imran's 13 wickets had been even cheaper. It was at this peak of form – in what was also a golden year for his team, hardly surprisingly – that he reached the record rating of 915 in the final drawn Test. Since then he has too often been unavailable for Pakistan, playing just twenty-six of their last forty-nine Tests, but while his absences have affected his rating – and perhaps stopped him from competing on more equal terms with Marshall and Hadlee – it has never dropped lower than 774, on his first game back after injury against Sri Lanka in 1985–86. His lowest before that was 654, back in 1980–81 against the West Indies. His average over the decade, 813, was third best. (Who was second? See below.)

G.F. LAWSON

Just as Dilip Vengsarkar was perhaps the most surprising of the leading batsmen, Geoffrey Lawson has not perhaps garnered a reputation for himself as one of the world's leading strike bowlers. Nonetheless there was a time, towards the end of Dennis Lillee's long and glorious career, when Lawson was very much regarded as his natural heir as Australia's leading strike bowler. And against England in 1982–83, when both Lillee and Alderman were injured in the first Test and ruled out of the series, Lawson carried the attack and took 34 wickets, mostly good ones, at just over 20. Match figures of 11 for 134 in the second Test pushed his rating up from 636 to 861, and a further 9 wickets at Adelaide gave him his highest rating. He stayed at around the 800 mark for the next two seasons, before losing form on the 1985 tour of England and thereafter confidence and fitness. In latter years he has been perhaps unfairly ignored by the selectors, but his surprise recall for the 1989 England tour brought an opportunity for redemption, which he grabbed gleefully. In the forty-one Tests he played in the Eighties, his average rating was 711.

J. GARNER

Whatever the cause of the recent drop in average ratings, one factor seems likely to have been the retirements in quick succession of Joel Garner and Michael Holding from the West Indian team. With two such superb bowlers suddenly out of the picture, life for batsmen can only have become easier – at least in terms of ratings, which tend to reward longevity rather than youthful promise. Garner's highest placed period came right at the beginning of the decade, most notably against England in 1980, when at Lord's he passed 900 for the only time (4–36 and 2–21). International batsmen probably still have nightmares about those high fast yorkers that brought so many of his 259 Test wickets. Although a slight deterioration was evident after England vanished from the scene in 1981, Garner was back at his very best for the next tour there in 1984, when he edged briefly above 850 again while taking 29 wickets. He hit his low-point, 705, when New Zealand toured the following winter (Marshall was unstoppable and Joel took just 10 wickets), but when he finally called it a day in 1986–87, he still had a 779 rating, making him 4th in the world. Over forty-five Tests played, he averaged 803 – the fourth best.

D.K. LILLEE

The ratings may not represent Lillee in his early, whirlwind-like days, but they certainly reflect his most consistent period. During the Eighties he was never out of the top ten, rarely out of the top five, and until his final series against Pakistan in 1983–84 he never dropped below 750 (his lowest point was 732 in the fourth Test). He hit 900 once, against Pakistan in the second Test of the 1981–82 rubber, and headed the ratings in the early months of 1982. More remarkably yet, he didn't miss any Tests in this period through injury until 1982–83, in what proved to be his penultimate series. (The 1982–83 Pakistan series he declined to take part in.) In twenty-nine Tests (he played another forty-one before 1980), he averaged 816, second only to Richard Hadlee. Sadly, there are no separate ratings for innings played with aluminium bats.

I.T. BOTHAM

To have rated more than 850 as both batsman and bowler is a unique achievement, and it's easy to forget just what a remarkable performer Ian Botham was in the early Eighties. He, Lillee, Garner and Kapil Dev dominated the bowling ratings in 1980 and 1981, but after starting at 906, and remaining over 850 for seven successive Tests, it was downhill for Botham thereafter. Edging gradually down to the 600s and high 500s (his average over all seventy-two Tests was 667), he then stabilized, not dropping below 500 until the final Test of the lost series against Pakistan in 1987. Having recorded his highest rating in his first Test of the Eighties, his lowest rating, 395, came in his last – another unique record. If we take the ratings seriously, then, it has *always* been true that Botham is never quite as good as he used to be.

C.E.H. CROFT

Like many West Indians, Colin Croft recorded his most impressive ratings against England. All four of the Tests in the 1980–81 series saw him exceed 850, with a peak of 899 in the fourth Test (the second having been cancelled), when he took 6 for 74 in the first innings. Eighteen months and only three Tests later, his career was prematurely ended by his decision to join a rebel tour of South Africa – a decision which also curtailed his first-class career. Who can tell whether he would have attained the same heights as his contemporaries Garner and Holding? In just fourteen Eighties Tests, though, he averaged 795.

KAPIL DEV

Much as Hadlee has kept the New Zealand bowling attack going almost single-handedly, so Kapil Dev has performed a similar role for India. Constantly twinned with an increasingly desperate selection of 'all-rounders' (bowlers who couldn't bat, and weren't too hot at bowling, either), he has kept his form and more importantly his fitness throughout the decade, missing only one Test – against England in 1984–85, when he was dropped for playing a silly shot in the previous match. In the other seventy-three, he averaged 741, less than his all-rounder rivals Hadlee and Imran but better than Botham. Like Botham, he recorded his highest place in his first match of the decade, against Australia in 1980–81, when he took 5 for 97 from a total of 406 (Greg Chappell scored a double century). His lowest scores, 569 (twice), both came rather later in the decade – in 1986–87 at home to Pakistan, and in 1988–89 in the West Indies – but his rating has been bobbing around at that level for a couple of years. With more than 300 wickets now to his name, though, Kapil Dev can never be underestimated.

M.A. HOLDING

For such a successful bowler – 249 wickets in sixty Tests since 1975–76 – Michael Holding's ratings are not on first glance as spectacular as those of his international bowling rivals. But despite just two matches above 850 – the higher, 865, earned after he had taken 32 wickets in three Tests in Australia in 1981–82 – he only once fell below 764 in all his subsequent Tests, and that only in his final appearance, after three Tests off. Clearly the shock of a rating as low as 728 was enough to hasten his retirement. His actual lowest, in a neat reversal of Botham's trick, was his first game – 652 against England in 1980 (not one of his more productive series). But his average rating of 785 (from forty-one Tests) is perhaps the most telling figure.

C.J. McDERMOTT

Another mildly surprising entry in this select band, Craig McDermott in fact made a considerable impact on his first tour, of England in 1985. 30 wickets (albeit at a cost of 30 runs each) were enough to make him the pre-eminent member of a well-beaten side. *Wisden* described him as 'the outstanding success' of the tour, 'fiery, strong and seemingly more mature than his 20 years'. That was exactly as we saw it – here was the answer to Australia's prayers. But, as in the case of Geoff Lawson, somehow it didn't turn out like that. After this impressive start – jumping to 850 in only his sixth Test, then 870 in his eighth – his form deserted him. Now slower and more disciplined, McDermott is one of many contenders for the Australian XI, and is unable to command a regular place. His lowest rating (at least since his first Test, a very creditable 384) came in his last Test to date, against the West Indies in 1988–89, when he registered 510. But although he seems to have been out of the picture for a long time, the 1989 tour of England actually represented the first time he had ever missed more than four consecutive Tests. In his twenty-three Tests so far, his average rating has been 669.

It would be churlish not to mention one other bowler, who never quite made 850, but did reach the heights of 847. Come on – are we that pernickety?

R.G.D. WILLIS

What's curious about Bob Willis' career – or at least the relatively small part of it covered by the ratings – is how much his bowling improved when he took over as captain. Pottering around in the 600s for most of 1980 and 1981 – even his amazing 8–43 at Headingley only gave him a rating of 691 – he jumped to 730 immediately on taking over as skipper against India in 1982, and reached the peak of his career – 847 and 3rd in the world – against New Zealand a year later. As soon as he lost the captaincy, after the lost Pakistan series in 1983–84, both his form and rating declined. Nevertheless, averaging 732 over his thirty-seven Tests within the period, his merry countenance and cheery manner brightened many a tour. Over four years after his retirement, England have never adequately replaced him.

THE TOP ALL-ROUNDERS

In Test cricket the Eighties were undoubtedly the decade of the all-rounder. Countries vied to unearth the next world-beater, with the inevitable result that we were plagued with bits-and-pieces players, none of them quite being good enough at either batting or bowling to retain their places in the long term.

The four who started the trend – Ian Botham, Imran Khan, Richard Hadlee and Kapil Dev – had one advantage over all these also-rans: they were all world-class bowlers capable, in patches, of world-class batsmanship. How then to define an all-rounder in ratings terms? Earlier we paid most attention to the batsmen or bowlers who, in their own field, exceeded 400 points, this figure becoming in the process an accepted threshold. All-rounders, then, should have more than 400 points as batsmen *and* bowlers: a not unreasonable criterion, but a hard one to satisfy. Indeed, besides the gentlemen above, only ten other players have managed it: A.R. Border (A), J.G. Bracewell (NZ), J.V. Coney (NZ), J.E. Emburey (E), M.D. Marshall (WI), Mudassar Nazar (P), G. Miller (E), R.J. Shastri (I) Wasim Raja (P) and S.R. Waugh (A). Of these, only Mudassar and Shastri have qualified consistently, although neither has ever performed as spectacularly as Botham and company (both of their ratings generally float around the 400–500 zone).

So, perhaps a little arbitrarily, I have invented an all-rounder rating, by adding together the player's batting points over 400 and his bowling points over 400. So if Hadlee has a batting rating of 583 and a bowling rating of 857, this gives him an all-rounder rating of 183 + 457 = 640. If either of the two standard ratings drops below 400, the all-rounder rating is reduced to 0.

The results of all this calculation are remarkably informative. The highest all-rounder ratings ever recorded by each player are as follows:

1. I.T. Botham (E)	877	(Bt 771, Bo 906, 1980, E v WI, 1st Test)
2. Imran Khan (P)	746	(Bt 633, Bo 913, 1982–83, P v I, 4th Test)
3. R.J. Hadlee (NZ)	704	(Bt 601, Bo 903, 1986–87, SL v NZ)
4. Kapil Dev (I)	602	(Bt 522, Bo 880, 1980–81, A v I)

Botham's pre-eminence rests on the fact that, unlike the other three, he has also reached the very top as a batsman. Imran's highest batting rating was 661 (in 1983–84), Hadlee's 650 (in 1983–84) and Kapil Dev's 635 (in 1982) – but Botham once hit 871, and spent a further fifteen Tests with a rating of 700 or higher.

The big man in action. Is it time for lunch yet?

As the table shows, though, Botham has been in steady decline since the beginning of the Eighties. Indeed, on his final Test appearance to date – the fifth Test against Australia in 1989 – he actually recorded a bowling rating of 395, which by these criteria means that he's no longer an international all-rounder at all. Botham's domination of the early part of the decade (his calamitous West Indian series of 1980–81 notwithstanding) was complete, but as his powers failed, so Imran and Hadlee took over. As we go to press, the two are very much neck and neck.

Botham's impressive early statistics, meanwhile, have been let down by the last few years, which show just how long he has been trading on past glories. In the average all-rounder ratings, he is a poor third with 490. Imran Khan, with 574, just pips Richard Hadlee (569) while Kapil Dev is a distant fourth (363). Still, the debate over which of them is the greatest all-rounder will continue, possibly for ever. What's clear is that Botham and Kapil Dev are no longer in the race, and with all four well over thirty, there aren't any new contenders. Where did the all-rounders go?

ALL-ROUNDERS CHART

	Botham	Imran Khan	Hadlee	Kapil Dev
80	786	*	*	*
80–81	562	346	435	271
81	629	*	*	*
81–82	657	393	409	441
82	708	554	*	501
82–83	563	686	427	410
83	464	*	513	*
83–84	451	**	616	439
84	409	*	*	*
84–85	*	*	617	409
85	411	*	*	*
85–86	321	508	624	333
86	276	*	615	308
86–87	294	616	644	284
87	225	637	*	*
87–88	*	620	657	294
88	*	*	*	*
88–89	*	598	582	303
89	37	*	*	*

Single stars indicate seasons in which the player didn't take part in any Test matches. The double star indicates a season in which Imran played two Tests but bowled in neither (he was still injured at the time).

DELOITTE ALGORITHMS

How, then, is it worked out? Individual ratings are calculated in two stages:

(i) After each Test match, a player is assigned 'Rating Values' which represent the calculated worth of his performances in that match. (In fact, a batsman gets a Rating Value for each innings he plays, while a bowler gets a pair of Rating Values for his overall performance in the match.)
(ii) Then the player's new Deloitte ratings (for both batting and bowling) are calculated from his previous ratings and from the Rating Values just assigned. Players playing their first Test match start with a Rating of 0, while those who started playing before 1979 are given an initial Rating derived from their averages at the time.

As can be imagined, both of these stages are mathematically complex, and took a long time to design, implement, test and refine. The result is a computer algorithm – or rather, pair of algorithms – of such length and intricacy as to make it incomprehensible to the averagely computer-illiterate cricket fan (e.g. me).

Even so, without two main constraints that the programmers set themselves, it could have been even worse. First, they decided that any variables they would use in the calculations would have to be entirely statistically based, and therefore clearly objective. If they started throwing in their own opinions of players' worth and achievements, all hell would break loose – not least from a lot of angry players. The consequence of this was that three important factors which would all have had to be assessed rather than measured – the pitch condition, the 'quality' of an innings, and the standard of fielding in a match – could not be considered. (This explains why such dismal innings as Broad's interminable 86 against Sri Lanka in 1984 proved so profitable in terms of ratings points.)

Additionally, they decided that it was practicable to work only from brief innings summary scorecards rather than from full ball-by-ball analyses. Their excuse for this was that they wished 'to keep the quantity of data required by the algorithm within sensible limits,' but I suspect that they were also keen to go home and see their families from time to time. Nevertheless, this self-imposed limitation removed three equally important sources of information from the algorithms: what time things happened, who bowled to whom and at what stage of the game, and the batsmen's scoring rate, both in terms of runs per minute and runs per ball.

This left, for batsmen, the following factors:

- Runs scored in each innings by the batsman
- Innings status (i.e. whether out or not out)
- Teams innings scores (including wickets fallen)
- Match result
- Opposition bowling strength

and for bowlers:

- Runs conceded
- Wickets taken (including which batsmen)
- Strike rate (balls bowled per wicket taken)
- Bowling economy (runs conceded per ball bowled)
- Team innings scores (including wickets fallen)
- Match result

Yet more factors were considered and finally rejected, mainly because no-one was entirely sure how important they were. These included the size of partnerships between batsmen, the method of dismissal of batsmen, and the team's margin of victory, rather than just the result.

DETERMINING THE RATING VALUES

For the sake of simplicity, the Ratings Values are no more than weighted innings and bowling analyses. Starting with, in the batsman's case, the number of runs scored in an innings, the figures go through a series of transformations that reflect the different weightings, and out at the other end pops the Ratings Value.

To start with, the number of wickets that fell in the match has to be taken into account. Incomplete innings have to be adjusted first, as 180 for 2 would very rarely be equivalent to 900 all out. A separate formula thus transforms the simple ratio of runs per wicket to the much more important sounding 'match pitch factor' (although, it should be stressed, the actual pitch is not being assessed in any way), and this formula is then used:

$$\mathbf{RV'} = \mathbf{RV}*\left(1 + \frac{\mathbf{Average}}{\mathbf{Match}}\right)/2$$

where **RV'** is the player's new Rating Value,
RV is the player's old Rating Value (i.e. runs scored),
Average is a researched average number of runs per wicket in previous Test matches (approximately 31), and
Match is the match pitch factor.

The Rating Value then goes through a similar transformation for each innings:

$$RV' = RV*\left(7 + \frac{\mathbf{Average}}{\mathbf{Innings}}\right)/8$$

where **Innings** is the innings pitch factor.

The opposition bowling is now evaluated, by averaging the abilities of the individual bowlers (derived from their current ratings), weighted according to the number of bowlers bowled by each in the match. Defining this value as **Quality**, we get:

RV' = RV***Average/Quality**.

The result now comes into play. Players on the winning side who scored more than our **Average** quantity (the average number of runs scored per wicket in all Test matches), are given a bonus –

RV' = RV + 0.5*(RV – **Average**)

– while each player on the losing side who scored less than the **Average** is penalized. If he scored less than half the **Average**,

RV' = **RV***0.5.

(Well, you've got to be cruel to be kind.) If he scored less than **Average**, but more than half it,

RV' = **RV** – 0.5*(**Average** – **RV**).

Not out players now get a bonus, derived from their previous Rating and added to their RV, and the figure produced is the final batting Rating Value.

A bowler's Rating Values are worked out by a similar method, although he has two for each innings, derived from his bowling figures – say 4 for 63. '4' then becomes what we'll call **RV**1, and '63' **RV**2. **RV**1 is then weighted according to the Ratings of the batsmen dismissed – if they were all tail-enders, for instance, '4' may suddenly become '3.1'. **RV**2, meanwhile, is altered by the same runs-per-wicket criteria as the batting **RV**s:

$$\mathbf{RV}2' = \mathbf{RV}2*(1 + \frac{\mathbf{Average}}{\mathbf{Match}})/2$$

and then by similar formulae for each innings.

The match result affects bowlers on the winning side who took more than 4.5 wickets and bowlers on the losing side who took fewer than 4.5 and conceded more than the average number of runs per wicket (our friend **Average**). Winning bowlers in the wickets get a bonus as follows –

RV1' = **RV**1 + 0.5* (**RV**1 – 4.5)

– while the expensive losers have their **RV**2 figure bumped up:

RV2' = RV2*(1 + 0.01*(4.5 – **Wickets**))

where **Wickets** is the number of wickets they took in the match.

Now strike rate rears its ugly head. Defining **Ratio** as the ratio of the bowler's strike rate to the overall match strike rate (i.e. both sides, both innings), we get:

RV1' = **RV1***(4 + **Ratio**)/5.

Economy is treated similarly. Defining **Economy** as the ratio of the player's economy to the overall match economy, we get:

RV2' = **RV2***(9 + **Economy**) 10.

That calculated, the bowler's Ratings Values are complete.

CALCULATING THE RATING

For batting, the Rating is calculated using a weighted average of all the player's Rating Values – the so-called 'geometric decay' factor. As a simple example, the standard (unweighted) average of 100 and 70 is simply calculated as:

$$\textbf{Aver} = \frac{(100 + 70)}{2} = 85$$

If you want to give more weight to the 70 figure, though, you can do it like this:

$$\textbf{Weighted Average} = \frac{(1 \times 100) + (2 \times 70)}{3} = 80$$

The resultant average is therefore influenced most by the most heavily weighted figures – just what's needed for the ratings. Weight the 70 by 3, for instance (and divide the whole lot by 3 + 1 = 4) and the weighted average drops to 77.5.

Extrapolating from this (and leaping into the algebra without fear or shame), we can put together a formula for the batting rating that looks a bit like this:

$$\textbf{Rating} = \frac{\textbf{RV1} + (k^*\textbf{RV2}) + (k^*k^*\textbf{RV3}) + (k^*k^*k^*\textbf{RV4}) + \ldots}{1 + k + k^*k + k^*k^*k + \ldots}$$

where **Rating** is the player's rating;
RV1, **RV2**, etc are the player's Rating Values for all his innings (with RV1 being the most recent); and
k is the decay constant and lies between 0 and 1.

This formula, as well as looking horrible, requires the individual Rating Values from previous matches, but with a little mathematical manipulation, we can alter this so that only the old rating and the new Rating Value come into the frame:

$$\textbf{New Rating} = \frac{k^*\textbf{Old Rating}^*(1 - k^n) + \textbf{RV}1^*(1 - k)}{1 - k^{n+1}}$$

(where n is the number of innings played by this player before this match).

k was eventually set at 0.95, the result of which being that each innings is weighted 5 per cent less in a player's rating than the previous innings. This means that a player playing perhaps eight innings per Test season has his most recent innings weighted approximately double those from the previous Test season, while innings of three years ago contribute only a tenth of the current innings. Crafty, huh?

The bowling rating is even more complex. How do you compare, say, 1 for 14 with 4 for 110? The ratings needed to be weighted in the same way as the batting ratings had been, but although a single performance could be defined simply as a single innings for a batsman, there was no equivalent definition for a bowler. The eventual choice was to use the runs conceded as a measure of the scale of a bowler's performance, so a bowler conceding 100 runs in a match had his RVs for that match weighted twice that of a match in which he concedes 50 runs. (In fact every 30 runs conceded corresponds to a single 'performance' by a bowler.) The decay factor (k) was different, too: 0.985 as opposed to 0.95. The final formula, suitably converted, was:

$$\textbf{New Rating} = \frac{(1 + k + k^*k + \ldots. + k^{n-1})^*k + (\textbf{RV}2/30)}{(1 + k + k^*k + \ldots. + k^{n-1}) + (k/\textbf{Old Rating}) + (\textbf{RV}1/30)}$$

where n is the number of 'performances' by this player in his career (as defined above). Now you see why they needed a computer.

NEW PLAYERS

The system works for all but the newest Test players, who for the first few games of their career have their ratings 'damped' by gradually decreasing percentages to stop them rising too high and too quickly. Without such a safety net, someone like Kuruppu of Sri Lanka, who scored 201 in his first innings, would have leapt even higher up the chart, and Hirwani's 16-wicket bag in his first Test against the West Indies would have been yet more profitable. But after ten innings (for a batsman) or 40 wickets (for a bowler), ratings are no longer damped – after then, players are on their own.

INDEX

Index

(*Bold print indicates photograph*)